Palgrave Insights into Apocalypse Economics

Series Editor
Richard Westra, Centre for Macau Studies,
University of Macau, Macau, China

This series is set to become the lodestone for critical Marxist and related Left scholarship on the raft of apocalyptic tendencies enveloping the global economy and society. Its working premise is that neoliberal policies from the 1980s not only failed to rejuvenate capitalist prosperity lost with the demise of the post-Second World War 'golden age' economy but in fact have generated a widening spectrum of pathologies that threaten humanity itself. At the most fundamental level the series cultivates state of the art critical political economic analysis of the crises, recessionary, deflationary and austerity conditions that have beset the world economy since the global meltdown of 2008–2009. However, though centered on work that critically explores global propensities for devastating financial convulsions, ever-widening inequalities and economic marginalisation due to information technologies, robotised production and low wage outsourcing, it seeks to draw on exacerbating factors such as climate change and global environmental despoliation, corrupted food systems and land-grabbing, rampant militarism, cyber crime and terrorism, all together which defy mainstream economics and conventional political policy solutions.

For critical Marxist and related Left scholars the series offers a non-sectarian outlet for academic work that is hard-hitting, inter/trans-disciplinary and multiperspectival. Its readership draws in academics, researchers, students, progressive governmental and non-governmental actors and the academically-informed public.

More information about this series at
https://link.springer.com/bookseries/15867

Paul Cooney

Paths of Development in the Southern Cone

Deindustrialization and Reprimarization and their Social and Environmental Consequences

palgrave
macmillan

Paul Cooney
Brooklyn, NY, USA

ISSN 2523-8108 ISSN 2523-8116 (electronic)
Palgrave Insights into Apocalypse Economics
ISBN 978-3-030-67672-8 ISBN 978-3-030-67673-5 (eBook)
https://doi.org/10.1007/978-3-030-67673-5

This Palgrave Macmillan imprint is published by the registered company Springer Nature Switzerland AG
The registered company address is: Gewerbestrasse 11, 6330 Cham, Switzerland

To my parents, Bill and Rose,
for teaching me the lessons of life,
without which, this book would not have been possible.

Acknowledgments

I am grateful to many friends, colleagues, and students over the years, from when this book went from an idea through to the current final version. As referred to in the book, there were several articles that I had written with colleagues that were used in several parts of the book. These colleagues include José Raimundo Trindade, Wesley Pereira, Sergio Rivero, William Sacher, Juan Santarcangelo, and Gilberto de Souza Marques. I also wish to thank Richard Westra for offering me the opportunity to have my book included in the Book Series on Apocalypse Economics, which he has organized.

In the final stretch run, a number of colleagues gave very useful feedback on versions of chapters, such as Joe Smith, William Sacher, Gilberto de Souza Marques, Tom Scheetz, Enith Flores, Giliad de Souza Silva, and José Raimundo Trinidade. Moreover, several colleagues assisted with data access and discussion, such as Giliad de Souza Silva, José Raimundo Trinidade, Thomas Sheetz, Juan Iñigo Carrera, and also a thesis student of mine at PUCE/Quito, Andres Oña.

Over the years, many other friends and colleagues have given me feedback on earlier writings or articles or provided me with insights and ideas from our discussions which were key for the book: Al Campbell, Marcelo Diniz, Mathías Eskenazi, Paolo Cipolla, César Do Campo, Elena Arengo, Paddy Quick, Steve Mathews, Danilo Fernandez, Joana Valente, Ricardo Lazzari, Adalmir Marquetti, Juan Grigera, Abelardo Mariña Flores, Ricardo Abduca, Pablo Varela, Leonardo Arengo, Patrick

Bond, Karina Forcinito, Mariano Treacy, Juan Kornblitt, Martin Miglio, Pablo Barneix, and Pablo Sisti.

I also benefitted from discussions with students of mine, whether in the Brazilian Amazon at the UFPA (Universidade Federal do Pará), or in Argentina, in the Province of Buenos Aries at the UNGS (Universidad Nacional de General Sarmiento) or at the Catholic University in Quito (PUCE).

Finally, and most significantly, over the last five years, and especially in this final stretch, I have had the unreplaceable support between assistance in editing, discussions, suggestions, and especially mental and moral support from my compañera, Enith Flores Chamba.

Quito, September 2021 Paul Cooney

Praise for *Paths of Development in the Southern Cone*

"This book offers an illuminating, comprehensive and original account of the accumulation strategies and economic trajectories of Argentina and Brazil. The troubles and tribulations of industrialisation and deindustrialisation in these countries are examined in great detail, across a historical arch spanning several decades, and in the context of the changes in the world economy. This book is essential reading for anyone interested in the political economy of Argentina and Brazil."

—Alfredo Saad-Filho, *King's College London*

"This book is a summation of Paul Cooney's last decade or so of work, explaining why the two most industrialised economies of South America are losing their core internally-oriented manufacturing potential, in favour of the export-oriented and extractivist circuits of capital (albeit with the latter suffering crises at the end of the global commodity super-cycle). The work is the most sophisticated about these two countries that I know of, and in the book, Cooney seeks to more formally introduce the 'reprimarization' concept. To do so, Cooney provides an excellent historical trajectory of these countries, focusing on both world economic dynamics and local class-forming processes. As well as anyone, he understands the dynamics within the main sectors: soy, cattle, mining, fossil fuels, and biofuels. He is particularly committed to a critique of the 'New

Developmentalism' thesis of former Finance Minister Luiz Carlos Bresser-Pereira, a critique with which I fully agree. He also utilizes Marxist political economy very fruitfully, particularly by employing David Harvey's concepts of rent and dispossession."

—Patrick Bond, *University of The Witwatersrand, Johannesburg, South Africa, Distinguished Professor of Political Economy, School of Governance*

Abbreviations

AAA	Alianza Anticomunista Argentina (Argentine Anticommunist Alliance)
AAPRESID	Asociación Argentina de Productores en Siembra Directa (Argentine Association of Zero Tillage Producers)
ABCD	Archer Daniels Midland (ADM), Bunge, Cargill, and Dreyfus
AFJP	Administradora de Fondos de Jubilaciones y Pensiones (Retirement and Pension Fund Administration)
BASA	Banco da Amazônia (Bank of the Amazon)
BCIA	Banco de Crédito Industrial Argentino (Argentine Industrial Credit Bank)
BNDES	Banco Nacional de Desenvolvimento Econômico e Social (National Bank of Economic and Social Development)
BOVESPA	Bolsa de Valores do Estado de São Paulo (São Paulo Stock Exchange)
BRICS	Brazil, Russia, India, China and South Africa
CESP	Companhia Energética de São Paulo (São Paulo Energy Company)
CGT	Confederación General de Trabajadores (General Confederation of Workers [Argentina])
CIFRA	Centro de Investigación y Formación de la República Argentina (Argentine Center for Research and Training)
CVRD	Companhia Vale do Rio Doce (CVRD); Vale do Rio Doce Company or just Vale.
DIEESE	Departamento Intersindical de Estatística e Estudos Socioeconômicos (Inter-Union Department of Statistics and Socioeconomic Studies)

ECLAC	Economic Commission for Latin America and the Caribbean
EJOLT	Environmental Justice Organizations, Liabilities and Trade
EPA	Environmental Protection Agency
EPH	Encuesta Permanente de Hogares (Permanent Household Survey)
FDA	Food and Drug Administration
FDI	Foreign Direct Investment
FHC	Fernando Henrique Cardozo
GATT	General Agreement on Tariffs and Trade
GDP	Gross Domestic Product
GMO	Genetically Modified Organism
GNP	Gross National Product
IAPI	Instituto Argentino de Promoción del Intercambio (Argentine Institute for Promoting Trade)
IBGE	Instituto Brasileiro de Geografia e Estatística (Brazilian Institute of Geography and Statistics)
IBGE/SCN	Instituto Brasileiro de Geografia e Estatística / Sistema de Contas Nacionais (Brazilian Institute of Geography and Statistics/National Accounts)
ICOMI	Industria e Comércio de Minérios S/A (Industry and Trade of Minerals Company)
ILO	International Labor Organization
IMF	International Monetary Fund
IMSS	Instituto Mexicano del Seguro Social (Mexican Institute of Social Security)
INCRA	Instituto Nacional de Colonização e Reforma Agrária (National Institute of Colonization and Agrarian Reform)
INDEC	Instituto Nacional de Estadística y Censos de la República Argentina (National Institute of Statistics and Censuses of Argentina)
INEGI	Instituto Nacional de Estadística y Geografía (National Institute of Statistics and Geography [Mexico])
INPE	Instituto Nacional de Pesquisas Espaciais (National Institute for Spatial Research, Brazil)
IPEA	Instituto de Pesquisa Econômica Aplicada (Institute of Applied Economic Research, Brazil)
ISI	Import Substitution Industrialization
ISSSTE	Instituto de Seguridad y Servicios Sociales de los Trabajadores del Estado (Institute of Social Security and Services for State Workers-Mexico)
MAI	Multilateral Agreement on Investment
MERCOSUR	Mercado Común del Sur (Southern Common Market, in practice, South American Common Market)

MMT	Methylcyclopentadienyl Manganese Tricarbonyl (a gasoline additive)
MNCs	Multinational Corporations
MRN	Mineração Rio do Norte (North River Mining Company, Brazil)
NAFTA	North American Free Trade Agreement
NTAE	Non-Traditional Agricultural Exports
OCMAL	Observatorio de Conflictos Mineros de América Latina (Observatory of Mining Conflicts in Latin America)
PAC	Programa de Aceleração do Crescimento (I y II) (Growth Acceleration Program I and II)
PEA	Población Económicamente Activa (Economically Active Population)
PMDB	Partido do Movimento Democrático Brasileiro (Brazilian Democratic Movement Party)
PND	Plano Nacional de Desenvolvimento (I y II) (National Development Plans: I and II)
PRI	Partido Revolucionario Institucional (Institutional Revolutionary Party)
PSDB	Partido da Social Democracia Brasileira (Brazilian Social Democracy Party)
PT	Partido dos Trabalhadores (Worker's Party-Brazil)
RR	Roundup Ready (Monsanto [Bayer] trademark for its patented line of genetically modified crop seeds that are resistant to its glyphosate-based herbicide, Roundup)
RRPE	Review of Radical Political Economics (journal of URPE-Union for Radical Political Economics)
SAPs	Structural Adjustment Programs
SEADE	Fundação Sistema Estadual de Análise de Dados (State System Foundation for Data Analysis)
SELIC	Sistema Especial de Liquidação e Custódia (Brazilian Federal Funds Rate)
SIDRA	Sistema IBGE de Recuperação Automática (IBGE Automatic Recovery System)
SOMISA	Sociedad Mixta Siderúrgica Argentina (Argentine Steel and Iron Works)
SPVEA	Superintendência do Plano de Valorização Económica da Amazônia (Authority for the Valorization Plan of the Amazon)
SRA	Sociedad Rural Argentina (Argentine Rural Society)
SUDAM	Superintendência do Desenvolvimento da Amazônia (Development Authority for the Amazon)
TCC	Transnational Capitalist Class
TCS	Transnational Capitalist State
TNC	Transnational Corporation

UAC	Unión de Asambleas Ciudadanas (Union of Citizen Assemblies-Argentina)
UIA	Union Industrial de Argentina (Union of Argentine Industry)
WTO	World Trade Organization
WWI	World War I
WWII	World War I
YPF	Yacimientos Petrolíferos Fiscales (Argentine State Petroleum Company)

Contents

List of Figures

CHAPTER 1

Introduction

This book presents recent development trajectories in the Southern Cone[1], namely, Argentina and Brazil, and how they have undergone transitions from two of the three most industrialized countries of Latin America through processes of deindustrialization and reprimarization, with a range of social and environmental impacts. In order to understand these shifts, the book begins with a look back historically at the processes of Import Substitution Industrialization (ISI) from the 1930s through the 1970s and then followed by the rise of neoliberalism. An examination of the specific experiences of transitioning to neoliberal trajectories, in the case of Argentina, with the arrival of the dictatorship of 1976, while for Brazil this did not occur until 1990, with the upset victory of Collor de Melo followed by Cardoso and the *Plano Real*.[2]

[1] The term Southern Cone refers to the southern part of South America and its definition varies from the more restricted group of countries-just Chile, Argentina and Uruguay, to a more inclusive definition including Paraguay and Brazil. This book concentrates on just two of the aforementioned countries: Brazil and Argentina, and thus employs the broader definition of the region.

[2] The *Plano Real*, or in English, the *Real* Plan, where *Real* is presently the Brazilian currency, was a neoliberal stabilization plan. Its primary aims were to cut inflation and attract foreign investment, and this was designed by Fernando Henrique Cardoso, while Economics Minister, prior to becoming President of Brazil in 1994.

P. Cooney, *Paths of Development in the Southern Cone*, Palgrave Insights into Apocalypse Economics,
https://doi.org/10.1007/978-3-030-67673-5_10

Through the implementation of neoliberal policies, particularly the pursuit of free trade policies and financial deregulation, industry came to be treated as expendable, as did the prospects of well-paid industrial jobs for workers. Though staggered or in steps, the implementation of another key neoliberal policy over recent decades, namely flexibilization of labor, associated with outsourcing by transnational corporations (TNCs) and a general weakening of labor rights, has contributed to an assault on workers globally and also here in the Southern Cone.

Beyond deindustrialization there has also been the more recently described trajectory of reprimarization, meaning the shift away from manufacturing industry and a return to the dominance of the primary sector as the motor of these economies. In the case of Brazil, it comes as quite a surprise to some, but the percentage of manufacturing in relation to their Gross Domestic Product (GDP) has dropped from over 35% in the second half of the 1980s to roughly 11% today and much of this latter shift has actually taken place with progressive governments in pursuit of a "new developmentalism".

In terms of the organization of the book, after this introduction, the second chapter addresses theoretical issues of relevance for the key themes of the book. The chapter begins with a general discussion of the concepts of center and periphery and the nature of dependency. This is followed by a discussion of the characterization of the present period of neoliberal globalization and the hegemony of transnational corporations (TNCs) and also examining the roles played by the International Monetary Fund (IMF), the World Trade Organization (WTO), and the rise of China in recent decades. Moreover, the relevance of the theoretical categories of ground rent and accumulation by dispossession are assessed in addition to the concept of the second contradiction of capitalism, linked to environmental concerns. Although these theoretical issues are initially presented in the next chapter, many aspects are only fully developed when presented in more detail in later chapters in the context of concrete examples.

In Chapter 3, there is a summary presentation of the historical background for both countries, beginning with the transition from agro-export economies, and culminating in the process of import substitution industrialization (ISI). For the first period of ISI, the relative importance of external and internal factors is evaluated. There is then the discussion of how industrialization goes through the phases of first producing light consumer goods, then consumer durables and eventually capital goods, and what the nature of these different phases imply. In the case of

Brazil, the periods of Vargas and Kubitschek are presented and then the third phase of industrialization under the military dictatorship, specifically during the Geisel years, is briefly summarized. In the case of Argentina, the particular role of Perón and the union movement, followed by various military governments, as well as Frondizi, are considered, and then an evaluation of the military coup of 1976, marking a clear shift toward neoliberalism and the dismantling of Argentina's industrial base.

During the 1970s is when a clear divergence between the Argentine and Brazilian paths occurs, the former beginning a process of deindustrialization and the latter still experiencing its third phase of industrialization. Nevertheless, the consensus is that the ISI model was exhausted by the 1970s. In any event, with the combination of the Volcker Shock[3] in 1980 followed by the debt crisis of the 1980s, it was evident that neoliberalism was to become entrenched in Latin America, and eventually across the globe. In fact, the neoliberal experiments in Argentina, Chile, and Uruguay laid the groundwork during the 1970s, and by the 1980s, almost all countries of the region were on a neoliberal tack, with the exception of Brazil, arguably a case of late neoliberalism, beginning in 1990.

In Chapter 4 the transition from ISI and the rise of neoliberalism is presented, as exemplified by the Mont Pèlerin Group, and the four different dimensions of neoliberalism are considered: political, economic theory, ideology, and the real economy dimension. A brief summary of the accumulation crisis of the 1970s, exacerbated by the oil crisis is presented, followed by an examination of the recycling of petrodollars for the promotion of debt, especially for Latin America, pushing some to industrialize (Brazil, Mexico) and others to deindustrialize (Argentina) and the steady shift toward finance. The combination of the increasing dominance of monetarism in economic analysis and policy, and the debt crisis, culminated in the establishment of a new phase of global capitalism, namely neoliberal globalization, dominated by transnational capital, as reflected in the Washington Consensus.

The fifth chapter concentrates on the history of Argentina's political economy from the 1970s up until the crisis of 2001, thus titled: Argentina—from Dictatorship to Depression. Here the major impacts

[3] The Volcker Shock was the huge increase in the federal funds rate in 1980, from 10.25% to 20%, whose aim was to end stagflation in the US, and is named after its author, who was the Chairman of the Federal Reserve at the time.

and shifts that began with the military government's implementation of neoliberal policies starting in 1976 with the economics minister Martínez de Hoz are examined, leading to the first wave of deindustrialization. This is followed by an analysis of the 1980s and the Alfonsín years in the transition to democracy, and the crisis of hyperinflation. The last part examines the intensification of neoliberal policies under Menem with the Cavallo Plan and convertibility, witnessing a second wave of deindustrialization, the reprimarization of the Argentine economy, and Argentina experiencing its worst economic crisis ever with an economic depression to start the twenty-first century.

The sixth chapter turns to examine Brazil and the transition to democracy in the mid-1980s, followed by the new Constitution of 1988 and then entering the phase of Late Neoliberalism, begun with Collor de Melo, followed by a more intense application of neoliberal orthodoxy with Cardoso, first as economics minister and then as president. It is during this period where Brazil's deindustrialization intensifies and the beginnings of reprimarization are established, and with it, the negative impacts for the majority of the population, the environment and a growing external vulnerability.

In Chapter 7, initially, the definitions of deindustrialization and reprimarization are discussed. This is followed by an analysis of the processes of deindustrialization in Argentina and Brazil. Then a detailed analysis of the deepening of reprimarization is presented, mainly reflected in the expansion of soy, mining, cattle, and petroleum, among other primary activities. These processes involved a clear role of the State, especially in terms of infrastructure projects and displacement of indigenous, local, and peasant populations. This shift was strongly tied to the increased role of China, both as a major trading partner, having become the main recipient of the primary exports of both countries, and playing a key role in financially supporting infrastructure projects. Moreover, the discussion of ground rent is crucial for understanding the increased role of extractive industries. The second half of the chapter enters into a discussion of reprimarization and the relevance of the category of accumulation by dispossession (Harvey 2003). In addition to a deepening of the theoretical discussion of the category of accumulation by dispossession, the concrete examples of cattle, mining and soy in Brazil and Argentina are examined. Related to these processes, especially in the Brazilian Amazon is the issue of deforestation and the implications for climate change. The role of both military and civilian governments in the processes of expropriation and ensuing social conflicts are examined, and how this ties into the criminalization of social resistance. In conclusion, a summary is presented of how these tendencies of deindustrialization and reprimarization transpired for both countries and the most significant consequences thereof.

In Chapter 8, the theoretical basis of neodevelopmentalism is presented and evaluated with respect to the tendencies of deindustrialization and reprimarization, as well as with regards to breaking from neoliberalism. This is then followed by an evaluation of the concrete examples of the two Kirchner governments in Argentina and the PT governments in Brazil. Although these new governments have often been described as transitioning beyond neoliberalism, the reality was more a move away from strict neoliberal orthodoxy and perhaps toward a "new developmentalism"trajectory at best, but with several elements of neoliberalism firmly in place. What became clear is the extent to which the trajectories being followed, involved a deepening of reprimarization, and extractivism. An evaluation of social issues and results for these periods is assessed, considering GDP, wages, employment, informal labor, poverty, and inequality, in addition to the social welfare programs, aimed to reduce social exclusion. Subsequently, an evaluation of environmental impacts and consequences, particularly of reprimarization, are presented, ranging from issues of air, water, and soil pollution to concerns over biodiversity, deforestation, and climate change.

For example, the most significant expansion in Brazil has been in the Amazon, where lumber, cattle, mining, and soy grew much faster than elsewhere in Brazil and came to have significant impacts. The most notable environmental impact is that of deforestation, which is very significant with respect to global warming, exacerbating the trend toward planetary catastrophe. In addition, the issues of hydroelectric dams are considered, as they continue to involve significant social conflict and environmental disasters in Brazil and elsewhere in the continent, and are strategically important for the electricity-intensive mining sector. There is also the significant issue of the use of transgenic crops, especially soy, but also cotton, corn, and wheat, and the associated agrotoxics and problems of erosion, not to mention air, soil, and water pollution, if not desertification, in the case of the Argentine Pampas. Finally, a general summary of what these new paths, so-called "neodevelopmentalism," have meant for the populations of Argentina and Brazil, the overall socio-environmental impacts, and anticipating the prospects in the short-term future. The latter is extended further in Chapter 9 and in the Conclusions.

The following chapter, presents a brief summary of the conservative governments that followed after the Kirchners in Argentina, and after the impeachment of Dilma in Brazil. An evaluation of the economic results of the Macri government is presented, followed by a summary of the impeachment process of Dilma and then the neoliberal shifts of Temer and Bolsonaro. The second half of the chapter attempts to provide an overall assessment of the problems of the current development paths, including the troubling and pessimistic situation for Mercosur, and then moves toward an analysis seeking to discern possible alternatives in the near future.

In terms of Argentina, there was a return to more orthodox neoliberal policies with the government of Macri, leaving the economy worse off than before, in a recession and with worsening inflation, reaching over 50%. The turn of events in Brazil has been even worse, with Temer reversing many workers' gains under the PT, rapidly implementing orthodox neoliberal policies. Unfortunately for Brazil, things became even worse with Bolsonaro winning the election, as Lula sat in jail, such that Brazil is going through a social crisis, as is all the globe, with the current COVID-19 pandemic, but experiencing one of the worst scenarios in terms of health and social outcomes. Brazil has truly become a tragic scenario and this will be considered in the conclusions, though with little expectations of being able to predict what exactly will be taking place in the short term.

Although Bolsonaro seems to clearly have fascist tendencies, so far it is not clear whether he could truly lead a fascist movement in Brazil, yet one should not underestimate the forces behind him, be it the military or the evangelical flocks. In fact, a threat of a real military coup is no longer excluded, especially during the unfolding of the COVID-19 crisis in 2020. Besides the sad number of deaths and the totally inadequate manner of dealing with this crisis, the new government has also aggressively accelerated expansion in the Amazon, with not just greater deforestation, but promoting increased burning of the forest and genocide even among several indigenous groups. This new scenario for Brazil provides a scary reality and a dark horizon regarding the near future for the most populous country of Latin America.

Lastly, in the conclusions, the problems with the current development paths are summarized, and then an open discussion is conducted with regard to what is necessary for an alternative to TNC-dominated neoliberal globalization, and what aspects would constitute an alternative development path. The analysis concentrates on specifically Argentina and Brazil, but also considers the possibilities of greater regional development in the future. Nevertheless, the most pressing concerns are surviving the COVID-19 pandemic and concomitant economic crisis. Evidently, this is a global crisis, but the pandemic is particularly problematic in Argentina and especially in Brazil. Besides overcoming the pandemic at a global level, there is the urgent need to get beyond or break from the current reactionary phase in Brazil with Bolsonaro. In any case, in the post-COVID-19 world, the urgent task will be considering and promoting alternative development paths and a process of transition beyond neoliberalism, if not capitalism.

CHAPTER 2

Theoretical Issues

The aim of this chapter is to present a brief introduction of the main theoretical issues which are relevant in order to understand the processes of deindustrialization and reprimarization which Argentina and Brazil have experienced in recent decades and moreover their socioenvironmental impacts. The next section addresses the issue of center and periphery and the nature of dependency experienced by Argentina and Brazil and how the nature of this dependency has shifted over time. This is followed by a discussion of neoliberal globalization and the role played by international institutions, particularly the WTO and IMF. The third section presents a discussion on the hegemony of TNCs in the global economy and the concept of the emergence of a transnational capitalist class (TCC), followed by the fourth section and the role of class alliances at different moments historically for Argentina and Brazil. The fifth section discusses the relevance of Harvey's concept of accumulation by dispossession, as adapted from Marx's concept of original accumulation. The sixth section argues for the theoretical importance of understanding the role of ground rent, and its implications for the insertion of peripheral countries in the world economy. The seventh section presents the important and novel contribution of O'Conner referred to as the 2nd contradiction of capitalism, addressing its relevance for the issue of the environment in the context of development and in particular, as related to the processes

P. Cooney, *Paths of Development in the Southern Cone*, Palgrave Insights into Apocalypse Economics, https://doi.org/10.1007/978-3-030-67673-5_1

of reprimarization being experienced by Argentina and Brazil in the present conjuncture. Through the forthcoming chapters, these theoretical issues will be further addressed and developed upon considering historical evidence. The section below enters the first theoretical discussion, which is around the concept of center and periphery and the nature of dependency.

2.1 Center–Periphery and the Nature of Dependency

It can be argued that both Brazil and Argentina correspond to countries of the periphery, based on the dialectical dichotomy of center–periphery. This relationship implies that countries of the periphery have a subordinate status, and are therefore both economically and politically dependent on the center; though distinct from direct political control, as was predominant in the case of the British Empire. Nevertheless, the center is taking advantage of the peripheral countries through a combination of political and economic domination, and involving the transfer of wealth from the periphery to the center through a range of mechanisms. The debate over the nature of this transfer mechanism is substantial and there is not a consensus in this regard. Nonetheless, the majority of those employing a Marxist approach consider that a key aspect of imperialist domination of peripheral countries is a transfer of wealth from the periphery to the center, and I argue that this is constitutive of the main basis of dependency.[1]

In order to understand the nature of dependency and how this has changed over a century, some will argue that one needs to first identify the nature of imperialism. This is understandable as there seems to be a yin and yang relationship between imperialism and dependency. However, there are many theoretical discussions, consider Harvey (2003), and Meiksens Wood (2005) regarding imperialism, which does not deal specifically with the impact on development or dependency for countries of the periphery, but rather concentrate on the nature of imperial hegemony, such as for the US, and relationships between countries of the center. This is not incorrect; however, only looking at that aspect is

[1] At this point, the term dependency is being used in a general sense and not in line with a particular author or approach within the dependency school, though the argument for three phases of dependency is my own interpretation, to the best of my knowledge.

an incomplete analysis of imperialism. In this regard, this book takes an opposite tack or rather the analysis is concentrating on the flip side of the coin. The aim is to seek to understand the changes that have taken place in Argentina and Brazil and why imperialist relations have kept these countries in a condition of dependency. Thus, this book puts more emphasis on the reality of peripheral countries and does not seek to fully examine or understand all aspects of imperialism. In spite of interest and importance, there is neither time nor space, and this book is not the appropriate place for that pursuit. Nevertheless, in order to understand the changing nature of dependency for any country, one must pay sufficient attention to both the internal and external forces; the latter, by necessity, includes imperial and transnational strategies. If one examines historical changes at the level of the global economy in recent decades, it should be evident that there is a need to examine both dimensions and to recognize the relevance of the particularities of each country and for specific periods, identifying the differences and similarities for distinct historical periods, but not ignoring the overall context which is imperialism.

Considering the changes that have taken place in the functioning of the global economy, given the hegemony of transnational production and the rules set out by the WTO, we are clearly in a new epoch. The views on globalization range from the neoliberal defenders of laissez-faire, to notable critiques, such as Hardt and Negri's *Empire* (2000), Sklair and Robinson's analysis of transnational capital, as well as the resurgence of the dependency school or approach. In examining the dependency[2] approach, although there have been numerous authors and debates over the years, due to space limitations, only a brief summary will be made of the dependency school, though including the examination of some of the new contributions made from the Latin American region in recent decades, especially from Brazil, Argentina, and Mexico.

The dependency approach or "dependency theory" was seen as quite controversial, especially in the US and Europe, but often due to confusion or conflation of what exactly constituted dependency and/or the dependency school, combined with intense debates with certain more polemical authors. The name of Andre Gunder Frank (1967),[3] among

[2] For a more in-depth discussion, see Cooney and Trindade (2017).

[3] In fact, Frank did not always clearly identify himself as a dependency theorist, nor always as a Marxist, this is in clear contrast to several Brazilian Marxist dependency theorists, such as Marini (1973).

other controversial writers, led many in the US and Europe to reject or ignore the school or debates. Although several of the criticisms were valid, there were many different theorists and debates around the school and at present I would argue that there is a need to recognize the positive advances and seek to employ the useful aspects of dependency theory as a tool for strengthening our understanding of the relations between the center and periphery today.

There has been a resurgence of discussions around dependency theory, especially in Brazil, including some of the original theorists, such as Dos Santos (1970) and Bambirra (1978) but also a new wave of younger scholars, such as Martins (2011) and Carcanholo (2017). This resurgence has also been present in other countries of Latin America, most notably in Argentina and Mexico, such as the work of Katz (2018) and Féliz (2019) from Argentina, and Osorio (2012) in Mexico, though originally from Chile. Most popular in recent years has been the evaluation of the contributions made by Dos Santos but especially the contribution of Ruy Mauro Marini and there are many followers of him today. Below is the general view of dependency as presented by Marini:

> ...the Latin American countries are connected to the capitalist center countries by means of a structure defined and established based upon an international division of labor in which the production relations of the periphery are transformed to guarantee the reproduction of dependency and imperialism. (Marini 1973: 109–113)

A major point stressed by Marini is the problem of "unequal exchange" and as argued by most dependency theorists, Latin American countries predominantly produce primary products or raw materials, with minimal value-added, for export. Martin continues presenting Marini's emphasis on the category of super-exploitation:

> He argues that since the capitalists of the periphery cannot obtain or develop advanced technology, they end up with lower levels of productivity compared to the 1st World. As a result, they seek to increase exploitation as a means of compensation and therefore their survival fundamentally depends upon the *mechanism of super-exploitation*. The latter Marini argues is achieved through increasing the intensity of labor, the length of the working day and by paying lower wages; all as a means of compensation so as to insure their profits. He describes this as a mode of production rooted

in "super-exploitation" of labor and that this constitutes the essential characteristic of production in dependent countries. (Martins 2011)

The main emphasis continues to be the structural problem of dependency and the necessity of super-exploitation, though applying it in the new context of TNC-dominated production via Global Value Chains and the worsening of prospects of "development." Recently, some dependency theorists, such as Féliz (2019) or fellow travelers, such as Katz (2018), have engaged in constructive criticism, while others appear to be more rigid or less critical of oversights made in the past. The point stressed by so many current dependency authors is the above-mentioned super-exploitation, especially given the growth of the informal sector and the increasingly precarious conditions for workers throughout Latin America. Although there are some "dependentistas" that have debated the validity of the category, it is generally not addressed, other than by critics. On the one hand, the choice of the term may be more from the political appeal than from theoretical rigor. In a strict sense, as described by Marx, super-exploitation is when the value of labor power is below the price of labor power. In empirical analysis, the latter can be measured as the wage but there have been very few attempts to measure the value of labor power separately, and usually not in the context of super-exploitation (see Bond 2006).

The dependency school continues with a critical analysis recognizing the structural imbalances that are the main basis for underdevelopment in the grand majority of countries and population of the globe. This approach correctly argues that the accumulation processes in the first world are the priority for the global economy and where the periphery is seen as secondary (whether workers or capitalists). The agro-export economies that dominated Latin America at the end of the nineteenth century was the initial dominant stage of dependency. In the case of countries such as Argentina, Brazil, and Mexico, a serious industrialization via ISI, implied a second stage of dependency, given the shift in production flows of surplus value and profits and the operations of MNCs (multinational corporations) within the countries industrializing. It can be argued that the present period of neoliberal globalization constitutes a new and third phase of dependency for those countries that experienced a significant, however, distorted or limited, industrialization which reflects the shift to reprimarization and thus a return to the dominance of the primary sector, especially oriented toward exports, such as minerals and oil, though often toward non-traditional agricultural exports, e.g., soy and flowers (Robinson 2008).

2.2 Neoliberal Globalization, TNCs, and the WTO

Neoliberal policies were being imposed by the mid-1970s for Argentina with the dictatorship of 1976, though for most of Latin America, they arrived only after the debt crisis of the mid-1980s, and not till the 1990s for Brazil. There are arguably four main pillars which constitute neoliberalism: (1) trade liberalization; (2) financial deregulation; (3) privatization of state enterprises; and (4) labor flexibilization. This set of policies reflected a push by the First World and the institutions that represent them, the IMF and World Bank, and they were key in undermining, and in fact reversing the ISI processes and social advances during the decades of industrialization. The debt crisis of Latin America in the 1980s was used as an opportunity to force countries of Latin America into adopting these pro-market neoliberal policies, a form of international legalized blackmail.[4] Thus, instead of continuing to foment and assist industrialization, they were fundamental in bringing about the first phase of deindustrialization and providing renewed support for landed oligarchies and, a new financial elite[5] and an eventual fusion of the two. These elites were willing to help make such a shift, especially with clear material gains involved. This is an example whereby external interests push or offer opportunities to internal forces to produce change with benefits for both, in spite of it being counter to the general development of a given country, and to the interests of the majority of its population.

Neoliberal globalization emerged through the 1980s and became well established through the 1990s. This was based upon the support, not just of the previously established institutions, namely, the IMF and World Bank, but now with the World Trade Organization, making it much

[4] This is the same type strategy and tactic that was used recently by the European Central Bank against Greece in 2015.

[5] During the early years of the dictatorship the term *patria financiera* was being used to refer to a new financial elite, growing in power and importance in terms of the political economy of Argentina; consider the Financial reform of 1977 (see Chapter 5). Evidently, it is the local example of the sector of finance capital, which has come to dominate first world economic policy in this period of neoliberal globalization.

harder for countries to pursue autonomous development paths, and thus reducing the feasibility of implementing serious national industrial policies.

In spite of its relatively low profile, it appears that the present day is even more dominated by the omnipotent WTO,[6] which replaced and essentially revamped the existing GATT (General Agreement on Tariffs and Trade) as of 1995. Even though it does not impose sanctions directly, its framework provides the capacity to eliminate to a very large extent the autonomy that any individual country has for implementing serious developmental policies, including industrial policies.

A very relevant example of how the WTO is a clear obstacle to autonomous development, as well as sustainable development, is described by Naomi Klein (2014)[7] regarding a plan by Ontario for the promotion of solar panels, in an attempt to promote renewable resources. In spite of having achieved major success for a number of years, including significant investment by foreign companies from multiple countries, because there was a provision for support of local jobs, the project was subject to sanctions via the WTO. Unfortunately, the WTO ruled against Canada, as a result of pressure from Japan and the European Union, criticizing the use of local content, and arguing that it violated WTO's rules, and as a result the program was scrapped. A huge step backward in terms of what Ontario was achieving in reducing our dependence on coal and as a result fossil fuel companies can also feel comfortable that such attempts to reduce our dependence on fossil fuels has a clear ally in the WTO. More importantly, for countries such as Brazil and Argentina the national treatment rules, imply that a government cannot provide any support for its local producers or workers, instead there MUST be equal treatment for national and foreign firms. Evidently, the biggest players, such as the US, Europe, Japan, and China are able to avoid these limitations and will tend not to be taken to court by Zimbabwe, Ecuador, or the Philippines. Had

[6] There have been numerous critical evaluations of the role of the WTO arguing that far from producing a level playing field, that it has clearly benefitted the TNCs and first world countries at the expense of local development and developing countries, which are disproportionately penalized (see Rodrik 2018; Khor 2006; Edelman 2020).

[7] A very relevant discussion of the role of the WTO against interests aimed at promoting renewable resources, all in the name of fair trade, and clearly jeopardizing what individual countries can do, including promoting sustainable development in terms of the environment and support of local initiatives (Klein 2014, pp. 65–69).

this institution been in place at the end of the eighteenth and through the nineteenth and twentieth century, it would have prohibited the great majority of industrialized countries from industrializing.[8]

2.3 Hegemony of TNCs in the Global Economy

The role played by TNCs is absolutely fundamental in understanding the process referred to as globalization, in particular, neoliberal globalization, where there is a clear class bias in favor of capital over labor, with the main beneficiary being the transnational corporations and the capitalist classes, especially in the financial sector, across the globe.

A major characteristic of this period of neoliberal globalization is that of the growing hegemony of transnational corporations.[9] There have been major theoretical contributions in this area made by Sklair (2001), Robinson (2004, 2008), and others. Most notable has been the work of Robinson, who argues that the hegemony of the TNCs is concomitant with the emergence of a transnational capitalist class and the decline in the autonomy of the nation-state. This is not equivalent to the end of the nation-state, but rather how TNCs come to play a greater role in the formation of national policies, especially in countries of the periphery. The specific analysis of Latin America and the nature of its insertion in the transnational production and financial system is presented in a book by Robinson on *Latin America and Global Capitalism* (2008). The evidence of such a new transnational class alliance is supported as several key dynamic sectors are examined, namely, (1) agro-industry, in particular soy and cattle, and in general Non-Traditional Agricultural Exports (NTAE); (2) mining and; (3) the energy sector, exemplified by oil and gas exploration, and biofuels. This analysis has helped to understand the specific shifts that have taken place in Argentina and Brazil, namely, the move toward reprimarization, combined with the deepening presence of TNCs and providing the basis for a new stage of dependency.

This theoretical argument provides a basis for understanding the "seemingly" contradictory posture adopted by so many political leaders

[8] See Chang (2002) for an excellent critique of free trade ideology and issues in development backed up with substantive historical evidence.

[9] Consider the stylized fact that 80% of all international trade is carried out between transnational corporations.

and dominant classes in the periphery, with respect to national interests, when their policies seem designed to accommodate the interests of TNCs of the center more than national firms. It is intended, that through historical analysis, this theoretical development regarding the emergence of a transnational capitalist class provides a useful tool for understanding these dialectical contradictions present in the current period of neoliberal globalization.

2.4 Role of Class Alliances

In Chapter 3 and subsequent chapters, the role of class alliances in Argentina and Brazil will be examined and it is argued that it constitutes a fundamental issue regarding changes in the nature of dependency and imperialism, not to mention the transition from agro-export economies to increasingly industrialized societies. Briefly, one can observe the role of landed oligarchies from the end of the nineteenth century and the dominance of the agro-export model, followed by a transition toward industrialization with the rise of a nascent industrial bourgeoisie. A major area of debate to be discussed and compared between the two countries will be the role of the industrial working class and whether or not a class alliance was established with the industrial bourgeoisie or not, during the periods associated with primarily Vargas and Perón.

Upon considering the transformations that took place with neoliberal globalization across the globe, but in particular for Argentina and Brazil, the hypothesis, just presented, of an emerging transnational capitalist class, will be discussed in light of more detailed empirical evidence. If such a case is deemed plausible, the nature of class alliances and political movements becomes quite distinct, as the relevant terrain can hardly be limited to that of nation-states or their respective national classes. A more in-depth discussion is not appropriate here prior to analyzing the historical trajectories pursued in more detail. Nevertheless, the relevance of this debate has serious implications for any discussion of class struggle in coming decades and whether it may require the mobilization of a transnational working class.

2.5 Role of Accumulation by Dispossession[10]

One of the new developments in recent years is the extension of Marx's category of original accumulation to a new broader theoretical category developed by Harvey (2003) in his book *The New Imperialism*, namely, accumulation by dispossession. Although Harvey applies this concept to a broad range of contexts, the relevance for this book, is whether it is applicable in the context of several processes associated with reprimarization. In fact, in the context of the Brazilian Amazon, the relevance of this concept was considered and it was argued that it was relevant for certain cases, though recognizing distinctions from the concept of original accumulation by Marx (Rivero and Cooney 2010). From the two quotations below, one can see how one could easily derive two definitions based on the section on "The Secret of Primitive Accumulation," in Chapter 26 of *Capital, Vol. I*. Marx first argues with reference to Adam Smith that:

> ...original accumulation (the "previous accumulation" of Adam Smith (Bk. II, Introduction) which precedes capitalist accumulation; an accumulation which is not the result of the capitalist mode of production but its point of departure. (Marx 1977, p. 873)

In the above definition there is no reference to forced expropriation of workers, unlike the following quote from the same chapter:

> So-called original accumulation, therefore, is nothing else than the historical process of divorcing the producer from the means of production. It appears as "original" because it forms the pre-history of capital, and of the mode of production corresponding to capital. (Marx 1977, pp. 874–875)

The point is not simply whether a new theoretical advance is absolutely consistent with Marx, but whether it is a contribution useful for understanding the present day. In this sense, Harvey argues that many of the extra-economic tactics and strategies which the State and Capital employ,

[10] It is worth noting that there have been a number of related interventions made by authors such as Luxemburg and Arendt, to whom Harvey makes clear reference, in his *the New Imperialism*, but also by other authors that are in debate over the concept and originality of Harvey's intervention. for these debates, see *Historical Materialism*, Vol. 14, No. 4, and *The Commoner* Nr. 2 (September 2001)—Enclosures, the Mirror Image of Alternatives.

using both legal and illegal means, and the use of violence to facilitate accumulation is not something that only occurred during the prehistory of capitalism, but rather that it continues till this day. Harvey argues that this has been the case in the instances of the removal of the commons or the processes of privatizations, or the elimination of property rights by ethnic peoples or workers in various parts of the globe so as to accommodate the interests of governments and TNCs, be it for mineral and oil extraction, or agricultural production.

There have been numerous instances throughout Latin America, including both Argentina and Brazil, in recent decades facilitating the expansion of cattle, soy, mining, hydroelectric dams, and petroleum extraction, among other raw materials, that have contributed toward accumulation by dispossession and also toward the process of reprimarization. Therefore, in the analysis in Chapter 7, Harvey's category is considered relevant for understanding the capitalist expansion taking place in both Brazil and Argentina.

Nevertheless, there is a need to be cautious with regard to the application of Harvey's concept, since many authors have employed it without careful scrutiny. For example, during the dictatorship in Brazil in the 1970s, the State, in conjunction with large-scale capitalists, carried out changes or manipulation of laws, combined with violence, in order to facilitate the eventual expansion of soy and cattle producers. This set of activities correspond to the category of accumulation by dispossession, however, once these large-scale soy farms or cattle ranches are in operation, the subsequent accumulation is not accumulation by dispossession, but merely normal capitalist accumulation. Yet, there are certain parts in Harvey's book and other writings which could suggest an interpretation, whereby all the subsequent accumulation corresponds to accumulation by dispossession. Nevertheless, Harvey has been critical of several of these loose interpretations or applications of his concept. (See the *Historical Materialism* Symposium in 2006.) Further debate will only become more fruitful once specific examples are presented and discussed in later chapters. An issue mentioned above, ground rent, a concept critical for understanding peripheral countries insertion in the world economy from the nineteenth century through till the present day, will now be considered.

2.6 Role of Ground Rent and Insertion in the World Economy

At the end of the nineteenth century, the majority of Latin America fit the agro-export model and countries like Argentina and Brazil were providing agricultural goods and raw materials, such as wool, leather, wheat, coffee, and rubber to the center. The integration with the capitalist world economy in the nineteenth century meant they had to import the great majority of manufactured goods. This reflects the standard center–periphery division where, by definition, countries in the periphery are technologically backward, especially with regards to manufacturing, in relation to that of the center. Therefore, in order to have a viable insertion in the world economy they needed to export raw materials and agricultural goods. It is important to recognize that a key reason why peripheral countries can compete in the area of agriculture and raw materials is due to the existence of differential fertility in land and differential productivity, in the case of mines or oil. One does not need to have the latest technology in order to have competitive conditions of production, in contrast to manufacturing.

The reality is such, that particular aspects of land, soil, or subsoil, are not generally reproducible, be it higher fertility of agricultural land or higher productivity of mines and oil wells, and this occurs in both countries of the center and periphery. Therefore, in spite of an inability to compete in manufacturing, exporting raw materials or agricultural products provided a means by which countries of the periphery could compete, if not dominate in a given sector. The category of differential rent, as well as absolute rent, as presented by Marx (1981) in Volume 3 of Capital, which derives from highly fertile land, such as the Pampas, or high productivity mines and oil wells, are the basis by which countries of the periphery could achieve capitalist accumulation.

The present period dominated by the hegemony of the TNCs has implied a major shift with respect to the possibilities of development for the majority of the Latin American region, if not the periphery in general. Given the rules of the WTO[11] and dominance of TNCs, the

[11] In particular, the WTO's national treatment obligation is a general prohibition on the use of internal taxes and other internal regulatory measures so as to afford protection to domestic production, and thus prohibiting many policies that industrialized countries used to foment national production between the eighteenth and twentieth centuries.

possibility of staying competitive in the manufacturing sectors has been incredibly reduced and to achieve competitiveness they are increasingly reduced to those sectors where natural fertility or productivity is an advantage, namely, where ground rent plays a role, such as minerals, petroleum, and soy. A clear example is the extraction of iron ore by Vale in Carajás in the Brazilian Amazon, where they have been able to produce a ton of iron ore for $15 while the best iron mines available in China cost $100 to produce a ton. This differential productivity clearly corresponds to the category of ground rent referred to above and thus constitutes Brazil's primary comparative advantage in the global economy; unfortunately, it is the opposite case when considering the world market for the manufacturing sector.

This has been a short presentation of why the theoretical concept of ground rent, as derived from Marx, is relevant today and how this contributes to a deeper understanding of why developing economies are shifting toward an increasingly primary production orientation, if not the trajectory of reprimarization, as will be further analyzed in Chapter 7.[12]

2.7 The 2nd Contradiction of Capitalism and the Environment

In considering the shift to reprimarization in Argentina and Brazil it is increasingly relevant to consider the impacts on the environment. The following issues are very much connected to the shifts toward reprimarization: (1) deforestation of the Amazon Rain Forest linked to lumber, minerals, petroleum, cattle, and soy expansion; (2) air, water, and soil pollution linked to the use of pesticides, as well as mining and oil extraction activities; (3) soil erosion as a result of mining and soy. In addition there are major socio-environmental issues around the expansion of hydroelectric dams, especially in Brazil, which is strongly tied to the expansion of mining in the Amazon and elsewhere. The discussion of the impact of capitalist expansion on the environment was one of the main contributions, among many, made by James O'Connor. In terms of theoretical issues, a major advance made by O'Connor was his presentation of the second contradiction of capitalism.

[12] For a more developed analysis of the role of ground rent from a marxist perspective and analyzing reprimarization in Latin America, see Trindade and Cooney (2019).

James O'Connor was one of the first established Marxists to make groundbreaking efforts in the area of ecology and has become associated with the concept of the second contradiction of capitalism from many of his writings dealing with the environment (O'Connor 1988, 1998). The main thrust of his argument is that there was the emphasis on class struggle that was linked to the first contradiction of capitalism, namely, between the productive forces and the relations of production. The second contradiction is that between, on the one hand, the productive forces and the relations of production, and on the other, the conditions of reproduction. The latter includes the land, air, water, and the environment in general and O'Connor also includes the reproduction of labor power.[13] As a result of increasing attention given to environmental concerns, in part thanks to O'Connor, the second contradiction has come to be more and more relevant in recent years. To a large extent it has been the negative environmental impacts of ever-expanding capitalism, exacerbated during the phase of TNC-dominated neoliberal globalization, producing major climate crises, if not a path of devastation and degradation that will take decades, if not centuries, to be reversed or in the worst-case scenario, the end of the human species, if the accelerating climate change is not put in check.

The analysis carried out by O'Connor forced many political economists to include considerations of the environment and ecology in their critical analysis of class and capitalist society. Nevertheless, it can be argued that certain aspects of his argument are flawed or that there are different views regarding the implications of the 2nd contradiction and this relates to the issue of cause and effect with respect to profitability and crises. In particular, what seems far from certain is the argument by O'Connor that the environmental impacts will necessarily lead to a decline in profitability for capitalist firms. It can be argued instead that it is more likely that the capitalist firms and global TNCs will be able to shift or defer the problem to local communities, workers or countries, and experience minimal negative impact in terms of their bottom line; recent history seems to be more supportive of this latter view.

[13] A number of Marxists, including myself, would argue against the inclusion of labor-power by O'Connor, since the productive forces are not just limited to machines or means of production but also include skilled or unskilled labor power.

The main thrust of such a critique of O'Connor is not in terms of the negative impacts on the environment, which derive from capitalist accumulation, and even more so today given the unparalleled power TNCs have in many corners of the globe. What can be questioned, is the mechanism by which this will impact the profitability of these firms. In general, it can be argued, that TNCs are able to elude the most serious negative effects such that their cost structure and profits are minimally affected by the damage that their accumulation has come to cause. In part this is a result of human rights taking a back seat to corporate rights, and their relative power being that much stronger.

Consider the example of mining, such as in Marapá in the Amazon in 1957, when Bethlehem Steel went there and extracted manganese for several decades, leaving the area devastated and the communities suffering, however, Bethlehem Steel had their amazing profits repatriated. Of course, there are some cases where a given mineral or product becomes too expensive to produce or not profitable as a result of worsening environmental conditions, but they will move on or seek an alternative. Unless there are serious changes to global laws, or the rules that tend to dominate trade (and investment) treaties, such as NAFTA, or the existence of an effective world court for environmental justice, it is the opposite that tends to take place, especially under neoliberalism; these corporations will remain minimally affected, especially with respect to profitability.

Evidently, one must examine each situation or environmental problem, case by case. In the context of global climate change, O'Connor's argument may have the greatest validity, although his argument is for a much broader range of environmental problems. In the instance of a strengthened global environmental movement that achieves advances at the level of laws and restrictions on the part of TNCs, then many of the damages and ecological devastation that has been caused by TNCs and others could clearly lead to impacts on profitability for capital. However, at the present moment, the world is very far from this being implemented. Nevertheless, if such conditions are achieved, not only could worsening profitability be a result, but perhaps a level of the political mobilizations could push us toward a post-capitalist world. In general, one should advocate or seek constructive criticism with respect to O'Connor and aim to advance theoretical discussion, especially political economic analysis which takes both class and environmental issues into account; as well as supporting or promoting political practice which involves a red-green front, as he had argued for.

For now, the TNCs generally are able to elude the serious legal and environmental problems, which could jeopardize their profitability. Nevertheless, it is important to recognize the relevance of the second contradiction, emphasizing the impact on the conditions of reproduction, and that this contradiction clearly impacts negatively upon the environment. It is the communities, particularly poor ones, but not only, that are impacted and as a result of this contradiction, could lead to social struggle and conflict and potentially undermine the smooth functioning of the system. So, O'Connor should be applauded for identifying the 2nd contradiction and also for elaborating upon it and the environment, raising consciousness, and pushing many an economist, Marxists included, to take into account the environment and ecological issues. However, there is a need to have a closer examination regarding the mechanisms of how such a contradiction is manifested in the real capitalist world. To the extent possible, this discussion will be revisited in later chapters, when dealing with environmental issues.

2.8 Final Considerations

This chapter has attempted to present an overview of theoretical issues which are of relevance for understanding the trajectories pursued by Brazil and Argentina in recent decades. In spite of it being quite limited, given the space limitations and the main topic of the book, it is hoped to have provided some insight to the background setting for theoretical discussions to be further elaborated upon in the coming chapters. Unfortunately, some of the theoretical issues were not discussed as deeply as preferred, given the fact that the empirical evidence necessary for these discussions has not yet been presented.

Beyond the issue of the relevance of the concepts center–periphery and dependency, the following theoretical topics were also considered: neoliberal globalization, the nature of the hegemony of TNCs, and the emergence of a transnational capitalist class, international institutions, in particular, the WTO, the relevance of the concept of accumulation by dispossession, the concept of ground rent in the context of reprimarization and lastly, the 2nd contradiction of capitalism and its relevance for the environment. The next chapter presents a historical analysis starting with the period of transition for both Argentina and Brazil, transitioning from agro-export economies at the end of the nineteenth century into the early phase of Import Substitution Industrialization during the first decades of the twentieth century.

References

Bambirra, Vania. 1978. *Teoría de la dependencia: una anticrítica*. Mexico City: Ediciones Era.

Bond, Patrick. 2006. *Looting Africa: The Economics of Exploitation*. New York: Zed Books.

Carcanholo, Marcelo Dias. 2017. *Dependencia, super-explotación del Trabajo y Crisis: una interpretación desde Marx*. Madrid: Ediciones Maia.

Chang, Han-Joon. 2002. *Kicking Away the Ladder—Development Strategy in Historical Perspective*. London: Anthem Press.

Cooney, Paul, and Trindade, José R. 2017. "Dependency Approach in Latin America: Confronting Challenges of the 21st Century." Presented at the *X Jornadas de Economía Crítica*, September 2017, UNGS, Buenos Aires, Argentina.

Dos Santos, Theotônio. 1970. "The Structure of Dependence." *American Economic Review*, LX (May), pp. 231–236.

Edelman, Marc. 2020. "Bringing the Moral Economy Back into the Study of 21st Century Transnational Peasant Movements." *American Anthropologist* Vol. 107, No. 3 (2005).

Féliz, Mariano. 2019. "Neodevelopmentalism and Dependency in Twenty-first Century Argentina: Insights from the Work of Ruy Mauro Marini. *Latin American Perspectives*, Issue 224, Vol. 46 No. 1, January 2019, pp. 105–221.

Frank, Andre G. 1967. *Capitalism and Underdevelopment in Latin America: Historical Studies of Chile and Brazil*. New York: Monthly Review Press.

Hardt, M., and Negri, A. 2000. *Empire*. Cambridge, MA: Harvard University Press.

Harvey, David, 2003. *The New Imperialism*. Oxford and London.

Historical Materialism Symposium. 2006. Vol. 14, No. 4.

Katz, Claudio. 2018. *La Teoría de la Dependencia, cincuenta años después*. Buenos Aires: Batalla de Ideas.

Khor, Martin. 2006. "The WTO's Doha Negotiations and Impasse: A Development Perspective." *Third World Network* (November): 16.

Klein, Naomi. 2014. *This Changes Everything: Capitalism vs. the Climate*. New York: Simon and Schuster.

Marini, Ruy Mauro. 1973. *Dialética da dependência*. México: Era.

Martins, Carlos E. 2011. *Globalização, Dependência e Neoliberalismo na América Latina*. São Paulo: Boitempo.

Marx, Karl. 1977 *Capital: Critique of Political Economy, Vol. I*. New York: Vintage Books.

———. 1981 *Capital: Critique of Political Economy, Vol. III*. New York: Penguin Books.

Meiksens Wood, Ellen. 2005. *Empire of Capital*. New York: Verso.

O'Connor, James. 1988, "Capitalism, Nature, Socialism: A Theoretical Introduction." *Capitalism, Nature, Socialism*, Vol. 1, No. 1.

———. 1998. *Natural Causes: Essays in Ecological Marxism*. New York: Guilford Press.

Osorio, J. 2012. "América Latina: o novo padrão exportador de especialização produtiva – estudo de cinco economias da região". In: Carla Ferreira, Jaime Osorio e Mathias Luce (orgs.), *Padrão de reprodução do capital: contribuições da teoria marxista da dependência*. São Paulo: Boitempo.

Rivero, S., and Paul Cooney. 2010. "The Amazon as a Frontier of Capital Accumulation: Looking Beyond the Trees." *Capitalism, Nature, Socialism*, Vol. 21, No. 4.

Robinson, William I. 2004. *A Theory of Global Capitalism—Production, Class and State in a Transnational World*. Baltimore: The John Hopkins University Press.

———. 2008. *Latin America and Global Capitalism—A Critical Globalization Perspective*. Baltimore: The John Hopkins University Press.

Rodrik, Dani. 2018. "The WTO Has Become Dysfunctional." *Financial Times*, August 5, 2018.

Sklair, Leslie. 2001. *The Transnational Capitalist Class*. Oxford: Blackwell.

Trindade, J.R., and Cooney, Paul. 2019. "Empresas Transnacionais, Territorialidade e Impactos Ambientais na Região Amazônica Oriental Brasileira." Presented at *ENEP XXIV*, Victoria, Brazil.

CHAPTER 3

Import Substitution Industrialization (ISI) in Argentina and Brazil

3.1 Transition from Agro-Export Economies Toward Industrialization

This first section of this chapter carries out an analysis for both the Argentine and Brazilian economies during the period of transition between the agro-export phase and the beginning of the phase of Import Substitution Industrialization (ISI). The previous phase is associated with the tendency for an economy to orient itself toward the production and export of primary goods and raw materials for the first world. In both cases, the insertion in the world economy is crucial for understanding the socioeconomic development for each country. As throughout the book, the aim is to analyze the trajectories of each country identifying the most salient similarities and differences between the Argentine and Brazilian experiences. In the section below, the historical background is presented, with emphasis on the state of industry for both countries prior to World War I (WWI). On the one hand, there is a common history, given the fact that both experienced Iberian colonialism, from the sixteenth century through the nineteenth century, and through the colonial expansion of extractive and agricultural activities constituting clear examples of agro-export economies. During the nineteenth century there had been changes in the composition of exports, as a result of their insertion in the world

P. Cooney, *Paths of Development in the Southern Cone*, Palgrave Insights into Apocalypse Economics,
https://doi.org/10.1007/978-3-030-67673-5_2

economy. Both countries provided a range of primary goods, such as raw materials, foodstuffs, etc., for Europe and the US, in general.

In Sect. 3.1.1 below, the development of Argentina's industry from the time of WWI until the beginning of the 1930s is presented, followed by a presentation of the situation for Brazilian industry during that same period. In each case, the debates around the impact of foreign factors or external shocks, such as the First World War and the Great Depression, are considered. It is evident that, since such factors lead to a disruption of imports for both countries, local industry was forced to respond and cover the gap as best as possible. One question which the analysis aims to provide an answer to is the following: at what point did industry transition from being merely nascent to more mature and established? Another important issue is that of shifts and the construction of new class alliances, which played a key role in fomenting changes which took place during this period.

The section below is a comparative analysis of the two experiences of transitioning toward industrialization, identifying similarities and differences between both trajectories. The expansion of the 1920s is relevant in the context of the debate mentioned above. Of major importance is the relation of both countries, Argentina and Brazil, with the dominant world powers: Great Britain and the US. The specific interaction with these world powers is examined with special emphasis on the nature of the dependency that exists between them, given their importance as their main destination for exports and as sources of investment. In the last subsection final considerations are presented with regard to the experiences of two of the most significant economies of South America during the phase of transition from the agro-export phase to the early stages of ISI, including some reflections regarding the relevance of such historical transitions, in light of the processes of deindustrialization in the present day.[1]

[1] See Cooney and Santarcángelo (2011), or Cooney (2020) and Trindade et al. (2016) for the case of just Brazil.

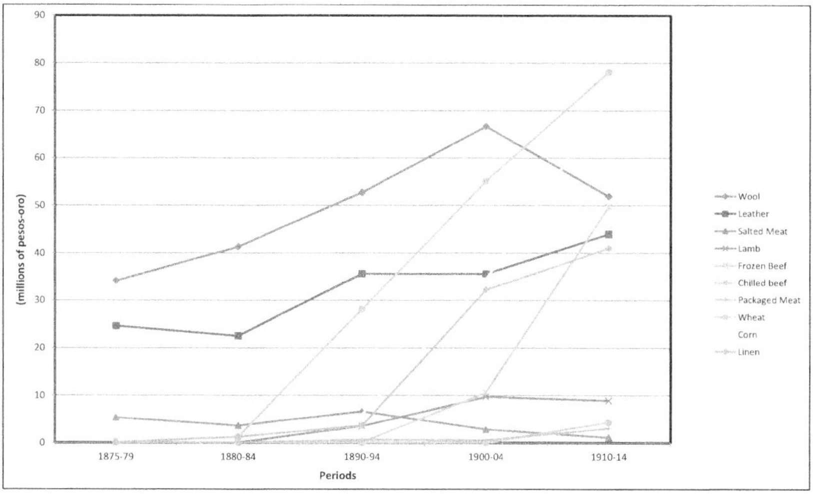

Fig. 3.1 Argentine Exports (1875–1914) (millions of *pesos-oro*) [based on the average prices for the period 1910–1914] (*Source* Graph is based on data from Diaz Alejandro 1975, p. 19)

3.1.1 Argentina

3.1.1.1 Agro-Export Economy[2]

During the period 1875–1895 the exports of wool and leather are dominant, being gradually replaced by wheat and corn toward the end of the century. Afterward, the export of frozen beef and linen grew rapidly, especially during the decade prior to WWI when railroads and refrigerated cars came to play a key role. In Fig. 3.1 the main Argentine exports are presented for this period. In the case of wheat, exports experience a strong increase reaching 28.1 million *pesos-oro*[3] in 1890–1894, and then 78.1 million for the period 1910–1914. Corn exports also showed a similar acceleration, reaching 72.4 million pesos-oro for the period 1910–1914. Two other cases of notable growth in this period are frozen beef

[2] This section has benefitted by the data and information incorporated from the following sources: Diaz Alejandro (1975), Arceo (2003), and Lazzari (2011).

[3] The Argentine currency was *pesos-oro* and an estimate of the exchange rate with the British pound sterling in 1882 is 5.04 *pesos-oro* for a pound sterling (see Alvarez 1929, p. 118).

and linen. In the case of beef, exports grew from 0.1 million pesos-oro in 1890–1894 up to 49.7 million pesos-oro in 1910–1914, primarily as a result of the increase of refrigerated rail cars. The key factors which explain these changes are demand, primarily from Europe; the availability of laborers, in particular, immigrants; the key role played by British capital; and the wealth generated, between ground rent and speculation fomented by rapid growth and finally the expansion of the internal market in Argentina.

In evaluating the growth of exports of beef compared to lamb it is worth noting how the former grew from 9 to 18 million *pesos-oro* during the period 1875–1914. On the eve of WWI, chilled beef began to be more important within Argentina's export profile. The development of refrigerated railcars gave Argentina the capacity to export meat and this was in part due to U.S. investment, but also due to the support and loans by the British.

A key aspect of the dynamic of the agro-export economy is the importance of being able to produce at a low cost, whether one is producing wool, leather, beef, wheat, coffee, or rubber, as in the case of Brazil. This was possible due to the combination of low wages and high fertility. The latter establishes the conditions for obtaining agricultural ground rent, which is fundamental for accumulation. Such conditions were available in the Argentine pampas,[4] at the end of the nineteenth century, and on that basis, they were able to receive a steady flow of capital both internally and from outside the country. The growth of agricultural ground rent facilitated the strong expansion of production in the pampas. This also came to promote land speculation, which strengthened even more the expansion in the pampas. As a consequence of the increases in rent and profits from land speculation there was a strengthening of the landed oligarchy.

3.1.1.2 Class Alliances

During the last decades of the nineteenth century and the beginning of the twentieth the oligarchy of the pampas was the hegemonic class in Argentina. The key question is: what was their relationship with the development of industry and the ascendant industrial bourgeoisie? Some argue that the agro-export oligarchy looked to put a brake on the advances

[4] The term used in Argentina for the pampas is often "*la pampa húmeda*", which is literally the humid pampa, referring to the presence of a sufficient amount of rainfall, in order for the land to be fertile, otherwise it would be too dry.

by industry while others argue that the industrial bourgeoisie arose out of this very same oligarchy. The hegemonic fraction of the landowning class diversified into different activities, such as finances, thus allowing this group to profit in periods of growth as well as in downturns of the economic cycles, analogous to hedging in the modern day. In such instances, the interests of the oligarchy became diversified and their sources of accumulation coincided with obtaining credit via foreign loans, leading to a feverish expansion of business and speculation.

The alliance which was established between the Pampean oligarchy and foreign capital was charged with providing goods and infrastructure at low cost. Thus, the development of national industry was dependent upon the behavior of the hegemonic fractions of capital, whether national or foreign. According to Lazzari (2011), and coinciding with the analysis of Dorfman and Schvarzer, a difference or opposition between the landowning class and the industrial bourgeoisie as social classes did not exist, and some families which were part of the hegemonic class actually began to invest in industry, using their profits obtained from agriculture, livestock, finances, or from speculation in order to expand into new profitable areas.

3.1.1.3 Nascent Industry

In the final decades of the nineteenth century, the industrial sector was in the process of establishing itself and was clearly subordinate to agriculture. According to Arceo (2003), between 1900 and 1913, manufacturing industry was growing at a cumulative rate of 7% annually, while the agricultural sector was only growing at 5%. Evidently, the role of imports of manufactured products continued to be strong, if not dominant, in many of the different branches, though with significant variations. For example, the percentage of consumption covered by local production was 37% in foodstuffs, while in metals and machines it was only 12% and in textiles and clothing it was 17.5%.[5]

As was the case for many countries, the chains of manufacturing industry which were able to advance further, had strong links to the agricultural sector, and thus the food and beverages sector played a major role. Nevertheless, in 1915, manufacturing industry constituted a mere

[5] These numbers are based upon the analysis carried out by Arceo for the year 1914 and are calculated excluding industrial production in Argentina which was subsequently exported (Arceo 2003, pp. 310–311).

13% of GDP, while the agricultural sector[6] was 35%. The economy was still under the control of the landed oligarchy and therefore responsive to the agro-export sector and its necessary accumulation.

A key factor for the expansion of nascent industry was the issue of available laborers. The combination of the flow of immigrants[7] together with population growth was important for the intense expansion, providing a labor force for growing manufacturing industry. The immigrant factor was even more important given the fact that many of the immigrant workers already had experience working in factories in Europe previously, in contrast to many of the Argentines in that period. The formation and growth of the argentine working class was crucial for the subsequent development of urban classes, which came to have greater demands of manufactured goods, and in this way, contributed to the expansion of the internal market in Argentina. Another factor was the increased demand for housing, especially with the flow of people migrating to the cities.

3.1.1.4 The Role of the State and Great Britain

An important aspect is the role of the State and, in particular, the connections and negotiations with international powers, especially Great Britain. Evidently, the driving force of the economy at the end of the nineteenth century and the beginning of the twentieth was the agro-export sector, which had the greatest sales to Europe and with Great Britain being the primary destination of exports. Besides the interest in imports, the providing of loans and investment was of major importance for Great Britain. Most significant in this regard was the expansion of the railroads from the last three decades of the nineteenth century onwards, in particular the refrigerated rail cars, primarily used for transporting beef.

According to Ford (2009), in the year 1875, the sectorial division of labor with Great Britain was the following: railroads, public services, and credit provided by the English, while Argentines would invest in landed property. Initially, the relationship with Great Britain was primarily commercial, and investment was provided to insure the export of wool to

[6] When the term agriculture or agricultural sector is used, it is including livestock, unless specified otherwise, as it is a translation of the term "agropecuaria" in Spanish or "agropecuária" in Portuguese.

[7] For information on immigrants in Argentina data from Solberg (1981, p. 196) was employed and he used official statistics of the National Ministry of Immigration (*Dirección Nacional de Migraciones*) for data on net immigration.

English textile firms. Afterward, British financial capital came to finance the development of the Argentine State, mainly for the projects involving infrastructure, such as for railroads. British finance capital came to gain a foothold in this way within the Argentine economy, which between the years 1880 and 1913 grew almost 20 times, reaching 1928 billion *pesos-oro* in 1913, which constituted 59.3% of all investment in Argentina.[8] The British were always able to count on the local governments in making the effort to insure the realization of significant profits, and at the same time, authorizing the tax exemptions and land grants to the extent required for the expansion of railroads. This has been a brief presentation of the period of transition from an agro-export economy to the beginnings of industrialization in Argentina; however, prior to considering the first phase of ISI, the transition from an agro-export economy for Brazil will be considered first.

3.1.2 Brazil

3.1.2.1 The Coffee Economy

For the majority of the nineteenth century the principal driving force of development in the Brazilian economy was exports, growing 214% between 1840 and 1890. In spite of sugar growing 33% and cotton 43%, the fivefold increase in coffee production implied that coffee was the primary motor of the economy. The evolution of the production of coffee, in terms of accumulation and the development of a wage-earning class, in contradistinction to slaves or subsistence peasants, is crucial in understanding the development of Brazilian industry. In addition to the Brazilians who became wage earners, there was a very significant impact from the flow of immigrants from Europe, especially Italy; similar to Argentina. According to Furtado, if the expansion of the coffee economy had been exclusively dependent on European immigrants, wages would have been higher. However, between immigrants and Brazilian laborers, the pressure for keeping wages down was much stronger; a clear case of an expanded industrial reserve army. During several decades the coffee sector had high profits and expanded rapidly, however, the world market had a limit and Brazil was already supplying 75% of it by the end of the century.

[8] The data on British investment in 1913 are from Solberg (1981, p. 198).

3.1.2.2 Nascent Industry[9]

At the end of the 1880s, there was a period of intense speculation, known as the *Encilhamento*. Some argue that the *Encilhamento* (1886–1894) was merely a period of speculation and hurt nascent industry while others argue that it, in fact, constituted the genesis of industrial capital. For example, the authors Mello (1982), Silva (1976), Cano (1977), and Aureliano (1981), all argue that the origin of industrial capital took place during this period of the expansion of coffee.

Suzigan argues that the evidence is most consistent with the perspective by Stein (1979) and that there had been significant investment during the period of the *Encilhamento*. Other authors, including Fishlow, argue that the delay in devaluing the currency (*mil-reais*) implied that machines were cheaper and thus provided incentives for investment in industry, importing machinery equipment from Europe and the US. After 1891, an increase in the prices of imports of consumer goods was registered, and this provided a stimulus for the production of such goods within Brazil, taking advantage of machinery that had been bought previously at much lower prices, as a result of the overvalued exchange rate.

As discussed earlier, the role of immigrants was fundamental for the expansion of coffee, but perhaps even more so for the development of Brazilian industry. From the end of the nineteenth century and the beginning of the twentieth, immigrants were brought in for the coffee plantations and the government assisted in providing them for the manufacturing industry[10] and for the establishment of free laborers. The different industries which took advantage of the availability of immigrant laborers and technicians were: matches, wheat mills, textiles, breweries, and shoe and hat makers.

In the case of Argentina it was seen how the landed oligarchy came to diversify its investment between speculation in land, finances, and industry. In a similar way, Suzigan describes the diversification carried out by the coffee oligarchy, or *cafeteiros*:

> The majority of capital invested in manufacturing in this period shows a direct or indirect link to the export economy. Direct investments of capital

[9] Much of this text is based upon a comprehensive analysis carried out by Suzigan (2000) in his classic text on Brazilian Industry.

[10] The term *indústria de transformação*, used in Brazil, is equivalent to the term manufacturing industry.

> from the coffee sector have been made in manufacturing in São Paulo during the 19th century in factories of cotton cloth, jute and wool and to a lesser extent in the metal machinery sector. (Suzigan 2000, pp. 128–129)

This is a key point with respect to the behavior of *paulista* capitalists and is consistent with the concept as developed by Wilson Cano (1977), in which the coffee plantation owners or *cafeteiros* came to adopt a network of activities as their basis of investment. For this period, the advance of basic manufacturing industries is linked to the process of accumulation of capital of the agro-export sector, dominated by the *cafeteiros*.

3.2 First Phase of Industrialization in Argentina and Brazil

3.2.1 *Argentine Industry (from WWI Till the 1930s)*

Analyzing Argentina after the First World War and the approach of the 1930s and the Great Depression, it is evident that Argentina begins its first phase of Import Substitution Industrialization or ISI. For some, this industrialization had been delayed, in the sense that Argentina had advanced in terms of production, growth, and GDP per capita comparable to Australia and Canada, anticipating an industrial takeoff. However, there had been a "great delay" in postponing this takeoff until the 1930s. One of the authors most well-known who participated in this debate over "the great delay" was Diaz Alejandro (1975).

Some authors try to argue that the period of WWI was positive in the sense that the War brought about scarcity in many goods and inputs, which had been imported and thus pushing local producers to fill this gap, given the growing internal market. Others argue the opposite, in that the war period was negative for industry due to the limitations of obtaining inputs and necessary products for their expansion.

3.2.2 *Development of Argentine Industry*

In Fig. 3.2, the graphs of total GDP and the percentage which corresponds to manufacturing industry can be observed. It shows how this percentage increased from 13% at the beginning of the century till almost 25% in 1946; a very clear tendency, in spite of variations. From the data

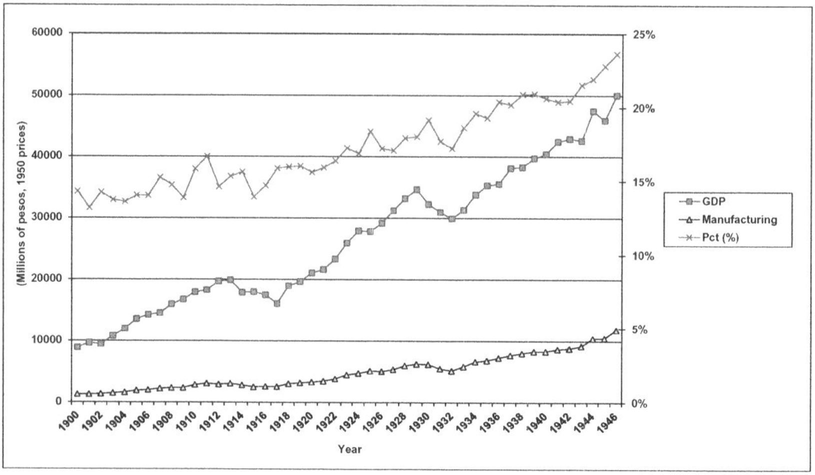

Fig. 3.2 GDP, Manufacturing industry, Argentina (1900–1946) (*Source* Data from ECLA 1958)

used for Fig. 3.2, it is evident, that although the Argentine economy was growing, the manufacturing industry was growing even more rapidly. Although this graph clarifies the situation for the manufacturing industry as a whole, when considering the 1935 Census sectorial data, Villanueva shows how food and beverages were still dominant with 37%; textiles 15%, metals, and by-products 5.6%; machines and vehicles 6.6%; that of chemicals 3.9% and petroleum and its derivatives also 3.9%.

The dominance of food and beverages makes sense at this stage since Argentina is transitioning from an agro-export-dominated economy and this is the industry most linked to that. As this period constitutes one of a changing nature or form of dependency, it is because previously Argentina was overwhelmingly importing manufactured goods and all which that entails as a country of the periphery. As a country industrializes, the dependency on importing manufacturing goods goes through a transition, and eventually multinationals (later on transnationals) come to operate within a country, thus shifting the dominant circuit of capital and the form of dependency. As will be observed through the subsequent decades, the capacity of Argentina's industry ends up providing more and more of its manufacturing needs, and in fact eventually surpasses the GDP contribution of agriculture in the national economy (see Fig. 3.3). This

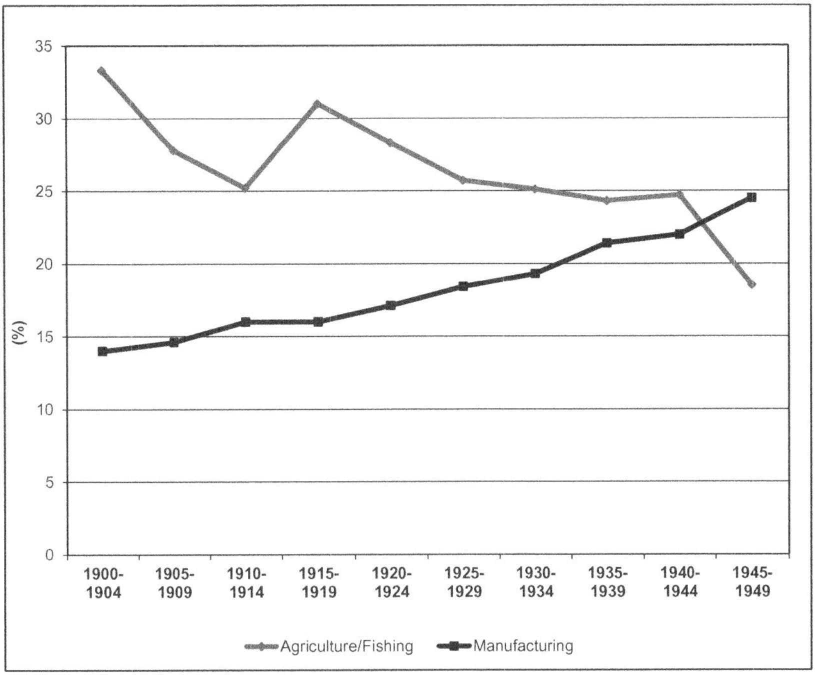

Fig. 3.3 Sectorial Participation of GDP (%) Argentina (*Source* Data from ECLA 1958)

is a reflection of a shift in terms of the specific insertion in the world economy and thus reduces the degree of dependency in terms of the impacts pointed to by Prebisch regarding terms of trade. An important aspect of this shift is the manner in which MNCs came to set up operations, while fomenting industry, in countries such as Argentina and Brazil. The relevance of the food and beverage sector at that time and perhaps even more so today is revealing and deserves attention in any discussion on development strategies.

Similarly, Di Tella and Zymelman (1967) presented results for various industries and highlighted the food and beverages sector. According to them, its percentage with respect to overall national industry had fallen during this whole period, from 38% in 1915–1920 and then 39.37% for the five-year period 1920–1924; afterward dropping to 36.54 for the next five-year period 1925–1929 and then even lower for the next one, 1930–1934, reaching 33.22%. On the one hand, one could say that for the period as a whole, the national percentage had declined, yet in absolute terms, it still continued to be the sector with greater growth and at a much greater absolute level of production.

3.2.3 *Shifts Within Agricultural Production and Toward Industry*

After the war it was no longer possible for Great Britain to maintain the same level of trade with Argentina and thus agro-exports fell sharply. By the time of the Great Depression, the push toward industrial diversification was not to be stopped in spite of agreements such as Roca-Runciman in 1933. One important factor was that the frontier of agricultural expansion in the Pampas had come to an end.[11] In other words, the extinction of new fertile lands, needed for generating agrarian rent, implied that the limits of the agricultural expansion, particularly for beef had been reached. There were also increasing problems with increase in the prices of land fueling speculation and thus an excessive use of mortgages.

This period witnesses a transition of an economy dominated by far by the agricultural sector, especially cereals and beef, which up to the present day continues to be important, but not to the level of prior to WWI. As a result of these changes in the countryside and with the help of US investment, sectors of the Pampean oligarchy diversified their production even more toward industry. One could really see this period as the first stage of ISI, even though the interests of the oligarchy corresponded with the development of industry in accord with the necessities of the agro sector. In this period there is not a clear distinction between an agrarian class and a new industrial class fighting for dominance, given that so many times the same persons or families were both the landowning oligarchy and the industrialists.

In any case, the growth of industry is undeniable and the eventual establishment of an industrial bourgeoisie was only an issue of time; comparing the participation of the largest sectors, for the period of 1900–1949, the reduction in the participation of agriculture and the growth of the manufacturing industry shows a very significant shift in Fig. 3.3, with industry surpassing agriculture in the mid-1940s at roughly 23%.

[11] See Díaz Alejandro (1975), Di Tella y Zymelman (1967), or Villanueva (1972).

3.2.4 Competition Between Great Britain and the US

A key problem for Argentina is that the destination of the great majority of their exports was Great Britain on the eve of WWI and reciprocally Great Britain was the principal investor in Argentina, whether for railroads, agricultural production, or loans to the government. After the war, the role of Great Britain suffered a major setback and was no longer able to maintain Argentine imports as it had in the past and in addition, the flow of capitals to Argentina were practically reduced to zero. In contrast, the US was willing to increase its flow of investment into Argentina during the 1920s and 1930s. The problem was that the main exports of Argentina were beef and grains, both products which the US also produced and even exported, and thus was not interested in importing them from Argentina. As it turns out, the shift of world finances from London to New York produced a dilemma for Argentina, namely continuing to require the flow of foreign capital but maintaining its trade surplus with England and a trade deficit with the US: a triangular problem, if you will. In fact, foreign investment expressed as a percentage of GDP, suffered a serious contraction compared to the period before the war, falling from 20.8% for the period 1910–1914 down to 3.2 for the period 1930–1935.[12]

With the financial crisis of 1929 and the plummet of world trade, the tendency toward protection increased notably. For example, Great Britain took measures which tended to protect the incipient beef market of the Commonwealth, that is to say, only buying meat from British colonies, which included Canada, Australia, and South Africa, among others. As a result, Argentina was excluded from these favorable conditions, and as a result there began the negotiations over the proposal of the Roca–Runciman Pact. Basically, Britain proposed to continue buying beef in exchange for Argentina maintaining protection of the investments in state enterprises (especially in the transport sector) and eliminating any tariffs for manufactured British goods.

Given the importance of exporting beef among other products to Great Britain, the Argentine government signed this pact in May 1933, which consolidated the power of the British firms involved in the refrigerated railcars and benefited notably the livestock sector, who together with

[12] See Di Tella and Zymelman (1967), Fig. 3.9.

the landed oligarchy were those that supported the project. The Argentine Rural Society (*Sociedad Rural Argentina*-SRA) made the following slogan famous "buy from those that buy from you"[13] as supporting the Pact. The Argentine Industrial Union *(Unión Industrial Argentina)*,[14] initially pushed to keep the tariffs against the free import of British goods which the Pact eliminated, but finally had to succumb and align themselves with the interests of the landed oligarchy, in support of the agreement with the minor demand that the policies would continue to protect a select group of products produced nationally.

The Pact was questioned by the sectors of the left, socialists and *Radicales*,[15] who denounced the negative impact of the agreement for consumers; they argued that as a consequence of the agreement, they were paying more to British than they would be to US counterparts. With this pact, Argentina showed itself siding with Great Britain in the context of open competition after the First World War between British and US interests, in terms of access to their local markets. Before moving on to the period of the 1940s and the arrival of Perón, the shifts in Brazilian industry, from the time of WWI through till the 1930s and the Vargas period will first be examined.

3.2.5 Brazilian Industry (WWI Through Till the 1930s)

For example, the shift from agro-export economies toward ISI could be argued to be essentially the result of outside factors, though strongly dependent upon internal factors. The theory of adverse shocks refers to when the world market stops providing basic goods for a peripheral country, such a country should try to produce these goods themselves out of necessity. This has been considered the case for both Argentina and Brazil with WWI being the 1st adverse shock. Effectively, there were

13 "The slogan in Spanish ("*comprar a quien nos compra*") translates as "buy from those that buy from you."

14 The translation of *la Sociedad Rural Argentina* (SRA) is the Argentine Rural Society, an institution which represented the landed oligarchy and over time agribusiness (see Chapter 5). The translation of *la Unión Industrial Argentina* is the Argentine Industrial Union and this institution has represented organized industry for decades in Argentina.

15 *Radicales* refers to members of the party *Unión Cívica Radical* which can be translated as the Radical Civic Union and has been one of the two main parties for over a century and is not particularly radical in terms of its politics.

the periods of growth of exports when the major expansion of industrial capital took place and it is also certain that the industrial capital originated in activities directly or indirectly linked to the export sector (be it coffee in Brazil or beef and wheat in Argentina).

Nevertheless, it is clear that the Great Depression of the 1930s (the 2nd adverse shock) constituted the inflection point in terms of industrial development for both Brazil and Argentina. The discussion tends to be around the issue of the impact of WWI and the Great Depression, in terms of adverse shocks, which came to have positive effects with respect to industrialization. It could be argued that for both Argentine and Brazilian industry, they were not sufficiently developed to weather the storm of the adverse shock of the war; distinct from what took place with the Great Depression of the 1930s.

In the following decade Brazilian industry developed significantly, although not all in a smooth manner. It may turn out to have been crucial that during this period there came to be the recognition on the part of both government and industrialists, regarding the need to foment the diversity and development of the industrial sector.

3.2.6 Coffee Crisis and Implications for Industry

Furtado argued that the policy of the defense of coffee consisted in the government and coffee producers' efforts in maintaining the price of coffee. This was accomplished by both the payment for warehousing the coffee and combined with the destruction of part of the harvest. The complicated mechanism of the defense of coffee functioned with relative efficiency until 1929, when the greatest coffee crisis hit, given the fact that the level of production was double that of the level of exports. Between the years 1925–1929, the exportable production of coffee increased from 15.8 million up to 28.5 million sacks of coffee (60 kilos per sack).[16] The average production for the period 1927–1929 was 20.9 million sacks of coffee, while exports were 14.1 million. The greatest gap was reached exactly at the time of the outbreak of the crisis of 1929 and the beginning of the world depression: in 1929: production reached 28.94 million sacks while exports were only 14.28 million. Given such a gap, the depression showed that the scheme of warehousing coffee was no longer sustainable.

[16] Source of this data was the Brazilian Institute of Coffee (*Instituto Brasileiro do Café*).

With the crisis of coffee and the problems of currency, the result was a major flight of capital and evaporating foreign reserves.

The First World War accelerated the process which made evident the need to diversify the structure of industrial production. This diversification intensified during the decade of the 1920s, partially stimulated by government incentives and subsidies. With the crisis of exports and the Great Depression of the 1930s, the link between the expansion of the export sector and the growth of the industrial sector was broken, even though the industrial sector continued being dependent on the former in so far as providing foreign exchange necessary for importing machines and equipment required for investment and production inputs.

It was evident that there had been a clear negative impact after 1929, given the crisis of coffee and the beginning of the Great Depression. The following period saw a renewed defense of coffee and an expansionist economic policy, producing increases in investment between 1933 and 1939. The recovery of manufacturing industry can be seen as a result of the implementation of anti-cyclical policies, the devaluation of the currency, which caused imports to be more expensive, and the push by the Vargas government. The latter made efforts to support nascent industry with infrastructural programs, tariff and subsidy policies, including tax exemptions, incentives, as well as credit. In this period, one could begin to see the positive results of efforts made by the Vargas administration in terms of industrial growth, and therefore it is clear that the process of ISI had truly begun, accelerating the diversification of industry by that time.

3.2.7 Summary of Early ISI Period for Argentina and Brazil

The main issues to be considered in this summary are the following: wage earners and immigrants, chains linked to the agro-export sector, the role of speculation and diversification, the impact of the rate of exchange, the role of the US and Great Britain, class alliances, the decline of the agro-export sector, the internal market, and the impact of "adverse shocks," namely, WWI and the Great Depression.

In terms of foreign trade, the agro-exports of both countries depended on Europe and the US in general. The role of the competition between Great Britain and the U S was rather important and yet quite different for Argentina and Brazil. Consider that which took place with the Roca–Runciman Pact; an attempt by Britain to maintain special relations with

Argentina, and thus worsening the relations between Argentina and the US.

A major shift in the 1920s was the expansion of U.S. investment, which continued into the 1930s with the establishment of manufacturing plants in both Argentina and Brazil. The growing presence of the US was to be expected and reflects the slow but sure transition between the British and U.S. empires. In any case, the role of Great Britain continued to be stronger in Argentina compared to Brazil, given the fact that Brazil did not need to export so much to Britain, as the primary destination of its exports (in particular, coffee) was the US. This situation was quite distinct for Argentina, which had to operate a new type of triangular trade: having a deficit with the US due to imports of manufactured goods, and a surplus with Britain with exports of primary agricultural products and thus a quandary as they depended on the US for investment. This was the period of transition of economies dominated by landed oligarchies, whether the coffee plantation owners of Brazil, or the Pampean oligarchy of Argentina, toward more industrialized economies.

The discussion over adverse shocks, both with WWI and the Great Depression, presents a solid argument for providing an incentive for industry. These results contradict those that argue that industry only began in the 1930s and that previously it was irrelevant. In the two cases, there had been a significant advance especially in the 1920s, which showed that the 1930s was a continuation of a process which had already begun. In both countries the role of a growing internal market was fundamental. On the one hand this was due to the growth of the working class with the expansion of wage earners, requiring more and more manufacturing products. On the other hand, it was due to the growing bourgeoisies, whether the industrialists or the landed oligarchy, with their increased demands for consumer goods, including luxury goods. Evidently, the conditions were better for the working class in Argentina compared to Brazil, obtaining higher wages and thus generating greater effective demand. There is no doubt that the expansion and degree of political intervention in the subsequent decades were greater and thus corresponded to the name of the process of Import Substitution Industrialization (ISI), which was a major advance for the development of industry and in general for both countries.

3.3 ISI in Argentina and Brazil

In considering the takeoff of Import Substitution Industrialization (ISI) it really begins with the second Vargas period in Brazil and the arrival of Perón on the national stage in Argentina. Although the first period of Vargas beginning with the coup in 1937 and the establishment of the *Novo Estado* witnessed a number of aspects associated with both stages of ISI, this section concentrates more on the changes which reflected the deepening of industry. Historically, the second stage of ISI is associated with the later governments of Kubitschek in Brazil and Frondizi in Argentina. This is clearly understandable given the level of industrial production and technological advance, which came in the late 1950s and early 1960s. Nevertheless, one should recognize that there were major accomplishments in terms of the growth and expansion of industry during the governments of Perón in Argentina and Vargas in Brazil, which is arguably the first phase of ISI.

3.3.1 Brazilian Industry in Vargas's Novo Estado *and Beyond*

Although Vargas was originally elected in 1934, he actually carried out a coup in 1937, forming the "New State" (*Estado Novo*) and remained in power until 1945, when due to military pressure he stepped down and called for elections. At this point Dutra became the President from 1945 through 1950. It was in 1950 when Vargas was reelected and remained in power until 1954, when under military pressure, he committed suicide, allegedly. At that point the existing Vice President took over, João Goulart, and then there were elections in 1955, at which point Juscelino Kubitschek won and began a new phase of intensive industrialization with his Plan of Goals (*Plano de Metas*), described below.

In spite of major advances, during this first stage of ISI, the process of industrialization remained limited and dependent on the export sector in order to continue advancing. It was during the second period of Vargas (1950–1954) when the development of heavy industry started to intensify and between the years 1956–1960 when heavy industry was finally firmly established in Brazil. This period is characterized by the attempt by the national state to reformulate economic strategy. New mechanisms of economic policy and planning were put into place to improve infrastructure: energy, transport, and other strategic industries, etc. In this sense, both direct and indirect state incentives were important for the infrastructure, strategic industries, and the auto parts industry; the latter laying the foundation for the future automobile industry linked to multinational capital.

Overall, the manufacturing sector grew at an annual rate of 6.3% between 1928 and 1955, with its percentage of GDP growing from 12.5 to 20% during this period. Another important development in Brazil was the establishment of new financial institutions formed during the period of ISI. These included the Agricultural Credit Program (*Carteira de Crédito Agrícola*) and the Industrial Bank of Brazil (*Banco Industrial do Brasil*); both established in 1937, and also the National Bank of Economic Development (*Banco Nacional de Desenvolvimento Econômico*)[17] formed in 1952. The latter has come to have a pivotal role for many aspects of Brazil's development and support for industry, and most recently with PAC, the program for the acceleration of growth.[18]

During the second period of Vargas, the deepening of the process of industrialization reached a qualitative shift and it could be argued that this is constitutive of the second stage of dependency, as discussed below. In other words, Brazil's insertion in the world economy was no longer simply being a provider of raw materials and agricultural goods. Their industry had grown significantly, especially in terms of consumer non-durables and the next phase was on the horizon, as seen below with the arrival of Kubitschek in power.

As argued in Chapter 2, the second stage corresponds to when MNCs (Multinational Corporations) from the US and other center countries, locate their plants inside the borders of peripheral countries such as Argentina and Brazil, in part to avoid protection but also in terms of controlling production and the flow of profits. The quintessential example of such an industry is that of automobiles. Therefore, there is a contribution on the part of foreign capital toward the processes of industrialization. However, the nature of dependency in this stage is no longer exporting only raw materials and agricultural products to the center, with the reverse flow of manufacturing exports to the periphery. It is more complex in terms of the necessity of importing more costly machinery in

[17] Originally BNDE was created in 1952, *Banco Nacional de Desenvolvimento Econômico*, and in 1982 it became the *Banco Nacional de Desenvolvimento Econômico e Social* (BNDES).

[18] PAC: *Programa de Aceleração do Crescimento*.

order to produce light and then durable consumer goods. In terms of external vulnerabilities, it is shifting along the production chain in terms of where there is a financial bottleneck. The only way to surpass it is being able to be in charge of (not necessarily absolute domination, nor autarky), the whole chain of production, which includes capital goods, not just consumer durables. This issue will be further addressed in forthcoming sections, but now the case of Argentina under Perón.

3.3.2 Industrialization Under Perón[19]

Prior to the 1940s, the earlier phase of industrialization in Argentina reflected expansion in the sectors associated with light consumer goods, such as shoes and textiles. Even though there was light metallurgy, there was very limited development of heavy industry. Similar to Brazil, the advances of technology had been limited and there tended to be an emphasis on the production of non-durable consumer goods. As described above, there was also the continued expansion of food and beverages, representing a close link to the agro-export sector.

As occurred for a number of countries, the anticipation or preparations for WWII gave a stimulus toward local industry around 1939. Similar to the adverse shocks of WWI and the Great Depression, the decline in international trade resulted in several world powers now needing to import industrial goods, as much of their available industrial capacity was oriented toward the war effort. Subsequently, through the war years and after, there was a lack of availability of many manufactured goods on world markets for countries of the periphery. The lack of available imports implied the need to bridge the gap through local production and thus Argentine industry was strengthened and became one of the more important sectors within the economy (see Fig. 3.3). Inevitably, there were clearly still limitations in terms of technological capacity and the dependency on a range of inputs from heavy industry, which still had to be imported.

During the first Perón government, there was a First Five-Year plan (*Primer Plan Quinquenal*) established for the period 1947–1951. During this phase of industrialization, given the significant role by the landowning oligarchy, and thus a structural condition which implied that much of

[19] This section relies significantly on the historical material in Kicillof (2011).

industry was directly connected to the agro-export sector. Peronism advocated for a break, employing the agricultural surplus to foment industrialization and also arguing for the simultaneous improvement in worker's living conditions and salaries, as well as the State providing greater social protection. Therefore, the Peronist project envisioned a role of the Peronist *(Justicialista)* party as well as unions to bring such a project to fruition. Critical goals of the Peronists' industrialization plan included the following: promotion of the internal market; reduction in external vulnerability; nationalization of public services; redistribution of income, and public works projects in the areas of health, housing, transportation, and education. However, in contrast to the plan's expectations, the resulting industrialization only worsened Argentina's external dependence. The main problem of the trade deficit was not surprising: an increased need for heavy machinery or other more advanced technological inputs, which grew as industrialization advanced. As for many countries and in other historical periods the problem of the balance of payments deficit came to be a major impediment.

According to Kicillof (2011, p. 15), an important institution for this period was the Argentine Institute for Promoting Trade (*Instituto Argentino para la Promoción del Intercambio*—IAPI), which allowed for the redistribution of the agrarian rent generated by the agro-export sector, which thus became an important source of revenue for the State. IAPI operated by acquiring primary products, such as cereals, meat and its by-products, and then exporting them. Thus, a key result of the first period of Perón was a redistribution of agrarian rent toward industry, combined with a significant increase in real wages for the growing industrial working class. The issue of wages reflects the historical struggles by the working class and unions, including anarcho-syndicalists, among others in Argentina, both prior to and during the period of Perón.

The protection of nascent industry was carried out through the implementation of tariff and non-tariff policies, including the state providing credit at lower rates. One of the institutions which left its mark on the pro-industry credit policy of Peronism was the expansion of funds channeled through the Argentine Industrial Credit Bank (*Banco de Crédito Industrial Argentino*—BCIA). This development bank was created in 1944 and reached its apex during the three year period from 1946 to 1949. Several state enterprises which were created or strengthened in this period were in the steel, shipbuilding, and armaments industries, most notably SOMISA,[20] an Argentine State Enterprise for Iron and Steel Production (*Sociedad Mixta de Siderurgia Argentina*) created in 1947 (Kicillof 2011).

Summarizing this first Peronist government, there was a notable increase in the participation of wage earners in national income, promoted via the increase in real wages, as well as through increased employment for labor. Achievements included the expansion of the economy, and the growth of labor's share of income, and both were associated with the expansion of industry, which had become the central driving force of the economy, replacing the role of the primary sector.

In spite of the attempt of a five-year stabilization plan in 1952 (*Segundo Plan Quinquenal*), after the crisis of 1949, the government was searching for solutions to go beyond the limitations of ISI, based only on light industry. As argued by Kicillof,

> The primary aims of this Plan were: a) provide the basis of further expansion of the base industries (capital goods and intermediate inputs for the following industries–petroleum, chemical and petrochemicals, and iron and steel); b) policies geared toward improving productivity of the agricultural sector (plus a devaluation of the peso); c) reduction of public expenditures; d) restriction on wages (limited to increases in productivity); e) promotion of the inflow of foreign capital. (Kicillof 2011)

However, during this second five-year plan, the first stage of ISI was confronting major limitations and restrictions and so with the fall in political support for Peronism, and the arrival of the coup in 1955, this phase of Argentine industrialization was brought to an end.

A key aspect of the advances made under Perón reflected the external conditions, be it world market prices, terms of trade, and Argentina's foreign exchange reserves, which Perón inherited when he first came to power. Argentina had to wait till the middle of the 1960s before their industry achieved a more complete profile. This was largely as a result of greater integration of the iron and steel industry, between the extraction of raw materials, such as iron and gas, through to the petrochemical complex, achieving a greater capacity for production and export of manufactured goods. In spite of some earlier resistance it was necessary to accept FDI so as to have sufficient capital to expand their manufacturing

[20] SOMISA- Sociedad Mixta de Siderurgia Argentina.

capacity. This was in spite of its limitations and strong criticisms by Perón early on, and would remain a point of contention, both for Argentina and Brazil, if not the periphery in general. The experience of Brazil under Kubitschek will be considered before elaborating further on the second stage of ISI in Argentina.

3.3.3 *The Next Stages of ISI in Brazil from Kubitschek through Geisel*[21]

Just as Vargas is associated with the takeoff of the first stage of industrialization, Kubitschek is associated with the deepening of industrialization. Efforts aimed at national development with significant state intervention resulted in the elaboration of the Plan of Goals by the Kubitschek government in 1956. This program promised to advance the equivalent of 50 years of progress in just five years. According to Vasconcellos et al. (1996), the Plan contained four basic objectives: (1) state infrastructure investments, with emphasis in the areas of transport and electricity; (2) incentives for the production of intermediate goods (steel, cement, coal, etc.); (3) stimulus for the establishment of consumer durables and capital goods sectors and, finally, iv) the construction of Brasília as the new national capital. The last item was seen as a crucial part of his overall development strategy, and it was aimed at reducing the overwhelming predominance of the South and Southeast within Brazil's economy. Two other areas in which Kubitschek aimed to make major improvements were foodstuffs and education, unfortunately these latter two achieved much less success.

According to Ianni (1986, p. 160), the Plan aimed at "transforming the economic structure of the country, in order to establish basic heavy industry and the reformulation of the real conditions of interdependence with world capitalism." Thus, national developmentalism played a major role in terms of the progress of the Brazilian economy, particularly during the 1950s. This was achieved as a result of an approach which provided the government and policy-makers with well-established theoretical tools, but also due to the capacity of putting such ideas into practice (Mantega 1984). In other words, as Bielschowsky (2004) argued, developmentalism was an economic ideology which provided support for the project

[21] Much of this section derives from an article I wrote with two Brazilian co-authors, see Trinidade et al. (2016).

of industrialization. The developmentalist ideology was accompanied by the dynamic development process involving the "substitution of imports" which, Tavares (2010, p. 51) argued "to be a process of internal development which took place and was oriented in accordance with external restrictions which became manifest primarily through the expansion and diversification of industry."

During Kubitschek's government (1956–1961), the Brazilian economy registered vigorous growth; GDP increased by 8% a year on average and the percentage of GDP in manufacturing rose by more than 4% in just four years, increasing from 21.3% in 1956 to 25.5% in 1960. The *Plano de Metas*, which developed during Kubitschek's government, aimed to install a broad and diversified range of industrial sectors and was for the most part successful. This was accomplished through state investments in key areas (petroleum, electric power, highways, ports, etc.); through the formation of state enterprises (auto parts, textiles, food and beverages, etc.) and also, or primarily, through multinational corporations (later on, TNCs) in dynamic sectors geared toward producing for Brazil's internal market (automobiles, pharmaceuticals, metal processing). The areas which clearly achieved major advancers during Kubitschek's government were the hydroelectric plants, navy construction, automobiles, electrical material, and heavy machinery; constituting the base for production goods in the country. During the period 1956–1962, GDP grew significantly at an average annual rate of 7.1%, strongly related to the rate of investment which reached 18% of GDP in 1958–1959. However, the low rate of growth of exports and the increase of imports caused a growing trade deficit, eventually causing inflation and a balance of payments crisis.

After taking power through a coup in 1964, the military government accelerated industrialization, with high tariff barriers. In fact, the process of diversification intensified during the so-called "Brazilian Economic Miracle" (1968–1973), a period of intense growth. Although GDP grew by 11% (See Fig. 4.2) it was achieved during the military dictatorship through both economic and political repression. During this period, the Brazilian economy and society consolidated what Oliveira (1988) described as the opposite of the Welfare State, based solidly upon the private appropriation of "public funds" and on a particular structural flexibility with regards to the use and disposition of the labor force.

Thus, the Brazilian economy went through an intense transformation process, from the decades of the 1960s through till the 1980s, consolidating an industrial park and implanting, or "transplanting," as

Oliveira prefers to describe it (1988), the principal industrial sectors which typify the 2nd industrial revolution. The two main programs supporting industry which were implemented in this period were two National Development Plans (PND I and PND II). It was during the government of Geisel (1974–1979) when the Second National Development Plan (PND II—*Plano Nacional de Desenvolvimento* II) was implemented with a particularly ambitious program for heavy industry.

Throughout this process, the State played a key role, articulating capitalist interests, facilitating expansion into key areas and mobilizing financial surpluses, and thus solidifying the process of Brazilian industrialization (Mattoso 1995; Tavares 2010). However, this pattern of industrialization was characterized by a strong discrepancy between the growth of productivity and real wages, in contrast to the classical Fordist model, as employed in advanced capitalist economies, where the two series tended to have similar growth rates. As a result of the high levels of GDP growth (Fig. 4.2) averages of 7.1, 6.6 and 8.8% for the 1950s, 1960s and 1970s, respectively, Brazil was achieving a doubling of GDP every ten years. Nevertheless, there were strongly contrasting results and significant variation between the peaks and troughs. This accelerated growth was based upon the production of durable consumer goods, primarily by the automobile industry. The consolidation of this "development model," which took place under the military regime from 1964 to 1985, was made possible as a result of extremely unequal wealth and income distribution. A key aspect of this process was the strengthening of the tendency toward more intensive exploitation of low-skilled labor.

This industrial arrangement had a necessary counterpart in terms of finance. The latter was strongly based upon government support, without which the industrialization process would not have been feasible. As Goldenstein (1994) points out, in the Brazilian case, besides providing financing, the State set up the basic nucleus of heavy industry from the time of Vargas's New State (*Estado Novo*) in 1937. Multinational capital was responsible for shifting the core of so-called "white industry" (consumer durables), thereby producing an economy characterized by an "internal internationalization" according to Coriat and Sabóia (1988), resulting in a massive presence of MNCs in the more dynamic production circuits.

The establishment of a "minimum wage" in the Brazilian economy reflects the objective of the State to control the labor force. This facilitated a monetary expansion of the economy, necessary for the restructuring of the labor market, and producing, as an end result, a wage structure, which provided the basis for more intense accumulation of capital in Brazil. The low levels of the minimum wage and its representativeness with respect to what the average employed Brazilian earns constitute one of the central elements of the exploitation of the labor force. This is intimately linked, on the one hand, with the low levels of skills and education, constituting a vicious circle, which exposes at the same time, two aspects of Brazilian "peripheral Fordism": the precarious conditions for the reproduction of the labor force and an organization of the productive process centered upon the intensive use of unskilled labor, a relationship which Lipietz (1988) described as common in the context of "bloody Taylorization" in the periphery.

The structural arrangement of Brazil's industry was quite functional for national development up to the end of the 1980s, considering the established international division of labor as well as the predominance of São Paulo with respect to the overall national economy. The latter came to be seen as increasingly problematic given the major changes that came as a result of neoliberal globalization in the ensuing decades. This was reinforced by the problems of the growth of industry in other parts of Brazil and the need for the expansion and incorporation of consumer markets in the Northeast, North, and Center-West regions of the country.

The sharing of productivity gains with wages was necessary for the achieving of the long-term growth cycle for the economies of the center, producing a solid balance between accumulation and mass consumption, constituting the classic example of Fordism. In the case of Brazil, the sustainability of the dynamic consumer durables industries was based upon credit being available for the middle and upper classes, and limited wages and consumption for the working class. Given the limited gains in wages, even in the most dynamic sectors, in spite of significant gains in productivity, Brazil continued to have a very unequal wealth and income distribution.

During the "boom" period (1968–1973), known as the "economic miracle," average wages grew at a rate below that of productivity gains, and the wage policy established by the military governments produced clear wage disparities and a strong squeeze of the principle segments of workers as described above (see Singer 1989; Sabóia 1985; Antunes 1992). It is worth noting that the differentiation between the wages of "skilled" and "unskilled" labor categories, as well as between technicians and management, which are functionally important to capital, is clearly evident throughout this period. According to Coriat and Sabóia (1988, p. 25), this demonstrates that the "gains of productivity are barely transferred to wages, and in a very unequal way."

The financing of accumulation was carried out based upon the State providing investment and guidance for maximizing economic growth. This was achieved through the collection of taxes, which had clear political constraints, combined with significant increases in government debt. The latter was first achieved through major increases in foreign debt, which the IMF promoted during the 1970s, and afterward through a combination of both internal and external debt. The nature of the relationship of the State with both transnational capital and large national capital could be viewed as a tripod, such that "public funds" were always capable of providing that dynamic mechanism necessary for private capital accumulation. At the beginning of the 1970s, the IMF was encouraging Brazil to take on foreign debt, but after 1980, the IMF did a 180-degree turn and Brazil's industrialization programs were forced to stop or be a setback after the monetarist Volcker Shock, which will be described in the next chapter. Before that, the next section examines the second stage of ISI in Argentina from Frondizi through till the military coup of 1976 when Argentina began a process of deindustrialization.

3.3.4 The 2nd Stage of ISI in Argentina from Frondizi till the Coup of 1976

It can be argued that the early phase of the second ISI was the period 1956–1963, which was when Frondizi was President and this happens to overlap almost exactly with the period of major advances carried out by Kubitschek. Frondizi is associated with the Developmentalist Project (*Proyecto Desarrollista*) and the beginning of the second phase of ISI. As argued by Kicillof:

> The main point of the developmentalist approach is rooted in facing the reality that the industrialization process with a base or foundation in heavy industry which would allow avoiding the problems caused during the first phase of ISI. Concretely, this meant avoiding the growth of light consumer goods which produced an external imbalance due to the growing need for importing capital goods. In order for Argentina to be able to abandon its state of underdevelopment, it became evident that it was unavoidable that the State would have to promote an industrialization based on heavy

> industry", through the use of industrial policy which included the promotion of industry through the use of tariffs and the expansion of public credit. (Kicillof 2011, p. 21)

There was a choice to exacerbate the class conflict domestically accommodating national capital or permit a greater dependence on foreign capital, reversing a previous position, and it was the latter that was chosen by the government. This is reflected in the 1958 Equity and Development Plan (*Plan de Equidad y Desarrollo*) which continued industrialization through an alliance of the local industrial bourgeoisie and foreign capital. Seeking to resolve the permanent problem of worsening stagnation of the argentine economy, this plan proposed the creation of a series of structural conditions whose aim was to benefit the production of durable consumer goods, intermediate goods, and certain capital goods, and in parallel, provide a strong incentive for the petrochemical industry. The principal source of financing of this project was foreign investment, though complemented by internal savings on the part of popular sectors. In this context, the dynamic sectors included the iron and steel industry, petrochemicals, fossil fuels (primarily oil and coal), and the automobile industry. At a secondary level there was significant growth for the following sectors: textiles, food and beverages, shoes, and lumber (See Kicillof 2011).

Toward 1961, the Frondizi government was also not able to elude the traditional problem: after significant industrial growth, there is always an eventual shortage of foreign exchange, and depending on primary exports, often a worsening trade deficit. The two main problems were a decline in the internal demand for consumer goods and the increase in the costs of capital goods. Therefore, Argentina was lacking foreign exchange in order to import more expensive inputs and capital goods, which were necessary to continue the expansion of nascent industry. It was in this manner that the end of the first phase of the Second Stage of ISI (1956–1963), resulted in stagnation together with a significant reversal of income distribution that had been achieved under Perón.

This is a standard case for a country in the periphery with serious external restrictions, given a decline in imports and thus a reduction in output and production. Toward the end of the 1950s, Frondizi pursued a greater influx of foreign investment with the object of accelerating capital formation and fomenting the vertical integration of the economy. Thereby, developing the basic industries, namely, steel, petrochemicals, automobiles, and others and achieving self-sufficiency in petroleum. As a result there was a significant increase in the demand for foreign exchange in order to pay for the imports required for this period, as well as for other financial transactions and services. Both of these are flows of wealth returning to the countries of origin, i.e., repatriation of profits. As stated earlier, the easy phase of the second stage of ISI had come to an end. The next period of industrialization to be considered is the military government of Onganía.

3.3.4.1 Onganía and the "Revolución Argentina"

Another negative phase came with the Argentine Revolution, established by the coup of 1966, bringing to power General Onganía and pursuing industrialization with recessive redistribution. The policy of the government was in fact to repress wages, in contrast to the previous government of Illia, a Radical, and also to repress any other type of social conflict. The intention of these policies was to reduce labor costs, providing the basis for industrial expansion. Some argue as a result of repressive policies, the year 1966 was marked by a deep recession which led to changes in Onganía's economic team and led to the implementation of the Plan Krieger Vasena (named after the Minister of Economics and Labor) in 1967.

In spite of the liberal orientation of the de facto government, the industrial complex not only benefitted by the repression of labor conflicts and thus lower wages and greater workplace control, but public investment played a key role as well. The action by the State was evident in the construction sector, where public works projects benefitted the overall efficiency of the economy. In the same sense, important initiatives were carried out for electric energy generation, such as the creation of the Northern Patagonia Hydroelectric Firm (*Empresa Hidroeléctrica Norpatagónica*), the other hydroelectric power plant, El Chocón, in Neuquén and the national grid connecting Greater Buenos Aires at the beginning of 1968, through the National Atomic Energy Commission with the nuclear plant Atucha I.

The interruption of the ISI model was not caused by its inherent exhaustion. Consider that between 1964 and 1974, the annual rate of growth of GDP at constant prices was roughly 5% and for the same period, manufacturing value-added expanded at an average annual rate of nearly 7%. Moreover, in 1975, the exports of industrial products represented roughly 20% of all exports in contrast to only 3% in 1960. After almost three decades of cyclical behavior (referred to as "stop and go"), in the decade between 1964 and 1973, the industry had continuous growth and with significant dynamism compared to other economic activities, and together with the growth of productivity, wages, employment, and exports. In this context, the metallurgy, chemical, and petrochemical sectors were the most dynamic sectors. Therefore, it was toward the end of the 1950s, when the process of ISI began to be strengthened, producing a strong structural change in the industrial sector and which became the motor of economic development for Argentina up through the mid-1970s.

3.4 Final Considerations

During the phase of the agro-export model, in the first stage of development, Argentina was able to position itself as one of the emerging countries of that period with better prospects for the future. Nevertheless, in the second stage, the process of ISI, which it began, later than the more advanced countries, such as Canada and Australia, it also experienced a satisfactory economic performance. With regards to Brazil, which had less of a favorable behavior or experience during the period dominated by the agro-export model, came to have greater growth than Argentina during the ISI period. This was a product of deliberate government policies and the stimulus which a rather large internal market offered, among other factors, including the relationship with the US.

Of relevance was the fact that Brazil had an advantage of obtaining the needed capital goods and financing from the US for its nascent industry, given the capacity for Brazil to export coffee to the US, which was the main purchaser of this commodity. This was also beneficial for the coffee *latifundistas* or plantation owners. In the case of Argentina, its industrial park was able to grow in the 1940s, by specializing in the production of non-durable consumer goods, primarily for local consumption though in part for export. In any case, it clearly was the case of light industry dependent upon the import of capital goods and essential inputs. It was at a disadvantage, as it did not have a key product like coffee, which the US needed to import, and in fact its primary exports competed directly with the US and its export interests, primarily beef and wheat.

As we turn to the 1970s, there is a general consensus that the Import Substitution Industrialization model had run its course. Many mainstream economists argued that the ISI model was exhausted and that there was a need to remove protection, eliminate subsidies, and institutional support for industry. It can be argued that the ISI model was not exhausted but rather a particular form of ISI was exhausted, one which reflected over-accommodation of foreign capital. There is a need to examine to what extent the model of ISI failed or whether or not a particular form of ISI failed, namely, one increasingly dependent on the role of MNCs or by the end of the 1970s, TNCs. The need for countries to increasingly orient their economies and accommodate the needs of transnational accumulation via global commodity chains and recognizing that as a result this was increasingly coming into conflict with autonomous or independent industrial policies in the periphery.

As discussed above, both Argentina and Brazil, had agro-export economies at the end of the nineteenth century and as argued above in Chapter 2, this constituted the initial dominant stage of dependency. This chapter presented the historical processes of change and how through the historical context of World War I and the Great Depression, an initial industrialization appeared. The specific trajectories of both Argentine and Brazil were examined, recognizing the similarities and differences between strategic trading partners and class alliances that led to the consolidation of the first phase of ISI. Moreover, the role of the two states and the Vargas and Perón governments reflected a shift toward deliberate policies promoting industrialization and a shift away from the dominance of landed oligarchies.

This is arguably a reflection of a second stage of dependency, namely one in which MNCs of the center were able to secure their advantages via foreign direct investment in industry and the establishment of a growing network of MNCs, operating within these countries, and no longer strictly dependent on these countries to merely provide raw materials and agricultural exports. In spite of advances in terms of industrialization, it is clear that the dependency on technology and foreign investment meant that even in the best-case scenario, these processes of ISI were incomplete and distorted, especially in the case of Argentina, where deindustrialization began even before a third phase of ISI could be embarked upon. The arrival of the military dictatorship in 1976, and the neoliberal transformation in Argentina is examined in Chapter 5. In the case of Brazil, it was not until the 1990s that neoliberalism came to dominate and as seen above the military government of Geisel was actually instrumental in pursuing the third stage of ISI, involving the production and export of capital goods.

As argued in Chapter 2, the present period of neoliberal globalization constitutes a new and third phase of dependency for those countries that experienced a significant, however distorted or limited, industrialization and this third phase reflects the shift to reprimarization and thus a return to the dominance of the primary sector, especially oriented toward exports. This will be examined further for both countries in Chapter 7, which addresses the trajectories of deindustrialization and reprimarization for both countries. However, first an examination of the rise of neoliberalism in general is taken up in Chapter 4 next.

References

Alvarez, Juan. 1929. *Temas de la Historia Económica Argentina*. Buenos Aires: Ateneo.

Antunes, Ricardo. 1992. *A rebeldia do trabalho: o confronto operário no ABC paulista: as greves de 1978/80* (2° ed.). Campina (SP): Editora da UNICAMP.

Arceo, Enrique. 2003. *Argentina en la Periferia Próspera. Renta Internacional, dominación oligárquica y modo de acumulación*. Buenos Aires: Universidad Nacional de Quilmes Ediciones.

Aureliano, L.M. 1981. *No limiar da industrialização*. São Paulo: Editora Braziliense.

Bielschowsky, Ricardo. 2004. *Pensamento econômico brasileiro: o ciclo ideológico do desenvolvimentismo* (5ª ed.). Rio de Janeiro: Contraponto.

Cano, Wilson. 1977. *Raízes da concentração industrial em São Paulo*. São Paulo: Difel.

Cooney, Paul. 2020. "Argentina y Brasil: tendencias de desindustrialización y reprimarización." PICTO in Sergio Emiliozzi and Karina Forcinito (compiladorxs), *Políticas de ciencia, tecnología e innovación: La emergencia de los instrumentos sectoriales en Argentina y Brasil*. Provincia de Buenos Aires: Ediciones UNGS.

Cooney, Paul, and Santarcángelo, Juan E. 2011. "La industria en Argentina y Brasil a comienzos del siglo XXI: Avances y desafíos." Trabajo presentado en las *Jornadas de Economía Crítica*, agosto 2011.

Coriat, B., and Sabóia, J. 1988. "Regime de acumulação e relação salarial no Brasil: um processo de fordização forçada e contrariada." *Ensaios FEE*, Vol. 9, No. 2, pp. 3–45.

Di Tella, Guido, and Zymelman, Manuel. 1967. *Las Etapas del Desarrollo Económico Argentino*. Buenos Aires: Editorial Universitaria de Buenos Aires.

Díaz Alejandro, C.F. 1975. *Ensayos sobre la historia económica argentina* (2ª ed.). Buenos Aires: Amorrortu.

ECLA. 1958. http://www.eclac.cl.

Ford, A.G. 2009. "Las inversiones británicas y el desarrollo de la economía argentina, 1880–1914." In: David Rock (ed.), *Argentina en el siglo veinte: economía y desarrollo político desde la élite conservadora a Perón-Perón* (pp. 33–64). San Isidro: Lenguaje Claro Editora.

Goldenstein, L. 1994. *Repensando a dependência.* Rio de Janeiro: Paz e Terra.

Ianni, O. 1986. *Estado e Planejamento Econômico no Brasil.* Rio de Janeiro: Editora Civilização Brasileira.

Kicillof, Axel. 2011. "Serie canal encuentro: La etapa agro-exportadora." Texto no publicado.

Lazzari, Ricardo. 2011. "Estrategias de acumulación de las clases dominantes de Argentina y Brasil bajo la dinámica cíclica de los modelos primario exportadores (1870–1914)." Trabajo presentado en las *Jornadas de Economía Crítica*, agosto 2011.

Lipietz, Alain. 1988. *Miragens e Milagres: problemas da industrialização no terceiro mundo.* São Paulo: Nobel.

Mantega, Guido. 1984. *A economia política brasileira.* Petrópolis: Editora Vozes.

Mattoso, J. 1995. *A Desordem do Trabalho.* São Paulo: Scritta.

Mello, J.M. Cardoso de. 1982. *O Capitalismo Tardio.* São Paulo: Brasiliense.

Oliveira, F. de. 1988. "A formação do anti-valor." In: *Novos Estudos CEBRAP*, No. 22. São Paulo: CEBRAP.

Sabóia, J. 1985. *A questão salarial.* São Paulo: Brasilense.

Silva, Sérgio S. 1976. *Expansão cafeeira e origem da indústria no Brasil.* São Paulo: Alfa Omega.

Singer, Paul. 1989. *A Crise do Milagre.* Rio de Janeiro: Paz e Terra.

Solberg, C.E. 1981. "Argentina y Canadá: Una Perspectiva Comparada sobre su Desarrollo Económico, 1919–1939." *Desarrollo Económico*, Vol. 21, No. 82 (julio–setiembre 1981).

Stein, S.J. 1979. *Origens e evolução da Indústria têxtil no Brasil—1850/1950.* Rio de Janeiro: Campus.

Suzigan, Wilson. 2000. *Indústria Brasileira: Origem e Desenvolvimento.* São Paulo: Editora Hucitec, Editora da Unicamp.

Tavares, Maria dá C. 2010. "O processo de substituição de importações como modelo de desenvolvimento na América Latina." In: J. Sicsú e P. Douglas (eds.), *Desenvolvimento e Igualdade: homenagem aos 80 anos de Maria da Conceição Tavares* (pp. 39–66). Rio de Janeiro: IPEA.

Trindade, J.R, Cooney, Paul, and De Oliveira, W. 2016. "Industrial Trajectory and Economic Development: Dilemma of the Reprimarization of the Brazilian Economy." *RRPE*, Vol. 48, No. 2, pp. 269–286.

Vasconcellos, M.A.S., et al. 1996. *Economia Brasileira Contemporânea: para cursos de economia e administração.* São Paulo: Atlas.

Villanueva, J. 1972. "El Origen de la Industrialización Argentina." *Desarrollo Económico*, Vol. XII, No. 47.

CHAPTER 4

Transition from ISI to Neoliberalism

In the last chapter we observed the transition from agro-export economies to the model of import substitution industrialization. This transition period involved a range of problems and issues reflecting transformations associated with any major economic shift, especially between rural areas and new urban centers, the move away from the motor of the economy being agriculture and cattle as in Argentina or coffee in Brazil to that of industry and the associated demographic and sociocultural changes. The period of ISI lasted from roughly the 1930s into the 1970s. The general consensus is that the ISI model became exhausted in the 1970s, however, as one looks more carefully there is a clear set of interests between the center countries and TNCs that preferred to promote neoliberalism and undermine industrialization in the periphery as opposed to a strict failure of the ISI model. In this chapter the historical rise of neoliberalism globally is presented, examining the factors that led to its rise. The implications for import substitution industrialization in Latin America and the growth of foreign debt in general are also presented, while the particular details of the transition to neoliberalism in Argentina and Brazil are discussed in subsequent Chapters 5 and 6, respectively.

P. Cooney, *Paths of Development in the Southern Cone*, Palgrave Insights into Apocalypse Economics,
https://doi.org/10.1007/978-3-030-67673-5_3

4.1 Rise of Neoliberalism

4.1.1 Ideological Dimension

The tendency of laissez-faire is always present in capitalism, although the degree of support varies depending on the historical context. For example, the State barriers limiting capital's mobility as identified by Adam Smith during the period of liberalism of the eighteenth century are quite distinct from those of the twentieth century. Nevertheless, there are always defenders of the freedom of capital, individual entrepreneurial freedoms, with strong private property rights, free markets, and free trade. They will argue in favor of the importance of the free movement of capital, not the free movement of people; the recent case of NAFTA being a clear example in this respect.[1]

The term neoliberalism can be traced back to a meeting in Paris in 1938, where von Mises and Hayek were both delegates.[2] They perceived FDR's New Deal and the moves toward a welfare state in Europe, as manifestations of collectivism which risked moving toward Nazism and communism. In the book, *The Road to Serfdom*, published in 1944, Hayek argued that government planning, by crushing individualism, would lead inexorably to totalitarian control. In 1947, Hayek and others founded the first organization that would spread the doctrine of neoliberalism—the Mont Pèlerin Society—it was supported financially by millionaires and their foundations, as "a kind of neoliberal international"[3]: a transatlantic network of academics, businessmen, journalists, and activists. The movement's rich backers funded a series of think tanks which would refine and promote the ideology. Among them were the American Enterprise Institute, the Heritage Foundation, the Cato Institute, the Institute of Economic Affairs, the Center for Policy Studies, and the Adam Smith Institute. They also financed academic positions and departments, particularly at the universities of Chicago and Virginia.

The Mont Pèlerin Society, based in Switzerland included other recognized members such as Milton Friedman, Popper, Stigler, and Knight and later on included such notables as Gary Becker and Charles Koch.

[1] In this sense, when one refers to laissez-faire, they should refer to laissez-faire pour capital!

[2] See Monbiot (2016).

[3] A term used by Daniel Stedman Jones in *Masters of the Universe: Hayek, Friedman, and the Birth of Neoliberal Politics* (2012).

In a certain sense, this group was a reaction to the advances made by the Welfare State, especially after WWII, but also the importance that communism and socialism and progressive movements came to have during the first half of the twentieth century. Ideologically, this group has a rather reactionary, and anti-communist inclination, supporting dictatorships, such as Pinochet, the Chilean dictator, and other authoritarian governments, provided they supported neoliberal policies.[4] The influence of the "Chicago boys," followers of Milton Friedman, is well documented in the case of Chile. There are many other cases but space does not allow further elaboration.

4.1.2 *Theoretical Dimension*

The theoretical dimension of neoliberalism present in economic theory is associated with the debates between the monetarists, most notably, Milton Friedman, and Keynesians, such as Samuelson and Galbraith, especially regarding the role of the State in the functioning of the economy, and also regarding the use of fiscal and monetary policy. Keynesians are associated with the defense of social programs and also with anti-cyclical policies in order to achieve or maintain full employment. The use of such policies is associated with the Phillips curve, but given the phenomena of stagflation, their usefulness came into question (see below). While there were no serious crises, the Welfare State continued to receive political support. However, toward the end of the 1960s and the beginning of the 1970s, symptoms of a world crisis began to appear, associated with the relative decline of the US and the U.S. dollar.

4.1.3 *The Real Economy Dimension*

The 1970s were a classic case of a crisis of accumulation though without a depression, as a result of the decline in profitability.[5] The US lost its capacity to compete as before, as a result of the lack of productivity growth experienced by the US compared to its major rivals, being

[4] Examples include the military dictatorships in Argentina, and Uruguay.

[5] See Marx (1981) for the main explanations of accumulation crises connected to falling profitability; key authors of the twentieth century include Mandel (1975), Shaikh (1978, 1987), Harvey (1982) among many others.

Germany and Japan.[6] Additionally, there was the issue of the public deficit, which increased significantly as a result of military expenditures in the Vietnam War. A decisive moment was right after France and other European countries pressured the US to make good on the dollar-gold standard, which resulted in Nixon breaking from the convertibility between the U.S. dollar and gold at $35 per ounce in 1971.

The evidence of problems of profitability in the US can be anticipated by the peak of the real stock market index between 1966 and 1967 and this correlated with the non-financial industrial rate of profit for the US, declining from the late 1960s until roughly 1982 (see Shaikh 1987). Thus, the crisis of profitability during the 1970s, laid the basis for a period of stagnation and also deindustrialization, predominantly in the U.S. Northeast and Midwest, which later became known as the Rust Belt. However, economic problems were not only afflicting the U.S. economy, but there were problems of declining profitability in the majority of advanced countries (see Shaikh 1983) and as a consequence led to a global recession.

A new phenomenon arose in this period, the combination of stagnation and inflation together, which later became known as stagflation. This came to be used as a strong criticism of the Phillips Curve, associated with the tradeoff between unemployment and inflation, as defended by Keynesians. The latter argued that during a period of recession one would have high rates of unemployment, but at least inflation would not be a problem. In contrast, it was argued that for periods of significant growth, inflation would be present, but with low rates of unemployment. The use of Keynesian anti-cyclical policies seemed to insure this tradeoff. However, by the mid to late 1970s, the phenomenon of stagflation undermined the Keynesian perspective and resulted in the rise of the monetarist school and then followed by the "supply siders" in the 1980s.

The monetarists also attacked Keynesians regarding the role of the State in the economy, arguing for the need of a more laissez-faire approach to insure growth and prosperity. A concrete result of this theoretical debate within academia spilled over to real politics, as witnessed by the increasing incorporation of monetarists into government positions. The most notable was forcing Carter in the last years of his term to accept Paul Volcker as the new Federal Reserve Chairman (1979–1987), and Volcker became renowned (or infamous) for the Volcker Shock, an

[6] See Brenner (1998). The Economics of Global Turbulence, *NLR* 229 May/June 1998.

unprecedented increase of the federal funds rate in 1980 from 10.25 to 20% and keeping it high through the early 1980s.[7] This can be seen as the turning point, with the beginning of the neoliberal period, associated with Reagan coming to power in the US and Thatcher in Great Britain.

4.1.4 Political Dimension

It is also important to recognize how the neoliberal perspective, though generally not mentioned explicitly,[8] was not just accepted by the elites, but rather it was also accepted by the populations of many countries, and therefore by the majority of those negatively impacted by it. For example, consider the support for right-wing populists such as Fujimori in Peru or Menem in Argentina. Part of the explanation derives from the perspective promoted by Margaret Thatcher—TINA (There is No Alternative). Unfortunately, given the nature of negotiations for countries of the periphery with the IMF, it does really seem that there is no alternative.

One sinister aspect, especially within the economic academy, is the argument of orthodox neoliberals that there is only one correct vision of the world, in spite of the use of this criticism against totalitarian Marxism (one world view),[9] and that other paradigms are worthless, be it Keynesian, Neoricardian, Institutionalist, or Marxist. This philosophy plays a serious role and continues to be active through to the present day. Nevertheless, given the failures of many neoliberal policies and growing challenges, it is not as strong as it once was given the occurrence of neoliberal crises during the 1990s and beyond: México in 1994, Asia in 1996–1997, Russia in 1998, Brazil in 1999, Ecuador in 2000, and Argentina between 2001 and 2003 and of course the "Great Recession" in 2008–2010. All the same it has shown significant resilience in spite of these crises, though this reflects the capacity of politicians to manipulate and the powers that be to prevent alternatives to neoliberalism to have

[7] The relevance of this Volcker Shock is particularly key as it meant a 180-degree turn by the IMF with regards to lending to countries in the periphery and is seen as the main catalyst behind the Latin American Debt Crisis; see below in Sects. 4.3 and 4.4. Also of note, though less significant, there was a smaller shock associated with Volcker in 1982.

[8] See Monbiot (2016), regarding the use of the term neoliberal and how by the mid-fifties it was no longer used by its defendants. Its return to use was most associated with a critique of neoliberal policies, starting in Latin America.

[9] The commonly used term in Spanish is *pensamiento único* for the dominant orthodox view in neoclassical economics.

a chance at truly succeeding, as in the case of Latin America in the last couple of decades.[10]

Presently, there have been more than three decades of neoliberal policies implemented in the majority of Latin American countries. In certain cases, such as in Argentina, Chile, and Uruguay, for more than forty years, clearly implying that enough time has passed in order to carry out an evaluation of the results of these policies. Brazil, as argued elsewhere, corresponds to "late neoliberalism,"[11] which only truly began in the 1990s with Collor de Mello. After the abovementioned chain of financial crises, the general problems of the neoliberal model had become more evident, even for mainstream economists, such as Stiglitz and Krugman, among others, who then became increasingly critical of the neoliberal perspective.[12]

4.2 Import Substitution Industrialization (ISI)

Neoliberals maintain that it is better to reduce the role of the state in order for the economy to function more efficiently, and to reduce impediments to free markets, such as tariffs and subsidies. This is part of the general critique of the developmentalist state, associated with implementing a proactive industrial policy and specifically the model of import substitution industrialization, with the use of tariffs and subsidies designed to protect nascent industry.

Investment rules oriented by ISI for many countries of the periphery reflected Mexico's 1973 Law for Promoting Mexican Investment and regulating Foreign Investment,[13] requiring at least 51% of investment to be national, and therefore limiting the total dominance of TNCs in peripheral countries. The policy pursued by many TNCs in the periphery prior to the mid to late 1970s was to set up shop as in a joint venture, yet

[10] Evidently, there are internal problems and not just external forces that need to be evaluated to explain the failure of the "Pink Tide" (progressive governments) in Latin America. These issues will be further discussed in later chapters.

[11] The term "late neoliberalism" is used for Brazil given the fact the implementation of neoliberal policies took place much later than the rest of Latin America, which was either the 1970s, or the majority with the debt crisis of the 1980s.

[12] Nevertheless, Krugman is still one of the renowned defenders of "free trade" as evidenced by his best-selling textbooks on International Economics and Trade.

[13] In Spanish, *Ley para Promover la Inversión Mexicana y Regular la Inversión Extranjera*, from 1973.

meeting the standard of 51% local investment in order to not have imports of their goods hurt by tariffs aimed at promoting local industry. This seemed to fit with both the national interest of fomenting local industry and yet accommodating TNC interests. Eventually TNCS pushed for free trade zones or export processing zones or other exceptions to the rules of investment, as in NAFTA.[14] This reflects the shifts in strategy on the part of TNCs, which eventually led to the WTO and the attempt of MAI (Multilateral Agreement on Investment) in subsequent decades (see below for more on TNCs).

Unfortunately, even with ISI, the periphery would still have to import a large amount of inputs and intermediate goods as part of the production demands of these joint ventures and often causing major balance of payments problems. Considering the case of Mexico, during the period 1970–1981 there was an average annual rate of growth of the economy of 6.7% and even more impressive, the average annual rate of manufacturing industry was 9.4% (Dussel 1997, p. 136). However, a growing problem is that light industry, primarily non-durable consumer goods, required intermediate inputs and machines to be imported, which tended to exceed the value of Mexican exports. In fact, the TNCs operating in Mexico were the main ones responsible for the increase of imported machines and other capital goods, and constituting 48.9% of the trade deficit in 1970 and 115% in 1980 (Dussel 1997, p. 126).

Advocates of laissez-faire or a free market economy claimed that ISI caused the alleged inefficiency of manufacturing and produced difficulties in promoting a dynamic economy. Many critics have argued that ISI, besides promoting inefficient firms, also led to rampant corruption and therefore decelerated economic growth. Undoubtedly, there were problems of corruption, but these problems have been the same, if not worse during the neoliberal period. However, in contrast to these claims, economic growth under ISI was much stronger for many economies compared to the neoliberal period.

Below GDP growth rates are presented for the cases of Brazil and Mexico, where ISI continued through the 1970s with major advances in industrialization. As can be seen in Fig. 4.1, Mexico had GDP rates of growth above 6% for the decades of the 1950s, 1960s, and 1970s,

[14] The industrialization associated with NAFTA must be put in historical context given the precedent of the Border industrialization Program in 1965; for more on this topic see Cooney (2001).

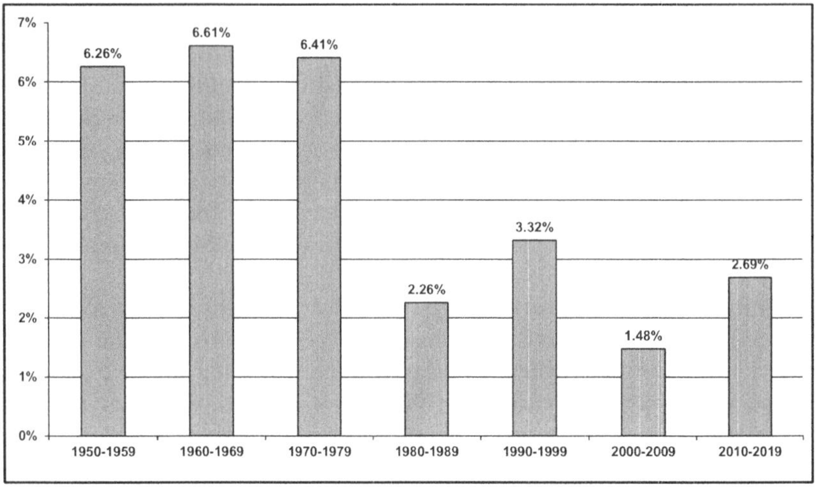

Fig. 4.1 Mexico's GDP Rates of growth by decade: 1950–2019 (*Source* INEGI [2005, 2020], World Bank [2020] and author's calculations)

while the neoliberal periods saw rates of 2.26% for the 1980s, 3.32% for the 1990s, 1.48% for the 2000s, and 2.69% for the 2010s. During the neoliberal period Mexico experienced three major crises and two depressions: the 1982 peso crisis, the peso crisis and depression of 1994–1995 and then the depression of 2008–2011. The jury is out and neoliberalism has a horrible track record in the case of Mexico.

Similar to the case of Mexico, we can observe in Fig. 4.2, how Brazil had GDP rates of growth above 6% for the decades of the 1950s, 1960s, and 1970s, while the neoliberal periods saw rates of 2.2% for the 1980s, 1.75% for the 1990s, 3.39% for the 2000s, and a mere 1.39% for the 2010s. The case of Brazil clearly shows a stark contrast in favor of ISI compared to neoliberalism with respect to the sacrosanct (for neoliberals) rate of GDP growth. Unfortunately, part of the Miracle growth in the 1960s and 1970s reflected a dictatorship and very repressed wages. Since the 1980s, the GDP growth rates on average have been rather low, with the exception of 2000–2009, when the PT was in power, though more importantly, when there was a commodities boom. As this ended in 2013 or so, it is not surprising that the growth rates have dropped as they have. This is discussed further in the coming chapters.

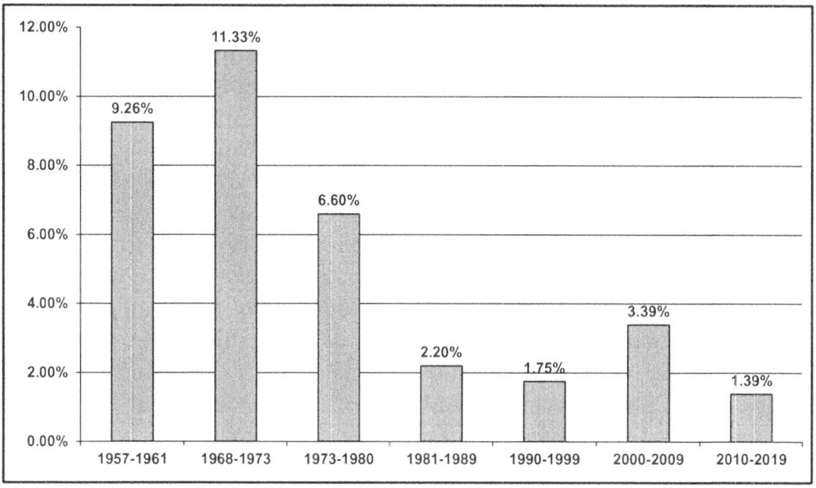

Fig. 4.2 Brazil's GDP Rates of growth by decade: 1957–2019 (*Source* IBGE [2020] and Banco Central do Brasil [2020])

Many mainstream economists argued that the ISI model was exhausted and that there was a need to remove protection, eliminate subsidies, and institutional support for industry. It is often argued that the ISI model was exhausted but the GDP growth rates were much higher than during neoliberalism.

4.3 The Shift from Industry to Finance; Petrodollars, the IMF, and Debt

During the decade of the 1970s, a great deal of capital seeking higher profits than that which industry could yield, became available, thus resulting in a significant transfer of capital from industry to financial markets. This was primarily due to the accumulation crisis (described above) in the advanced economies. International financial markets played a particularly strong role starting from the mid to late 1970s through the 1980s and 1990s and continues up until the present day, and there has been a shift away from foreign direct investment (FDI), particularly plant and equipment, and toward more speculative investment.[15]

From the mid-1970s, many industrial firms sought to shift investment away from industry and oil was a key destination, in addition to finance. In fact, between 1973 and 1974 there was a quadrupling of the price of oil on world markets, going from $3 to $12 a barrel. However, given the recessionary tendency globally, there was an excess of "petrodollars," profits generated from oil sales and seeking additional destinations for investment. The IMF and World Bank came to the rescue with a plan for the recycling of these petrodollars in the form of promoting debt and costly infrastructure projects to countries of the periphery.

In the case of the three most industrialized economies of Latin America, Argentina, Brazil, and Mexico, this debt increased by a factor between 6 and 10 times (see Fig. 4.3). For Brazil and Mexico, the increase in debt was viewed as key for the further industrialization already underway, and thus viewed as wisely spent investment for the future. Unfortunately, for Argentina, which had already begun its neoliberal transition in 1976, the debt was used for the process of deindustrialization (see Chapter 5 below).

As seen in Fig. 4.3, in just one decade, between 1970 and 1980, Brazil's debt increased by a factor of more than 10, from US $6.24 to US $64.26 billion, and then in just four more years it reached US $ 102.13 billion, an increase of almost another 60%. In the case of Mexico, the foreign debt increased by a factor of eight between the years 1970 and 1980, from US $7.09 to US $57.57 billion, and then it increased by another 65% between 1980 and 1984, reaching US $ 94.96 billion. In the case of Argentina, the increase was almost six-fold between 1975 and 1984, growing from US $8.08 to US $46.9 billion. As seen below, in spite of the advance of industry in Brazil and Mexico, the IMF's 180-degree turn, tied to the Volcker shock, seriously changed the prospects of development for these two major economies of Latin America and bringing to an end the experiment of ISI in Latin America for good.

[15] An example of the growing role of finance in the global economy is given by the increase in the percentage of US investment in finance compared to overall investment: after having a roughly stable level of 15% from the 1950s through to the 1970s, it grew steadily from the end of the 1970s and peaked at around 27% in 1989. See Brenner (1998).

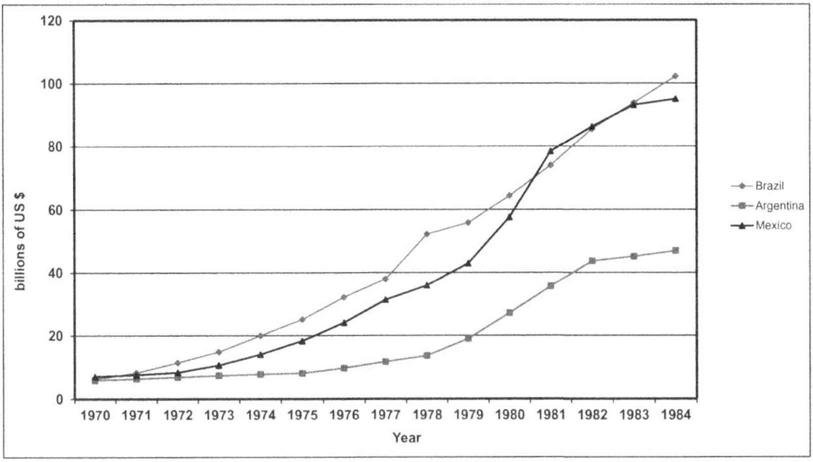

Fig. 4.3 Expansion of Foreign Debt for Argentina, Brazil and Mexico: 1970–1984 (millions of US $) (*Source* Banco Central do Brasil [2008], INDEC [2008], and World Bank [2020])

4.4 The Debt Crisis, the IMF, and the Four Pillars of Neoliberalism

Unfortunately, as a number of countries of the periphery were deepening their level of industrialization and building up infrastructure often with the support of loans from the IMF, the World Bank or the Inter-American Development Bank,[16] the rules of the game changed, as monetarists came to hold sway and push toward austerity and structural adjustment programs. As mentioned above, the infamous Volcker shock, argued to be the monetarist solution to the new problem of stagflation, increased the federal funds rate to 20%. This meant that all foreign debt for the countries of the periphery suddenly had a much larger burden as the rate of interest increased from 10.25 to 20% in a matter of months. In fact, the total foreign debt was only US $29 billion for all of Latin America in 1970 but this ballooned to US $159 billion by 1978, and then after the Volcker Shock it reached an outrageous US $327 billion by 1982 (See Sims and Romero, 2013). In general, most debtor countries struggle

[16] More commonly known in Spanish as BID (Banco Inter-Americano de Desarrollo).

to just make their interest payments, rarely actually paying off part of the principal. Therefore, the IMF's promotion of debt and recycling of petrodollars through the 1970s can be seen as the primary cause, more than anything else, for the Latin American debt crisis, however, it was the Volcker interest rate hike that was the catalyst to the debt crisis.[17]

During the 1980s, this influence led to imposed recessions both in the core economies but particularly in the "global south," especially after the Mexican debt crisis of 1982–1983. For Latin America as a whole, the 1980s were known as the "lost decade" and in the case of Brazil, from 1981 to 1989 annual GNP growth was a mere 2.2%. The IMF used the debt crisis as leverage for pushing countries to adopt SAPs (Structural Adjustment Programs) or, in other words, neoliberal policies. The four basic pillars of neoliberalism are arguably trade liberalization, financial deregulation, privatizations of public enterprises, and the flexibilization of labor. Each of these pillars will now be considered.

4.4.1 *Financial Deregulation*

Financial deregulation has tended to be associated with policies which attract or accommodate foreign capital. It has often been argued by mainstream economists that one major obstacle for developing countries was the low rate of savings, and that in order to achieve adequate levels of investment efforts were needed in order to provide a healthy environment for foreign capital.[18]

There are several policies associated with financial liberalization. The most significant is the relaxation of the minimum of 51% for the national share of investment in any given national firm, thus allowing foreign capital to clearly be the majority owner for national firms. Financial liberalization also includes deregulation or elimination of controls with respect to repatriation of profits and royalties, tax breaks, or exemptions. Another major policy shift associated with improving the environment for foreign

[17] This is not to deny blame for many Latin American governments, but they were not alone by any means, and the loans promoted by the IMF were often to military governments, not known for using these funds for social programs, rather more likely used for arms purchases and repression of their own populations.

[18] Examples from a liberal or neoliberal view abound over the years; be it the original Mont Pèlerin Society, such as Hayek or Friedman, W.W. Rostow back in the 1950s or authors such as Krueger in the present day.

investment is the strengthening of the local currency.[19] This is seen as necessary in order to calm foreign investor's fears of suddenly having their assets denominated in *pesos* or *reais* drop sharply in dollar terms because of a devaluation of the local currency. This is often achieved through the combination of high interest rates and overvalued exchange rates, which has been the case for several Latin American countries in recent years.[20]

However, an overvalued currency is cause for concern, especially when an unanticipated external shock takes place and a crisis of confidence ensues, such as the currency crisis of 1999 in Brazil.[21] In such cases, it is not clear whether the devaluation or the fear of devaluation will cause a crisis; consider the cases of Mexico in 1995, Brazil in 1999, and Argentina in 2001. Furthermore, overdependence on foreign investment is not something truly desirable, given the ever-present threat of capital flight, especially without capital controls in place.

When considering foreign direct investment, it is crucial to distinguish between portfolio investment and investment in new physical plant and equipment. If portfolio investment dominates, due to such a high level of liquidity, a minor shift or fear of a shift can lead to a rapid and devastating capital flight, such as the cases of Mexico in 1994 and Argentina in 2001.[22] In addition, there is empirical evidence of financial deregulation being strongly correlated with capital flight and corruption.[23]

4.4.2 Trade Liberalization

In spite of the predominance of finance during the present period of neoliberal globalization, the push for free trade seems to be the true mantra of *laissez-faire* advocates. In general, when countries of the periphery eliminate or reduce tariffs, national industry is negatively impacted because of the problems of competing with 1st world TNCs. It is much more difficult to compete against TNCs which have the most advanced technology and therefore much lower costs without protective

[19] With regards to exchange rate policy, there is a difference between the interests of neoliberals in the first world, which are at times defenders of devaluations and at other times defenders of convertibility or the pegging of a currency with the dollar.

[20] See Gala (2006) or Bastos (2006).

[21] The currency crisis is described in further detail in Chapter 6.

[22] See Cooney (2007a, 2008b).

[23] See Basualdo, E. M. (2003) and Guillén Romo, Héctor (2002).

tariffs. It is therefore a myth that through the elimination of tariffs, there will be an "even" playing field, in spite of claims by the defenders of free trade. The less industrialized countries need to resolve the problem of promoting and developing their own technology (R&D) in order to avoid the dependence connected to importing high-tech and advanced technology, which tends to be the most expensive imports in terms of foreign exchange.

In most of the discussion around free trade, scant reference is made to the historical record, namely, that none of the advanced economies (G7+) achieved success by pursuing the free trade model advocated today, but rather through a combination of incentives for nascent national industry and with significant tariff and non-tariff barriers. The strongest examples are the US, Germany, Great Britain, Japan, and South Korea. As opposed to following a free trade approach for development, the most developed economies practiced policies which the Washington Consensus assured developing countries to be a formula for failure. According to Chang,

> A closer look at the history of capitalism, reveals a very different story ...when they were developing countries themselves, virtually all of today's developed countries did not practice free trade (and *laissez–faire* industrial policy as its domestic counterpart) but promoted their national industries through tariffs, subsidies, and other measures. (Chang 2007)

Chang shows that despite their rather strong stance of encouraging other countries to adopt free trade, the US and Britain "...were in fact often the pioneers and frequently the most ardent users of *interventionist* trade and industrial policy measures in their early stages of development."[24] Unfortunately, the hypocrisy of countries such as the US and institutions such as the WTO, IMF, and World Bank has not been sufficiently challenged by either the media, economists, or the countries that are suffering the consequences thereof. The reality is that if a given country, say Argentina, was to implement tariffs and subsidies, as was done by the US and Great Britain, namely, supporting local nascent industry, other countries could sanction them for not treating foreign firms the same way as their national firms. This is part of the unacceptable conditions that come with being a member of the WTO.

[24] Ibid., p. 23. For a more extensive reading on this issue, see Chang, Há-Joon, *Kicking Away the Ladder-Development Strategy in Historical Perspective* (London: Anthem Press, 2002a).

Although they do not use the word sanction, instead referring to facilitating dispute resolution, and thus providing the international framework for the US or China to take Argentina to court, for simply trying to support their local industry. Examples abound and several were referred to in Chapter 2.

4.4.3 *Privatizations*[25]

From the middle of the 1980s, the IMF and other international institutions pushed the countries of the periphery to privatize their public enterprises. Besides arguing they were not efficient, they also argued that as a result of selling these enterprises they would improve their fiscal accounts. Clearly, there is an increase in revenue for the short term, however, once these public enterprises are sold, they will not generate any future revenue as in the past, other than through taxes from the privatized firms. Such sales only help pay for the services of the debt during a few years for foreign banks.

The argument supporting privatization, or the selling off of public enterprises, is that the private sector is more efficient, that running operations like a business instead of a bloated bureaucracy translates to lower costs, greater efficiency, and better products and services. The theory goes that corporations can deliver government services better and at a lower cost than the government. Privatization does not mean that the government definitively severs itself from operational practice either; in addition to providing funding through the award of government contracts, the relationship between government and private industry strengthens and grows through privatization, owing to the close, incestuous relationship between the two manifested clearly through the phenomenon of the "revolving door."

Privatization transforms the provision of public goods and services for the welfare of the public into profit-making enterprises, essentially subverting the defining mission of the state to serve the public interest writ large. According to the myth, privatization provides a way to increase the efficiency in serving the common good of citizens. According to neoliberal practice, however, privatization adds a new purpose to the state: providing fresh sources of profit for private capital. Neoliberalism sells the efficiency myth but delivers the profit reality.

[25] This section relies upon the following sources: Wrenn (2016), Cooney (2007a, 2007b, 2008b).

A major example of the push toward privatizations is the experience of Mexico. According to a report by the World Bank, a total of $US 31.4 billion was received for the Mexican privatizations between 1990 and 1998. Between the years 1982 and 1995, Mexico went from having 1155 state enterprises to only 185. The sold enterprises included railroads, telephone, natural gas, electrical energy provider, administration of satellites, ports and airports, sugar refineries, and banks. A major disadvantage brought about by these privatizations was the subsequent unemployment as a result of laying off so many state workers. For example, during the period 1982–1993, the public enterprises reduced the number of paid employees to 429,000 and laid off 765,730 workers. After 1993, many additional workers were laid off as well.[26]

In addition to privatizing these public enterprises, Mexico also privatized its system of Social Security. The decision was approved in 1995 and as of 1996 the system of retirement and pensions (the Mexican Institute of Social Security: el Instituto Mexicano de Seguro Social (IMSS), and the Institute of Security and Social Services for State Workers (Instituto de Seguridad y Servicios Sociales para los Trabajadores del Estado—(ISSSTE), were also privatized. Thus, the 36,487 contributors that had Social Security initially, were affected and afterward some 9 million 42 thousand of ISSSTE lost their coverage. In total more than 50% of the population of Mexico was affected by this decision. Finally, these privatizations implied that public enterprises and Mexican resources that were under State control were auctioned off to private interests, with foreign TNCs dominating the acquisitions. The final result of privatizations is a growing tendency of foreign domination of the Mexican economy.

In the subsequent chapters, an assessment of the impacts of neoliberal policies will be considered, first analyzing Argentina in Chapter 5 and then Brazil in Chapter 6. As the details of privatizations will be elaborated upon there, to avoid repetition, only a very brief summary is presented for both countries. During the years 1991–1998, when Menem was President, Argentina sold off approximately US $31 billion worth of public enterprises (Rock 2002, p. 68). The state enterprises privatized in this period included the national oil company (YPF), the national airline, Aerolíneas Argentina, the electric and gas utilities, water, and the railroads. As in most countries of the periphery, the privatization processes have been clear examples of major corruption and swindling of public

[26] See Ortega (2002).

assets, and Argentina was no exception, especially for the cases involving debt–equity swaps (Azpiazu and Schorr 2004). Given the class bias of neoliberal policies, it is not surprising that these privatizations involved both the laying off of workers, causing increases in unemployment, and also the privatization of Social Security programs, hurting workers in their retirement years.

In the case of Brazil, according to Rocha (2002), between the years 1996 and 2002 a total of US $30.9 billion in foreign direct investment was used for privatization of Brazilian state enterprises. The main sectors that involved the privatization of state companies were: electricity, telecommunications, gas, and finance. In contrast, the government claims to have received total revenues of almost $90 billion from its auction of public assets. A more detailed analysis of Brazil's privatizations will be presented in Chapter 6: Late Neoliberalism in Brazil.

4.4.4 Flexibilization of Labor

The last of the four pillars of neoliberalism is one which took longer to implement and for good reason. If governments had attempted to implement flexibilization of labor early on in the transition to neoliberalism, there would have been much more resistance to it, among other neoliberal polices, much sooner. Unfortunately, over the decades it has come to be as extensive as the other three and shamefully being pursued and adopted by many "progressive" governments, even if the worse versions are from conservative forces. In spite of the neoliberal claims that this will improve the job market for workers, in general the reforms associated with the flexibilization of labor are designed to undermine unions and other worker organizations, make it much easier for bosses or capitalists to hire and fire at will. Overall, flexibilization of labor has produced a reduction in the rights won by workers over decades, promoting the informal labor market (reaching levels as high as 60% in Brazil in 1999, and almost 50% in 2004 in Argentina),[27] increasing the tendency of outsourcing of workers especially to accommodate the TNCs operating within Latin America and further weakening the levels of wages throughout the region with few exceptions.

The neoliberal policy pushing for the flexibilization of labor is one of the clearest examples of the "pursuit of the restoration of class power" as

[27] For more detail on the informal economy, see Chapter 8 or Cooney (2013).

Fig. 4.4 Share of assets held by the Top 1% of the US population: 1922–1998 (*Source* Dumeníl and Lévy [2004])

expressed by Harvey (2005). In support of this claim, Harvey borrows the empirical presentation by Duménil and Lévy (2004) showing the recuperation of economic wealth by the U.S. capitalist class during the period of neoliberalism: the share of assets held by the top 1% of the U.S. population during the period 1922–1998 (see Fig. 4.4). It can be observed that during the late 1920s, the wealthiest 1% had close to 50% of all U.S. assets, however, between the Great Depression, the New Deal, WWII, and Keynesian policies in the post-WWII period, not to mention worker and union mobilizations, this percentage fell below 25% by the mid-1970s. After that point in time, it is clear that as a result of neoliberal policies, that class struggle was active in the sense that the capitalist class obtained a major recovery of its lost wealth and by the twenty-first century had returned to own more than 35% of all U.S. wealth. Such a result is both impressive and disturbing. The next topic to be examined is the role of TNCs in this period of neoliberal globalization.

4.5 Neoliberal Globalization and the Role of TNCs

In evaluating and in fact identifying the main characteristics of neoliberal globalization, the silent actors often have the most prominent roles, be it the World Trade Organization, the IMF, or TNCs. The transnational corporations (TNCs) were able to transform the production processes across the globe with numerous negative consequences for the majority of working classes in most of the world as they achieved major improvements in their profitability. The result was the end of the alternative represented by ISI and the implementation of neoliberal policies, often leading to a general worsening of the living conditions of their respective populations throughout Latin America. Associated with the increasing domination of TNCs across the globe is the emergence of a transnational capitalist class (TCC), as has been argued by Robinson and Sklair (Robinson 2004, 2008; Sklair 2001). The increasing hegemony of TNCs is transforming national into transnational spaces with major implications for struggle and resistance against these seemingly all-powerful global corporations. This has been concomitant with the expansion of transnational commodity chains across the globe, and the subsequent decline in terms of the importance or relevance of national policies, be it industrial, commercial, or financial, given the imperative to accommodate the interests of TNCs and the new TCC. This has had a clear impact in terms of the decline in autonomous industrial policies and the shift toward deindustrialization, reprimarization and neo-extractivism.[28]

4.6 A Summary of the General Impacts of Neoliberalism in Latin America[29]

Defenders of neoliberal "reforms" argue that through the opening up of the economy instead of stagnant statist development, Latin America would achieve an expansion of trade and investment and thus obtain significant increases in growth rates and even GDP per capita. As a result, there would also be improvements in levels of income and wages and thus lower levels of unemployment and poverty and indigence. Some have even argued that the environment would also improve, as claimed by

[28] The term reprimarization does not really apply to countries that never had a serious industrialization and thus a further intensification of the primary sector would be more adequate, though an increasingly used term is that of neo-extractivism. A common reference is Gudynas (2015) referring to the processes dominated by TNCs of extracting minerals, oil and other natural resources, and at times including agribusiness. A more detailed discussion of these terms is presented in Chapter 7.

[29] A good portion of the material in this section is from the piece by Cooney (2008a) on the General Law of Capitalist Accumulation and Inequality in Latin America and employing data from ECLAC (2004).

the defenders of NAFTA. It can be argued that the key point historically was the debt crisis in Mexico in 1982, after which most Latin American countries began to implement neoliberal policies and reorient their economies.

The principal measuring rod for economic success, for neoclassical economists, when considering development, is the growth of the GDP and they maintain that through neoliberal policies countries would be able to break from the "slow" performance experienced as a result of policies associated with the ISI model. However, as seen above, the rates of growth since the beginning of the 1980s have been approximately 1–2% and at times negative and including depressions in the cases of Argentina and Mexico, compared to the rates of growth of at least 5–6% or more during the ISI period. Given the significant increases in population, the recent rates of growth of GDP per capita were even lower and often negative (ECLAC 2004).

Turning to other socioeconomic measures: during the 1980s real wages generally declined, although in the 1990s there was a range of experiences, where increases were often followed by declines. In the case of Argentina, as of the middle of the 1990s, real wages did not return to 60% of the level they had in the middle of the 1970s, which was when the shift to neoliberalism began.[30] In the case of Mexico, manufacturing real wages still were roughly 70% of the level attained in 1980 (See Cooney 2001, 2008b). The general level of urban unemployment in Latin America was 7.3% in 1990, but grew to 10.8% in general in 2003, with cases such as Argentina growing from 7.4% in 1990 to 19.7% in 2002, or Colombia, from 10.5% in 1990 increasing to 17.6% in 2002. (ECLAC 2004; Cooney 2008a); these two are both examples of more industrialized countries.[31]

The general level of poverty in Latin America was 40.5% in 1980 and then grew to 48.3% in 1990, but afterward to 44% in 2002 (ECLAC 2004). Although the level of poverty in rural areas experienced a similar behavior the results are far from being encouraging: the level of poverty was 59.9% in 1980, grew to 65.4 in 1990, and afterward slightly

[30] Figure 5.2 shows the real wages of Argentina from the early 1970s on.

[31] Argentina was clearly one of the top three Latin American countries that experienced industrialization and Colombia was at times cited as the fourth or fifth. Unfortunately, both countries have experienced serious deindustrialization, Argentina starting in the 1970s and with a second round in the 1990s under Menem, while Colombia's period of deindustrialization has been during the last twenty to twenty-five years.

improved and dropped to 61.8% in 2002. There was also a similar pattern for levels of indigence: from 18.6% in 1980, increasing to 22.5% in 1990 and afterward falling to 19.4% in 2002. Associated with the problem of poverty, is the noticeable increase in informal employment with lower wages and less stable income, especially during the crisis of 2008–2010. For example, in Greater Buenos Aires, the level of informal employment reached 38% of all employment in 1999, and it is estimated that these jobs have incomes 45% less than the equivalent in the formal sector (Rapoport 2000, p. 1021).

It is common for "mainstream" economists to argue that neoliberal reforms will bring about a boom in growth, first causing an increase in inequality but through the "trickledown" effect inequality will be reduced with time. Examining such changes in Latin America from the middle of the 1980s through 2002–2003, one can see a clear tendency of increasing inequality, though with some exceptions such as Colombia and the Dominican Republic. Notable increases of inequality of income occurred in Costa Rica, Mexico, Venezuela, and Argentina; the last being the most notable, for example, the highest decile had 30.9% of national income in 1980 and this grew to 40.7% by 2002.

Although the statistics presented are clear evidence of the worsening economic situation in Latin America in general, it is necessary to recognize that certain countries experienced improvements. For example, in El Salvador and Guatemala there were clear reductions in unemployment from 1990 to 2003. There was also a significant drop of poverty in Brazil, El Salvador, Guatemala, Panama, and especially Chile, where poverty declined from 45.1% in 1987 to 18.8% in 2003.[32] This section was a brief evaluation of the results of neoliberal policies in Latin America, concentrating on the period from 1980 through 2006, and for 18 countries, which corresponded to the analysis by ECLAC (2004).

4.7 Conclusion

This chapter began with an examination of the historical rise of neoliberalism in general, considering the following four dimensions: ideological, theoretical, the real economy, and lastly the political dimension. This was followed by an examination of the last stages of import substitution industrialization (ISI) in Latin America, debating the nature of the exhaustion

[32] Part of this decline reflects the shift in the definition of poverty by the World Bank in recent decades.

of this model, especially given the superior performance in terms of GDP growth rates for the more industrialized countries and the contradictory role played by TNCs. Subsequently, the scenarios of the promotion of debt by the IMF and World Bank, often through the recycling of petrodollars were presented and then followed in early 1980 with the Volcker shock. The latter produced a 180-degree turn by the IMF which went from pushing and promoting debt to suddenly discouraging industrial expansion and demanding greater payments on the part of countries of the periphery. This combination led to the Latin American debt crisis and became the main means of leverage by the IMF to promote or force countries to adopt neoliberal policies; the four main pillars being trade liberalization, financial deregulation, privatizations, and last but not least, the flexibilization of labor.

In the next chapter, the case of Argentina is studied, one of the first neoliberal experiments, having shifted earlier than many countries, namely, in 1976, when the military junta took power. The subsequent decades of this neoliberal experiment will be evaluated and the trajectory of this experiment can be described as going from a dictatorship through two waves of deindustrialization and finally plummeting into an economic depression.

References

Azpiazu, D., and Schorr, M. 2004. "Los impactos regresivos de las privatizaciones en la Argentina: ¿"errores de diseño" o funcionalidad frente a los intereses del poder económico?". In: R. Boyer and J. C. Neffa (eds.), *La economía argentina y su crisis (1976–2001): visiones institucionalistas y regulacionistas*. Buenos Aires: Miño y Dávila.

Banco Central do Brasil. 2004–2021. https://www.bcb.gov.br/.

Bastos, P.P. 2006. "Controle de capitais: uma comparação internacional." Presented at the *3rd Latin American Political Science Congress*, Unicamp, Campinas, Brazil, September 2006.

Basualdo, E.M. 2003. "Historia económica: Las reformas estructurales y el plan de convertibilidad durante la década de los noventa, El auge y la crisis de la valorización financiera." *Revista Realidad Económica*, Número 200, 16 de noviembre -31 de diciembre 2003, Buenos Aires.

Brenner, Robert. 1998. "The Economics of Global Turbulence." *New Left Review*, Special Issue 229, May/June 1998.

Chang, Han-Joon. 2007. "Kicking Away the Ladder: The Real History of Free Trade." In: Anwar Shaikh (Ed.), *Globalization and the Myths of Free Trade: History, Theory and Empirical Evidence*. New York: Routledge.
Cooney, Paul. 2001. "The Mexican Crisis and the Maquiladora Boom—A Paradox of Development or the Logic of Neoliberalism." *Latin American Perspectives*, Vol. 28, pp. 55–83.
———. 2007a. "Argentina's Quarter Century Experiment with Neoliberalism: From Dictatorship to Depression." *Revista de Economia Contemporânea*. Rio de Janeiro, Vol. 11, No. 1 (January/April).
———. 2007b. "Evaluando el Neoliberalismo en América Latina: Los casos de Argentina, Brasil y México." Presented at the *XII Encontro da SEP*, June 2007.
———. 2008a. "Uma Avaliação Empírica da Lei Geral da Acumulação Capitalista no Período Atual de Globalização Neoliberal." *Revista de Economia UFPR (Curitiba)*, Vol. 35, pp. 51–76.
———. 2008b. "Dos décadas de Neoliberalismo en México: resultados y retos." *Novos Cadernos NAEA*, No. 11, pp. 15–42.
———. 2013. "El Estado del Mercado de Trabajo Informal en el Cono Sur: los casos de Argentina y Brasil" presented at the *VI Jornadas de Economía Crítica*, Mendoza, Argentina.
Dumeníl, G., and Lévy, D. 2004. *Capital Resurgent: Roots of the Neoliberal Revolution*. Cambridge, Massachusetts: Harvard University Press.
Dussel, E. 1997. *La Economía de la Polarización—Teoría y Evolución del Cambio Estructural de las Manufacturas Mexicanas (1988–1996)*. México, D.F.: Editorial Jus.
ECLAC. 2004. *Statistical Yearbook for Latin America and the Caribbean*. http://www.eclac.cl.
Gala, Paulo. 2006. "Dois padrões de política cambial: américa latina e sudeste asiático." Presented at the *3rd Latin American Political Science Congress*, Unicamp, Campinas, Brazil, September 2006.
Gudynas, Eduardo. 2015. *Extractivismos. Ecología economía y política de un modo de entender el desarrollo y la Naturaleza*. 1ª ed. Cedib y ClAES, Lima.
Guillén Romo, Héctor 2002. "México: del desarrollo "hacia adentro" al desarrollo "hacia afuera." *Realidad Económica*, Vol. 191 (octubre/noviembre, 2002), pp. 56–77.
Harvey, David. 1982. *Limits to Capital*. London: Penguin Books.
———. 2005. *A Brief History of Neoliberalism*. Oxford: Oxford University Press.
IBGE. (Instituto Brasileiro de Geografia e Estadística) 2016–2021. https://www.ibge.gov.br/. Accessed July 2021.
INDEC. 2003–2021. https://www.indec.gov.ar/. Accessed July 2021.
INEGI. (Instituto Nacional de Estadística, Geografia e Informática) 1999–2007. https://www.inegi.gob.mx.

Mandel, E. 1975. *Late Capitalism*. London: Verso.
Marx, Karl. 1981 *Capital: Critique of Political Economy, Vol. III*. New York: Penguin Books.
Monbiot, George. 2016. *How Did We Get into This Mess?: Politics, Equality, Nature*. London: Verso.
Ortega, Max. 2002. *Política Laboral y Movimiento Sindical. El Primer Año del Gobierno Foxista*. México: Editorial Itaca.
Rapoport, M., et al. 2000. *Historia económica, política y social de la Argentina (1880–2000)*. Buenos Aires: Ediciones Macchi.
Robinson, William I. 2004. *A Theory of Global Capitalism—Production, Class and State in a Transnational World*. Baltimore: The John Hopkins University Press.
———. 2008. *Latin America and Global Capitalism—A Critical Globalization Perspective*. Baltimore: The John Hopkins University Press.
Rocha, Geisa M. 2002. "Neo-Dependency in Brazil." *New Left Review*, No. 16.
Rock, D. 2002. "Racking Argentina." *New Left Review*, No. 17 (September/October 2002), London.
Shaikh, Anwar. 1978. "An Introduction to the History of Crisis Theories." In: *U.S. Capitalism in Crisis*. New York: Union for Radical Political Economy.
———. 1983. Mimeo from Advanced Political Economy 204–205, New School for Social Research, New York.
———. 1987. "The Falling Rate of Profit and the Economic Crisis in the U.S." In: Robert Cherry et al. (eds.), *The Imperiled Economy, Book I*. New York: Union for Radical Political Economy.
Sims, Jocelyn, and Jessie Romero. 2013. "Latin American Debt Crisis of the 1980s: 1982–1989." *Federal Reserve History*. https://www.federalreservehistory.org/essays/latin-american-debt-crisis.
Sklair, Leslie. 2001. *The Transnational Capitalist Class*. Oxford: Blackwell Publishers.
Stedman Jones, Daniel. 2012. *Masters of the Universe: Hayek, Friedman, and the Birth of Neoliberal Politics*. Princeton: Princeton University Press.
World Bank. 2018–2021. https://data.worldbank.org/.
Wrenn, Mary V. 2016. "Immanent Critique, Enabling Myths, and the Neoliberal Narrative." *Review of Radical Political Economics*, Vol. 48, No. 3, pp. 452–466.

CHAPTER 5

Argentina's Quarter Century Experiment with Neoliberalism: From Dictatorship to Depression

5.1 Introduction

After experiencing the worst economic crisis in its history with the hyper-inflation and recession of 1989, Argentina then set yet a new historical mark not only for its own history, but for the world's, having experienced the largest debt default by any country ever in 2002.[1] The experience of Argentina provides a rather sobering evaluation of neoliberal policies for two reasons. Firstly, it was one of the earliest neoliberal experiments, along with Chile and Uruguay, making the shift in the mid-70s, compared to most other countries in Latin America, that shifted to the neoliberal trajectory in the 1980s. Secondly, Argentina was recognized as having the highest standard of living and income per capita in Latin America

[1] It is interesting to note, that this is not the first time that Argentina suspended payment on its foreign debt, in fact their ninth default was in 2020, and the first time was in 1891.

This chapter is substantially derived from an article published in the *Revista de Economia Contemporânea* with the same title (Cooney 2007a).

P. Cooney, *Paths of Development in the Southern Cone*, Palgrave Insights into Apocalypse Economics,
https://doi.org/10.1007/978-3-030-67673-5_4

for several decades[2] but as a result of neoliberal policies implemented through the last quarter century, its trajectory shifted and culminated in an economic depression with over 50% of the population living below the official poverty line, and almost one quarter of all Argentines in a state of indigence.[3]

In order to understand how Argentina could go from one of the most "developed" countries of the periphery, and then a poster child for neoliberalism, to reach the crisis of 2001 and enter a depression in 2002 requires an historical perspective of the last quarter century in Argentina. This chapter attempts to identify why the crisis occurred when it did, but also to understand how the underlying shifts in the political economy of Argentina over more than two decades led to the possibility of such a crisis.

Despite mainstream economists being in denial, the drive toward a neoliberal economic model, as advocated by both the Argentine elite and the IMF, has had a clear class bias and thus led to a marked decline in the standard of living for the majority of Argentines. The particular type of neoliberalism, which Argentina pursued, involved a shift in trajectory toward agro-industry and finance at the expense of manufacturing, and thus produced two waves of deindustrialization and therefore a greater vulnerability of the Argentine economy to globalization in the 1990s, especially once they had to accommodate the rules of the WTO.

This chapter first evaluates the period of the dictatorship from 1976 to 83 and the drive by the IMF and the military junta for the implementation of neoliberal policies. Secondly, the transition to democracy and the more heterodox economic policies of Alfonsín are considered, followed by the crisis of hyperinflation. The latter led to the support for Menem and the eventual "Convertibility Plan," pegging the peso to the U.S. dollar. The period of the 1990s observed a renewed emphasis on neoliberal policies under the Menem and De la Rúa administrations. After considering the experience of the 1990s leading up to the crisis, the overall impact of a quarter century of neoliberal policies on Argentine workers is presented.

[2] Although Argentina's GDP per capita has been in decline since roughly 1914, it was still clearly ahead of other Latin American countries prior to the dictatorship of 1976.

[3] Although official data (INDEC) back in the early 2000s was the source of the estimate of 25% for the level of indigence, data is often changing or subject to different methodologies and with political interests behind certain shifts, and therefore other or later estimates show a lower value.

This is followed by a detailed look at the period preceding the outbreak of the crisis at the end of December 2001. The next to last section assesses the role of the Argentine elite and the IMF over the last quarter century, and in particular, the latter, given the track record of recent years with the string of financial crises worldwide, not just in Argentina. Lastly, the failed neoliberal experiment of the last quarter century is summarized followed by an overview of the economic and political developments which took place as Argentina emerged out of the depression of 2002.

5.2 The Dictatorship of the 1970s, the IMF and the Shift to Neoliberalism

In 1975–1976, Argentina was enduring a period of chaos and uncertainty, in large part derived from the economic and political instability after Perón's return to power in 1973, followed by his death in 1974. There were serious divisions within Peronism: from the neo-fascist AAA (*Alianza Anticomunista Argentina*) on the right and through to the *Montoneros* guerilla movement on the left. Some degree of class peace was achieved between the Peronist labor unions and the national bourgeoisie, but only temporarily. After Perón passed away in July 1974, Isabel Perón inherited a crisis which reached its nadir in June 1975, when the Economy Minister Rodrigo attempted an IMF-style shock treatment to try and rein in inflation (*el Rodrigazo*). After failing to achieve the desired outcome, the government then allowed an adjustment of 140% for nominal wages and inflation subsequently spiraled into hyperinflation.[4]

It was at this point, that Isabel Perón's government was negotiating for an IMF payment as reserves were in need of replenishment, given the country's economic crisis. The IMF would not come through with a previously arranged tranche despite efforts and several trips by her economic team to Washington. It is evident that at the height of the crisis period, the IMF should have helped to provide some stability and pushed Argentina to have new elections, as opposed to supporting a military coup.

Just one week after the military coup of March 1976, and without having to negotiate or send a delegation, the Argentine junta was able

[4] Given the political instability in Argentina, Isabel Perón's government lacked a clear economic approach, attempting both orthodox and heterodox policies.

to obtain over US$100 million dollars from the IMF. In addition to this show of support for a government willing to implement and impose neoliberal policies with an iron hand, the IMF came through with the largest loan ever to a Latin American country (US$260 million dollars), just five months later (Schvarzer 1986, pp. 45–46).

As seen above in Chapter 3 during the period between the 1930s and 1976, Argentina, pursued the economic policies known as import substitution industrialization (ISI). Of note, from the middle of the 1960s, Argentina was experiencing a new phenomenon—the growth of industrial manufacturing exports. In fact, they had reached over two thirds of all exports in 1973 (Kosacoff and Azpiazu 1989, p. 109). However, when the military junta came to power in March of 1976, the new government had a change of plans and the importance of Argentine industry would never be the same. This was evident in the economic policies implemented by the junta with its new economics minister, Martínez de Hoz. These neoliberal policies reflected a shift toward a laissez-faire approach, and were strongly associated with economists from the University of Chicago, such as Milton Friedman and Robert Lucas.[5] The dictatorship carried out a transformation called the Process of National Reorganization (*El Proceso de Reorganización Nacional*), which was a reactionary political and economic agenda.

The junta sought a radical restructuring of the Argentine economy, namely liberal orthodoxy in new clothing, aiming to achieve a more dynamic insertion into the global economy. The junta intended to shift support away from manufacturing industry and toward agriculture and agribusiness. They argued that the rent from agriculture, primarily beef, and grains, was no longer going to be used as a subsidy for manufacturing industry, but rather for the development of agribusiness with greater value-added. They contrasted themselves with the recent military government of Onganía in the late 1960s, claiming that the previous flawed approach was a Keynesian-oriented ISI and that a more radical liberalization, namely monetarist policies and state terror, was required to achieve success economically.

[5] Although there is a stronger association of Chile with the University of Chicago and the infamous "Chicago boys," the shift that took place in Argentina was also clearly influenced by Chicago's conservative economists and advocates of the free-market and neoliberal policies.

There are three key factors, which explain this approach by the junta. One represented a shift of support by the junta toward being more supportive of the landowning oligarchy/agribusiness as opposed to manufacturing industrialists. At an institutional level, this was reflected in the government allying itself more with the Argentine Rural Society (*Sociedad Rural Argentina*, SRA), which represented the landowning oligarchy, than with the Industrial Union of Argentina (*Union Industrial de Argentina*, UIA), which represents industrialists. There was also the opposition to ISI policies, arguing against the advantages for the industrialists, but also opposed to the growing percentage of the Argentine working class becoming middle class. According to the neoliberal perspective of economic orthodoxy, as described by Smith:

> Argentina's industrialization had been fueled by artificially high wages, unrealistically low public sector prices, exorbitant public spending (especially on social welfare and education) and systematic discrimination against Pampean agrarian producers in favor of subsidies to urban industries catering to mass consumption. (Smith 1989, p. 234)

That which the junta sought to eliminate corresponds with many of the main aims of Fordism as achieved in the more advanced countries of the center, but it is an understandable posture from the perspective of the elites of the periphery wishing to maintain their class privilege, unfortunately requiring the terror of the state to achieve it.

The second factor reflected the junta's obsession with stamping out dissent in general, but especially among organized workers. Most notably was the memory of strikes in Rosario and Cordoba in the late 1960s and early 1970s and especially, the *Cordobazo* in 1969.[6] The junta was committed to eliminating the industrial park in Argentina because it was seen as facilitating labor unrest; this was the price to be paid to avoid communist subversives from taking power.

The third factor is accommodating transnational capital, since foreign TNCs would benefit if Argentina concentrated on producing primary products and agribusiness, thus leaving automobile, steel, and heavy

[6] The *Cordobazo* was a week-long working class-led rebellion in the major city of Cordoba in 1969.

manufacturing to imports or from local production by the TNCs.[7] Responding to foreign interests, a new extremely liberal foreign investment law was put into place in order to attract transnational capital.

In spite of the continued advances of industrialization in countries such as Brazil and Mexico during the 1970s, the case of Argentina reflects political opposition, both locally and internationally toward the continuation of ISI. Therefore, as mentioned in the previous chapter, the argument for the exhaustion of the ISI model, contributed to reduced support for ISI among much of the populace, when in fact, the problems of industrialization are more complex and require an understanding of the different phases of dependency in the periphery.

The economic and social policies pursued by the military government had a very negative impact on Argentine manufacturing. Between 1975 and 1981, the manufacturing share of the GDP declined from 29 to 22%, and industrial production as a whole went down by 17% (Smith 1989, pp. 251–253). Similarly, between 1975 and 1980, industrial employment declined by more than 26% (Canitrot 1981, p. 188). The result of the neoliberal policies of the junta began the first wave of deindustrialization in Argentina. When referring to deindustrialization, it is the decline in manufacturing industry, which is distinct from agribusiness or agroindustry or mineral extraction which is often seen as industrial though not manufacturing. This issue will be addressed again in Chapter 7 when the discussion of deindustrialization and reprimarization is examined in detail. In any case, one must be careful with respect to the data one is accessing or analyzing in order to present a trend toward deindustrialization. If not explicitly mentioned, when the term deindustrialization is used in the book, it refers to the decline in the percentage of manufacturing in relation to GDP.[8]

At one level the process of deindustrialization would not seem to be in the best interests of the Argentine bourgeoisie, however, that is based on the idea that the interests of the Argentine bourgeoisie are strictly tied to the expansion of Argentine industrial manufacturing capital. The reality is that a result of the shift away from manufacturing and toward agribusiness, such as seed oils, including soy, the *Proceso* facilitated a

[7] Examples of TNCs producing in Argentina during this period are Ford, Renault, Warner Lambert, Philips, Siemens, and Brown Boveri.

[8] A discussion of the definitions of deindustrialization and reprimarization is at the beginning of Chapter 7.

restructuring of the Argentine capitalist class. In line with the argument of Robinson (2008), this is constitutive of the emergence of the second tier of the transnational capitalist class (TCC), which is predominant in the periphery. Thus, in Argentina, this resulted in tying local interests, such as Pampean landowners, to global interests and global value chains and international finance. As a trend over time, many more of these members of the elite or TCC came to have more and more of their investment portfolios in international finance and agribusiness and less and less in national manufacturing.

On the one hand, after 1976 there was not simply a return to an agro-export-oriented economy, instead there was the pursuit of a more internationally oriented dynamic agro-industrial sector with strong ties to the global economy. Moreover, the changes in government economic policy tended to benefit transnational corporations and the most powerful national corporations, such as, Bunge & Born, Macri, Perez Companc, etc.,[9] and by design the less powerful Argentine manufacturing firms unable to weather the cold shock of international competition were considered expendable.

One of the most important neoliberal policies that Martínez de Hoz implemented was the Financial Reform of June 1977 (*Reforma Financiera de 1977*), which abolished control of interest rates, and removed many financial regulations regarding credit and investment, though generating mixed results. On the one hand they were able to build up foreign reserves but were not able to resolve the problem of inflation. In hindsight, it can be argued that it was a failure of the monetarist policies but this was not admitted officially.

The reform of June 1977 had been strongly pushed by Argentina's financial elite, referred to in Argentina as *la patria financiera*[10] and was also supported by the IMF. This financial reform greatly facilitated the shift from manufacturing to finance, promoted financial speculation, and created an atmosphere conducive to lax financial controls and capital flight. In fact, during the military dictatorship there was an estimated

[9] For example, Martínez de Hoz was a member of more than 10 directorates of agribusiness and industry and put into place the plan which had been devised by major companies, months before, in planning for the coup (Sevares 2002, p. 32).

[10] *Patria financiera* (literally translated as financial fatherland) represents Argentina's financial elite, which has had increasingly significant links with transnational capital, especially finance and agribusiness.

US$28 billion in capital flight (Minsburg 2001, p. 148). Another telling example of both the lack of financial controls and the impunity on the part of the junta: during the negotiations with the IMF for a standby agreement, US$10 billion simply vanished from the records out of a total of US$40 billion debt, and was referred to as a "financial Hiroshima" according to one World Bank official (Smith 1989, p. 249). This is also revealing with regard to the IMF's willingness to look the other way with a military government pursuing the neoliberal model, however corrupt they may be. Such an oversight would have produced a scandal with the democratic Alfonsín government, just a couple of years later.

As presented in Chapter 4, from the mid to late 1970s, the IMF and other international financial institutions were promoting countries to take on debt due to excess petrodollars and this was when Argentina's debt first began to increase significantly. It grew from US$9.7 billion dollars in 1976 to US$45 billion dollars in 1983. In Fig. 5.1, one can see a sharp

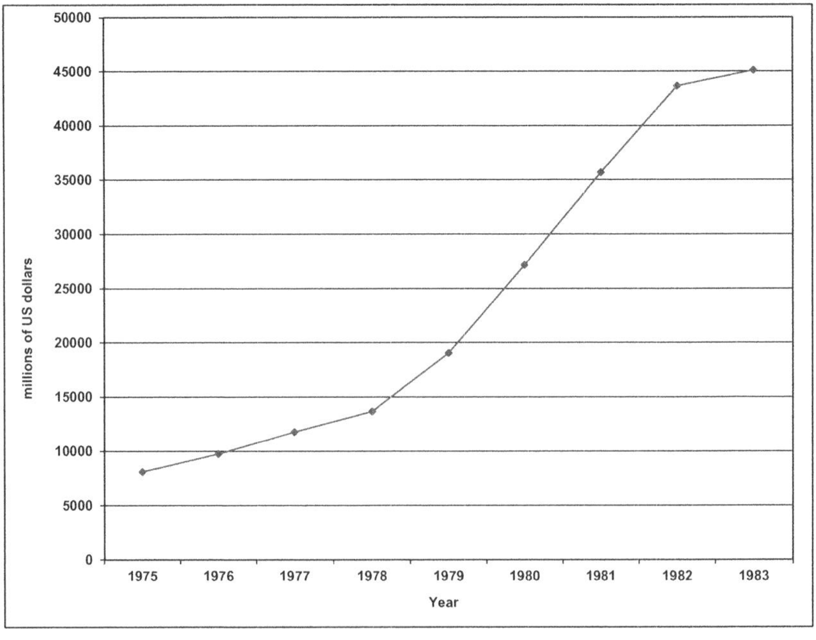

Fig. 5.1 Argentina's Foreign Debt (1975–1983) (millions of US$) (*Source* Ministerio de Economía, Argentina, 2005)

increase in the growth of debt around 1978, resulting in a 363% increase of foreign debt between 1976 and 1983, the years of the military dictatorship. Although both Brazil and Mexico, like Argentina, saw their foreign debt ballon, (in fact, by a factor of 10 between 1970 and 1981, see Fig. 4.3), at least such debt led to a growth and expansion of manufacturing in contrast to Argentina's deindustrialization.

Though all three countries had crises in the early 1980s, Brazil and Mexico had crises of growth and expansion, while Argentina had a crisis of shrinkage. It should be pointed out that part of Argentina's debt increase in this period was due to a drastic financial reform implemented by Domingo Cavallo in 1982, who was then president of the Central Bank. Within just six months, 40% of the private sector's debt (~US$6 billion dollars) was converted to public debt (Smith 1989, p. 247).

It is also important to note the shift that took place after 1982 with regard to the availability of foreign credit. After Mexico's debt crisis in 1982, the IMF and other lending institutions shifted 180 degrees with regard to credit policy for the third world. In the graph above, this can be seen by the leveling off between 1982 and 1983. This was a manifestation of the shift toward monetarist policies in general, but especially in the US, where interest rates were pushed upward arguably to control inflation, starting with Paul Volker's appointment to the head of the Federal Reserve under Carter in 1979. After Volker's initial "shock" treatment in 1980, an increase of the federal funds rate from 10.25% to 20%, this caused major increases for the foreign debt of many countries, Argentina among them.[11]

In addition to the process of deindustrialization and the negative impact on manufacturing, the financial reform and other neoliberal economic policies of the dictatorship led to a much greater economic instability and eventually three-digit inflation in 1982. At a more concrete level, Argentina was experiencing a fiscal crisis of the state, but from a long-term view, this crisis reflected the problems associated with a shift from ISI to a neoliberal accumulation strategy, an economy more dependent on finance and agro-industry than on the manufacturing base of the past. In addition, the working classes of Argentina anticipated a clear improvement economically, regaining some of the ground lost

[11] As discussed in Chapter 4, the Volcker Shock is associated with the 180° turn which the IMF took with respect to lending to countries in the periphery, and was clearly linked to the debt crisis.

during the repressive military regime, however, the capitalist class and the *patria financiera* had no intention of relinquishing their gains of recent years. This was the difficult context that Alfonsín inherited as Argentina transitioned to democracy.

5.3 The Transition to Democracy and Hyperinflation—The Alfonsín Period

Thus, Alfonsín was expected to help right the wrongs of the previous military government and improve Argentina's ailing economy. A major problem was the different expectations by competing social classes regarding the future of the economy. After years of social exclusion, the working classes were demanding an improvement of real wages having experienced a major decline in their purchasing power, such that it was below that of the decade of the 1960s. Although GDP in 1983 was roughly equivalent to that of 1970, Argentina's population had grown by 22%, implying a significant deterioration in per capita income. From capital's viewpoint, fixed investment had fallen more than 30% compared to the average of the 1970s, ironically much of this was due to the neoliberal model, which many capitalists had advocated.

The Alfonsín government, feeling confident after the elections, attempted to be more independent from both domestic and outside forces and to forge ahead with an economic solution without having to make concessions to the Peronists or other political parties, or other established institutions, such as the SRA, UIA, or CGT.[12] Thus, Alfonsín and his economics' minister, Ricardo Grinspun chose to break from the strict neoliberal orthodox approach and pursue a heterodox variant which would reinvigorate the economy and also allow for a more equitable distribution of income. This was in spite of and counter to the IMF's calls for economic orthodoxy-growth first, followed by redistribution.

In 1984, Alfonsín took the bold step of suspending all debt payments on the principal and systematically delaying interest payments. The battle of economic policy with the IMF continued through the year, but given the balance of payments crisis, the new government was forced to shift

[12] SRA (*Sociedad Rural Argentina*), UIA (*Union Industrial Argentina*), and the CGT (*Confederación General de Trabajadores*) General Workers' Federation.

from brinkmanship to conciliation and sign a traditional orthodox adjustment plan with the IMF in September 1984. The resulting IMF austerity plan proscribed real wage increases, eliminated price controls, and forced Argentina to liberalize trade restrictions.

In 1985, the annual inflation rate had reached 1000%, but after introducing the Austral Plan with the new economics minister, Juan Sourrouille, Argentina finally had a reprieve, as monthly inflation rates dropped from 30 to below 5%. Nevertheless, over the next couple of years, inflation continued to be a growing problem and eventually escalated into the crisis of hyperinflation of 1989. Throughout Alfonsín's tenure, there had been a rocky relationship with the IMF, as his administration was more willing to assert their preferred set of policies. However, given the continued problems of a growing debt burden and galloping inflation, time after time, the Alfonsín government had to succumb to the demands of the IMF for neoliberal austerity plans. Although, Argentina often did not follow these plans to the letter, the net result was more a set of orthodox policies, rather than heterodox ones, as the government originally advocated.

This resulted in a continuity of neoliberal economic policies as pursued by the dictatorship and then Menem. The Alfonsín administration began with the intention of pursuing economic growth combined with income distribution, as just mentioned, however, through the course of the 1980s, due to pressure from both the local elites, as well as the IMF, they came to pursue "anti-inflationary" policies that prevented increases in real wages, not just nominal wages. Alfonsín also attempted to control workers wage demands using the discourse of democratization of the unions as a means of weakening unions. On the one hand, there was an economic incentive to control wage demands, but there were also political motivations, given the strong association between the CGT and the Peronist party, the main opposition to Alfonsín's Radical party.[13]

Dinerstein presents an analysis of how economic policies even under a democratic government can constitute a weapon of repression against the working classes of a country. She argues that

[13] Alfonsín's push for the democratization of the Peronist-dominated CGT, reflected a political rivalry, not just a concern for transparency within the CGT, which was and still is something necessary for Argentine workers' interests.

> The transition to democracy was only the political expression of the *other* transition: from economic instability to the legitimisation of the terrorism of money in the form of *stability* in the 1990s. The struggle for and against the legitimisation of the terrorism of money over the political took the form of hyperinflation. Hyperinflation became the means of both the valorisation of capital and the repression of labour. Faced with the burden of the interests of the external debt, in 1989 the government's impossible aim of simultaneously satisfying social demands and subjugating itself to the mandate of the IMF, the World Bank and its creditors asserted itself as 'distrust' in the national currency and produced a financial crisis. (Dinerstein 2003a, pp. 12–13)

At the height of the crisis in 1989 the rate of inflation reached 4-digits (4923%), the percentage of Argentines living below the poverty line was approaching 50% and there was overall instability (INDEC 2003). The result was a period of chaos, with looting, police repression, and fear of a social rebellion. After the elections of 1989, instead of accommodating Alfonsín with an interim loan till the president-elect, Carlos Menem took office, the IMF pushed for Alfonsín to resign before completing his term in office. The climate of economic instability and particularly hyperinflation produced an atmosphere that allowed Menem to gain the support to further and deepen the neoliberal process of economic transformation begun in 1976.

5.4 Neoliberalism Under Menem and the Impact of Globalization

In March 1991, the Menem administration implemented an economic plan known as the *Plan Cavallo*, named after the economics minister, Domingo Cavallo. This plan bore striking resemblance to that of the economic policies pursued by the dictatorship and Martínez de Hoz back in the 1970s.[14] This is because they were both fundamentally neoliberal, as reflected by the main elements being: financial deregulation, reform of the state, trade liberalization, and the flexibilization of

[14] It should not be such a surprise given the fact that Domingo Cavallo was the Central Bank President during the later years of the dictatorship.

labor; reflecting the general pro-capital bias.[15] The Menem administration was committed to an accumulation model with its base in finance and agribusiness, sacrificing manufacturing, and thus producing a second wave of deindustrialization in the manufacturing sector.

5.4.1 Convertibility and Financial Reforms

The one aspect of the *Plan Cavallo*, which was not rooted in fundamental neoliberal policy, was the pegging of the peso to the dollar at a rate of one-to-one, commonly referred to as *convertibilidad* or convertibility.[16] Although inconsistent with a pure *laissez-faire* orthodoxy, but consistent with how neoliberalism is practiced, convertibility was accepted and supported by the IMF and Washington, right up until 1998. This was seen as a shrewd and successful ploy, by encouraging Argentines to bring their U.S. dollars "out of the mattresses" and to trust the national currency and banks again. Though risky, it turned out to be extremely effective in ending the hyperinflation of the late 80s and early 90s. There was finally a sense of stability, which had great psychological appeal after the country had endured a period of hyperinflation, as discussed above. The country was desperate for some level of economic stability and thus willing to see if the neoliberal *Plan Cavallo* could work.

The pegging of the peso to the dollar, also known as a currency board,[17] was a clear advantage for foreign investors since they would not have to worry about instability or sudden devaluations causing major losses on their investments denominated in pesos. There was an increased confidence in the Argentine bond market, as well as in the economy as a whole. The down side of convertibility was that Argentine goods, especially manufactured goods, were more expensive on the world market and

[15] As the economic policies laid out by the Menem administration were practically identical to the economic policies pursued by the dictatorship, the influence of Milton Friedman and others, such as Lucas, from the University of Chicago, was reflected in the policies pursued by Argentina.

[16] Initially it was 10,000 australes = 1 dollar, and after Argentina changed its currency it was 1 peso = 1 dollar.

[17] A currency board refers to pegging a local currency, such as the Argentine peso to the U.S. dollar, which was one-to-one for most of the 1990s.

imports were cheaper for Argentines, and thus contributed to a worsening trade deficit. The impact of convertibility on imports and exports is further discussed in the section on trade liberalization below.

One of the four main neoliberal pillars is financial deregulation, implying the elimination of restrictions on foreign investment, and also on the outflow or repatriation of profits, royalties, etc. This clearly facilitated the flight of capital, be it foreign or domestic. Basualdo estimated total capital flight to be US$115 billion between 1980 and 2001, in a graph which shows a very clear correlation between capital flight and the expansion of foreign debt and interest payments (Basualdo 2001, p. 37). The problem of capital flight is a clear example of how financial deregulation leads to insufficient control of capital movement for many countries, not just Argentina. Financial deregulation produces an environment, which increases external vulnerability for a country, leaving it more prone to crisis when a certain degree of confidence by international investors is lost.

5.4.2 Privatizations of Public Enterprises

Another of the key pillars of neoliberalism, privatizations, or the selling off of public enterprises, played a significant role during the 1990s in Argentina. During the period 1991–1998, Argentina sold off a total of some US$31 billion worth of public enterprises (Rock 2002, p. 68), though the majority of which was sold off between the years 1991 and 95. Although this improved the fiscal balance for those years, this was partially offset due to the debt–equity swaps agreed to by the Menem administration. However, this meant that after 1994 there was not only nothing left to sell, but also these resources that could have been a steady source of revenue, such as, the national oil company (YPF),[18] would be providing no future income, other than taxes.[19] Besides YPF, the Argentine government also sold off the national airline, the electric and gas utilities, water, the railroads, and many other public enterprises.

Another major concern was the manner in which the privatization process took place, often lacking transparency and clearly favoring the

[18] YPF-*Yacimientos Petroleros Fiscales*; "National Oil Company."

[19] Although it can be argued that taxes paid by the privatized companies provide a source of revenue, it is almost certainly a smaller amount than the potential net revenue generated by a public enterprise.

transnational corporations and local conglomerates, as evidenced by the majority of the state enterprises being sold below their worth or involving debt–equity swaps (Azpiazu and Schorr 2004). Although the drive toward privatizations was coming from the Peronist party, the IMF provided a significant external push by strongly advocating these policies and supporting TNCs in subsequent negotiations.[20]

It was during the military dictatorship of 1976–1983, when public enterprises were deliberately undermined, being disproportionately impacted by budget cuts. There had been a growing need for the renovation of physical capital that did not take place, "arguably" because of the level of the State's indebtedness. Changes in management occurred on a regular basis because of political shifts causing a lack of continuity in terms of management and leadership and therefore their ability to serve the public declined and the quality of service worsened. Such an impact is independent of being a public or private enterprise. Instead of privatizing public enterprises, the junta or the Menem government could have made their functioning a greater priority, and given them the infrastructure necessary to perform well, as with any private firm providing services.

Privatizations of state enterprises had a rather significant impact on unemployment in Argentina, especially in the provinces. A total of over 110,000 workers were laid off between the years 1990 and 93 (Duarte 2002, p. 76). This increase in unemployment had the greatest impact in the poorer provinces.[21] It should come as no surprise that after the wave of privatizations, these provinces were having greater problems with their budgets. Additional impacts of neoliberal policies on workers, are discussed below in Sect. 5.5.

5.4.3 *Privatization of Social Security*

Another neoliberal policy supported by, but not as strongly demanded by the IMF, is the privatization of Social Security programs. Unfortunately for Argentina, the Menem administration, with support from the World Bank, partially privatized its Social Security system in 1994. Payroll taxes

[20] Even in 2005, we see the pressure by Rodrigo Rato of the IMF on the Kirchner government regarding privatized firms and TNCs operating in Argentina.

[21] According to Rock (2002, p. 71) "In the poorest parts of Argentina –the northern provinces of Salta, Jujuy and Formosa-per capita income among the poor had fallen to the levels of Bangladesh and Nepal by the late 1990s."

that had previously gone to the government for the Social Security system were instead diverted to private accounts. This resulted in a significant reduction in tax revenue. According to the IMF (1998) the reduction of revenues corresponded to roughly 1.0% of annual GDP, which would result in a total of roughly US$18 billion for the years 1994–2000.[22] However, other research has included additional revenue shifts and estimate that the lack of revenue received by the government between 1994 and 2000 was approximately US$52 billion (See Basualdo, 2003, p. 22) and Damill et al. (2004, p. 303).

At the time, the Menem administration tried to ameliorate concerns for the lack of revenue by arguing that the revenues obtained by the privatization of public enterprises would help during the transition period of privatizing Social Security. The reality was that much of the revenue anticipated by the privatizations was lost through debt–equity swaps, as mentioned above and thus Argentina had to borrow in order to make up for the lost revenue. This was not an ideal time to have to increase borrowing as the U.S. Federal Reserve increased interest rates in February 1994 going from 3 to 6% during the subsequent months, and then came the string of financial crises—Mexico (94–95), South East Asia (96–98), Russia(98), and Brazil(99).

It is ironic that one of the policies pushed by the IMF, namely privatization of Social Security, was one of the contributing factors to the fiscal crisis that Argentina was experiencing during 2001, and when needing a loan, the IMF forced them to cut the benefits in its traditional Social Security program by 13% in September of 2001. It is yet another example of how the neoliberal policies pushed by the IMF are often irrational as they often are against the interests of the country, they allegedly are aimed to help.[23]

[22] Using the estimation of percentages in Table 5.1 of Baker and Weisbrot (2002) and the series for GDP from INDEC, an estimate of just over US$18 billion was the result.

[23] Nevertheless, what may appear to be irrational makes sense when considering that the interests of the elites of peripheral countries are increasingly aligned with the transnational capitalist class, in contrast with the interests of the grand majority of the populations of their own countries.

5.4.4 *Trade Liberalization*

Since the military junta came to power in 1976, there has been a drive for trade liberalization, through the reduction of tariffs, and elimination of non-tariff barriers. These tendencies were extended and deepened as of 1990 under the Menem administration. The tariff structure established as of 1991 was 22% for consumer goods, 15% for inputs, and 5% for capital or intermediate goods not produced in Argentina. The goals were initially 20, 10, and 0, respectively in 1991, as advocated by the IMF and GATT.[24] The objective of reducing the maximum tariff in a period of 4 years to 20% and eliminating non-tariff barriers, such as quotas, licenses, and import restrictions, was practically achieved around the beginning of 1991. Other trade barriers were completely removed with the exception of restrictions on auto imports, which not coincidentally, was by far the most dynamic sector during the 1990s.[25]

The result of these trade policies meant more problems for local industry, which now had to compete with much cheaper imports, and no longer with the protection of tariffs, etc. The lowering of tariffs and elimination of trade regulations made the Argentine economy more vulnerable to the cold shock of global competition. Between 1992 and 1999, Argentina had a trade deficit in every year except for 1995 and 1996, when the "tequila effect" of the Mexican peso crisis forced Argentina to keep imports in line with exports, as shown in Table 5.1.

Despite the frequently used argument that the currency board prevented Argentina's exports from growing, they basically doubled between the early 1990s and late 1990s. During the 1990s, between 24–31% of Argentina's exports were going to Brazil, and the overvaluation of the *Real* between 1994 and 1998, did play a role in the growth of Argentina's exports. The problem had more to do with the increase of imports, which grew from 4 to 8 billion in the early 1990s to over 30 billion by 1997–1998. This consistent and substantial imbalance between exports and imports resulted in an accumulated trade deficit of over US$18 billion between 1991 and 1999 as seen in Table 5.1 (INDEC 2005).

[24] GATT—General Agreement on Trade and Tariffs.

[25] There were also other factors related to regional industrial strategy within the context of Mercosur.

Table 5.1 Argentina's Trade Balance 1991–1999 (millions of US$)

Year	*Exports*	*Imports*	*Net Exports*
1991	11,978	8,275	3,703
1992	12,235	14,872	–2,637
1993	13,118	16,784	–3,666
1994	15,839	21,590	–5,751
1995	20,963	20,122	841
1996	23,811	23,762	49
1997	26,431	30,450	–4,019
1998	26,434	31,377	–4,943
1999	23,309	25,508	–2,199
Total	174,117	192,740	–18,623

Source INDEC (2005)

It is important to recognize that after 1995, Argentina was a member of the WTO and therefore by default, had a neoliberal trade policy. The upshot being that any attempt to promote or foment local or national industry, that did not give the same conditions to foreign firms, was potentially subject to sanctions, through the WTO dispute settlement mechanism. Any industrial policy which gives subsidies or tax breaks to the nascent industry is in violation of the current WTO rules, in spite of this having been the dominant path of industrialization of all 1st world countries (Chang 2002a). Connected to this, is the fact that the growth of exports, is dominated by primary goods, not manufactured goods, as was the case in the early 1970s. This discussion of manufacturing and primary sectors will be further developed in Chapter 7.

The problem of the growing trade deficit is arguably due to the combination of trade liberalization, declining prices of soy and agricultural products, and the currency board, not just convertibility. In the section below, the shift away from manufacturing toward agribusiness is examined and it is evident that after two waves of deindustrialization, Argentina was increasingly vulnerable to a more competitive world economy.

5.4.5 *Deindustrialization Revisited*

As mentioned above, prior to 1976, industrial manufacturing exports had reached over two-thirds of all Argentine exports. However, with the two waves of deindustrialization, one under the military junta and the other under Menem, the role of manufacturing in the Argentine economy experienced a significant decline. For example, during the Menem years, according to Rapoport, manufacturing as a share of GDP went from 30.9% in 1989 down to 17.1% in 1998 (Rapoport et al. 2000, p. 1026).[26] Estimates based on census data show that manufacturing jobs declined by 32.6% from 1,132,499 to 762,992 between 1991 and 2001.

These statistics constitute evidence of the second wave of deindustrialization in Argentina.[27] Since 1976 there was an emphasis on agribusiness and the lack of a national industrial policy to promote technological change in manufacturing within Argentina. The Menem government, just as the military government, claimed that it was committed to trade liberalization through tariff reduction and the elimination of tariff barriers, in order to force Argentine industry to be able to compete internationally. This fairy tale formula rooted in the myth of "free trade" unfortunately held sway during the 1990s in Argentina. The reality is that a few large firms, such as Perez Companc and Bunge & Born (since 2001, Bunge Limited) were able to weather the storm of imports, but for the majority of Argentina's manufacturing firms this meant hardships and, in some instances, disaster. For firms trying to export, convertibility only exacerbated the problem.

For a quarter century, there was a serious disarticulation of Argentine manufacturing industry, increasing the difficulty to compete in an ever more globalized world market. This is both reflected in the growing dependence on consumer and capital goods imports, and the extent to which Argentina's exports are dominated by raw materials and agricultural products. A key problem with an overdependence on agricultural products is they experience more frequent and greater price variations. For example, Argentine agricultural exports benefited until 1996 with a gradual increase of prices in international markets, which was some compensation for the overvalued peso. However, this tendency began to reverse in 1997, as there was a decline in the prices of agricultural products on world markets, since the global economy was entering a recession.

[26] The value of 30.9% in 1989 seems to be a serious overestimation as other estimates indicate a value nearer to 22%, but the decline down to 17% coincides with official data from a few years ago. This discrepancy may have to do with the hyperinflation of 1989 (almost 5000%) and an estimate, even official, could have been way off at the time, and then adjusted later on.

[27] Some argue that the process of deindustrialization was continuous from 1976 through till 2003, as opposed to there being two waves (see analysis of the data in Chapter 7).

From that point on, sales of Argentine products began to stagnate in value terms, although they continued to grow in physical terms (Rapoport et al. 2000, p. 999).

During the beginning of the twenty-first century, agricultural production has grown in general, due to a series of transformations for various crops, resulting in increased yields and total area cultivated. In general, the crops that grew the most were destined for export and also those that introduced technological innovations in production. Such changes have often been employed in order to maintain competitiveness in the world market. It is worth noting that as of 2003, Argentina was only second to the US with respect to producing genetically modified crops, primarily corn, cotton, and soybeans.

Since the early 1980s, seed oils[28] and cereals have been the most important crops in terms of their value of production and export share. In fact, by the end of the twentieth century they constituted roughly one quarter of Argentina's exports (INDEC 2003). In recent years, wheat, corn, sorghum, soybeans, and sunflowers have all increased their yields and area cultivated significantly, thus causing a reduction in the area cultivated for other crops. This expansion can be called the "agriculturalization" of Argentina, since this is at the expense of livestock farming.[29] In contrast to the growth and expansion in agriculture, livestock production experienced a general stagnation, with lower growth and a reduction in the number of heads of cattle or other livestock. In the case of beef, there has been a decline in domestic consumption, which exports have not been able to compensate for, but in fact the expansion of soy has also led to the reduction of beef production.

In addition to the impact for workers in manufacturing due to deindustrialization, neoliberal policies have also led to changes in agricultural production, contributing to a worsening of the conditions for workers overall; the next section considers the general impact on workers due to neoliberal policies in Argentina during the 1990s.

[28] Seed oils (*oleaginosas*) include corn, sorghum, soybean, and sunflower oils.

[29] In this regard, one needs to distinguish between the term *agropecuaria* in Spanish, which includes livestock, and just agriculture which excludes the latter.

5.5 Neoliberalism's Impact on Workers

Given the class bias associated with neoliberal policies, it is imperative to look at the overall impact on the Argentine working class, especially since Menem became president. First, as mentioned earlier, there were major layoffs, totally more than 110,000, as a result of the privatizations that took place. Secondly, the decline in manufacturing led to a reduction of over 369,000 jobs from 1991 to 2001, a 33.9% loss in total manufacturing employment.[30] As a result of the two waves of manufacturing deindustrialization, Argentina went from over 1.5 million manufacturing jobs in 1974 down to roughly 763 thousand jobs in 2001, a loss of 50%. Thirdly, the shift toward more efficient and technologically advanced techniques in agribusiness, during the 1990s, also contributed to an increase in unemployment, although this was balanced out in part due to the increase in agricultural production.

Throughout the decade of the 1990s, as manufacturing jobs were declining, the growth of informal jobs grew significantly. For example, informal work in Buenos Aires and surroundings (*Gran Buenos Aires*) grew to reach 38% of all employment by 1999 and such jobs are estimated to have incomes 45% less than formal employment (Rapoport et al. 2000, p. 1021). As increased numbers of people competed for fewer jobs and the better paid manufacturing jobs were being lost, the growth of the informal sector resulted in a decline in real wages for the majority of the Argentine "working" class. The clearly negative impact on industrial real wages over the last forty years can be seen in Fig. 5.2. Nevertheless, the level to which real wages overall have declined has been even more significant for the reasons just mentioned.

For the decade of the 90s as a whole, unemployment grew from 6% in 1991 to almost 14% in 1999, according to the government's definition, and 28% when combined with underemployment (Basualdo 2003, p. 14). Between real wages dropping significantly during the dictatorship, followed by stagnation and decline in the 1990s, as of 2001 they were not even 84% of the level they had reached in 1976. At the nadir of the depression, unemployment was more than 20%, and combined with underemployment, almost 40% (Svampa and Pereyra 2004, p. 90) and real wages had declined at least another 18% through 2002. Given these problems of unemployment, and in particular the laying off of

[30] This is based on a calculation using data from INDEC (2005) and Basualdo (2003).

Fig. 5.2 Industrial Real Wages 1960–2002 (1960 = 100) (*Source* INDEC data [2005, 2020] worked on with the assistance of Iñigo Carrera)

state workers there was a new and expanding movement of unemployed workers or *piqueteros*,[31] in the provinces and also in Buenos Aires.

According to official statistics, in 2003 over 53% of the population was below the poverty line and the level of indigence was more than a quarter of the population (INDEC 2003). Such statistics provide some sense of just how bad things were in Argentina, but they still don't capture the suffering experienced by the people living through this depression. These statistics are all the more shocking if one is familiar with Argentina, having had one of the highest standards of living within the periphery. Unfortunately, one of the characteristics of many countries of the periphery is that economic crises that lead to depressions, not just recessions, are much more common than they should be.[32]

[31] There are several different *piquetero* organizations, but they prefer to be referred to as unemployed workers rather than just a reference to a specific strategy they employ, namely, picketing or blockading of highways. For more information on the different organizations see Dinerstein (2003a, b) or Svampa and Pereyra (2004).

[32] The term depression is often avoided by mainstream economists, and unfortunately many progressives follow suit, however, it is a distortion of the facts to describe what

Although the underlying cause of such economic crises is rooted in the capitalist system, the more immediate problem has been the growth of foreign debt. Before turning to an examination of the growth of the foreign debt and the specific role of the IMF, a detailed presentation of the events leading up to the crisis in 2001 follows below.

5.6 Argentina at the Abyss

When Fernando De la Rúa took office as president in December 1999, Argentina had already been experiencing a recession for more than a year. Within his first year, he was confronted with an even more difficult task of staving off the impending economic crisis due to a range of factors including a growing trade deficit, in part caused by the currency board, but also the declining prices on world markets for agricultural goods, and the foreign debt which was spiraling out of control.

There had been problems in the third quarter of 2000 as bond rates soared. For better or for worse, the IMF stepped in with an aid package. In early 2001, President De la Rúa reshuffled his cabinet, bringing back Domingo Cavallo[33] as economy minister. The arrival of Mr. Cavallo at first cheered investors, given his pro-business stance. However, he tried to implement a range of both orthodox and heterodox policies but to no avail. Through 2001, Argentina's reserves continued to decline as the recession reached its third year.[34]

By the middle of 2001, unemployment was approaching 20%, and given the worsening situation, the *piqueteros*, increasingly used the tactic of blocking highways in order to prevent goods from getting to Buenos Aires, be it for local consumption or exports. They were demanding jobs, as many had been laid off due to privatizations, but also due to several years of recession. There had even been several incidents of government office buildings being burned down in provinces where public employees had been laid off or not paid for months. As the year advanced, the

took place in Argentina between 2001 and 2003, roughly between 10–11% drop in GDP, as merely a recession.

[33] Domingo Cavallo served as Central Bank President under the dictatorship in the early 1980s and as economics minister through most of the 1990s when Menem was in power, and briefly with De la Rúa.

[34] Argentina's foreign reserves dropped from US$25 billion to below US$15 billion between 2000 and 2001.

pending crisis loomed, much of industry was shut down, and unemployment and poverty continued to increase. Then came a run on the banks, the declining reserves took another drop and so Cavallo became desperate and instituted the *corralito*,[35] restricting people's access to their bank accounts and thus alienating almost everyone, but especially the Argentine middle class. The last straw was when the IMF reneged on a payment to Argentina of US$1.3 billion at the beginning of December 2001. This state of affairs led to the spontaneous street protests of the *cacerolazos* (the banging of pots and pans) and an increase in the highway blockades of the *piquetero* movement in Buenos Aires and across the country. By mid-December, there had been a general strike and rioting had occurred throughout Argentina as popular anger mounted against both Economics Minister Cavallo and President De la Rúa. On December 19, in spite of the declared state of siege, the Plaza de Mayo in Buenos Aires was the culmination of the popular insurrection and after just ten hours both Cavallo and De la Rúa were forced to resign, and escaped in a helicopter in the wee hours of December 20.

The first interim president, Rodriguez Saá, tried to go back on a promise that he would not run in the next Presidential election, and thus alienating many in the Peronist party. The combination of street protests and infighting within the Peronist party led to his quick demise. After a crazy two weeks of rioting, looting, and protesting, there were a total of 32 people killed, and five different presidents.[36] When the dust cleared, Eduardo Duhalde was the provisional president and despite some initial populist promises about breaking from the neoliberal model, he effectively served as the caretaker while Argentina defaulted on its foreign debt, devalued the peso to a fourth of its previous value and entered into a full-fledged depression.

The primary economic mechanism that caused Argentina's multiyear recession to turn into a depression was a generalized lack of confidence, causing firms, both Argentine and foreign to hold off from investment. The increased concern for a coming devaluation, reduced the confidence

[35] The *corralito* was a measure which prevented people from withdrawing more than $250 a week or $1000 a month from their bank accounts.

[36] The list of five different presidents between December 20, 2001 and January 2, 2002 were Fernando De la Rúa who resigned on December 20 followed by Ramón Puerta, Adolfo Rodríguez Saá, Eduardo Camaño, and finally Eduardo Duhalde who was in office from January 2, 2002 till May 25, 2003, replaced by Néstor Kirchner.

of both investors and consumers. In the case of consumers, no one was willing to buy durable goods, a house, or a car, fearing the loss of a job in the near future, and this exacerbated an already declining demand. The crucial step or catalyst shifting from recession into a depression came from the IMF's refusal to provide a previously arranged payment, followed by the desperate attempt by Cavallo to limit a run on the banks with the *corralito* which was a clear signal to Argentines of an impending devaluation.

During 2002, GNP declined by 11% (Iñigo Carrera 2004, p. 65) and at one point more than half of the population was living below the official poverty line (INDEC 2003). Duhalde succeeded in weathering the storm and preventing another acute social crisis and thus keeping the peace until Argentina signed an "interim" agreement with the IMF in January 2003 and lasted until Nestor Kirchner became president in May of 2003. This has been a brief summary of the unfolding of events during the period leading up to the crisis of December 2001 and the depression that ensued in 2002. The next section presents the case that the explosion of foreign debt during the 1990s was the most significant factor leading up to the crisis of 2001, and that both the Argentine elite and IMF share the blame for the crisis.

5.7 Foreign Debt and the Role of the IMF

Foreign debt is the component of Argentina's fiscal budget that had been the most out of control, and the immediate cause of the economic crisis in 2001. It grew at an incredible rate, having been less than US$10 billion in 1976 (as can be seen in Fig. 5.1) to balloon to US$146 billion in 2000. Most significantly, it more than doubled from 1993 to 2000, going from US$72 billion to US$146 billion (see Fig. 5.3).

The extent to which this was a growing problem for Argentina is further illustrated by considering the foreign debt as a percentage of GDP, which grew from 30.5 to 52%, between 1993 and 2001, which can also be seen in Fig. 5.3. This debt spiral was caused in part by the increase in U.S. interest rates, especially after the U.S. Federal Reserve raised short-term rates in February 1994, which doubled from 3 to 6% during the following year. This also affected Argentina's risk premium, exacerbating the impact of the increase in interest rates. A second major factor causing interest rates to increase worldwide, and subsequently increasing Argentina's debt, was the impact of the Mexican, Asian, Russian, and Brazilian

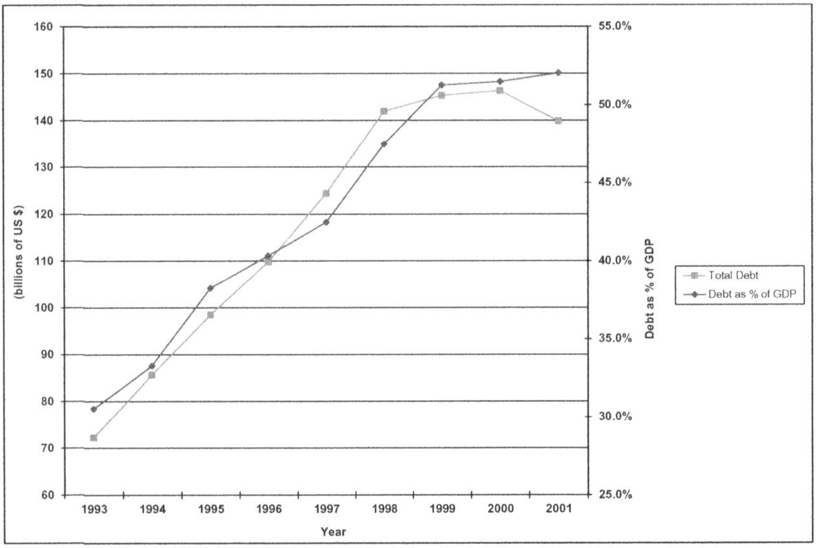

Fig. 5.3 Argentina's Foreign Debt (1993–2001) (billions of US$) (*Source* Ministerio de Economía, Argentina, 2005)

financial crises between 1995 and 1999 (Cibils et al. 2002, pp. 1–2). In fact, the interest payments that Argentina made during the 1990s total over US$60 billion and in 2000 alone were almost US$10 billion dollars (Weisbrot and Baker 2002, p. 4). As seen in Fig. 5.4, interest payments as a share of the GDP more than doubled, growing from 1.23% in 1993 to 3.4% in 2000. In contrast, government primary spending excluding interest payments as a share of the GDP tended to decline or stay steady through the 1990s, oscillating around 18.5% (see Fig. 5.5).

Thus, the IMF argument that Argentina was being fiscally irresponsible is not supported by the facts, unless fiscally irresponsible corresponds to making good on its debt payments for the IMF. Consider the claim on April 10, 2002 by the IMF's Anoop Singh[37] "In our view, failures in fiscal policy constitute the root cause of the current crisis." (Cibils et al. 2002, p. 3). It is rather amazing how the IMF portrays the situation despite such clear evidence to the contrary.

[37] Anoop Singh was the IMF Director of Special Operations in Buenos Aires in 2002.

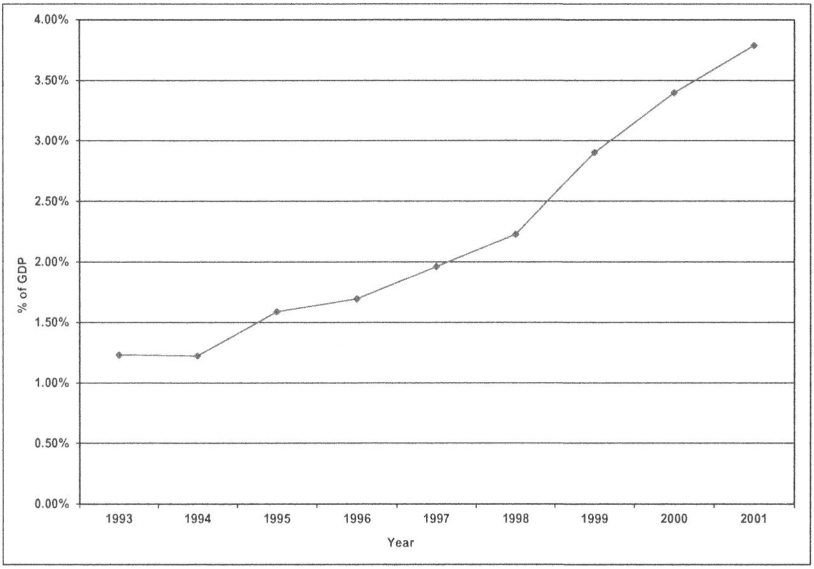

Fig. 5.4 Interest Payments as % of GDP (1993–2001) (*Source* Ministerio de Economía, Secretaria de Hacienda, Argentina, 2005)

In Section II, it was seen how the IMF, by not coming through for Isabel Perón, played a key role in bringing about the end of her administration. The military junta had to struggle less with the IMF because they were strongly committed to implementing neoliberal policies supported by the IMF and they had no problem using repression to do so. However, once Alfonsín was president in 1983, the IMF expressed displeasure with regard to his economic strategies, which were introducing some variants on the orthodox neoliberal model. Once Alfonsín did the unthinkable and suspended all payments on the debt principal, the IMF flexed its muscles and was able to force Argentina to "return to its senses" and get back on the neoliberal track. At the point where hyperinflation was peaking at almost 5000% and the country was enveloped in crisis, the IMF was one of the strongest advocates for Alfonsín to resign and let Menem take over.[38] They did not try to accommodate Argentina with an interim loan

[38] Some could argue that the argument presented here is avoiding criticism of Alfonsín, especially as there were attempts to increase interest rates so as to roll-over debt and

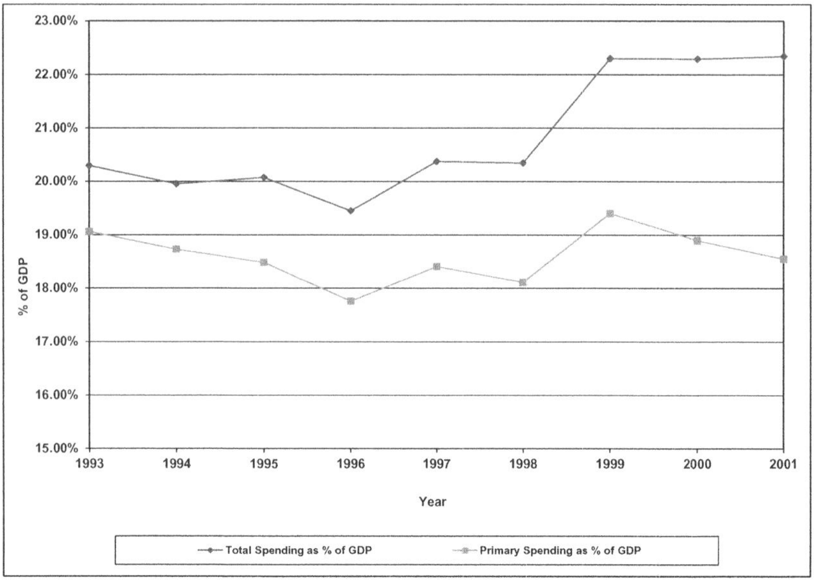

Fig. 5.5 Government Spending as % of GDP (1993–2001) (*Source* Ministerio de Economía, Secretaría de Hacienda, Argentina, 2005)

and wait a couple of months so as to have a smooth democratic transition to the next president. Instead they played a clear role in assisting those fomenting chaos and fear to force the Argentine people to support Menem's orthodox neoliberal approach. The IMF also gave full support for the Menem administration and the currency board through 2001 and yet attempt to deny any responsibility for the current crisis (Cibils et al. 2002, p. 6).

Despite his campaign claims advocating a shift from neoliberal policies, De la Rúa was following an orthodox economic plan as well from when he took office in 1999. Even though the De la Rúa government brought back the neoliberal guru, Domingo Cavallo, the IMF still let them down

reach the next election. Nevertheless, it is the international context of, first imperialism, and secondly institutions, such as the IMF, that impose their will, as banks, seeking their profits, not the development of countries of the periphery.

at the end of 2001, by reneging on a payment and thus forcing the immanent crisis. As Argentina was at the abyss, ready to fall into an even deeper crisis and depression, the lender of last resort, namely, the IMF, instead of offering a hand, gave Argentina a push.

As Argentina's foreign debt was spiraling out of control, shouldn't the IMF have been saying no to further loans or suggesting some other policies so that they didn't have to keep coming up with bailouts. It appears that the IMF, just like a good loan shark, is quite content to just keep collecting the interest, even if none of the principal ever gets paid off. The IMF was conceived as the lender of last resort, to help countries avoid financial crises. Based on this criterion, for the period from 1994 to 2002, the IMF has a poor track record—a string of financial crises, which they have not been able to prevent or provide solutions for afterward. Mexico had its worst economic crisis at the time in 1994–1995, followed by the Southeast Asia Financial Crisis of 1996–1997, then Russia in 1998, Brazil in 1999, Ecuador in 2000, and then Argentina in 2001–2002—the largest debt default in world history at the time!

5.8 Conclusions

The economic and social crisis that Argentina experienced has a number of causes. Most significant has been the pursuit of neoliberal economic policies for over a quarter century, combined with the impact of globalization dominated by transnational corporations. Throughout this period, the Argentine elite, the IMF, and TNCs have been proactive in pushing this project and thus bear the greatest responsibility for the negative impacts caused by it. It was during the dictatorship of the late 1970s, when Argentina began a process of deindustrialization in manufacturing due to both the neoliberal economic program and the clear shift away from manufacturing toward agribusiness and finance. It is evident that Argentina has become much more vulnerable to the threat of global competition and the oscillations of world market prices, having eliminated the majority of its controls for trade and other industrial policy tools. Similarly, financial deregulation, combined with the pegging of the peso to the dollar, led to a wave of foreign investment, capital flight, and an increasingly speculative and unstable environment. These changes caused Argentina to be more susceptible to the ripple effects of financial shocks, such as the Mexican Peso crisis, and more prone toward financial crises itself.

The impact of deindustrialization over 25 years combined with the more recent reprimarization, was seen as contributing to a worsening trade balance as imports were growing increasingly more than exports. By the mid to late 1990s, the growing trade deficit had been identified as significantly contributing to balance of payments problems. In order to maintain reserves, and keep paying the interest on foreign debt, loans from the IMF were increasing and combined with U.S. interest rate hikes, resulted in Argentina's debt doubling from US$72 billion to US$146 billion between 1993 and 2000.[39]

Despite there being other factors than the trade deficit which caused Argentina to borrow more, as well as other causes of the trade deficit, many emphasized the currency board as the principle cause of the crisis. It has been argued that Argentina should have delinked the peso from the dollar years earlier, but this is more easily said than done given the memory and fear of hyperinflation and a lack of confidence in the national currency. Menem did not wish to delink the dollar from the peso because the fear of devaluation would have produced a political crisis while he was still in power. Instead he was able to postpone the inevitable and the crisis hit when the opposition, the *Radicales*, were in power. This reflects Menem's support inside and outside the country, as he was able to shift the burden to the next administration, and the rest is history.

The rebellion of December 19–20, 2001 reflected a general dissatisfaction with almost all established political parties, as expressed in the popular slogan: "Get Rid of them all!" (*¡Que se Vayan Todos!*). During 2002 there was hope for significant political change in the air, between the street protests of the *cacerolazos*, the organized unemployed workers or *piqueteros*, and the birth of popular assemblies seeking to redefine politics in a new way. There was an increasing level of economic autonomy, between the wave of occupied factories, the growth of barter clubs, and the increased role of local and regional currencies, not to mention at the international level, Argentina had broken its pact with the IMF.

Nevertheless, Argentina came out of default by signing an interim agreement with the IMF in January 2003, despite a brief (roughly 9 hours) default in September 2003. Having hit bottom in 2002, Argentina's economy inevitably saw improvements thereafter, achieving 9% GNP

[39] As referred to above, increases in U.S. interest rates were also due to the financial crises in Mexico, Asia, Russia, and Brazil and secondly, Argentina's country risk was subsequently impacted, further exacerbating the growth of Argentina's debt.

growth in 2003. The growth that has occurred since the nadir of the depression was significant in improving the serious problems of unemployment and poverty. Nevertheless, as to be evaluated and discussed in subsequent chapters, even the shifts in the economic trajectory which took place under the Kirchner governments, the so-called new developmentalism, was not enough to return the middle and working classes of Argentina to pre-crisis levels

Although Néstor Kirchner provided a certain amount of hope for Argentines, his set of economic policies have been a mixed bag. In his discourse, Kirchner has been quite confrontational with the IMF at times and also with certain TNCs, but when it comes to economic fundamentals, he accommodated the IMF by agreeing to a 3% or greater budget surplus. As Argentina was coming out of a depression, it made no sense to generate a budget surplus instead it is the time that you expect to have a budget deficit in order to bolster the economy through government spending. No center country would agree to have a budget surplus in such a period. This is not just an issue or problem for Argentina, it is an international issue, and if other countries were more supportive, the IMF's hand could have been forced. There had been much hope that the Lula administration would be a clear ally in challenging the IMF, but it became evident that Brazil did not want to rock the boat and chose to stay more aligned with the neoliberal track.

In the political arena, Kirchner made several positive changes reflecting the sentiment of the population, such as regards to the military and police abuses. However, one would hope that the failures of a quarter century of the neoliberal model would resonate among leaders in government, not just among *piqueteros*. Unfortunately, the role of the Argentine elite and the IMF is still active in attempting to keep this failed model going. Further discussion of the Kirchner governments and the attempt of a new development trajectory will be examined in depth in coming chapters.

References

Azpiazu, D., and Schorr, M. 2004. "Los impactos regresivos de las privatizaciones en la Argentina: ¿"errores de diseño" o funcionalidad frente a los intereses del poder económico?". In: R. Boyer and J. C. Neffa (eds.), *La economía argentina y su crisis (1976–2001): visiones institucionalistas y regulacionistas*. Buenos Aires: Miño y Dávila.

Baker, Dean, and Weisbrot, M. 2002. "The Role of Social Security Privatization in Argentina's Economic Crisis." *Center for Economic and Policy Research*, April 16, 2002, Washington, DC.

Basualdo, Eduardo M. 2001. *Sistema político y modelo de Acumulación en la Argentina*. Buenos Aires: Universidad Nacional de Quilmes.

———. 2003. "Historia económica: Las reformas estructurales y el plan de convertibilidad durante la década de los noventa, El auge y la crisis de la valorización financiera." *Revista Realidad Económica*, Número 200, 16 de noviembre–31 de diciembre 2003, Buenos Aires.

Canitrot, Adolfo. 1981. "Teoría y práctica del liberalismo. Política antiinflacionaria y apertura económica en la Argentina, 1976–1981." *Desarrollo Económico*, No. 82, pp. 131–189.

Chang, Han-Joon. 2002a. *Kicking Away the Ladder—Development Strategy in Historical Perspective*. London: Anthem Press.

Cibils, A., Weisbrot, M., and Kar, D. 2002. "Argentina Since Default. The IMF and the Depression." *Center for Economic and Policy Research*. Briefing paper, September 3, 2002. Washington, DC.

Cooney, Paul. 2007a. "Argentina's Quarter Century Experiment with Neoliberalism: From Dictatorship to Depression." *Revista de Economia Contemporânea*. Rio de Janeiro, Vol. 11, No. 1 (January/April).

———. 2007b. "Evaluando el Neoliberalismo en América Latina: Los casos de Argentina, Brasil y México." Presented at the *XII Encontro da SEP*, June 2007.

Damill, M., Frenkel, R., and Juvenal, L. 2004. "Las cuentas públicas y la crisis de la convertibilidad en la Argentina." In: R. Boyer and J.C. Neffa (eds.), *La economía argentina y su crisis (1976–2001): visiones institucionalistas y regulacionistas*. Buenos Aires: Miño y Dávila.

Dinerstein, A. 2003a. "The Battle of Buenos Aires. Crisis, Insurrection and the Reinvention of Politics in Argentina." *Historical Materialism*, Vol. 10, No. 4, London.

———. 2003b. "Power or Counter Power? The Dilemma of the *Piquetero* Movement in Argentina Post Crisis." *Capital & Class*, Vol. 81, London.

Duarte, M. 2002. "Los impactos de las privatizaciones sobre el mercado de trabajo: desocupación y creciente precarización laboral." In: D. Azpiazu (ed.), *Privatizaciones y Poder Económico*. Buenos Aires: Universidad Nacional de Quilmes.

INDEC. 2003–2020. www.indec.gov.ar/. Accessed July 2020.

Iñigo Carrera, Juan. 2004. "La crisis de la representación política como forma concreta de reproducirse la base específica de la acumulación de capital en Argentina." *Revista da Sociedade Brasileira de Economia Política*, No. 27, Rio de Janeiro.

International Monetary Fund. 1998. "Argentina: Recent Economic Developments." IMF Staff Country Report No. 98/38, Washington, DC.

Kosacoff, B., and Azpiazu, D. 1989. *La industria argentina: desarrollo y cambios estructurales*. Bueno–s Aires: Centro Editor de América Latina.

Ministerio de Economía, Argentina, 2005. https://www.argentina.gob.ar/economia.

Minsburg, N. 2001. *La economía pos-menemista- ¿atrapada sin salida?* Buenos Aires: EUDEBA.

Rapoport, M., et al. 2000. *Historia económica, política y social de la Argentina (1880–2000)*. Buenos Aires: Ediciones Macchi.

Robinson, William I. 2008. *Latin America and Global Capitalism—A Critical Globalization Perspective*. Baltimore: The John Hopkins University Press.

Rock, D. 2002. "Racking Argentina." *New Left Review*, No. 17 (September/October 2002), London.

Schvarzer, Jorge. 1986. *La política económica de Martínez de Hoz*. Buenos Aires: Hyspamerica Ediciones.

Sevares, J. 2002. *Por qué cayó la Argentina-Imposición, crisis y reciclaje del orden neoliberal*. Buenos Aires: Grupo Editorial Norma.

Smith, W.C. 1989. *Authoritarianism and the Crisis of the Argentine Political Economy*. Stanford: Stanford University Press.

Svampa, Maristella, and Pereyra, S. 2004. "La experiencia piquetera: Dimensiones y desafíos de las organizaciones de desocupados en Argentina." *Revista da Sociedade Brasileira de Economia Política*, No. 27, Rio de Janeiro.

Weisbrot, M., and Baker, D. 2002. "What Happened to Argentina?" *Center for Economic and Policy Research*, January 31, 2002, Washington, DC.

CHAPTER 6

Late Neoliberalism in Brazil

6.1 Introduction

As presented in Chapter 4, neoliberalism arose as an ideology in the middle of the twentieth century and came to dominate economic policies worldwide during the 1980s. The four key dimensions involved with the rise of neoliberalism were considered: ideological, political, and economic, both the theoretical side and the real economy side. The main factors which facilitated the rise of neoliberalism in Latin America during the 1980s were the debt crisis, the strong influence of the IMF, and the role of the Washington Consensus. Many political leaders employed a rhetoric which defended reforms as necessary in order to pursue a modern open economy with free markets, free trade and eliminating burdensome regulations and subsequently implemented neoliberal policies in their countries. The key policies included the liberalization of trade, financial deregulation, privatizations, and labor flexibilization.

A significant part of this chapter is based upon my chapter in Richard Westra's book *Confronting Global Neoliberalism: Third World Resistance and Development Strategies*, see Cooney (2010).

P. Cooney, *Paths of Development in the Southern Cone*, Palgrave Insights into Apocalypse Economics, https://doi.org/10.1007/978-3-030-67673-5_5

In spite of the claims of advocates of neoliberal policies, of higher growth, increases in wages, lower poverty and improvement in the environment, the empirical evidence presented with respect to many of these claims was in fact the exact opposite of what they had predicted, as seen previously in Chapter 4. The general results from 1980 through the beginning of the 2000s for Latin America were: low rates of GDP growth, low wages, an increase in unemployment and poverty for the majority of Latin American populations, and financial crises, recessions, and even depressions for much of the region.[1]

It is important to note that the transition to neoliberalism took place in different periods and with differences across a range of countries. For the majority of Latin America, this shift took place during the first half of the 1980s, but in the case of the Southern Cone, for example both Chile and Uruguay had military coups in 1973, Argentina in 1976 and these were followed by the implementation of neoliberal policies. In contrast, in Brazil, the shift to neoliberalism occurred only as of 1989 when Collor took office and for this reason it is considered "*late neoliberalism.*"[2]

As discussed in Chapter 3, after the crisis of 1929, a profound transformation took place with respect to the pattern of accumulation in Brazil. The economy had been following a model of an agro-exporting country, with minimal industry. Shortly afterward, however, industry began to gain autonomy and a new development model was adopted in Brazil: import substitution industrialization (ISI). This model was also pursued by other countries in Latin America, such as Argentina, Mexico, and Colombia, as they attempted to achieve greater economic autonomy after the Second Great Depression, especially given the reduced role played by the US and Europe with respect to the international economy. Other countries, outside of Latin America also had notable success with the ISI model, such as Egypt, Turkey, Iran, and South Korea, among others.

Several of the key points of ISI in Brazil, described in Chapter 3, will be reconsidered for the subsequent discussion, yet seeking to avoid too much

[1] See Cooney (2008a) "Uma avaliação empírica da lei geral da acumulação capitalista no período atual de globalização neoliberal," *Revista de Economia* UFPR, v. 35, n. 1. 2009 and Cooney (2007b) "Evaluando el Neoliberalismo en América Latina: Los casos de Argentina, Brasil y México," presented at the XII Encontro de SEP, June, 2007 in São Paulo.

[2] The term "Late neoliberalism" implies that Brazil began its neoliberal phase later than other countries, not that it is a later phase of neoliberalism.

redundancy. The basic idea of ISI was to strengthen national industry by reducing imports of manufactured goods and producing them locally. Brazil pursued the ISI model beginning with the Revolution of 1930 led by Getúlio Vargas after the crisis of 1929–1933, first for light manufacturing, by transferring a large proportion of the surplus generated by agriculture—particularly coffee—and using it to subsidize manufacturing industry. During Vargas' second period (1950–1954) the development of heavy industry began to intensify and from 1956 to 1960 heavy industry was finally established in Brazil.[3]

Vargas is clearly seen as the president with which ISI began in Brazil but it was Juscelino Kubitschek (1956–1961) where there was a deepening of industrialization, especially with the famous program called the Plan of Goals (*O Plano de Metas*) as presented in Chapter 3. Finally, it was during the military government in the late 1960s and early 1970s when Brazil experienced an accelerated and third stage of ISI, in particular the government of Geisel (1974–1979) with the ambitious program for heavy industry, known as the Second National Development Plan. As discussed in Chapter 4, during the 1970s, the IMF was encouraging Brazil to take on foreign debt, for the purpose of extending their industrialization, but as a result of the Volcker shock in 1980, the IMF did a 180-degree turn and came to discourage ISI. Thus, Brazil, among other countries, were forced to stop or be setback due to the monetarist shock.

The growth of GDP had been rather strong between the 1950s and 1970s, as evidenced by Fig. 4.2, and especially during the period known as the "miracle" from 1968 to 1973, when the rate of growth was over 11%. Even when the ISI model was in decline in the 1970s, the rate of GDP growth was 6.6%, which is three to four times the rate of growth achieved during the neoliberal period.[4] Now we summarize the factors which led to the general shift from ISI toward neoliberalism in Brazil.

During the 1970s, several economic problems arose that were associated with ISI and the role of the state in the functioning of the economy in Brazil. The dominant problem was the balance of payments crises, reflecting persistent trade deficits as well as problems of fiscal management and corruption. According to Saad-Filho and Morais (2002), "...the

[3] Overall, the manufacturing sector grew at an annual rate of 6.3% between 1928 and 1955, with its percentage of GDP growing from 12.5 to 20% during this period.

[4] See Fig. 4.2 for a comparison of GDP growth rates.

three main problems associated with ISI in Brazil were: (1) the fiscal crisis of the State, (2) the alleged inefficiency of the manufacturing and services (especially financial) sectors, and (3) the difficulty in promoting a sufficiently dynamic national system for innovations" (Saad-Filho and Morais 2002, p. 4).

Unfortunately, as Brazil was deepening their level of industrialization and building up infrastructure often with support of loans from the IMF, the World Bank, or the IDB,[5] the rules of the game changed, as monetarists came to hold sway and push toward austerity and structural adjustment programs. From 1981 to 1989 annual GDP growth was a mere 2.2%.

Although the shift toward neoliberalism began with the government of Collor, the most significant changes took place during the period associated with the former Economics Minister and then President Fernando Henrique Cardoso: 1994–2002. The range of neoliberal policies implemented is examined for Brazil below, starting with the period beginning in 1990, and identifying the socioeconomic impacts overall. In addition to presenting several macroeconomic measures, such as rates of GDP growth, foreign direct investment (FDI), and foreign and internal debt, an evaluation is made of several key social indicators: real wages, unemployment, poverty, and inequality.

The above was a short summary of the ISI period for Brazil derived from Chapter 3 and then the transition to neoliberalism in general, as presented in Chapter 4, and in the next section, a more detailed account is presented of the particular case of the late transition to neoliberalism in Brazil, referred to as "late neoliberalism," considering Collor de Melo and Cardoso and the *Plano Real*.

6.2 Late Neoliberalism in Brazil

Although the monetarist *Plano Cruzado*[6] was implemented in 1986 and there was also the reform of the financial system in 1988, it can be argued that Brazil only began pursuing the neoliberal model in earnest as of the 1990s when the government of Collor de Melo came to power.

[5] Inter-American Development Bank.

[6] The *Plano Cruzado* (Cruzado Plan) was a monetarist economic plan aimed at reducing inflation, which was out of control (168%) in 1986, and which also introduced the new currency—the *cruzado*. For a brief and concise summary, see Filgueiras (2000).

6.2.1 Collor de Melo

Between the end of the dictatorship in 1985, the experience of the debt crisis in the mid-1980s, and the problems of hyperinflation at the end of the 1980s, Brazilians were ready for a change as reflected in the more progressive Constitution of 1988. After Lula and the PT (*Partido dos Trabalhadores*—Worker's Party) won the first round of the election in 1989, it seemed that a shift to the left was finally about to take place. However, thanks to manipulation by the media, and the alleged US's meddling, Lula and the PT's victory was postponed, and the conservative Fernando Collor de Mello pulled off the second-round victory.

Though later than many other countries in Latin America, Brazil was finally making the shift toward neoliberalism, although during the short-lived administration of Collor,[7] the neoliberal policy of most significance was trade liberalization, which was implemented gradually starting in 1990. The impact of the shift in import tariffs on domestic industry and employment was stark. The decline of average tariffs from over 40% to less than 15% in just 6 years is evident in Fig. 6.4 in the section discussing the impact of trade liberalization for Brazilian industry. Starting with the Collor government, at the end of 1991, the subsequent administrations continued neoliberal policies aimed at controlling inflation and attracting foreign capital.

6.2.2 Plano Real[8]

A major problem for Brazil, like several other Latin American countries,[9] was hyperinflation, which having exceeded 2000% in 1994,[10] was the principal justification for the *Plano Real*. In addition to introducing a new currency, the *Real*, the *Plano Real* involved programs that included fiscal reform, elimination of inflation indexation, an overvalued exchange rate, initially pegged at parity with the U.S. dollar, high interest rates, and

[7] In 1992, Collor was impeached due to a corruption scandal, forcing him to leave office two years early.

[8] This section incorporates a number of key points and statistics from the article: Rocha, G. M. "Neo-Dependency in Brazil", *New Left Review*, v. 16, July–August (2002).

[9] A number of the well-known cases of hyperinflation in Latin America in recent years include Argentina, Bolivia, Brazil, Mexico, Nicaragua Peru, and Venezuela.

[10] Rocha (2002, p. 6).

a large inflow of foreign capital, much of which was speculative. As Rocha aptly describes in her 2002 article on "neo–dependency" in Brazil:

> The Plano Real, however, was much more ambitious in conception than a mere scheme for stabilization. From the outset, its central premise was that only by slashing inflation could an attractive investment climate be created for foreign investment by multinationals in Brazil.[11]

The rationale was that significant flows of foreign direct investment (FDI) were necessary for Brazil to achieve long-term growth, and that the *Plano Real*—as Cardoso maintained—would also improve productivity and effectively help national industry to be more competitive on the world market. The government argued that a healthy investment climate to attract foreign investors could be achieved through the elimination of inflation. Indeed, after reaching monthly rates of 50% in June 1994, rates of inflation fell to 6% in July of 1994 thanks to the *Real* Plan. Therefore, in that sense, it was a success. The Cardoso government, which began in 1995, argued that FDI would help government finances and Brazilian industry. This was quite a tall order given FDI's dubious history for the periphery, but this argument continued to have currency, despite the inevitable failure, as seen below.

Brazil experienced an unprecedented financial liberalization during the 1990s; a major feature of which was the encouragement of short-term funds. Accommodating foreign capital became the main emphasis of an economic policy which was based on an overvalued currency, trade liberalization, and high rates of interest. As in the cases of Argentina and Mexico, this kind of financial liberalization was key for the shift to the new model, but the increase in FDI also increased the external vulnerability (see section below). The neoliberal policies were responsible for Brazil's new insertion in the world economy. In fact, Brazil went from having the third largest trade surplus in the world during the 1980s—only behind Japan and Germany—to be an economy with a trade deficit, immediately after the *Real* Plan was adopted.

De Oliveira and Nakatani (2007) argue that instead of promoting growth, the *Real* Plan achieved the opposite. Growth for Cardoso's first term was just 2.6% and an even lower 2.1% for the second term, similar to the first years of the Lula government, which was 2.6%. In fact, over the

[11] Ibid., p. 7.

period 1996–2005 the average growth rate has been just 2.2%. It is even worse when considering GDP per capita growth in Brazil—only 0.7% for the same period.[12]

6.2.3 *Cardoso's Government*

Even though Collor was the first Brazilian president to initiate the shift toward neoliberal policies,[13] it was really Cardoso, as economics minister, who was key in designing and implementing the *Real* Plan described above. Although Collor achieved the initial trade liberalization and some deregulation, it was Cardoso's presidency that clearly put Brazil solidly on the neoliberal path, especially in terms of financial deregulation. The shift to accommodate foreign capital was unequivocal, with major influxes of foreign investment as well as imports shortly after becoming president.

6.2.4 *Foreign Direct Investment*

As evident in Fig. 6.1, the net flows of foreign direct investment increased significantly from a mere US$2.1 billion in 1994 to US$10.8 billion in 1996, more than a fivefold increase in just 2 years. Portfolio investment constituted a significant part of this increase: 46.5% of the total in 1993, growing to 58% in 1994, then 45.9% in 1995, and then declining to 32.4% in 1996.[14] Total FDI increased even more, growing to over US$32 billion by 2000. However, between 2000 and 2003, this flow plummets down to just over US$10 billion and then surges back up from 2004 to 2007 reaching over US$34 billion in 2007. Such volatility calls into question the logic that FDI flows reduce Brazil's external vulnerability and insure stability and economic growth.

The *Real* Plan also attracted short-term speculative funds, reaching a net total of some US$23 billion. In fact, in addition to one of the

[12] According to De Oliveira, and Nakatani (2007) "From 2005 through the third quarter of 2008, there was a clear increase in GDP growth: roughly between 4 and 5%, but as of the fourth quarter of 2008, there was a drop of 3.6% due to the world economic crisis."

[13] The trade liberalization and deregulation which Collor implemented were in fact conditions for restructuring Brazil's foreign debt under the Brady Plan (Rocha 2002, p. 6).

[14] Ibid., p. 9.

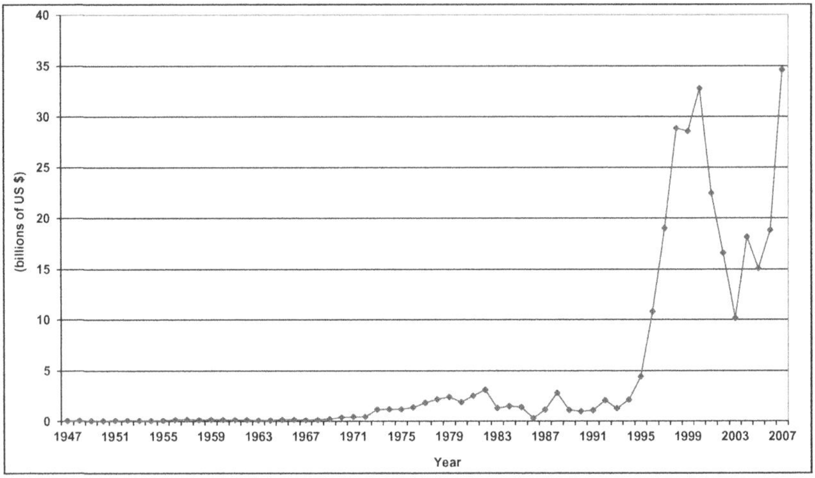

Fig. 6.1 Foreign Direct Investment in Brazil: 1947–2007 (billions of US$) (*Source* Banco Central do Brasil, 2010)

highest rates of interest worldwide, the government permitted absolute freedom of capital movement and particularly advantageous tax-exempt mechanisms known as CC5s, which are bank accounts for non-residents with free access to floating exchange rates.[15] In fact this is a significant aspect of the context which led to the currency crisis of 1999.

6.2.5 *Currency Crisis of 1999*

After the economic crisis in Russia during 1998, as in the case of the "tequila effect" caused by the Mexican crisis, the Brazilian economy felt the impact of another external shock. As Rocha (2002) describes:

> This time international confidence was only restored—temporarily—when the US orchestrated an IMF bailout of $41.5 billion to postpone the now inevitable currency collapse till after Washington had made sure of Cardoso's re-election in October 1998. (Rocha 2002, p. 14)

[15] Ibid., p. 9.

However, after the election it was only a few more months before the inevitable collapse in the form of an intensive speculative attack on the *real* in January 1999. Billions of dollars a day were taken out of the country, thereby forcing the Cardoso government to let the *real* float on world markets. The exchange rate anchor that had been the centerpiece of the *Plano Real* was undermined, and $50 billion in foreign reserves were lost in an attempt to prevent the inevitable devaluation: an eventual loss of two fifths of its value with respect to the dollar.[16] According to De Oliveira and Nakatani

> External vulnerability and the international financial crises of the 1990s brought down the economy in late 1998. After the currency collapse in early 1999, macroeconomic policy was changed, with three main priorities: low inflation, free-floating exchange rates, and generation of primary surpluses to avoid more debt. (De Oliveira and Nakatani 2007, p. 3)

In spite of the crisis of 1999, the neoliberal approach remained intact, both for the remainder of the Cardoso government and into the Lula administration, contrasting sharply with Lula's election rhetoric critical of Cardoso's policies.

6.2.6 *Lula's Government*

After losing three consecutive presidential elections, Lula and the PT finally won in October 2002. Despite the platform of the PT describing their commitment to social justice and worker's rights and criticisms of the policies of the Cardoso government, there was more of a continuity of policies pursued by the Lula government rather than a solid break with the past, as many Brazilians both expected and hoped. Yet the infiltration of neoliberal ideas within the economic policy formulations of the PT go back to the 1990s, so it was not a simple case of the PT shifting its perspective once it came to power. As 2003 progressed, there was general disillusion among Brazilian progressives, as the possibility of serious change dropped off the horizon, in spite of the PT's campaign promises. Nevertheless, the Lula government implemented a number of social programs in order to counter or ameliorate the worst aspects of neoliberal policies (see Sect. 8.5).

[16] See Rocha, 2002: 15.

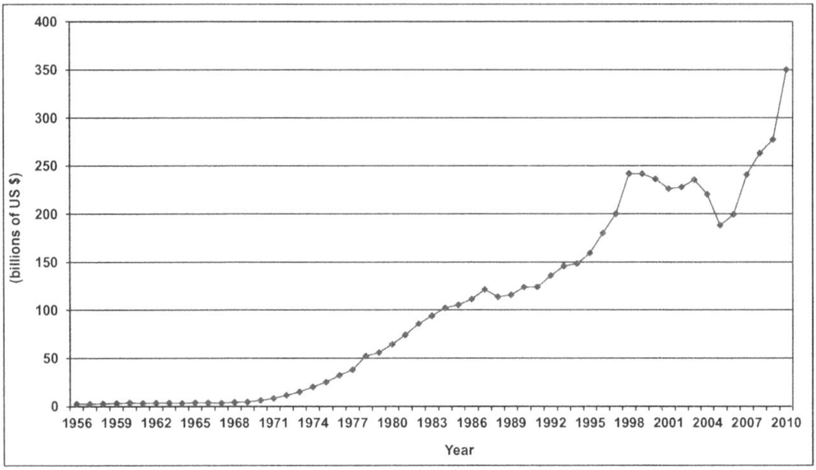

Fig. 6.2 Brazil's Foreign Debt: 1958–2010 (billions of US$) (*Source* Banco Central do Brasil [2011])

6.2.7 External Vulnerability,[17] Foreign Debt, and Internal Debt[18]

The results of the policies that combined an overvalued *real* with extremely high rates of interest can be seen as a success from the point of view that, in the short run, it minimized external vulnerability, thanks to significant increases in foreign reserves and FDI. In addition, there was a reduction of the foreign debt from US$241 billion in 1998 down to US$188 billion in 2005, although this went back up to US$240 billion in 2007, as seen in Fig. 6.2. Since the end of the Cardoso administration, the foreign debt as a percentage of GDP fell from 45.87 to 21.28% in December 2005. In the same period, the foreign debt service fell from 10.09% of GDP to 6.11%. However, in order to achieve these improvements, Brazil has been reducing external debt at the expense of increasing internal debt, thereby giving the appearance of reduced external vulnerability. However, the internal debt is being increased substantially and

[17] See Saad-Filho and Morais (2002), for a very good discussion about Brazil's external vulnerability as a result of neo-monetarist policies.

[18] Much of the analysis related to Internal Debt is based on two articles by Carlos E. Carvalho (2004, 2007).

at rates of interest significantly higher than those by which the foreign debt is being paid down. The rate of external debt tended to be around 4%, while the rate of internal debt is contracting at almost 13% annually (Carcanholo 2007). Therefore, the shift from external to internal debt is a situation that is actually worsening the overall indebtedness for governments in the future.

The internal debt grew from 13.9% of GDP in 1991 to over 51% in 2006, which was a rather significant increase. One of the major increases took place during the first years of the *Real* Plan when it went from 20.8% in 1994 to 39.2% in 1999, after the currency crisis. During the Cardoso government from 1999 to 2003, it showed a relative stability. With the exception of 2004, the public internal debt grew continually during the Lula government from 41.2% at the end of 2002 to 51.6% of GDP in October 2006, which implied a real increase of 25% in just four years. (Carvalho 2007, p. 82) This increase was not as drastic because it was accompanied by a drop in the external public debt as a result of the overvalued *real* and the strategy of accumulating international reserves by the Central Bank. It was therefore possible to reduce the net debt of the public sector during this period.

The net public debt (external and internal) grew significantly from 32.5% of GDP in 1994 to a maximum of 57.3% in 2002. Although the percentage of GDP decreased slightly in recent years, the absolute value continued to grow. Fig. 6.3 shows the strong growth of the internal debt from roughly US$600 billion to US$1600 billion during the period 2001–2007, and the increase of internal debt is much greater than the decrease of external debt.

The nature of internal debt is that it tends to be short term and valued at higher rates of interest, and accommodating, in particular, foreign investors. The problem created by this phenomenon is that the burden taken on by the government—and therefore the Brazilian people—implies a worsening of the debt situation overall. It is therefore critical to examine the basis behind the shift from foreign debt to internal debt, identifying the primary beneficiaries and the probable losers. The former tends to correspond to foreign investors and the Brazilian elite, while the latter is the great majority of working-class Brazilians.

For example, as the financial crisis in the US was worsening in October 2008, causing a growing uncertainty on world markets, Brazil lost over 10% of its international reserves in just a few weeks. Shortly thereafter, as much of the globe, Brazil's economy entered a recession, during the world economic crisis of 2008–2010. In terms of GDP, Brazil suffered one of the largest drops in GDP in the fourth quarter of 2008:

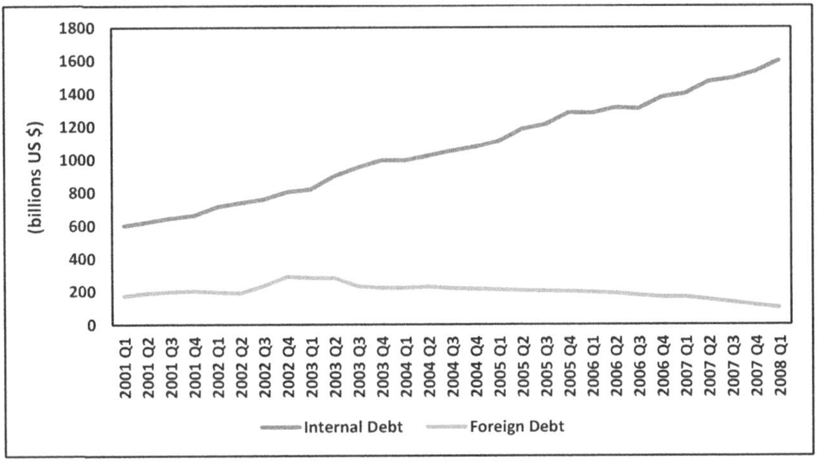

Fig. 6.3 Brazil's Foreign and Internal Public Debt: 2001–2008 (billions of US$) (*Source* Brazil's Central Bank, 2009)

−3.6%. In terms of Brazil's labor market, which is further discussed below, formal employment was at its worst level in 10 years, and those requiring unemployment insurance reached a record level—17%, as unemployment increased 14% between October 2008 and January 2009, and reached 15.1% for the six major metropolitan areas as of March 2008. The worsening of the situation in Brazil after the Great Recession is discussed further in Chapter 8. The section below presents the socioeconomic impacts of trade and financial liberalization from the end of the 1980s through to the eve of the Great Recession.

6.3 Socioeconomic Impacts of Neoliberal Globalization (1990–2007)[19]

A major concern for the Brazilian economy is the extent to which it is pursuing a development trajectory oriented toward the interests of TNCs operating in Brazil, whether they are manufacturing, agribusiness,

[19] The period 1990 through 2007 was chosen since 1990 corresponds to the beginning of neoliberalism in earnest with Collor de Melo and through 2007 as this is prior to the Great Recession of 2008–2010.

or financial firms, and often at the expense of national interests. As a result of the trade and financial liberalizations, national industry has more difficulties in competing successfully. First, with the highest or close to highest rates of interest in the world, resulting in an average of 14.56% between 1999 and 2020,[20] the costs of borrowing are greater, and therefore reduce the competitivity of national firms. Second, the elimination of tariffs implies a far more difficult terrain in which to compete against foreign TNCs within Brazil, far from the "level playing field" claimed by "free trade" advocates. Third, foreign TNCs are often granted far better terms than national firms: various regulations or taxes are relaxed for TNCs or foreign investors, but not for local firms. This reflects the degree to which governments also avoid special breaks for local firms given the potential of sanctions or discipline via WTO rules. Finally, with an overvalued currency, imports are much cheaper and it is more difficult for Brazilian products to compete either at home or in world markets.

As national industry encounters more problems, this has repercussions for wages and profits and therefore, income in general. With a decrease in the overall output level of Brazilian manufacturing, there will be a decline in both manufacturing jobs and a lack of growth of real wages for manufacturing employees. For example, Brazil lost more than one million industrial jobs during the period 1989–1997 alone. Such declines are consistent with relatively stagnant real wages and a significant increase in the informal economy, not to mention pressure for the flexibilization of labor both from outside and within Brazil. Thus, even if unemployment may begin to decline, the tendency is that better paid jobs in Brazilian manufacturing will be replaced by precarious, lower paid informal work, which is not a positive trend for the Brazilian economy, in fact it was roughly 60% through most of the 1990s and only dropped to below 50% in 2010 (see Fig. 8.11). The discussion of the informal economy is presented in Chapter 8.

Therefore, an increasing concern, as was the case of Argentina, is the reversal of Brazil's industrialization, as the economy is increasingly oriented toward agro-exports and much less oriented toward manufacturing industry. In fact, Brazil's ranking in terms of competitivity and industrial capacity and industrial exports has been falling compared to

[20] https://tradingeconomics.com/brazil/interest-rate.

other developing countries during recent years.[21] For example, between the years 1989 and 1999, Brazilian manufacturing exports as a percentage of world exports declined from roughly 0.8% down to 0.5%, while Brazil's exports of raw materials grew from around 2.2% to more than 3% of world exports.[22] There are a number of different factors responsible for these changes and in the next chapter the processes of deindustrialization and reprimarization in Brazil and Argentina will be examined in detail. For now, however, it is worth considering the impact of neoliberal trade policy and the lack of support either via an industrial policy or the lack of protection available for Brazilian firms.

6.3.1 *Trade Liberalization*

The clearest measure with respect to trade liberalization is the reduction in average import tariffs, which fell from more than 40% in 1988 down to only 13% in recent years (see Fig. 6.4). The worst example is that of capital goods which have tariffs approaching 0%, with certain exceptions. This basically makes it impossible for national high-tech firms to survive within Brazil.

6.3.2 *Privatizations*

A major part of the justification by Cardoso of the Plan Real and the pursuit of FDI was to generate a change and improvement in Brazil's competitiveness and to improve the overall situation for the country, along the lines of what he had referred to as dependent development, emphasizing development. Upon examining the reality more closely, the emphasis is on accommodating TNCs and the Brazilian elite which is constitutive of the transnational capitalist class, though second tier members, and some improvement in the coffers of the government for fiscal purposes, but the issue of improving the quality of life for the majority of Brazilians was not on the top of this agenda.

Turning to the privatizations which took place, Rocha (2002) argues that a major part of the increase of FDI was linked to the privatizations. Instead of investment which would lead to new plant and equipment and

[21] See Folha de São Paulo 10 November 2007.

[22] Pochmann (1996).

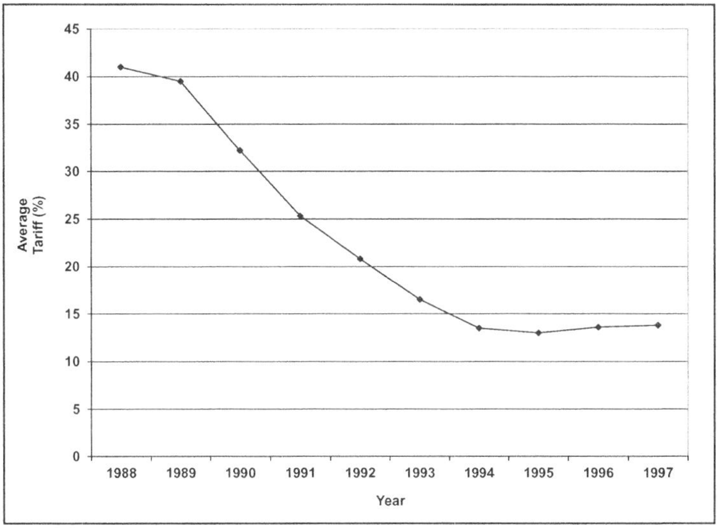

Fig. 6.4 Average Import Tariffs (%) Brazil 1988–1997 (*Source* Ministério de Fazenda, 2008)

improvements, a significant portion of the FDI was only interested in asset purchases and maybe a sale at another date, speculation more than an interest in improving technology and expanding production.

According to Rocha, privatizations totaled almost US$31 billion during the period 1996–2002. The main public enterprises sold were utilities: electricity, gas, and telecommunications, and also finance. Rocha claims that this total

> …would be higher if transactions financed with Brazilian resources were included, as the BNDES has financed many foreign acquisitions of privatized state firms at very low interest rates through a presidential decree of 24 May 1997. For its part, the government claims to have received total revenues of nearly $90 billion from its auction of public assets. (Rocha 2002: 21–22)

It seems bizarre that the Brazilian Development Bank is going to provide loans to foreign firms at low interest rates to buy national assets at low prices for the benefit of Brazilians. This appears quite illogical, but in fact it makes sense if one considers that the winners are not just TNCs, but the elite, including Cardoso and friends, that identify with the advance of transnational capital, not national capital or the interests of the majority of the population of Brazil. It seems that Cardoso understood marxism rather well, and how to make a profit of it; a good student of his own analysis, as argued by Rocha, just not a good president for the Brazilian people, but for the Brazilian and transnational elite he was excellent.

The levels of fraud and government manipulation of information clearly in the favor of the private firms purchasing Brazilian state enterprises varies significantly but none is as outrageous as the case of *Vale do Rio Doce*. The example of the privatization of *Vale do Rio Doce*,[23] is one of the worst examples of how the public was ripped off and Vale, though of Brazilian origin, has often operated as any other TNC in a country of the periphery. In spite of extracting millions from Carajás in the Amazon, and after pleas by Lula, they refused to place a steel mill in Brazil and instead set it up in China. The amount received by the government for Vale was a mere R$3.3 billion, and yet its value was listed as R$10 billion by Merrill Lynch at the time. However, given all of its subsidiaries and taking into account its extremely valuable mineral ore deposits, some have estimated its value at over R$100 billion (Biondi 2000), which is not so surprising given the fact that Vale is the second largest mining TNC on the planet.

In various sectors of the economy, there was a notable increase in the degree of internationalization of production. The presence and domination of foreign TNCs were most evident in the following sectors: foodstuffs, automobiles, computers, pharmaceuticals, hygiene and cleaning, plastics, and rubber, among others.[24]

A gauge of just how connected the push for FDI was with the processes of privatizations is the statistic that for the period "between 1995 and

[23] Cases of human rights abuse, environmental devastation, and extreme negligence on the part of Vale are discussed in Chapters 7 and 8, especially with respect to the environment and the Amazon.

[24] For an excellent analysis of globalization, denationalization and the growing influence of foreign firms in Brazil, see Reinaldo Gonçalves, *Globalização e Desnacionalização* (São Paulo: Paz e Terra, 1999).

1998 FDI accounted for 42.1% of the accumulated value of privatizations" (Rocha 2002: 22). Rocha goes on to describe transactions and operations by the Brazilian government which seems unreal, not only undermining national interests, but also some of the high-level capitalist investors. Moreover, very often the initial privatization also involves Brazilian partners, such as O Globo or Bradesco only to see them sell their shares later on to a foreign firm. This phenomenon was very common in Mexico and also Argentina and often with foreign firms or banks in Spain and Italy being the main beneficiaries, among others.

The government was very proactive in the privatizations of the state phone company Telebrás, to Telecom Italia. In addition a notable example is how "the Cardoso regime has actively assisted this displacement of domestic capital: in 1999, for instance, the BNDES advanced half the purchase price ($360 million) of the São Paulo energy company CESP-Tietê to the American Company AES, cutting out the historical Brazilian group Votorantim controlled by Antônio as Ermírio de Moraes, once described by a US scholar as a 'one-man national bourgeoisie'" (Rocha 2002).

Besides privatization, another mechanism of denationalization was through mergers and acquisitions, totally 1,233 by TNCs during the years 1995–1999 and combined with the devaluation of the local currency, the *real*, meant practically fire-sale prices for foreign TNCs. As national industry encounters problems it leads to a spreading of problems for other parts of the Brazilian economy: a decline in employment, wages, and income, and the overall capacity for the economy to grow.

6.3.3 *Growth*

As pointed out by De Oliveira and Nakatani, although the Lula government seems to have achieved the economic fundamentals in accordance with the IMF and the Washington Consensus this did not lead to significant growth as expected.[25] In fact, for the period of 1996–2005, Brazil only grew at an annual rate of 2.2% and during 2005 as the world grew at a rate of 4.3%, Brazil only reached 3.2%. Nevertheless, during the last couple years of the Lula administration, growth improved, reaching between 4–6% annually for 2006–2007. Yet, as just mentioned, in spite

[25] See F.A. De Oliveira and P. Nakatani (2007).

of an international situation much more favorable than during the years of the Cardoso administration, growth was not that much better. The second period of Lula and the government of Dilma are discussed in the next two chapters.

As presented in Fig. 4.2 and mentioned above, the growth rates of the allegedly stagnant ISI period were much stronger than during the neoliberal period. The rates for the decades of the 1950s, 1960s, and 1970s, were in the range of 6–7%—to over 11%, while the neoliberal period evidenced rates of GDP growth of slightly more than 2% or even less than 1.8% in the early part of the twenty-first century. However, there are many other socioeconomic aspects to be considered other than GDP when assessing economic well-being, such as wages, employment, poverty, and inequality.

6.3.4 *Wages*[26]

Wages is one of the most important variables for assessing the welfare of the majority of a population, and unfortunately, it has been suppressed for decades, if not centuries, in Brazil. Nevertheless, between 1955 and 1986, the real wage in Brazil was growing at a rate similar to productivity.[27] However, the overall trajectory since then has changed and in general there is a significant gap between the growth rate of productivity and that of wages. The average income for wage–earners, which roughly corresponds to the real wage, and as can be seen in Fig. 6.5, fell between 1985 and 1992, after which it grew slightly until 1997, and then fell again until 2002. Since then, it has been stable or stagnant at roughly 50–55% of the value it had in 1985. During the initial period of neoliberalism in Brazil, with Collor and then Cardoso, it is not much of a surprise that average wages remained below their level in 1985, however, with the PT (Workers' Party) coming to power, many anticipated a significant increase, instead of a minor improvement. Thus, according to this data, the real wage for Brazilian workers in 2007 was still roughly 50% of the value it

[26] According to DIEESE (Inter-Union Department for Statistics and Socioeconomic Studies), the minimum wage is now R$415/month, however they estimate that the necessary minimum wage corresponds to R$2,026 as of August 2008 (see www.dieese.org.br).

[27] See Marquetti, 2004.

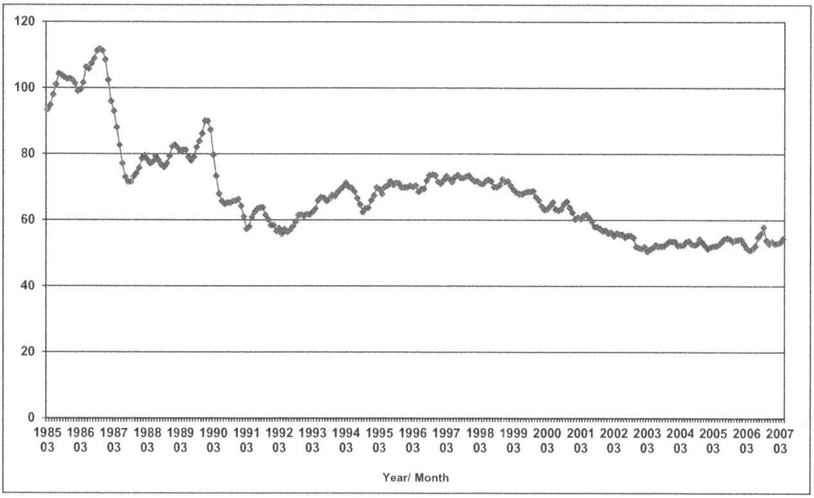

Fig. 6.5 Average Real Income for Wage–Earners in Brazil: 1985–2007 (1985 = 100) (*Source* SEADE/DIESSE, 2007

had when the ***dictatorship ended!*** This will be revisited in Chapter 8 along with other relevant socioeconomic variables.

6.3.5 Unemployment and Underemployment

As discussed above, the combination of high interest rates, the overvalued *real* and the trade liberalization which began in 1990, brought about the elimination of firms with high costs and low profitability and a concomitant increase in the rate of unemployment.[28] As can be observed in Fig. 6.6, urban unemployment grew from less than 5% in 1990 up to almost 14% in 1999 and between 1990 and 1997, 1.9 million people lost formal jobs in industry and roughly another half million in services. Between 1990 and February 1999 the losses totaled 3.2 million people. The employment situation clearly became more precarious, whether one considers job losses or the growing dependence on the informal market,

[28] The measure of unemployment used here is including underemployment, which is actually a more accurate measure of the lack of available jobs in an economy.

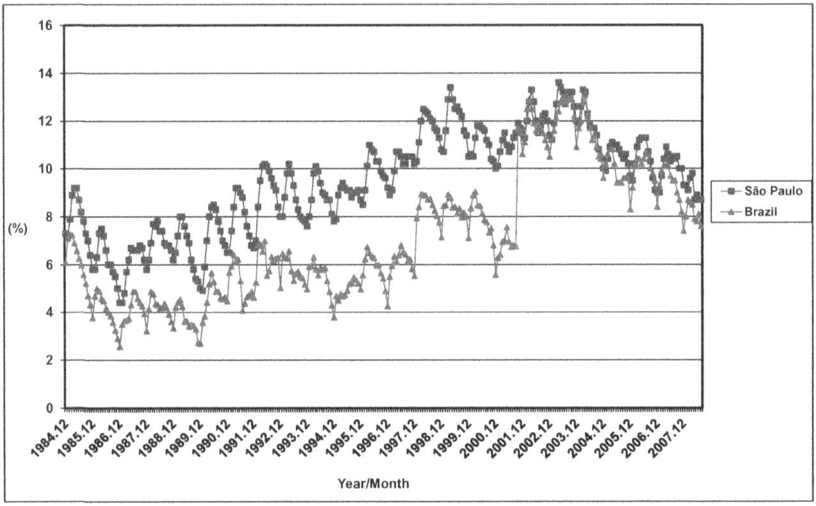

Fig. 6.6 Rates of Urban Unemployment in Brazil and São Paulo: 1984–2008[30] (*Source* IBGE; SEADE, 2008)

which grew to be as high as 50% in certain metropolitan areas, and much worse in rural areas.[29]

Although the IBGE has expanded its definition of unemployment, progressive economists tend to have more confidence in estimates by DIEESE or SEADE[31] which estimated total unemployment to be 14.2% in 1998 and 18.3% in 1999.[32] Independently of which data source one

[29] For an analysis of the deterioration of the labor market in Brazil and the growth of the informal economy see Pochmann, M. *O Trabalho sob Fogo Cruzado* (São Paulo: Editora Contexto, 1999).

[30] The two data series are open urban unemployment, which is inclusive of underemployment, however, prior to 2001; the values for Brazil and São Paulo are clearly lower compared to subsequent years. This is because a new methodology was adopted by the IBGE in 2001, using a broader definition for the open unemployment series. One should also take note that unemployed workers that stop looking for employment are not included in the unemployment rate.

[31] SEADE (Fundação Sistema Estadual de Análise de Dados) translated as the State Foundation for Data Analysis, which is based in São Paulo.

[32] See Cano (1999, p. 277).

uses, there has been a clear tendency for unemployment to increase during the neoliberal period beginning in 1990, although there was a clear reduction in the years during the Lula administration. This tendency of reduced unemployment switched to a worsening situation once the world economic crisis became manifest in September 2008. During the last quarter of 2008 and the first quarter of 2009, Brazil lost between one and one and a half million jobs, and as mentioned above, unemployment for the six major metropolitan regions reached 15.1% in March 2008. The employment situation during and after the crisis is examined in greater detail in Chapter 8.

6.3.6 *Inequality*

For convenience and popularity, the dominant measure of inequality—the Gini coefficient—is considered for Brazil. In 1976, the Gini coefficient for Brazil was 0.62, and this value was only surpassed during the period of hyperinflation in 1989 (0.635). Since then there has been a generally downward trend to reach 0.57 in 2005. As can be seen in Fig. 6.7, the movement over thirty years has been slight, with some recent improvement. Although just 4 or 5 years ago, Brazil was the fourth most

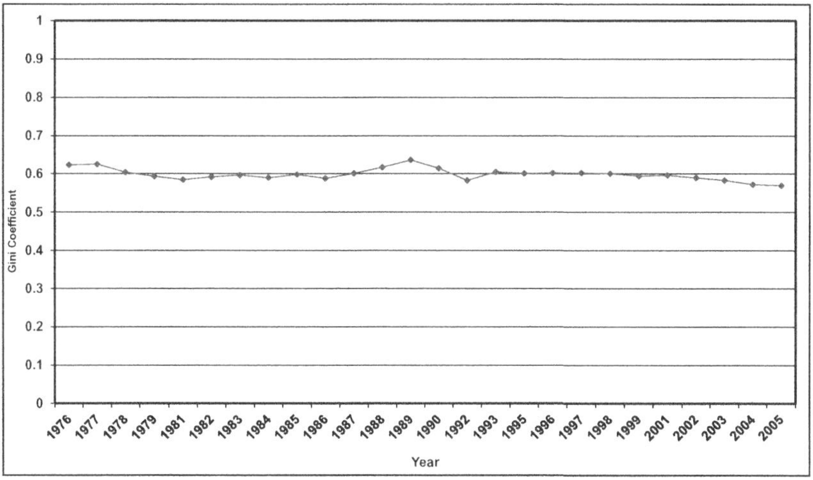

Fig. 6.7 Gini Coefficient in Brazil: 1976–2005 (*Source* IBGE, 2007)

unequal society in the world and it has improved to be the 9th or 10th most unequal, this is hardly anything to celebrate, given the severe inequality coefficient that continues to persist in Brazil. Undoubtedly, this recent improvement is directly related to the social welfare program *Bolsa Família*,[33] unfortunately, the great majority of Brazilians have not experienced a significant improvement with respect to their economic status or livelihood.

6.3.7 Poverty

Today more than ever, one must be extremely cautious when considering data on poverty, given the dominance and ideological bias reflected in the methodology used by the World Bank. Not only is the World Bank methodology used by many government statistics' offices, but also by many economists, even progressives. The contrast of different estimates for poverty in Brazil is quite significant as the World Bank cites 17.4% for 1990, while IPEA estimates 42% and ECLAC 48% for the same year—a huge difference. Unfortunately, the World Bank is committed to showing that globalization has reduced poverty significantly worldwide when exactly the opposite has taken place. The three main criticisms are (1) the absurdly low poverty line $1.25 in the US in 2005 (US$1 per day in 1985), as the basis for the international poverty line, (2) the use of general inflation indexes when the basket of basic goods, namely just those goods relevant for poor or nearly poor people's consumption should only be considered,[34] and (3) a generally inconsistent methodology for collection of data and definition of poverty across countries.[35]

According to IPEA, which employs the World Bank methodology, there has been a significant decline in poverty over the last 30 years, going from nearly 50% in 1976 to almost 30% in 2005. Although desirable, this seems quite dubious, once one looks at the reality in Brazil on the ground as well as considers the statistics just presented: real wages and unemployment. During the last twenty years unemployment alone increased to over 10% and as seen above, once underemployment is

[33] The *Bolsa Familia* and other social programs implemented under the PT administrations are discussed in Chapter 8.

[34] The difference between the general index for inflation and the index of food items only was roughly 70% during the period 2007–2008.

[35] See Pogge and Reddy, 2003.

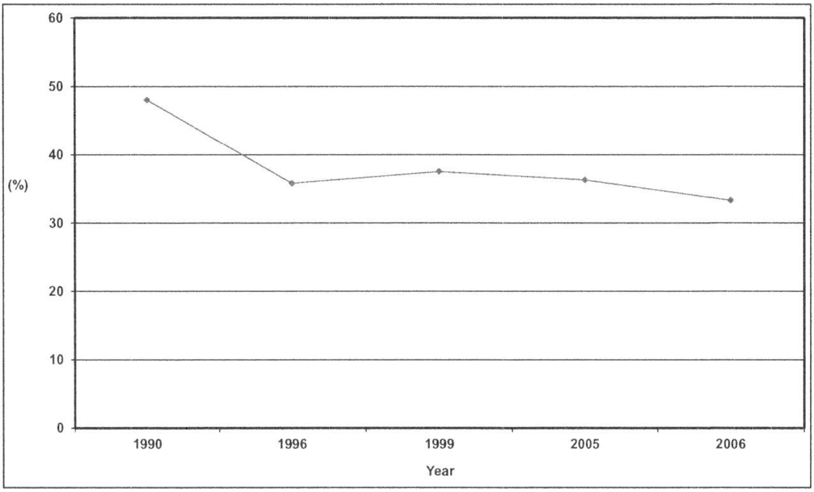

Fig. 6.8 Poverty in Brazil 1990–2006 (*Source* ECLAC, 2008)

included it reaches between 12 and 14%, and real wages are only 50% of what they were in 1985. Therefore, much lower real wages, a significantly worse employment situation, especially considering the increase in informal employment, a minimal improvement in inequality, suggests a clear basis for an increase in poverty, far from a decline of 20%.

Given the strong bias involved with the World Bank methodology, a preferred source of poverty data for Latin America is ECLAC,[36] which is shown in Fig. 6.8. Despite the fact that poverty grew during the 1980s in Brazil, a reduction is evident since the 1990s. Given the introduction of social programs aimed at alleviating the situation for the poorest in Brazil, it can be argued that these improvements are primarily related to such social programs which aimed to counter the most deleterious impacts of neoliberal policies.

[36] ECLAC (Economic Commission for Latin America and the Caribbean), Statistical Yearbook for Latin America and the Caribbean (www.eclac.cl) (2004).

6.3.8 *Winners and Losers Under Neoliberalism in Brazil*

In evaluating the overall impact of the implementation of neoliberal policies in Brazil from the beginning of the 1990s through till the arrival of the PT, it is crucial to identify the main beneficiaries and those that were socially excluded or experienced a worsening economic situation. The evaluation regarding the period after 2002 through to the present will be considered in Chapters 8 and 9.

The neoliberal macroeconomic policies of increasing the rate of interest and an overvalued exchange rate were designed to increase and accommodate foreign capital coming into Brazil, especially evident through the implementation of the *Real* Plan. In addition, there has been significant deregulation, reduction of taxes, and easing the process of repatriation of profits, royalties, etc. Thus, it is clear that the TNCs and foreign financial corporations operating in Brazil have benefited substantially. Brazilian banks have also clearly benefited, achieving record high profits in multiple years during the first decades of the twenty-first century. The Brazilian elite which have investments in the Brazilian stock market (BOVESPA) and in international financial markets have also benefited substantially from the neoliberal macroeconomic policies. Though discussed in greater detail in Chapter 8, much of the elite who were initially critics of a PT government, fared quite well in general since the Lula government came to power in 2003, however, their greed among other factors, helped bring the far right to power in 2016, and the victory of Bolsonaro in 2018.

In addition to Brazilian banks, the IMF and other international banks have clearly benefited from Brazil's neoliberal orientation.[37] For example, under Lula, Brazil was maintaining its primary surplus at a rather high level, approximately 4–5% of GDP, in order to ensure the payment of the foreign debt, even higher than originally requested by the IMF. Unfortunately, this implies that by putting aside money to pay debt service and accommodate foreign banks, there is less money available for social programs. As described above, the shift from external toward internal debt is increasing Brazil's external vulnerability and is benefiting those that own this debt while compromising future generations of Brazilians

[37] As will be discussed extensively in Chapter 8, the PT governments began with more continuity with the neoliberal policies of the Cardoso period, and over time tended to be more developmentalist, and less neoliberal, though with varying degrees.

that will have to pay for it through taxes or be denied social services because of fiscal constraints.

Although there has been record profitability for Brazilian banks, the situation for the majority of Brazilian manufacturing firms is another story. In order for Brazilian manufacturing to become more competitive, many firms went out of business or had to layoff many workers, as reflected in the decline in manufacturing employment, and also in the limited growth of Brazilian workers' wages, and then followed by a decline. In addition to the problem of under and unemployment, well-paid employment remains quite difficult to find in Brazil, and the growth of jobs has tended to be much stronger in the informal sector. It can be argued that this latter and non-desirable result is associated with neoliberal globalization in Brazil, as in so many other countries.

6.4 Conclusions

This chapter began by examining the period of import substitution industrialization in Brazil, followed by the neoliberal transformations which took place in Brazil, and which came to dominate the economic policies across the globe, and particularly in Latin America. Undoubtedly, the debt crisis at the beginning of the 1980s was a key moment in the shift from ISI to neoliberalism. The debt crisis provided the leverage necessary for the IMF and the World Bank to force many countries to adopt neoliberal policies, namely, privatizations, trade liberalization, financial deregulation, and the flexibilization of labor. However, Brazil made this transition much later than most other countries, as it really began with the arrival of Collor in 1990, and for this reason the term "late" neoliberalism has been used.

Although the neoliberal transition started with Collor, the more substantial shifts began with the *Plano Real* as well as other policies implemented during the Cardoso government. Despite the advances made in reducing inflation, the problems of neoliberal policies became evident with the outbreak of the currency crisis of 1999. Although there was substantial continuity of neoliberal policies under the Lula administration, the shifts associated with the PT administrations will be addressed in more detail in Chapter 8 which analyzes the attempt to shift to a new development trajectory, namely, neodevelopmentalism.

The third section presented a discussion regarding the socioeconomic impacts of the neoliberal policies from the early 1990s through to the beginning of the PT government. As seen in Chapter 4 and above, the neoliberal period in Brazil experienced much lower rates of growth than the ISI period: roughly between one quarter and one third of the rates during the ISI period. There was also a major reduction in wages during the neoliberal period, such that Brazilians are earning half of what they earned at the end of the dictatorship back in 1985. Under and unemployment have clearly worsened in this period and lastly, though inequality has improved slightly and poverty moderately, it is difficult to argue that the overall situation for the majority of Brazilians has improved under neoliberalism, and what slight gains were achieved have been reversed between the period of the Great Recession and especially now with the results of the neoliberal policies of Temer and Bolsonaro.

In Chapter 8, the social and environmental impacts of the "new development" paths in both Argentina and Brazil are examined, namely the periods dominated by the PT in Brazil and the Kirchners in Argentina. Then, in Chapter 9, an analysis is presented of the swing to the right and to a return of or deepening of neoliberal policies in both countries. In the case of Argentina, the rightward shift associated with Macri is examined and the recent return of the Peronists to power in 2019, with the election victory of President Alberto Fernandez with Cristina Fernandez de Kirchner as vice president. In the case of Brazil, Chapter 9 analyzes the impacts under Temer and Bolsonaro and the present crisis which includes the COVID-19 pandemic, and the economic crisis, if not depression, which the world faces for the future. As Bolsonaro is turning out to be even worse than Trump, Brazil is experiencing an unprecedented social disaster, between the combination of decades of neoliberal policies, and the unchartered territory of the current global pandemic, not to mention an extremely incompetent and dangerous proto-fascist leader. First, however, an examination of the new trajectories of deindustrialization and reprimarization are presented in the next chapter.

References

Banco Central do Brasil. 2004–2021. https://www.bcb.gov.br/.

Biondi, Aloysio. 2000. O *Brasil privatizado II: O assalto das privatizações continua*. São Paulo: Editora Fundação Perseu Abramo.

Cano, Wilson. 1999. *Soberania e Política Econômica na América Latina*. São Paulo: UNESP.

Carcanholo, R. 2007. "La Experiencia Brasileña: Deuda Externa, FMI y Política Económica." *Revista de SEPLA*, No. 1, set. 2007.

Carvalho, Carlos Eduardo. 2004. "Dívida pública: um debate necessário." In: João Sicsú, L.F.R. Paula, R. Michel (orgs.), *Novo-Desenvolvimentismo: Um projeto nacional de crescimento com equidade social*. Rio de Janeiro: Fundação Konrad Adenauer.

———. 2007. "A Dívida Interna: Custos, Restrições ao Crescimento, Alternativas." IEEI versão revista, April 24, 2007.

Cooney, Paul. 2010. "Late Neoliberalism." In: Richard Westra (ed.), *Brazil: Social and Economic Impacts of Trade and Financial Liberalization in Confronting Global Neoliberalism—Third World Resistance and Development Strategies*. Atlanta: Clarity Press.

———. 2007b. "Evaluando el Neoliberalismo en América Latina: Los casos de Argentina, Brasil y México." Presented at the *XII Encontro da SEP*, June 2007.

———. 2008a. "Uma Avaliação Empírica da Lei Geral da Acumulação Capitalista no Período Atual de Globalização Neoliberal". *Revista de Economia UFPR (Curitiba)*, v. 35, pp. 51–76.

De Oliveira, F.A., and Nakatani, P. 2007. "The Brazilian Economy Under Lula: A Balance of Contradictions." *Monthly Review*, Vol. 58, No. 8 (February).

ECLAC. 2008. http://www.eclac.cl.

Filgueiras, L. 2000. *História do Plano Real*. São Paulo: Editorial Boitempo.

Gonçalves, R. 1999. *Globalização e Desnacionalização*. São Paulo: Paz e Terra.

IBGE (Instituto Brasileiro de Geografia e Estadística). 2010–2021. www.ibge.gov.br/.

Marquetti, Adalmir. 2004. "A Economia Brasileira no Capitalismo Neoliberal: Progresso Técnico, Distribuição, Crescimento e Mudança Institucional." *Seminário USP/IPE*.

Pochmann, Mario. 1996. "Efeitos da internacionalização do capital no mundo do trabalho no Brasil." In: Enrique de La Garza Toledo y Carlos Salas (eds.), *NAFTA y MERCOSUR: Procesos de Apertura Económica y Trabajo*. Ciudad de México: CLACSO.

Pogge, Thomas, and Reddy, Sanjay. 2003. "Unknown: The Extent, Distribution, and Trend of Global Income Poverty." http://www.socialanalysis.org/.

Rocha, Geisa M. 2002. "Neo-Dependency in Brazil." *New Left Review*, No. 16.

Saad-Filho, A., and Morais, L. 2002. "Neo-Monetarismo Tropical: A Experiência Brasileira nos Anos Noventa." *Revista de Economia Política*, Vol. 22, No. 1 (85).

SEADE. 2007–2008. ((Fundação Sistema Estadual de Análise de Dados). https://www.seade.gov.br/.

CHAPTER 7

Deindustrialization and Reprimarization

7.1 Introduction

This chapter analyzes the current development paths that have been pursued in the two most industrialized countries of the Southern Cone, namely Brazil and Argentina, in recent decades. It has been argued that both countries have been pursuing new developmentalism[1] and yet that which has dominated in reality are the processes of deindustrialization and reprimarization. In order to understand these tendencies and their implications, the specifics of each country are examined. The chapter begins with a brief summary of the historical experiences of industrialization in both Argentina and Brazil, followed by a summary of neoliberal globalization and how the roles of the IMF, the WTO, and TNCs, contributed to these tendencies. This is followed by an evaluation of the processes of

[1] In English, the term neodevelopmentalism is used as often as new developmentalism and they should be seen as synonymous here in this book. In Spanish the term is *neodesarrollismo* and in Portuguese *novo desenvolvimentismo*.

Portions of this chapter are based upon my chapter titled "Current paths of development in the Southern Cone" in Westra (editor), *The Political Economy of Emerging Markets: Varieties of BRICS in the Age of Global Crises and Austerity* (2017).

P. Cooney, *Paths of Development in the Southern Cone*, Palgrave Insights into Apocalypse Economics, https://doi.org/10.1007/978-3-030-67673-5_6

deindustrialization and reprimarization for both countries and a discussion of their definitions. Moreover, a detailed analysis of these tendencies for both countries is carried out for extensive periods.

Section 7.6 of this chapter advances the discussion of the theoretical concept of accumulation by dispossession by David Harvey and evaluates its relevance in understanding the processes of reprimarization in both Argentina and Brazil. This is carried out through a more thorough analysis of the expansion of primary activities, namely, the sectors of transgenic soy production, cattle, and mega-mining, and analyzing the role of the State and transnationals, through legal and illegal means, in expropriations of local populations.

In the next chapter the tendencies of deindustrialization and reprimarization and their connection to the current development path, namely "neodevelopmentalism" will be analyzed for both countries. This will involve a more detailed discussion of development paths, with an evaluation of the political economy of the governments of the PT in Brazil with Lula and Dilma, and the Kirchners in Argentina, and the shift toward reprimarization and subsequent social and environmental impacts.

7.2 From ISI Through Neoliberalism to Deindustrialization

As seen in Chapter 3, both Argentina and Brazil were two of the most industrialized countries of Latin America given the history of the transition to ISI from the 1930s through the 1970s and into the 1980s for Brazil. On the one hand, both countries were able to advance through several stages of ISI, though Brazil achieved a more advanced level for a number of reasons. A key difference was the political support historically for a greater role of the State in Brazil, both in terms of industrialization, and its role in the economy overall. In fact, Brazil continued industrializing through the 1970s, with its military government of Geisel, while after the military coup in Argentina, the government of Videla not only began the implementation of neoliberal policies, they also began the process of deindustrialization.

The specific histories of the arrival of neoliberalism were analyzed in Chapters 4–6, and it is clear that this process took place at different paces and with nuanced histories. Nevertheless, the onslaught of neoliberal globalization and the hegemony of transnational corporations were such that by the 1990s both countries were on the same track, deindustrializing and well along their way with respect to reprimarization. In earlier chapters it was observed how the IMF encouraged the expansion of debt for countries such as Argentina, Brazil, and Mexico, which led to increased industrialization for Brazil and Mexico, but unfortunately to deindustrialization for Argentina. Though the debt crisis was used by the IMF as leverage to force countries to adopt neoliberal policies, in the case of Argentina, it was the military coup of 1976 which facilitated this shift. Unfortunately, after Argentina came out of the dictatorship, the first democratically elected President, Raúl Alfonsín, attempted to pursue a heterodox approach, but was thwarted at every turn by the IMF with neoliberal reforms (see Chapter 5).

The historical changes which took place in countries such as Argentina and Brazil with the end of ISI, and the shift toward neoliberalism, though with distinct trajectories, resulted in major steps backward for the processes of industrialization and development for the populations in both countries. The transition toward neoliberal globalization, complicated the conditions for manufacturing industry and industrial workers. For example, the process of trade liberalization strongly impacted the processes of ISI, eliminating or reducing protection and subsidies for national industry and thus exacerbating competition without achieving major productivity gains, or improvements for workers. Another aspect which impacted the manufacturing sector was financial deregulation, resulting in the shifting of the proportion of investment into speculative activities and thus negatively impacting both manufacturing production and employment. Lastly, the push toward privatizations led to major layoffs of public employees, and the selling off of many productive state enterprises to transnational capital.

A key aspect of neoliberal globalization has been the role of transnational corporations and the manner in which they have transformed the processes of production for the whole planet. Associated with the increasing domination of TNCs, there has been the emergence of a transnational capitalist class (TCC), as argued by Robinson (2004).[2] This has been concomitant with the expansion of transnational commodity

[2] The discussion of the concept of a TCC and transnational State was presented in Chapter 2, but due to space limitations, a further elaboration will not be presented here. Nevertheless, in the instances, which provide strong evidence, its relevance will be identified. For further discussion, Robinson argues that there is evidence of an emerging

chains across the globe. Given the imperative to accommodate the interests of TNCs and the new TCC, there has been a decline in terms of the importance or relevance of national industrial policies. Between transnationalization and the implementation of neoliberal policies, there was a clear end to the alternative represented by ISI.

The transformations achieved by TNCs are quite significant when considering the growth of outsourcing, whether in industry or in agriculture. Although outsourcing initially sounds positive for industrial expansion, it implies an increasingly precarious situation, whether for the firms of the periphery or the industrial workers, in free trade zones such as in Manaus or Tierra del Fuego. Therefore, the acceleration of technological change facilitated the shifting of production toward countries in the periphery where labor costs and benefits as well as tax burdens, were much lower or cheaper. The shifting of production also reflected locations where environmental restrictions and regulations were lax or minimally enforced.

The policy of an overvalued currency, whether through convertibility (Argentina) or the highest interest rates in the world (Brazil), reflected the monetarist perspective of controlling inflation and thus wages, in addition to the advantages for an emerging transnational capitalist class. The rate of exchange came to play a key role in the processes of deindustrialization and reprimarization of the Brazilian economy during the decades of the 1990s and 2000s, as will be seen below, but first Argentina will be considered.

7.3 Argentina's Deindustrialization[3]

As seen in Chapter 3, Argentina pursued ISI from the 1930s through to the 1970s and in spite of several coups and military governments, achieved some serious advances. For example, from the middle of the 1960s manufacturing goods grew such that they came to occupy two thirds of exports in 1973 (Kosacoff and Azpiazu 1989, p. 109). However, when the junta came to power in March 1976, the new government had

transnational capitalist class, and provides solid empirical analysis for the case of Latin America (Robinson 2008).

[3] Much of this text is presented in Chapter 5, though in more detail, and much of this is derived from the analysis of deindustrialization in Argentina in the text Cooney (2007).

other plans and the importance of Argentine industry would never be the same. This was evident in the neoliberal economic policies implemented by the junta with the new Economics Minister, Martínez de Hoz. A major goal of the military government was to shift their support away from manufacturing industry and toward agribusiness. It was argued that the rent from agriculture, principally from cattle and grains, would be used for the development of agribusiness instead of subsidizing the less efficient manufacturing industry.

As described in Chapter 5, when referring to deindustrialization, it constitutes the decline in manufacturing industry, which is distinct from agribusiness (or agro-industry) and mineral extraction, which is often seen as industrial, though not manufacturing. In fact, the term is misleading since industry can be seen as not just including manufacturing, but also agribusiness and mining. However, it is the historical shift away from manufacturing, which is often associated with industrialization and a return to the domination of the primary sector, although this sector includes activities such as the processing of grains or production of seed oils, which corresponds to agribusiness, but which are not associated with manufacturing industry, and the industrialization achieved through ISI.

The definition of the term reprimarization used in this book is the shifting of the motor of the economy away from manufacturing back to the domination of the primary goods sector. Even though the processing of raw materials, such as soy, wheat, and other cereals and grains, correspond to industry, they are clearly an extension of the primary good sector and thus reflect its current domination. Nevertheless, it is important to note, that they generate more value added than many other agricultural and extractive activities, in general.

Although, technically, the milling and grinding of soybeans is officially industrial, in this book, it is considered to be a part of the extended primary goods sector, and in this sense, its expansion is constitutive of reprimarization. Evidently, one has to examine and continue paying attention to the trends of value added, as well as the treatment in terms of tariffs and trade treaties of these different categories, but when the term reprimarization is used, it is referring to a general trend away from manufacturing industry (associated with industrialization, be it the center or the periphery) and once again toward the domination of the primary sector and related activities.

Three principal factors were identified as key in the shift away from manufacturing toward agribusiness during the 1970s. In summary, they

Fig. 7.1 Argentine Manufacturing Industry as a % of GDP: 1950–2019 (*Source* INDEC [2013, 2020])

were: (1) the change in alliances, away from the industrial bourgeoisie and a shift back to the landowning oligarchy, but now more modernized and fused with transnational agro-industry and finance, the latter often referred to as the *patria financiera*[4]; (2) the obsession on the part of the junta in eliminating the worker's resistance in general, even if this meant eliminating the industrial park in Argentina, given its association with concentrated organized workers and unions[5]; and (3) accommodating large capital, including foreign TNCs, the latter preferring Argentina to concentrate on primary goods production and leaving industrial activities, such as automobiles, steel, and heavy industry to TNCs operating locally.

Summarizing the process of deindustrialization as presented previously, the military dictatorship clearly had a very negative impact on Argentine industry, especially the manufacturing sector. In Fig. 7.1, it can be

[4] In Chapter 5 we referred to *patria financiera*, as a concentration of financiers, which over time has had increasing links to agribusiness.

[5] Most notable was the memory of the strikes and popular uprisings, such as the confrontations in 1969 in Córdoba (*el Cordobazo*), Rosario, Tucumán, etc. at the end of the 1960s and the beginning of the 1970s.

observed that the highest value of this series was almost 29% in 1971, and that prior to the dictatorship it was approximately 28% and during the military government this declined to 22% by 1981. Moreover, industrial employment also experienced a drop of more than 26%, and industrial production as a whole dropped 17% (Smith 1989, pp. 251–264). This constituted the first wave of deindustrialization in Argentina, while the second wave occurred during the government of Menem, when industry declined from roughly 22–15% in terms of GDP, and manufacturing jobs declined by 32.6%, from 1,132,499 to 762,992 between 1991 and 2001 (INDEC 2013)

In Fig. 7.1, the first series (INDEC 2013), downloaded from INDEC in 2013, goes from 1950 to 2012, while the second series (INDEC 2020) was what was readily available from INDEC in 2020, and goes from 2004 through 2019. They overlap from 2004 through 2012, and the value of the second series is greater in 2004, with a value of 18.93, while the earlier and more complete series only has a value of 16.8, roughly a difference of 2 percentage points. They seem to converge for the value of 16 between the years 2008 and 2009. Although they are very close for a couple of years, in the year 2012, the new series has a value 1% lower, and this is the last year of the previous series. Since both series are from INDEC, the differences are most likely due to changes in the methodology of calculating inflation, and thus impacting estimates of real production. Due to time limitations, not to mention lack of access to the underlying data, the data from the first series (INDEC 2013) will be considered valid through till 2009, and afterward the INDEC 2020 series, since it extends further, will be referred to. The upshot in terms of a trend in the decline of manufacturing as a percentage of GDP is after a maximum of roughly 29% in 1971, it has fallen by more than half to a value of 13% in 2019.

The factors contributing to a significant decline in manufacturing from when Menem took office in 1989 till the crisis of 2001, were the overvalued peso during the period of convertibility, high rates of interest, implying greater costs for industrial firms, and the pursuit of free trade policies instead of a national industrial policy.

After the depression of 2001–2003, between destroyed capital and extremely low wages, during the government of Nestor Kirchner, industry recovered, and according to the data for the series above, the manufacturing percentage increases by at best 1.5%. Overall, between the beginning of Nestor's government and when Macri took over is a decline of more than 2%, and this is giving the Kirchners the benefit of the doubt, given the data discrepancies.[6] There was significant debate whether or not the Kirchners' governments were promoting manufacturing industry or not, however, one must be specific about which period. In any case, this discussion, the social impacts of deindustrialization and the debate over development paths will be addressed in Chapter 8.[7]

7.4 A Difficult Trajectory for Brazilian Industry at the Outset of the Twenty-First Century[8]

In the first decade of the twenty-first century, Brazil evinced an image of a complex emerging economy, constituting the sixth largest economy worldwide, in terms of GDP. Nevertheless, the fact that the manufacturing sector was declining in terms of GDP since the mid-eighties, points to the fact that globalization was producing significant changes in the productive structure. This also reflects policy changes made in the decade of the 1990s and which continued into the first decade of the new century. Overall it is indicative of the transformations that have been taking place across the globe as the result of several decades of neoliberal globalization.

The historical presence of international capital in Brazil, primarily in the form of foreign direct investment (FDI), has constituted an important aspect in the formation of Brazil's industrial park. Gonçalves (1999) notes that "foreign capital found a favorable and liberal" atmosphere, with clear advantages and with national capital being subordinate to its interests. The presence and inflows of foreign capital into the Brazilian economy, was particularly accentuated during the 1990s, especially after the implementation of Cardoso's *Plano Real*. In large part, this was a result of the drive toward privatization of public enterprises in important sectors

[6] One must recognize, as I always tell my students, data is dirty, and the fact that there are multiple official data series and multiple approaches of underlying assumptions, or data manipulation, the "real" or "true" data series is always subject to interpretation. This is not an excuse to use any data series, but even when one carries out painstakingly careful calculations, there will still be debates as to what is correct. Such is science!

[7] There are some authors who seek to argue for a resurgence of manufacturing in certain countries of Latin America, such as Argentina, however, the data and the reality are clearly not in favor of such an argument (See Santarcangelo 2019).

[8] Portions of the text in this and the next section derive from my publication with José Trindade and Wesley Pereira, which is useful for further analysis of the process of Reprimarization in Brazil (see Trinidad et al. 2016).

of the economy, such as in mining and telecommunications. According to Gonçalves (1999, p. 15), the participation of foreign capital, in terms of the value of output, increased from 10% in 1995 to roughly 15% in 1998. As analyzed in Chapter 6, the increased role of foreign capital is evident when considering the major increases of foreign direct investment: from US $2.1 billion in 1994 to US $10.8 billion in 1996; more than quintupled in only 2 years and later reaching US$34 billion in 2007, generating significant financial fluctuations in the Brazilian economy (See Rocha 2002).

The consequent denationalization of the Brazilian economy resulting from the large presence of TNCs, and combined with WTO restrictions regarding subsidies and protection, reduced the capacity for the Brazilian industry to compete and also increased the external vulnerability of the Brazilian economy. As observed in the previously mentioned work (Gonçalves 1999, pp. 177–190), the weakening of the Brazilian productive base was partly caused by accommodating foreign TNCs, especially through privatizations. Thus, instead of providing new productive investment as a result of FDI, there was only a transfer of ownership of previously existing state assets to foreign transnationals. Therefore, the productive base came to be managed according to the logic of global productive efficiency, namely decisions aimed at reinforcing the networks of global capital, not the interests of national industry.

Another key aspect to consider is the growing presence of agribusiness and extractive sectors in Brazil; this tendency dates back to internal shifts in the early 1990s, but also reflects the institutional changes, such as the increased role of the WTO. There have been a number of important measures adopted and also instruments employed which accommodated agribusiness in recent decades. In particular, there has been significant use of rural credit for investments in agricultural mechanization and research oriented toward the production of grains and seed oils in the Brazilian Cerrado,[9] carried out by the state enterprise Embrapa.[10] There has also been a strengthening of the agribusiness chain linked to the food and

[9] The Cerrado is an area situated in the Center-West of Brazil, associated with the biome of savannah and is constituted by the states of Mato Grosso, Mato Grosso do Sul, Goiás and Tocantins (see map, Fig. 15 in Chapter 8).

[10] *Embrapa (Empresa Brasileira de Pesquisa Agropecuária)*, is translated as the Brazilian firm for Agricultural Research.

beverages sector, and this can be observed in Figs. 7.4 and 7.5, as well as in the export profile for the decade of the 2000s, as will be seen below.[11]

There is a general sense that after several decades of industrial growth, Brazil became a clear leader and industrial powerhouse of the region and it is still viewed as the strongest industrial economy of Latin America. However, there has been a growing discussion regarding Brazil's deindustrialization in the past as well as in the present. In this sense, it is important to examine one of the prevalent measures of deindustrialization, namely the value added in manufacturing as a share of GDP in percentage terms. Brazil's manufacturing industry achieved its maximum percentage of GDP, in terms of total output, in 1985, at almost 36%, reflecting the impact of the 2nd National Development Plan (II PND), as discussed in Chapter 3. This Plan was the last significant effort during the ISI period for employing government planning in the formulation and implementation of development policies and actions, giving special importance to the coordination of industrial policies and complementarities of productive chains.[12]

Figure 7.2 presents the contribution of manufacturing value added as a percentage of GDP. The highest level attained was 35.9% in 1985, followed by a downward tendency bottoming out at roughly 14% in 1998.[13] This was followed by a slight recovery to almost 18.5% in 2004, but then falling in recent years, dropping to 12.55% in 2012, and currently in 2019 down to 11%.

Shall we conclude that this tendency demonstrates a permanent process? Not necessarily. Since transformations in several sectors have been significant, there has been growing concern about the direction of industry going forward. However, it would only be through the establishment of a well thought out industrial policy that the present trajectory

[11] For the debate on agribusiness and recent developments see Bunker and Ciccantell (2005), IPEA (2012).

[12] For an analysis of these aspects, see Castro and Souza (1987) and also Carneiro (2002).

[13] In spite of the fact that the IBGE simply presents one series, it is worth noting that there was a methodological change in the Brazilian National Accounts in the year 2008 for data as of 1995. Therefore, the period from 1995 to 2012 is not consistent with the earlier series for the period 1947–1995, which is reflected in the significant drop in the series between 1994 and 1995. Ideally there would be two separate series presented, reflecting the two methodologies. Assuming the new methodology to be more accurate, the value of 35.9% in 1985, would probably be slightly adjusted downward.

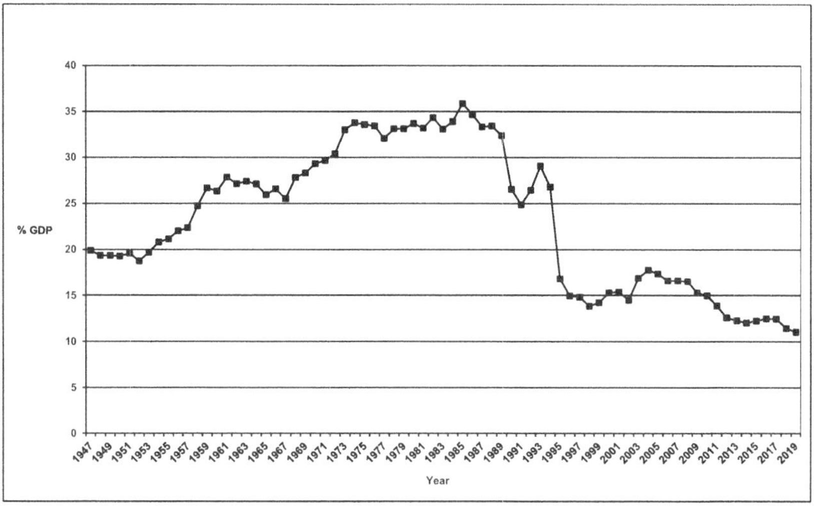

Fig. 7.2 Brazilian Manufacturing Industry (% GDP), 1947–2019 (*Source* IBGE/SCN 2020)

could be changed. Evidently, there is concern over Brazil's current export profile, and the nature and level of their current integration with China, reflecting the selling of primary goods in return for importing manufacturing goods. In addition, there is a great level of uncertainty with respect to the current economic situation for the global economy at present, given the COVID-19 pandemic. However, the discussion of possible scenarios will be postponed till later chapters for now, and recent changes for Brazilian industry will first be examined.

The main issue is the increase of the degree of dependence of the economy in relation to agribusiness and mining, to the detriment of manufacturing.[14] This is also reflected in the priorities of the government's investment in infrastructure such as hydroelectric dams, as part

[14] It should be pointed out that in general agribusiness has greater economic impacts in terms of employment and income than mining.

of the PAC.[15] For example, the growth rates of both agribusiness and mining had been strong due to the high prices in commodity markets, particularly since the mid-1990s, reflecting the rapid growth of China and its growing importance in the world economy. On the one hand, the commodities boom ended around 2013 or so and secondly, the current crisis associated with COVID-19 implies nothing is really certain for the next year or more.

A major concern is how this downward tendency in manufacturing will develop in the medium and long term, and whether it portends a growing and permanent primarization of the Brazilian economy. In any case, it does not mean that there was not important growth for a number of industrial sectors. However, before examining specific high growth sectors, the overall expansion of production, employment and productivity for recent years in the manufacturing sector in the aggregate is presented in Fig. 7.3.

As can be observed, with 1996 as the base year, production increases by roughly 50% between 1996 and 2010, however, with manufacturing employment increasing 64%, the net result is a decline of productivity to 91% of the value in 1996. Therefore, it is evident that Brazilian manufacturing was in a crucial period where improvements in terms of technological change were needed in order to bring about a reversal of this troubling downward trend,[16] beginning in 1998. Since that period Brazilian manufacturing productivity did make a turnaround. According to IEDI the productivity of the manufacturing industry grew at an annual average rate of 1.38% between 2010 and 2017, in spite of declines in 2012 and 2015. Therefore, this was clearly a major improvement compared to the data from 1996 to 2010 observed in Fig. 7.3. Unfortunately manufacturing employment declined at an annual rate of −1.28 over this same period (2010–2017) (IEDI 2018, pp. 6–7).

Although the growth rate of the absolute value of gross output between 1996 and 2010 for Brazilian manufacturing overall was almost

[15] PAC (*Programa de Aceleração do Crescimento*) can be translated as the Programme for Accelerated Growth, and reflects a clear push in support of government investment in infrastructure by the Lula and Dilma administrations, in contrast to their predecessor Cardoso.

[16] It is worth noting that the gap between productivity levels in Brazil and the US, measured by a percentage of the US productivity levels, was as low as 27% in 1950 but the gap was reduced to 45% by 1980. Unfortunately, since that time, the gap has increased again and the measure is down to a mere 25% in 2017 (IEDI 2018, p. 6).

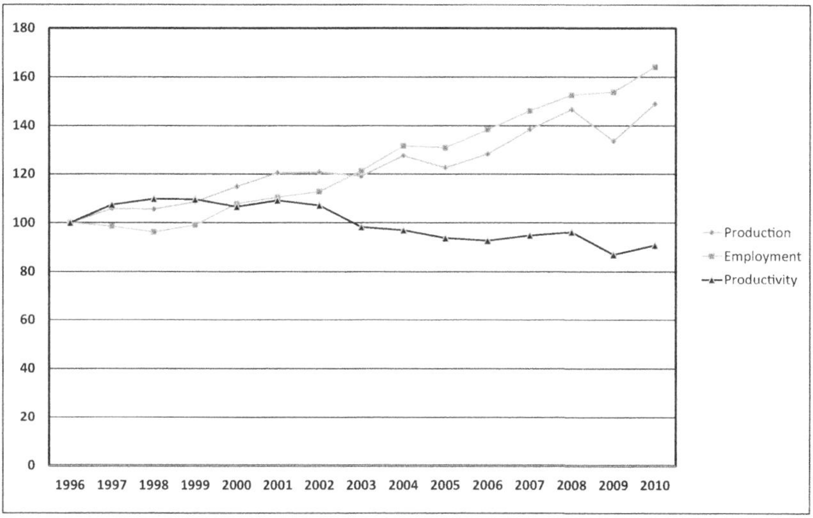

Fig. 7.3 Production, Employment and Productivity in Brazilian Manufacturing: 1996–2010 (1996 = 100) (*Source* Based on data from IBGE [Annual Industrial Firm Survey, 2012] and FGV 2012)

50%, several industries fared much better. As is evident in Fig. 7.4, through the period 1996–2010, of greatest significance in absolute terms was the food and beverages sector. Although its growth rate was only 5% above the average, it constituted 20% of the value of total manufacturing output, both in 1996 and 2010. The industry with the highest growth rate was that of petroleum and related products, growing by more than 114% during the period 1996 to 2010 and representing 9% of all manufacturing industry in 2010. The automobile sector experienced the second highest rate of growth for the period: an increase of 88%, and constituted 12% of the value of total manufacturing output in 2010. The metallurgy sector was also quite notable: experiencing 82% growth for the period and constituting 7% of all manufacturing industry. The sector machinery and equipment did not exhibit high growth, only 22% in the 15-year period, but is included in the graph because of its weak performance and it being one of the sectors associated with manufacturing and heavy industry.

Referring to the more recent study by IEDI again, between 2010 and 2015, there were two sectors with the most significant concentration of

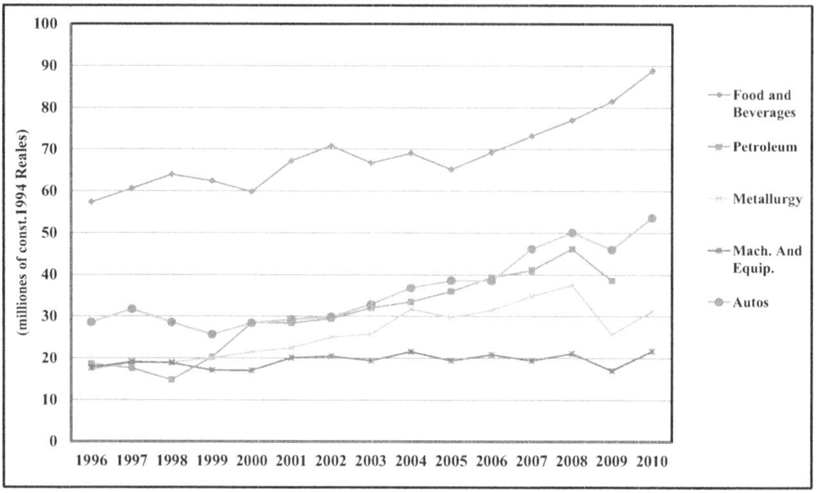

Fig. 7.4 High Growth Industries in Brazil, Value of Gross Output in 1996–2010 (millions of constant 1994 *Reais*) (*Source* IBGE Annual Firm Survey [2012] and author's calculations)

value added and were from just two sectors, both of which correspond to those categorized as intensive in natural resources: (1) the food and beverages sector and (2) coke, and petroleum and biofuel derivatives. As a result, the only sectors to show an increase in terms of importance in manufacturing value added were those that were intensive in the use of natural resources; yet another example of the tendency of reprimarization (IEDI 2018, p. 8).

It is important to observe that the main manufacturing sectors in Brazil are traditional ones, with minimal interaction with recent developments in more innovative sectors. Both the chemical and the automobile industries went through an intense process of productive restructuring in the last two decades, with the adoption of new production processes or with technological modernization, intensifying the denationalization process, and removing from the market the few industries dominated by national capital (see Gonçalves 1999).

In addition to the importance of the growth of key manufacturing industrial sectors, it was shown above that the increase of manufacturing employment was 64% above the levels of 1996. In order to examine the distribution of employment by sector, Fig. 7.5 presents the pattern of employment for those sectors with higher rates of growth of employment for the period 1996–2010. As one can see below, the sector which generated the largest number of jobs was by far that of food and beverages, which grew from 16% of all industrial employment to over 19% in 2010, growing at a rate of 95% for the period. The second most significant sector in terms of employment generation is clothing and accessories, which grew from 8% of all manufacturing jobs to almost 10% through this period, with a growth rate of 93%.

The other sectors of significance in terms of growth were metal products which grew at 92% for the period, and reaching almost 7% of all manufacturing employment; this is followed by the automobile sector which grew by 82% and reaching almost 7% of all manufacturing jobs as well. Lastly, is the nonmetallic minerals sector, which grew at a rate of 74% and approaching 6% of manufacturing employment in 2010. Moreover, the IEDI (2018) study for the period 2010–2015, also only showed increases in manufacturing employment for sectors with intensive use of natural resources, the largest increase being for the food and beverages sector. These results and those of Fig. 7.5 provide additional evidence

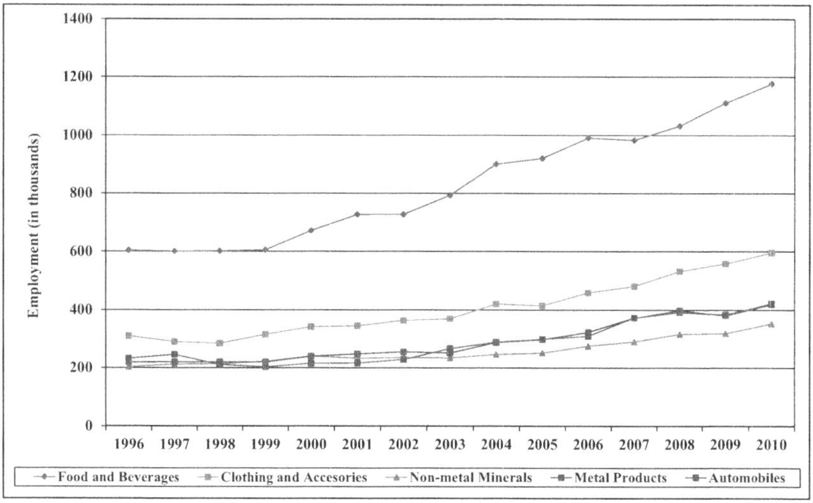

Fig. 7.5 Brazilian Manufacturing Sectors w/High Employment Growth: 1996–2010 (*Source* IBGE [Annual Firm Survey, 2012] and author's calculations)

regarding the shifts in orientation of the Brazilian economy since the end of the 1980s, and this tendency reflects a particular insertion in the current world economy, such that Brazil has increasingly become a producer of primary goods or manufacturing goods with low levels of value added, as reflected in the increasing weight of the food and beverages sector.

The current trajectory is a result of the structural changes which the Brazilian economy experienced since the end of the 1980s and specifically the framework established by the global neoliberal order since the 1990s, reflecting a particular type of insertion in the world economy: mainly as producer and supplier of primary goods with low value added. The necessary change to this pattern is fundamental for a new type of insertion of Brazil in the global economy, in order to avoid continuing along the path of dependent development with increased external vulnerability and recurring crises.

Unfortunately, this tendency of a third phase of dependency, as described in Chapter 2, constitutes another shift, but this time moving away from industrialization and expansion of manufacturing toward agribusiness, distinct from that of an economy dominated by agro-exports, though once again with the domination of primary production and a few related industries that produce some improvement in value added, such as food and beverages.

The same sector which was key in the transition from just agricultural exports, namely coffee, sugar, rubber, etc., in the 1930s, toward industrialization. The unfortunate reality is that this is the sector of industry with the largest percentage of production and employment even though we are approaching 100 years since the earlier phase, when this was also the case. However, as discussed in detail for the case of soy further below, the agribusiness sector is also dependent on a greater foreign presence, as in inputs for agriculture, be it the transgenic seeds, fertilizers, pesticides, hormones, etc., and soy harvesters. The upshot is that less of the differential rent associated with these primary activities stay in Brazil (or Argentina) and especially given the tendency of the emerging transnational capitalist class, this implies that the orientation of Brazilian capitalists and elite are looking more and more outward, not inward or thinking about development as in the ISI period.

The tendencies of deindustrialization witnessed for both Argentina and Brazil, though for distinct time periods, have contributed toward an overall tendency of reprimarization. The next section elaborates on the specifics of these shifts for both countries and identifies the factors that have been crucial, from the amazing growth of China and their demand for raw materials to the roles played by TNCs and the WTO.

7.5 The Current Tendency Toward Reprimarization in Argentina and Brazil[17]

During the first decades of the twenty-first century, the *commodities* boom could be seen as a great advantage in terms of capacity for countries to export agricultural products, minerals, and other raw materials. The dynamic of growth of both the agribusiness sector and other primary good sectors, such as minerals and petroleum, clearly contributed to the reprimarization of both these economies. On the one hand, it can be argued that Argentina actually began this process at the end of the 1970s, while Brazil made structural changes starting at the end of the 1980s. In any case, since the beginning of the 1990s, the economic policies being implemented in the two countries clearly reflect the framework of neoliberal globalization. These processes are also strongly influenced by the options, or lack of options, that come as a result of the rules regarding protection and subsidies to which they must adhere as members of the WTO, which have been in effect since 1995, when both countries entered the organization. The upshot is that in general, independent industrial policies, fomenting local industry in a serious way, are no longer feasible for countries of the periphery. The possibilities of competing in manufacturing at a global level have changed significantly, between the WTO framework and major advances in productivity (see footnote 16 above).[18]

Very much related to the WTO control is the need to accommodate transnational capital and thus fit into the global value chains of TNCs. The latter dominate the industrial and development policies of both countries, in part, as a result of the increasing role of the transnational capitalist class, whether that involves foreign investors, Argentines or Brazilians. Given the transnational dimension of the economic interests of local politicians, it can be argued that current governments accommodate TNCs more than their own national companies, as opposed to the traditional national

[17] See Trindade et al. (2016) and Cooney (2016).

[18] In fact, if the WTO rules were in effect in the nineteenth century, it is unlikely that either the U.S., or Germany could have come to have the success they did in competing against Great Britain (Chang 2002a). See discussion in Chapter 2.

interests associated with the ISI period (Robinson 2004), and this is not just the productive sector, but also for the financial sector.

For both countries, a major concern is the increased degree of dependence of the economy with respect to agribusiness, mining and other extractive sectors, and at the expense of the manufacturing sector. In this sense, the rates of growth for the primary sectors have been higher as a result of the commodities boom on world markets in the last decade or so. For many countries, their relation with China was the most notable change of trade relations since the beginning of the twenty-first century, especially for the continents of Africa and Latin America. The two cases of Argentina and Brazil experienced a very strong growth of trade with China during the last decade, and China continues as the primary trading partner of Brazil in 2021, and as the second most important trading partner for Argentina.[19]

China is interested in securing the supply of a range of raw materials and in order to achieve this they are insuring solid trading partners, such as Brazil and Argentina. Moreover, China is providing loans and expertise for infrastructure projects in addition to purchasing lands and brokering development projects, reflected in deals and treaties with Brazil and Argentina, such as in July 2014. Their main interest is obtaining control over primary products: soy and related products, beef, and other food products, petroleum, natural gas, and several minerals, etc. The concern of this development is that the two countries are orienting themselves so as to concentrate growth in the raw materials sector more and more, and secondly in the industrial sectors with low technological content and based on natural products, such as the food and beverage sector.

As mentioned above for Brazil, the manufacturing sector with the most growth and dynamism in recent decades is the food and beverages sector, which grew almost 280% during the period 1996–2007, in absolute terms, and generated more manufacturing employment: reaching almost 21% of all industrial employment in 2006. In the case of Argentina, the food and beverage sector has had the largest levels of total investment for the period 2003–2010, reaching 23.62% of all industrial investment in Argentina. There has been less consistent growth since the crisis of 2008–2010 and subsequent recessions, but given the reprimarization tendency it

[19] By 2012, China became the primary trading partner for Brazil for both imports and exports and is the second most important trading partner for Argentina for exports, and third for imports (Slipak 2014, 49).

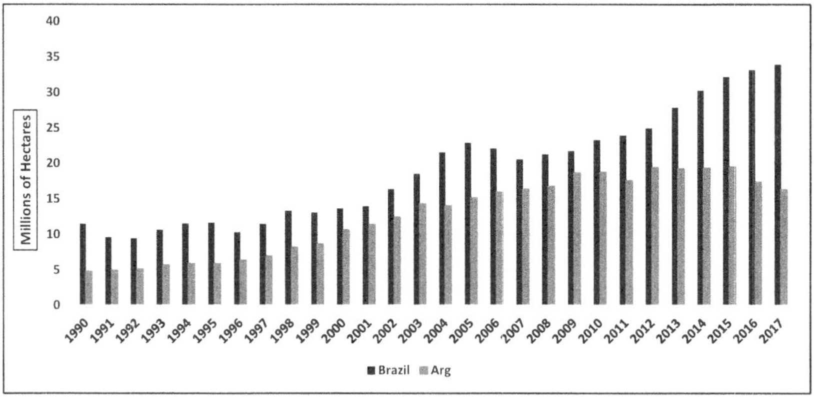

Fig. 7.6 Area Harvested for Soy in Argentina and Brazil: 1990–2017 (millions ha) (*Source* IBGE/PAM [2020] and INDEC/INTA [2020])

is expected that the food and beverage sector will continue to be the most dynamic industrial sector going forward, and most likely even through the COVID-19 crisis.

7.5.1 *Soy in Brazil and Argentina*

As has been referred to, the expansion of seed oils (*oleaginosas*) and in particular, soy, has been emblematic of the tendencies of reprimarization. In Fig. 7.6, it is quite evident how significant the expansion of soy has been for both Brazil and Argentina. The expansion of the area harvested of soy in Brazil grew an impressive 284% for Brazil between 1991 and 2019, and in the case of Argentina the growth was 231% between 1991 and 2017, with maximums of 29 million hectares in a year for Argentina and almost 37 million hectares in 2019 for Brazil. This shows why they are two of the primary producers and exporters of soybeans and derivatives at present.[20] In terms of genetically modified soybeans, in Argentina they constitute practically 100%, while in Brazil it is 96% or more.

[20] At the end of 2020, Brazil was the largest producer of soybeans with 37% of world production, followed by the US with 31% and Argentina was 3rd at 14%. In terms of exports, there are several different products, but the largest exporter is Brazil, followed by the US and with Argentina third.

7.5.2 Soy, Pesticides, and GMOs[21]

The famous Green Revolution began in the late 1960s, and is associated with the introduction of new varieties of grains, cereals, and seed oils and biotechnology was key for a number of crops, including soy. The shift toward a more intensive use of biotechnology reached a more mature stage in the 1990s. This was with the introduction of a technological package including genetically modified zero-tillage seeds (GMOs [22]), more agrochemicals, such as fertilizers, pesticides, and herbicides (Teubal 2006), especially glyphosate. In Argentina, this shift led to a significant replacement of cattle for soy and wheat, especially the former and the increasing role of the ever more dominant GMOs and toxic cocktails.

The genetically modified seed "Roundup Ready" is a variant of a soybean seed particularity resistant to glyphosate. As a result, the intensive use of RR "*zero tillage*" seeds increased productivity and reduced the level of erosion initially. According to AAPRESID—"This change to no-tillage planting was very rapid: from representing less than 25% of the area planted in 1997, it came to represent almost 80% in 2011, reaching levels nearing 100% in provinces such as Santiago del Estero, Salta and Corrientes" (AAPRESID 2012). The growing expansion of zero tillage, the transgenic seeds and pesticides increased land concentration in Argentina significantly: 82% of the producers occupy only 13% of the land, while 4% of the large producers occupy 65%. As of 2011, six major export companies dominate all the value chain production of soy and 50% of the lands are in the hands of 2% of the property owners (CIFRA 2011). The growing dynamism of no-tillage transgenic seeds and pesticides created a productive agrarian structure even more strongly concentrated, as much in terms of property as in terms of production. The expansion of the agricultural frontier and the monoculture has clearly benefitted these large private firms operating in Argentina and they have also arranged to manipulate the tax structure to further improve their profits (Treacy 2014).

A key factor is the transnationalization of inputs, in which a small clique of TNCs achieved consolidation as providers of seeds, fertilizers, and pesticides and other inputs and thus capturing an increasing portion

[21] The discussion in this section on soy in Argentina has benefitted from discussions with Mariano Treacy as well as the following text: Treacy (2014).

[22] GMO. Genetically Modified Organism.

of the ground rent generated by such activities, and derived from the higher fertility of the soil of the pampas. In spite of its importance, a more extensive analysis of the details of ground rent for soybean production will not be elaborated here,[23] nor the process by which a portion of agrarian rent is captured. Nevertheless, it is imperative to mention, that as a result of the growing use of agrotoxics, the Roundup Ready transgenic seeds, "no-tillage" machines, etc., there is an increasing and not insignificant proportion of agrarian rent, previously retained locally, now being passed on to the TNCs. This has fundamental implications with respect to the control of surplus value and the possibilities of sustainable development in the future (see Chapter 10). Two other sectors which are also classic examples of ground rent and in which the differential rent derives from the conditions of the subsoil rather than the soil itself, are mining and petroleum extraction.

The deregulatory climate of the 1990s saw an increasing presence of transnationals and consolidations in the global food industry. In the case of Brazil this was primarily in the food retail sector and the poultry, beef, and soy processing industries, with beef and soy having particular significance for the Amazon (see discussion below). Wilkinson (2009) observes the major role that TNCs have played in the increased centralization of the soy processing industry: for example, global agribusiness giant Bunge purchased Ceval, which since 1986 has been Brazil's largest soybean processor, while U.S.-based Archer Daniels Midland (ADM) took over the soy processing operations of Perdigão and Sadia, two Brazilian meat processing companies that merged in 2009 to create Brazil Foods, a TNC in its own right that is said to rival major U.S. transnational agribusiness firms.

As a result, Wilkinson (2009) notes that the majority of the country's soy crushing and trade is now in the hands of the four leading global players: ADM, Bunge, Cargill, and Dreyfus, known as the ABCD of cereals and grains, and which in recent years have increased their influence and size considerably (Kejsefman 2014). In the seed industry of Brazil, the dominant TNCs are Monsanto (Bayer), Syngenta, and Dupont industry, a fact that is quite pertinent for the soy industry, where genetically modified seeds now account for at least 96% of production.

[23] The basic discussion was presented in Chapter 2, but for further discussions of ground rent in the cases of agriculture, mining and petroleum, see Trindade and Cooney (2017).

These TNCs are playing the same role in Argentina, where the ABCD group is trying to dominate, although they are needing to compete more with China, whose influence continues to grow in both Argentina and Brazil. In fact, according to Haro Sly (2017, p. 8) "As China has become a global player in genomics and agrochemicals, that is, buying Nidera, Syngenta, Atanor, producing 40% of the world supply of generic glyphosate." These developments evidently put additional pressure on chemical companies, such as Bayer/Monsanto[24] among others in the field of agrochemicals.

The concern over reprimarization increases the more that Argentina is dependent on China and this is reflected in both China's policies and attitude. In addition, 68% of Argentina's exports to China are concentrated in soy and its derivatives. As could be expected, China is primarily exporting manufactured products to Argentina and glyphosate is one of the leading imports from China, and this is clearly linked to Argentina's reprimarization tendency (Haro Sly 2017, p. 8). In 2007, Argentina still had a trade surplus with China, however minor, but since then it has been negative and worsening, totaling (−24 US $ billion) between 2007 and 2014 (Oviedo 2015, p. 121), and when Argentina pushed to export crushed soy, China refused, preferring to import just soybeans or cakes (raw materials) and therefore the crushing (manufacturing) would be done in China, which involves much more value added; insuring Argentina knows its place within the hierarchy of the global economy!

In addition to the decline of manufacturing industry and the strong growth in primary activities, the reprimarization tendency has been clear for Argentina in terms of their export profile. It is worth recalling that roughly 67% of their exports were manufactured goods in 1973. In contrast, in 2016, the top ten items exported constitutes 56% of all exports and among these, primary exports (soy products, wheat, corn, beef and seafood) came to a total of 46%, and thus only 10% corresponded to manufactured goods (Schorr and Ortiz 2020, p. 84). This is a ratio of almost 5 to 1 in favor of primary products to manufactured goods. A comparison with exports in 1973 clearly shows the degree to which Argentina has experienced reprimarization. In the next section: Reprimarization and Accumulation by Dispossession, the expansion of soybeans in

[24] As Bayer purchased Monsanto in 2019, including Monsanto may seem unnecessary, however, I still consider it important to continue referring to Monsanto for the time being.

Argentina is further examined, given its increased role within the Argentine political economy. In fact, due to limited fertile land in Argentina, compared to Brazil, cattle have been increasingly compromised by the expansion of soy, while the opposite has taken place in Brazil.

As is discussed below, the primary expansion of cattle has been in the Amazon, although the beef is not the highest quality. Therefore, the lower quality beef is sent (exported internally) to the south and southeast of Brazil, while the higher quality beef from the south (e.g., Rio Grande do Sul) is exported. The available territory for both soy and cattle in Brazil is substantially more than that available in the fertile region of the Pampas (*Pampa Húmeda*), although there has been an expansion of soy production in a number of provinces outside this region, such as the Chaco. Recently, there has also been an expansion of soy in new regions in the north and northeast of Brazil, referred to as Matopiba and is composed of the states Maranhão, Tocantins, Piaui, and Bahia.

For more than twenty years, there has been an increase in the ratio of primary goods compared to manufacturing goods in Brazil's export profile. Solid evidence of the reprimarization tendency in the Brazilian economy is provided by Fig. 7.7, which presents the ratio of primary

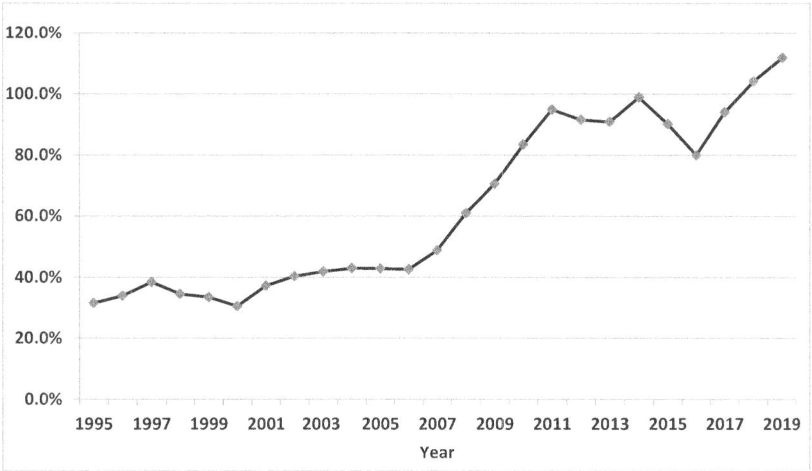

Fig. 7.7 Ratio of Primary to Manufacturing exports (%) (Brazil: 1995–2019) (*Source* MDIC [2020])

exports in relation to the percentage of manufacturing exports. Since 1995, the ratio of primary to manufacturing exports grew from roughly one third to one in 2014, the greatest acceleration taking place since 2007. Since 2014, the exports of primary goods dropped for a couple years and then rebounded as of 2016 and reaching a ratio of approximately 1.1 in 2019, as primary exports have now surpassed manufacturing exports. Moreover, the changes in Brazil's export profile is evident when one considers that during the period of ten years (1999–2009), exports grew roughly 318% overall, while exports of primary goods grew at 525%.

Having observed the shifts in terms of production and exports for both Argentina and Brazil, in this section, the evidence was arguably clear regarding the reprimarization tendency. The next section examines reprimarization in the context of the discussion of accumulation by dispossession,[25] considering a number of concrete examples. Although relevant for the discussion of reprimarization, petroleum and related products will only be presented and analyzed in Chapter 8, in the discussion around environmental impacts and consequences.

7.6 Reprimarization and Accumulation by Dispossession[26]

In this section a further discussion of Harvey's concept of accumulation by dispossession is developed and then evaluated in terms of its relevance in the context of reprimarization in the Southern Cone, namely for Argentina and Brazil. As described above, the tendency toward reprimarization is concentrated in a number of key sectors, namely soybeans, and derivative products, minerals, including gold, copper, aluminum, among others, fossil and biofuels, the lumber industry, livestock and other agribusiness, etc. After the theoretical presentation, the case of the Amazon is considered, both historically and during recent decades. Throughout this section, particular attention is given to the role of the State, especially for the expansion of cattle and soy in both Brazil

[25] A theoretical presentation of accumulation by dispossession was first considered in Chapter 2.

[26] Portions of this section are based upon a chapter written by myself and William Sacher (Sacher and Cooney 2019) as well as other papers presented with William Sacher (Cooney and Sacher 2015) and with José Trindade (Cooney and Trindade 2016).

and Argentina and also in examining large-scale mining as examples of accumulation by dispossession. Prior to examining specific cases in Argentina and Brazil, a more in-depth discussion of Harvey's concept of accumulation by dispossession will be presented.

7.6.1 *The Concept of Accumulation by Dispossession in Harvey*

As described in Chapter 2 above, in Harvey's book, *The New Imperialism*, he derives a new theoretical term clearly linked to Marx's category of original accumulation. He cites Luxemburg and Arendt, who both argued that this concept is relevant in analyzing historical transformations involving major dislocations of populations and the privatizing of the commons, and thus crucial for our understanding of accumulation in modern capitalism. For example, he refers to the following interpretation by Arendt:

> The processes that Marx, following Adam Smith, referred to as 'primitive' or 'original' accumulation constitute, in Arendt's view, an important and continuing force in the historical geography of capital accumulation through imperialism.... If those assets, such as empty land or new raw material sources, do not lie to hand, then capitalism must somehow produce them." (Harvey 2003, p.143)

As Harvey points out, the transformative processes involving fraud, pillage, and violent uprooting of thousands of freeholders, as in pre-capitalist England, continued to exist well beyond the establishment of capitalism in many parts of the globe and through to the present day. Harvey further argues for the need to analyze those historical processes that do not fit into a strict economic interpretation of capitalism's functioning "under conditions of peace, property and equality." He points to the limitation of Marx's analysis in Capital, where the assumptions made correspond to classical political economy, namely, the establishment of capitalist markets, rule of law, etc. In light of this limitation, Harvey introduces the new concept of accumulation by dispossession:

> The disadvantage of these assumptions (classical political economy) is that they relegate accumulation based upon predation, fraud, and violence to an "original stage" that is considered no longer relevant or, as with Luxemburg, as being somehow "outside of" capitalism as a closed system. A

> general re-evaluation of the continuous role and persistence of the predatory practices of "primitive" or "original" accumulation within the long historical geography of capital accumulation is, therefore, very much in order, as several commentators have recently observed. Since it seems peculiar to call an ongoing process "primitive" or "original," I shall in what follows substitute these terms by the concept of "accumulation by dispossession. (Harvey 2003, p. 144)

Harvey argues that Marx's analysis of original accumulation includes a range of processes. These include, "the commodification and privatization of land, and the forceful expulsion of peasant populations…suppression of rights to the commons; the commodification of labour power." (Ibid. p.145). Marx is describing the process of the enclosure movement in Great Britain, the converting of freeholders and peasants into wage laborers, and thus establishing the basis for the capitalist mode of production. In contrast, Harvey goes on to include in his concept, contemporary and current forms of accumulation that operate "extra-economically," that is to say, without resorting to the exploitation of wage labor, or basic capitalist accumulation. Among these current forms, Harvey identifies methods that do resemble those described by Marx in Capital, and others that do not.

However, he argues that in recent decades, with the implementation of the neoliberal project, the methods of accumulation by dispossession have multiplied and diversified, leading to a "new wave of enclosing the commons" (Harvey 2003, p. 148), that is to say, an extension of the commodification of public goods, of nature and of life, to new domains (through, for instance, bio-piracy, the green economy or the privatization of public services (Harvey 2003, p. 148). The privatization of state-owned companies, for example, has led to "special deals," in which private capitalists purchased public assets at fire-sale prices, and then take advantage of buying cheap to maximize their profits. Given what appears as a laundry list of items, compared to original accumulation, it could be argued that there is a need for a strict sense of Harvey's accumulation by dispossession, since the all-inclusive broad definition goes too far, becomes diluted and thus loses its analytical power, as has been argued by Brenner and others (Brenner 2006, pp. 101–102; Ashman and Callinicos 2006, pp. 119–120; Fine 2006, p. 143; Buck 2009, p. 98). Nevertheless, for the purposes of the analysis in this chapter, this discussion is not essential, as we are concentrating on the expropriation of populations for the purpose of activities associated with reprimarization.

7.6.2 The Role of the State

The expropriation of peasant and indigenous populations is another way of acquiring at a very low price, large tracts of land, whose control is essential for the implementation of, for example, extractive mega-mining or petroleum projects or access to land necessary for major agribusiness expansion. These processes, as Marx argued, require the use of deception, physical and symbolic violence, and even war. According to Harvey, in recent decades, waves of dispossession generated a "volatile mix of protest movements" (Harvey 2003, pp. 166–167), which are not constitutive of the typical struggle between capital and labor, but of a struggle against "accumulation by dispossession." Along with Marx, Harvey highlights the importance of the role of the State in these processes, as it provides political, financial, military, judicial, and moral support to the accumulation of capital through dispossession, and argues that the state, which has both a monopoly of violence but also dictates laws and whether or not to enforce them was crucial for the establishment of capitalist relations and continues to be so for the continued expansion of capital across the globe. According to Harvey:

> The state, with its monopoly of violence and definitions of legality, plays a crucial role in both backing and promoting these processes and [...] there is considerable evidence that the transition to capitalist development was and continues to be vitally contingent upon the stance of the state. The developmental role of the state goes back a long way, keeping the territorial and capitalistic logics of power always intertwined though not necessarily concordant. (Harvey 2003, p. 145)

Harvey argues that the increased relevance of accumulation by dispossession is in part a result of the global crisis of accumulation of the 1970s. In the decades that followed, the dispossession of common and public goods is seen as a mechanism of accumulation by dispossession which allowed the capitals of these countries to proceed with multiple "spatial-temporal fixes" thanks to neoliberal policies imposed by multilateral agencies in numerous countries, particularly of the global south (for instance using debt as leverage to impose neoliberal policies). There is substantial debate over the extent to which accumulation by dispossession has become the dominant form of accumulation (Ashman and Callinicos 2006, pp. 108–109; Fine 2006, p. 144; Dunn 2007, p. 10) and exactly at what point does accumulation by dispossession end and normal accumulation begin, as in the case of the State securing access and a concession to a transnational mining company which then extracts minerals and wealth for several decades, for example.

Of course, addressing the "dominant" character of "accumulation by dispossession" as a contemporary accumulation process would require a more precise definition of the concept. And the possible excessive "broadness" of the definition given by Harvey of accumulation by dispossession may allow him to affirm its dominance (Brenner 2006, p. 102). Although we find these debates relevant, we prefer not to elaborate any further upon them and instead reflect on the adequacy of Harvey's concept in understanding the process of reprimarization in the context of Argentina and Brazil.

7.6.3 Accumulation by Dispossession and the Amazon[27]

One of the areas where accumulation by dispossession is arguably rather relevant in Brazil is the Amazon Rain forest. The principal activities associated with these processes at present are mega-mining, soy, and cattle ranching, where TNCs have been operating since the end of the 1950s. Moreover, major transformations have taken place as a result of the expansion of soy and livestock farming, beginning with the military dictatorship during the 1970s and 1980s. During this period there was an effort made by the Brazilian State to promote the migration of large landowners toward the Amazon, and also for migrant workers from the Northeast of Brazil arriving in search of work (see Bunker 1985) and then producing the problematic phenomenon of *grilagem* (see below). In the discussion below it will become evident that these processes of accumulation by dispossession have clearly paid off for the elite and the Brazilian State; after several decades of the expansion of soy, cattle and mining, there has been an extraordinary amount of rent and profits extracted from the Amazon.

[27] This discussion of accumulation by dispossession in the Amazon is derived substantially from an article written with Sérgio Rivero for CNS (see Rivero and Cooney 2010).

First, however, we consider the fact that noncapitalist socioeconomic formations have existed in the Amazon for centuries (and arguably still do, though to a much lesser degree). As one considers the transformation of noncapitalist into capitalist production relations, an argument for employing the category of original accumulation could be and has been made. Periods of capitalist expansion in the Amazon require both workers—whether they be peasants, *caboclos*, *colonos*, or *seringueiros*[28]—and the ability of capitalists to obtain access to land or subsoil occupied by either peasants, indigenous groups, or traditional communities. They need this land in order to obtain property rights and ensure full control of production on the land, which serves as a key input, whether for rubber tapping, lumber, agricultural and cattle production, or mining and oil extraction.

The historical process of driving people off their land in the Amazon is consistent with Harvey's concept of "accumulation by dispossession." However, if the primary aim of the capitalists or *latifundiários* (landowners) is to obtain access to the land rather than the formation of wage laborers, Marx's category of original accumulation even in the broad sense (see Chapter 2) does not apply. For the case of capitalists who have been accumulating land for decades in São Paulo, Goiás, or the South of Brazil, and who are simply expanding geographically, the strict sense of original accumulation clearly does not apply.

In any event, many of these changes through to the present day unfortunately involve the use of force and violence. As Marx pointed out, "In actual history, it is a notorious fact that conquest, enslavement, robbery, murder, in short, force, play the greatest part [in enforcing property rights]." In other places and periods, existing property rights are often not enforced but ignored, and new rights are established in favor of the dominant classes, be they feudal lords, slave owners, or Amazonian *fazendeiros* (plantation owners).

[28] In this chapter the word *caboclo* refers to mixed populations of the Amazon. The term, *seringueiro* refers to the population involved with rubber extraction. In the case of the term *colono*, in the context of rubber extraction, it refers to the population of peasants that migrated from the Northeast to escape the droughts to the Amazon, during the rubber boom period, while in the 1970s, the term *colonos* also included smallholders (*mini-latifundiárias*) that migrated from the South and Southeast of Brazil to the Amazon. These definitions are somewhat schematic; a discussion about the meanings and anthropological weight of these denotations can be found in Brondizio (2004).

The current processes of expansion in the Amazon do not correspond to original accumulation in the strict economic sense that Marx wrote about for pre-capitalist England, but it does clearly fit with the concept of accumulation by dispossession as elaborated by Harvey, because the historical processes involving expropriations of populations through violence and fraud, result from the needs of capitalist accumulation. This is true whether the capitalists need wage laborers for agricultural production or simply want control of the land for production purposes and/or speculation. The transformation taking place in terms of dominant social relations of production in the Amazon is forcing large numbers of peasants or riverine people to move to the city and become informal laborers. The upshot for them is a transformation of the relations that had previously dominated them and their families' lives.

Thus, much of the *caboclo*-peasant population were northeastern migrants who came to collect rubber or were part of the unemployed urban population in the Amazon after the end of the first rubber cycle. These people produced and used the land, but unlike the white Americans that settled in the U.S. frontier, they didn't have property rights. The social relations that persisted in the Amazon riverine area strongly reflected the land property rights and social norms and institutions produced by these relations. This situation is in very clear contrast to the patterns of white settler colonies, which also involved the undermining or genocide of non-white traditional societies.

In fact, the formal control of the land is the key issue that defines the occupation patterns in the Amazon region. The concession of large areas to local political leaders was necessary to establish land property rights in favor of the *latifundiários*. In contrast to the US, disposable land in the Brazilian Amazon was at the end of the nineteenth century under formal control by the merchant class or the State, which explains the subsequent accumulation processes there. In the Brazilian Amazon, four forces competed over the use of the land: (a) the native indigenous population, which was the weakest of these forces; (b) the caboclo-peasant population that settled mainly in the riverine areas or near the cities; (c) the formal landowners, who partly abandoned the production systems once the rubber cycle came to an end (the collapse from 1910 to 1912); and (d) the government, which used the public lands as political capital in order to negotiate support with the elites. These four competing forces disputed the space in the region, while the control of the production process varied depending on the demand for Amazonian products (mainly rubber, at the end of the nineteenth century). After the bust of the rubber boom in 1912, the main economic basis for the Amazon region became the *caboclo*-peasant production system, which persisted up until the 1960s.

7.6.4 *The Military Government (1964–1985) and Policies of Expropriation*

After the coup of 1964, the military government implemented several policies and initiated major projects aimed at transforming the Amazon in order to lay the groundwork for an enormous expansion of agriculture, cattle production, and mining. This involved the shifting of alliances, creating new institutions or transforming existing ones, facilitating major migrations, and expropriating the land and resources of local populations through both legal and illegal means. In 1966, the military government began its "Operation Amazonia" (*Operação Amazônia*) by implementing a new set of laws and establishing new institutions.

The Brazilian government set up SUDAM (the Development Authority for the Amazon), which provided major fiscal incentives to landowners and capitalists from other parts of Brazil, mainly from the states of Goiás and São Paulo. The precursor to SUDAM was SPVEA (the Authority for the Valorization Plan for the Amazon), which was seen by many as having failed to achieve the changes desired by the federal government. A major difference between the two institutions was the shifts in the alliances established with local elites. The military government came to have greater influence in the region with SUDAM while the local elites lost ground in terms of their influence, which was greater with SPVEA.

Another key institutional change, also in 1966, was the conversion of the Credit Bank of the Amazon (*Banco de Crédito da Amazônia*) into BASA (*Banco da Amazônia*), which had very strong ties to SUDAM. Operation Amazonia's main achievement was to turn national and international capitalists into major landowners (*latifundiários*) for the agricultural and livestock production projects in the Amazon. Some have argued that SUDAM's policy of fiscal incentives effectively resulted in a counter agrarian reform. For example, Costa argues that the result of the policies of the military was not just a failed agrarian reform but the reverse, an increase in land concentration for the wealthy. He argues that "as a result of the modernization of *latifúndios*, the migration ... led to new structures for peasants.... in the Amazon." (Costa 2000: 80) As further elaborated below, the military government encouraged the migration of peasants from the Northeast states and the south/southeast, in part to ameliorate serious land conflicts, which had been taking place from the end of the 1950s. The result of these migrations, combined with shifts of local Amazonian populations led to a new structure for the peasant populations, namely that of family agriculture.

During the 1970s, as a result of the programs and laws that had been implemented, combined with major efforts to improve infrastructure in the region—primarily highways, such as the Trans-amazon Highway (BR-230) and BR-163—huge areas became available for speculation. The fiscal incentives and profits resulting from increases in land prices generated extra profits for landowners, which initiated new patterns of land use, mainly low-productivity ranching. The logic of such investments was to open the forest to make pastures not simply for cattle production itself, but to appropriate the land as well, and therefore obtain the rents and gains associated with incentives, subsidies, and land prices. Thus, the key issue was not cattle production, but land itself as a commodity, if not in fact, as capital. Though the newly created pasture could only support low occupation rates (much less than 1 head/hectare), prices for occupied land rose rapidly, producing speculative gains for the landowners, which permitted the expansion of more capitalized agricultural production in the ensuing decades.

As mentioned above, from the end of the 1960s throughout the 1970s, a large number of capitalists and landowners took advantage of the incentives SUDAM offered and moved from the states of São Paulo and Goiás to the Amazon, mainly to Mato Grosso, Pará, and Rondônia. This migration combined with a migration of landless peasants had a significant impact on the region. For example, in 1991 Mato Grosso had the sixth largest migrant population in Brazil, Pará had the eighth largest, and Rondônia the ninth largest. In 1991, over 62% of the population of Rondônia had been born in another state; for Mato Grosso this proportion was roughly 46%, and for Para, 18.43%.

One of the main mechanisms SUDAM used in its fiscal incentives was *grilagem*, the usurpation of lands by generating land titles, which trumped any legal claim by those who had occupied and worked the land previously. Thus, expropriation came about through the migration of capitalists and landowners from the south, who were given a title through corruption of the land title authorities (*cartórios*) or INCRA (the Institute for Colonization and Agrarian Reform), which was allegedly "regulating" land titles. Many of these large landowners and capitalists—often recent migrants to the Amazon—claimed that no one before them had a title for a specific piece of land, and therefore it was now theirs, even if a family had been living there for generations. This "legal" usurpation also gave them the right to forcibly remove the occupants (*posseiros*) or indigenous groups that had been occupying the land. This necessarily involved a significant amount of violence and was often done by *jagunços*, henchmen hired by the private landowners. In several regions, such as Mato Grosso, the violence was characterized as genocide of indigenous groups (see Oliveira 2005). The government also at times employed the army for the expropriation of peasants and indigenous populations.

Lands were also being distributed to smallholders or farmers (*colonos*), particularly in areas near the Trans-amazon Highway (BR-230) and in the southwestern part of the Amazon region. These new farming regions were set up as a direct result of the military's colonization projects and initially comprised properties of 100 hectares. Most of the colonists that came to the Trans-amazon region were from Brazil's northeast. The small farmers that came to the southwestern Amazon were from the southern states of Brazil. The government promoted this colonist frontier, which became the foundation of the country's agrarian policy, which in turn spurred rapid modernization in the south and southeast of Brazil.

The workers who migrated to the Amazon were principally from two regions: the northeast states, mainly from Maranhão and Ceará, and the south/southeast, e.g., the states of São Paulo, Paraná and Rio Grande do Sul. Those from the south tended to be small landowners who had lost their lands due to mechanization, because they couldn't afford to spend money on expensive machinery and as a result couldn't compete, while those from the northeast often migrated because of difficult economic conditions such as prolonged drought.[29] The military government enticed migrants to "populate" the Amazon with the slogan "*homens sem terra para a terra sem homens*" (people without land for the land without people). Encouraging mass migration to the Amazon from the northeast and south of Brazil was also an attempt to reduce increasing

[29] For an excellent analysis of the problems of drought, hunger and famine in Brazil, India and China, connected to the *El Niño* effect, see the extensively researched book by Mike Davis, *Late Victorian Holocausts*, 2017.

social conflicts over land, that were occurring in those regions during the 1970s.

The mass migrations to the two frontiers quickly began the process of clearing land to create pastures for cattle, an activity that became the main land use in the region for both large and small landowners. Hecht (1985) lays out several factors that explain the prevalence of cattle ranching in the Amazon, a particularly ecologically destructive practice in that region. Given the fact that around 70% of land use is pasture, ranching is the main deforestation driver in the Amazon. In addition to deforestation, ranching leads to increased pasture, worsening the problem of soil lixiviation—the separation of nutrients from the base soil. Thus, cattle ranching exacerbates the problem of soil impoverishment more than other agricultural practices.

Cattle ranching provides three additional sources of income for ranchers: increases in the price of land due to speculation, government incentives and subsidies, and income obtained from selling timber. The Brazilian government's subsidies and incentives for cattle ranching gifted the new landowners with huge profits. Cattle ranching has also been attractive for small farmers, who saw cattle as a low-risk asset. Aside from being quite flexible and easily adapted to different types of terrains, cattle are a relatively liquid asset with low maintenance costs.

7.6.5 *Agribusiness, Accumulation, and Dispossession*

At the end of the 1980s, the production patterns of the Amazon region started to change, with a rapid growth in capital-intensive agriculture, particularly soy plantations. From 1990 to 2007, the gross value of soybean production in the Amazon region grew by 21% per year, while cattle herds were growing at rates of 7% per year. The combination of the expansion of ranching and soy is a qualitative advance compared to the previous frontiers of colonization and land speculation. Both cattle and soy are strongly integrated with global markets and are far more capitalized than the other activities that dominated the region up through the 1970s and 1980s. In summary, the processes of accumulation by dispossession fomented by the military government laid the groundwork for a qualitatively new phase of capital accumulation, analogous to what was achieved with original accumulation, insofar as what followed constituted the establishment of full-fledged capitalist production for the first time in the Amazon, constituting a new phase of capitalist accumulation in the Amazon.

In terms of cattle expansion in the Amazon, between 1990 and 2006, cattle herds in the Amazon grew at an annual rate of 6.74% compared to an average annual growth rate of just 0.57% for the rest of Brazil (see Fig. 7.8). Most of the growth in Brazilian cattle—an increase of more than 180% in 16 years—occurred in the Amazonian states of Mato Grosso, Rondônia and Pará, where deforestation is greatest. Evidently the growth of domestic and foreign demand for beef, is a key factor explaining expansion, it is also influenced by other factors, such as the continual reduction in transportation costs, increases in productivity, and the relatively low price of land in the Amazon.

The highly capitalized soybean plantations represent a new pattern of production that is very different from the traditional agriculture practiced by small producers (*colonos*). The area of soybean plantations accounted for roughly 30% of the total area of annual crops in 1990. Between that time and 2004, it expanded to cover half of the total acreage in annual crops and remained so till 2007. The participation of the Amazon in

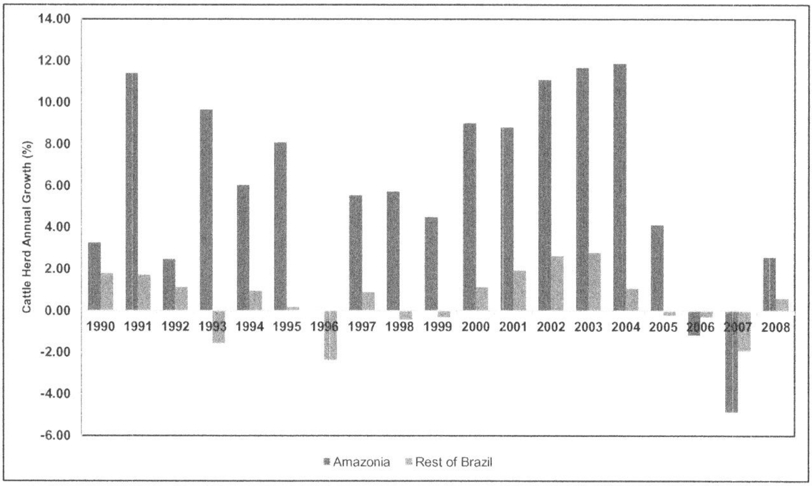

Fig. 7.8 Brazil and the Amazon: Annual Cattle Herd Growth Rates (1990–2008) (*Source* IBGE [2010]—Municipal Livestock Production [http://www.sidra.ibge.gov.br])

total production of soybeans in Brazil grew from 16 to 30% between 1990 and 2007. Of this total area, 25% was in the state of Mato Grosso, where soybean production grew from 1.5 million hectares in 1990 to 5.1 million hectares in 2007, making it the most important area of soybean production in Brazil.

Prior to the establishment of the soybean plantations, these areas were most likely occupied by cattle ranchers. The increasing dominance of soy appears to have shifted cattle production to other regions of the Amazon. As with cattle ranching in the Amazon between 2000 and 2007, the land used for soybean plantations grew by an average rate of 9% a year, whereas the average growth of plantations for the rest of Brazil was roughly 3% a year. The expansion of intensively capitalized agriculture occurred mainly in Mato Grosso, the Brazilian state with some of the best transportation infrastructure, which was initially promoted by the military government. Mato Grosso has been the region with the greatest productivity for soy production in Brazil, if not on the planet, yet several other Brazilian states have significant production of soy, such as Paraná.

Although the discussion of environmental impacts of reprimarization is to be addressed in the next chapter, a couple of points related to production and deforestation deserve mentioning here. In order to understand the connections between cattle, soy, and deforestation, it is necessary to consider the dominant pattern or sequence taking place in the Brazilian Amazon. The first step is the removal of the forest for lumber, in order to establish the basis for livestock production. Cattle, as mentioned above, comes to deplete the soil of its nutrients and also cause erosion, therefore before a transition to soy takes place, there is the introduction of a crop, such as rice, in order to facilitate the recovery of the soil's nutrients, and finally the planting of soy, with the higher profitability. With regard to deforestation, cattle are usually seen as the main driver but in fact one must look carefully at the sequence which involves soy, especially as the area cultivated for soy has quadrupled in the Amazon between 2006 and 2018 (Rodrigues 2018). Moreover, in recent years, given the growth in the demand for ethanol, the production of corn has expanded notably in parts of the Amazon, as well as among other parts of the North and Northeast of Brazil. Further discussion of the links between land use and deforestation and other environmental issues in the Amazon will be presented in the next chapter.

One of the last points that deserves attention with respect to accumulation by dispossession is clarifying the real difference between what constitutes the latter and what constitutes standard production and accumulation, which takes place after the process of accumulation by dispossession, although the standard accumulation is predicated on the completion of the previous process. In other words, the accumulation by dispossession in previous decades in the Amazon, put into place the fundamentals for the current phase of accumulation with respect to the boom of commodities, be it soy, cattle, or minerals. Once the extraction of minerals begins normal operation or the production of soy, etc., then this is normal accumulation, even if its functioning required a previous phase of accumulation by dispossession. Many followers of Harvey and in certain instances in his own texts, there is a conflation of these two distinct types of accumulation.

With respect to Argentina, the role of the State, even after the dictatorship, was also key during several decades, perhaps with fewer notable examples of displacement or expropriation of peasants or indigenous populations through the use of force and violence, but more through the use of manipulations for accessing land, privatizations, and buyouts. There exists on the other hand a growing concern regarding what type of development is preferred, especially considering socioenvironmental issues, in particular with respect to soy. In addition, soy is very capital intensive. Haro Sly (2017, p. 5) has pointed out that "For each 1000 Ha, the soybean crop employs 15 workers while for the same size sugar cane employs 350 workers and the citric crop employs 1,300 workers." She also makes the point that due to the high level of mechanization, there have been increased shifting of unemployed, from rural areas to the cities, as soy has expanded.

In this section, concrete historical examples were presented to justify the relevance of the concept of accumulation by dispossession by Harvey. It seems quite relevant, especially when considering what took place in the Amazon under the military dictatorship and how this facilitated the expansion of lumber, soy, and cattle. Notoriously absent from this list is that of mega-mining, which is the topic of the next section.

7.6.6 *Mega-Mining and Accumulation by Dispossession*[30]

Evidently mineral extraction is a major example of reprimarization in the Amazon, and the category of accumulation by dispossession clearly fits, especially in a case like Bethlehem Steel in Amapá in 1957. Although this book is concentrating on Argentina and Brazil, the importance of mining in Latin America in the first decades of the twenty-first century is quite pertinent; and thus, the relevance of accumulation by dispossession and mega-mining in general will be considered before turning to specific cases in Argentina and Brazil, including the Amazon.[31]

The exploitation of minerals, oil and gas are traditionally sectors in which the rates of profit can be very high, especially where ground rent is incorporated into profits. The initiation of these extractive activities requires, in turn, processes of dispossession and often plunder, in particular land grabbing, control and occupation of large areas of land and of natural resources like water. For capital, the less expensive the inputs, and the greater the control over land ownership, the more profitable their investments become. In this sense, the so-called "mining codes" promoted by the World Bank and promulgated in the global south in the eighties and nineties and beyond offered a legal framework tailored for transnational mining capital (Sacher 2015).

On the other hand, in the 2000s, the rise in the prices of numerous raw materials linked to the outstanding growth in China, led to a "mining super-cycle." In this context, the number of mining exploration and exploitation megaprojects skyrocketed in the global South. For instance, Latin America today concentrates 30% of the investment in global mining exploration (S&P Global 2018). Due to mega-mining's tendency toward larger and larger scale production, there is a need to have more and more territories available to implement these projects.

New deposits are often identified in indigenous or peasant territories, with a set of specific cultural and ecological concerns. Under these circumstances, dispossession of local people, land, resources, and basic material

[30] Portions of this section are based upon a chapter written by myself and William Sacher (Sacher and Cooney 2019). It is worth noting that a previous systematic review of the academic literature that analyzes the socioenvironmental conflicts associated with mining megaprojects, in light of the concept of Accumulation by Dispossession can be found in Sacher (2015).

[31] The term mega-mining refers to large-scale or mega-scale mining and derives from the established use in Spanish of *megaminería*.

conditions of life is necessary for the installation of large-scale mining in a given territory (Gordon and Webber 2008, pp. 67–68). The main forms of dispossession associated with mega-mining are: dispossessions of lands and territories, of communal goods, and natural resources. Several Latin American scholars argue that the mega-mining boom of the last 20 years, as a whole, is an example of accumulation by dispossession and that the numerous anti-mining struggles that have multiplied in the region and on a global scale in the same period can be interpreted as responses to this accumulation mechanism. Processes constitutive of accumulation by dispossession associated with large-scale mining have been documented in many territories, in the global north and south, and can often be understood, as Harvey suggests, as one solution for transnational capital—be it from the US, Canada, Europe, Japan, and now even from China—to find highly profitable new opportunities of investment (Sacher 2017).

For local communities, the economic consequences of the production of a "mega-mining space" may be dramatic. For instance, in many cases, due to pollution and the hoarding of land by companies, the capacity of agricultural production is lost. Soon the local economy revolves around a business piloted by foreign interests and a productive activity that in many cases has little to do with local needs. Of course, all these impacts are commonly associated with mining. Nevertheless, given its increasing magnitude, the industrial model is likely to lead to negative impacts for a much larger proportion of the population, land, and surrounding environs.

From that perspective, the extension of the area dedicated to the "mega-mining space" exceeds by many orders of magnitude the area typically affected by local or in many cases national mining installations. The dynamics of capital at the global level and the physical conditions imposed by the increasingly lower quality of deposits, jointly lead to an extensive industrial model that needs an increasingly larger area to be developed and implemented. In Latin America as well as other regions of the world, mega-mining has been synonymous with the hoarding of tens of millions of hectares in the form of mining concessions. These appropriations of land are usually associated with the violent expropriation of peasants, indigenous and artisanal miners and massive losses of commons and collective, and private lands, including individual private lands.

In the concrete case of Argentina, Galafassi (2010) cites the example of the Mapuche[32] lands and protected lands which were concessioned, "with the argument that the subsoil is the property of the State." Machado Aráoz (2010) shows how the dynamics of dispossession needs to be understood from different dimensions: physical, economic, environmental, and socio-cultural, such as in Catamarca, Argentina in the copper and gold mine Bajo de la Alumbrera.

In Brazil, one of the principal examples of reprimarization is the significant presence of large-scale mining projects or mega-mining in the Amazon. Mining constitutes close to 75 if not 80% of the exports of the state of Pará, (the second largest state of the Brazilian Amazon) and is the largest economic sector in terms of GDP. A key aspect is the high mineral content in the mines such as Carajás, the largest open-pit iron mine in the world and which is six times more productive than similar mines in China. This result is reflected in the particularly high differential rents obtained by foreign or Brazilian TNCs operating in the Amazon.

Moreover, the State and the large Brazilian banks have played a crucial role in the development and control of the mining sector during recent decades. This process constitutes another example of accumulation by dispossession in the Amazon. The structure of the mining sector was established at the end of the 1960s, but experienced changes during the last three decades, resulting in extraordinary profits through the exploration of natural resources in the region. Three of the most successful corporations in this sector in the Amazon are the following: Indústria e Comércio de Minérios Inc. (ICOMI); Mineração Rio do Norte (MRN); and the Companhia Vale do Rio Doce (CVRD),[33] more commonly referred to as simply Vale (Cooney and Trindade 2016).[34] In fact,

[32] The Mapuche is an indigenous nation whose territory extends between parts of Argentina and Chile and which existed prior to both colonial states, and whose territorial sovereignty has been threatened or violated by several companies and by both the Argentine and Chilean governments.

[33] ICOMI (Indústria e Comércio de Minérios Inc.) can be translated as Mineral Industry and Commerce; MRN (Mineração Rio do Norte (MRN) can be translated as North River Mining; and lastly Vale or CVRD (Companhia Vale do Rio Doce) can be translated as Sweet River Valley Company. It is interesting to note that there is a Sweet River Valley Investment company in the US, which at one point in time had roughly 51% ownership of Vale.

[34] These three mining sites are identified in the map of the Amazon in Fig. 8.14 on p. 216.

during the dictatorship expropriations of populations occurred in several instances in order for mining firms to gain access to land with mineral deposits, for example, the case of Vale do Rio Doce. Unfortunately, Vale continues to employ violence and uses repression even in the present day, contracting private security firms, that have attacked families in the city of Parauapebas in the state of Pará, that have been camped out. They attacked families totaling 150 people, using tear gas and rubber bullets, and injuring over 20 peasants, including children and elderly people. This has been going on since 2016, given the fact that Vale obtained the land through an irregularity in order to gain access to a mine (See Angelo 2020).

Although the areas where concessions have been granted for mining exploration and extraction, they almost never end up fully dedicated to mining activities. Instead, the companies that acquire such legal titles may claim a series of benefits and rights as owners of the land. In the first place, once it is officially registered, a concession title may immediately become an asset for the mining company. Second, by law, a concession title also generally guarantees unconditional access to the subsoil, the right to cross, occupy and use private properties and commons, and the possibility of forcefully displacing the populations living on the land. The tens of millions of hectares which have been granted concessions in the region, therefore represent a latent threat for any community living in the affected territories. In addition, the limits of a mining concession are usually defined from offices of companies and the government in large urban centers, without consulting or notifying the affected populations.

The concession of land for mega-mining activities leads to a de facto commodification and grabbing of the land in a very classical colonial manner. In other words, mining concessions can be seen as analogous to the massive dispossession of land in England between the fifteenth and eighteenth centuries, namely the enclosure movement, as described by Marx in Volume 1 of *Capital* (Marx 1977). In the case of mining mega-projects under construction or in operation, the populations and communities living in territories where mining TNCs are operating are often forced off their land by different coercive means. The latter are strategies designed by the State and mining companies, pushing the local populations to abandon their agricultural and other productive activities. The similarities with the dispossession processes that occurred in Europe in past centuries are striking, for instance with those that Marx described in his famous articles on the debates on "the law on wood theft" in the Rhenish Diet in Germany, providing evidence of the criminalization process of the traditional collection of firewood in the commons (Bensaïd 2008).

Latin America is probably the region with the most virulent and organized social protests against mega-mining projects, and some of the most notable in Argentina, such as the cases of Bajo de la Alumbrera in Catamarca, Meridian Gold in Esquel in Chubut, and Barrick Gold in Famatina in Cordoba. With the generalization of the mega-mining model and its extensive and intensive characteristics, the social unrest associated with mining projects in the region has reached unprecedented levels during the last two decades. Several sources show its continuous increase, for instance the Observatory of Mining Conflicts in Latin America (OCMAL 2020) counted a total of 245 mining conflicts throughout Latin America, while another initiative, the Atlas of Environmental Justice (EJOLT 2020) speaks of a total of 248 conflicts associated with several mining activities. However, social movements of resistance to mega-mining are often in the context of great power asymmetry; for example, comparing the power of communities and social movements on the one hand and transnational mining capital on the other hand (Svampa 2012, p. 19).

This struggle can be interpreted as social resistance to the extensive "accumulation by dispossession" processes associated with mega-mining. An important example of resistance to mega-mining and other activist issues, often related to reprimarization in Argentina is the organization the Union of Citizen Assemblies (UAC) which has been organizing movements of resistance to mega-mining, oil exploitation, large dams, urban pollution, and industrial monocultures since 2006. Further examination and discussion of the environmental impacts and associated social conflicts related to mega-mining projects in Argentina and Brazil will be elaborated on in the subsequent Chapter 8 addressing Social and Environmental Impacts of "New Development" Paths.

7.6.7 *The Role of the State Revisited*

As mentioned previously, the State has played a key role in processes associated with reprimarization, and also involving the expropriation of populations from their lands, and this continues to the present. In fact, most recently, 2019–2021, there has been an intensity of expropriations, especially among indigenous populations, under the Bolsonaro government, showing little regard for human rights and rather full support for criminal acts including burning down villages, as in August of 2019. Although the discussion of Bolsanaro's government will be considered in Chapter 9, it is worth noting that the current push by his government is similar to that of the military government in the 1980s and is not only expropriating populations, but there is increased evidence of actively seeking genocide for certain communities. In any case, in the next chapter, part of this discussion will be considered in the evaluation of both social and environmental impacts of new development paths.

Another relevant function of the current State is the development of the hydroelectric dams, which are fundamental for generating electricity for the processing of minerals. This has brought about serious social and environmental conflicts during recent years. Similarly, this issue will be analyzed more fully in Chapter 8 as well. However, it is pertinent to at least mention the most significant cases, extensively documented in terms of current conflicts around these dams in Brazil: Belo Monte, in the State of Pará and Rio São Francisco in the Northeast of Brazil. Lastly, an additional sector of major importance in terms of reprimarization, expropriations and the role of the State is that associated with petroleum and also biofuels, such as sugar and corn. This discussion will be presented in the context of environmental impacts of the current development path in the next chapter, including its links to the issue of climate change.

7.7 Conclusions

In the present chapter, we began with a quick summary of the impacts of neoliberal globalization, and in particular the role of TNCs and the WTO and how these set of factors combined with specific historical contexts led to the tendencies of deindustrialization and reprimarization in Argentina and Brazil. The processes of deindustrialization were first considered, reviewing the end of ISI and the arrival of neoliberal policies for both countries and with distinct trajectories and periods. The definitions of deindustrialization and reprimarization were also laid out and explained for greater clarity throughout the book. The impacts for manufacturing industry were examined and the steps in the process moving toward reprimarization were analyzed. The following section then examined the processes of reprimarization, presenting evidence of this transition.

Section 7.6 analyzed the relevance of Harvey's concept of accumulation by dispossession in the context of reprimarization in Argentina and Brazil, including more detailed theoretical and empirical analysis. In particular, the sectors examined were those associated with reprimarization, namely soy, cattle, and mining, and from an earlier period, the case of rubber extraction. In the last decades, there was a "quantum leap" in the magnitude of the mining operations, as well as the concessions granted to mining TNCs, not to mention the disproportionate expansion of soy and cattle in the Brazilian Amazon, or the exponential expansion of soy in the Pampas and other parts of Argentina. It can be argued that these dispossessions were necessary conditions for large-scale projects, anticipating high profitability, especially considering the role of ground rent.

Consistent with the analysis of the State by Harvey and Marx, was the evidence of the Argentine and Brazilian State employing legal and extra-legal means and violence in support of the needs of the TNCs. Therefore, from the analysis in this chapter it can be concluded that Harvey's theory of "accumulation by dispossession" contributes to our understanding of the dynamics at work in the occupation and appropriation of lands and resources by TNCs associated with the tendency toward reprimarization for the cases of Argentina and Brazil.

It is not clear what the exact development trajectories for both Argentina and Brazil will be in coming decades given the fact that the COVID-19 pandemic is the largest wrench thrown into the functioning of the global economy. Moreover, given the difficulties which the Fernandez Presidency faces after Macri's return to more neoliberal orthodoxy and IMF dependence, and the prospects for Brazil with the current proto-fascist Bolsonaro in power, the future looks bleak and more uncertain. In any case, the continuity of reprimarization seems to be a certainty. Although such a strategy could have success in the short run, depending on trends in the global economy, historically, the prices of primary goods tend to be more volatile and associated with declining terms of trade, as argued by Prebisch. Evaluating the future prospects and trying to interpret the potential scenarios given the present pandemic will be addressed or speculated upon in the last chapter. It appears that the political hegemony of finance-dominated neoliberal views will continue globally for the moment, and unfortunately, in spite of economic failure, the neoliberal politicians are still in power, whether in the US, Europe or China, or in most countries in Latin America.

References

AAPRESID (Asociación Argentina de Productores en Siembra Directa). 2012. Evolución de la superficie en Siembra Directa en Argentina. www.aapresid.org.ar/.

Angelo, Maurício. 2020. "Novo ataque de seguranças da Vale a agricultores acirra conflito pela terra no Pará". Reporter Brasil (June 27).

Ashman, S., and Callinicos, A. 2006. "Capital Accumulation and the State System: Assessing David Harvey's, The New Imperialism." *Historical Materialism*, Vol. 14, No. 4.

Bensaïd, Daniel. 2008. *Les dépossédés- Karl Marx, les voleurs de bois et le droit des pauvres*. Québec: Lux Éditeur.

Brenner, Robert. 2006. *What Is, and What Is Not, Imperialism? Historical Materialism*, Vol. 14, No. 4, pp. 79–105.

Brondizio, E.S. 2004. "Agricultural Intensification, Economic Identity and Shared Invisibility in Amazonian Peasantry: Caboclos and Colonists in Comparative Perspective." *Culture & Agriculture*, Vol. 26, pp. 1–24.

Buck, Daniel. 2009. "On Primitive Accumulation and Its Shadowy Twin, Subsumption." *Human Geography*, Vol. 2, No. 3.

Buenos Aires Times. 2020. "China Overtook Brazil as Argentina's Largest Trading Partner in April." 6 April. Accessed at https://www.batimes.com.ar/news/economy/china-overtook-brazil-as-argentinas-largest-trading-partner-in-april.phtml.

Bunker, Stephen G. 1985. *Underdeveloping the Amazon*. Chicago: University of Chicago Press.

Bunker, Stephen, and Paul Ciccantell. 2005. *Globalization and the Race for Resources*. Baltimore: Johns Hopkins University Press.

Carneiro, R. 2002. *Desenvolvimento em crise: a economia brasileira no último quartel do século XX*. São Paulo: Editora UNESP, IE – Unicamp.

Castro, Antonio Barros De, and Francisco Eduardo Pires De Souza. 1987. *Economia Brasileira em Marcha Forçada*. Rio de Janeiro: Paz e Terra.

Chang, Ha-Joon. 2002. *Kicking Away the Ladder—Development Strategy in Historical Perspective*. London: Anthem Press.

CIFRA. 2011. "Rentabilidad, empleo y condiciones de trabajo en el sector agropecuario." *Documento de Trabajo*, N. 8, febrero.

Cooney, Paul. 2007. "Argentina's Quarter Century Experiment with Neoliberalism: From Dictatorship to Depression." *Revista de Economia Contemporânea*. Rio de Janeiro, Vol. 11, No. 1 (January/April).

———. 2016. "Reprimarization: Implications for the Environment and Development in Latin America: The Cases of Argentina and Brazil." *RRPE*, Vol. 48, No. 4.

———. 2017. "Current Paths of Development in the Southern Cone: Deindustrialization and a Return to the Agro-export Model." In: Richard Westra (ed.), *The Political Economy of Emerging Markets Varieties of BRICS in the Age of Global Crises and Austerity*. New York: Routledge.

Cooney, Paul, and Sacher, W. 2015. "Reprimarización en Argentina y Brasil y la relevancia del concepto de 'acumulación por desposesión'." Presented at the VIII JEC, Rio Cuarto, Argentina.

Cooney, Paul, and Trindade, José R. 2016. "Reprimarización, Minería Transnacional y el Medio Ambiente en la Amazonia Brasileña." Presented at the *IX Jornadas de Economía Crítica*, agosto 25–27, 2016, Cordoba, Argentina.

Costa de Assis, Francisco. 2000. *Formação Agropecuária da Amazônia: os desafios do desenvolvimento sustentável*. Belém: NAEA.

Davis, Mike. 2017. *Late Victorian Holocausts: El Niño, Famines and the Making of the Third World*. New York: Verso.

Dunn, B. 2007. "Accumulation by Dispossession or Accumulation of Capital? The Case of China." *Journal of Australian Political Economy*, Vol. 60.

EJOLT. 2020. *Environmental Justice Organisations, Liabilities and Trade*. www.ejolt.org. Last visited July 12, 2020.

Fine, Ben. 2006. "Debating the 'New' Imperialism." *Historical Materialism*, Vol. 14, No. 4, pp. 133–156.

Galafassi, Guido. 2010. "Megaminería en Patagonia, Argentina, saqueo y nuevos cercamientos en un renovado proceso de acumulación por desposesión." In: G.C. Delgado (ed.), *Ecología política de la minería en América Latina*. México: UNAM-CEEICH.

Gonçalves, R. 1999. *Globalização e Desnacionalização*. São Paulo: Paz e Terra.

Gordon, Tedd, and Webber, Jeffery. 2008. "Imperialism and Resistance: Canadian Mining Companies in Latin America." *Third World Quarterly*, Vol. 29, No. 1, pp. 63–87.

Haro Sly, Maria José. 2017. "The Argentine Portion of the Soybean Commodity Chain." *Palgrave Communications*.

Harvey, David, 2003. *The New Imperialism*. Oxford and London.

Hecht, Susan. B. 1985. "Environment, Development and Politics: Capital Accumulation and the Livestock Sector in Eastern Amazonia." *World Development*, Vol. 13, No. 6, pp. 663–684.

IBGE (Instituto Brasileiro de Geografia e Estadística) 2010–2021. www.ibge.gov.br/. Accessed July 2021.

IBGE/SIDRA. 2010–2020. www.sidra.ibge.gov.br/. Accessed July 2020.

IEDI (Instituto de Estudos para o Desenvolvimento Industrial). 2018. "A Produtividade Industrial no Período Recente." Julho 2018.

INDEC. 2003–2020. www.indec.gov.ar/. Accessed July 2020.

IPEA. 2010–2021. www.ipeadata.gov.br/. Accessed July 2021.

Kejsefman, I. 2014. "El 'nuevo' agro argentino: Transformaciones productivas en el sector y la inserción de la Argentina en el actual capitalismo mundial (1990–2012)." *mimeo*.

Kosacoff, B., and Azpiazu, D. 1989. *La industria argentina: desarrollo y cambios estructurales*. Buenos Aires: Centro Editor de América Latina.

Machado Aráoz, H. 2010. "El Agua Vale Más que el Oro. Grito de resistencia descolonial contra los nuevos dispositivos expropiatorios." In: Delgado Gian Carlo (ed.), *Ecología política de la minería en América Latina*. México: UNAM-CEEICH.

Marx, Karl. 1977 *Capital: Critique of Political Economy, Vol. I*. New York: Vintage Books.

MDIC. 2012–2020. http://www.mdic.gov.br/sitio/. Accessed December 2020.

OCMAL. 2020. *Observatorio de Conflictos Mineros de América Latina*. www.ocm al.org. Last visited July 12, 2020.

Oliveira, A.U. de. 2005. "BR-163 Cuiabá-Santarém: Geopolítica, grilagem, violência e mundialização." In: *Amazônia Revelada: Os descaminhos ao longo da BR-163*. Brasilia: CNPq.

Oviedo, Eduardo Daniel. 2015. "Actors in the Argentina-China Soybean Trade and in Chinese Immigration to Argentina." In: E. Dussel Peters and Ariel C. Armony (coord.), *Beyond Raw Materials-Who Are the Actors in the Latin America and Caribbean-China Relationship?*

Rivero, S., and Paul Cooney. 2010. "The Amazon as a Frontier of Capital Accumulation: Looking Beyond the Trees." *Capitalism, Nature, Socialism*, Vol. 21, No. 4.

Robinson, William I. 2004. *A Theory of Global Capitalism—Production, Class and State in a Transnational World*. Baltimore: The John Hopkins University Press.

———. 2008. *Latin America and Global Capitalism—A Critical Globalization Perspective*. Baltimore: The John Hopkins University Press.

Rocha, Geisa M. 2002. "Neo-Dependency in Brazil." *New Left Review*, No. 16.

Rodrigues, Sabrina. 2018. "Área de cultivo de soja na Amazônia quadruplicou desde 2006." *O Eco*. https://www.oeco.org.br/noticias/area-de-cultivo-de-soja-na-amazonia-quadruplicou-desde-2006/. Accessed August 16, 2020.

Sacher, William. 2015. "Megaminería y Desposesión en el Sur: un análisis comparativo." *Íconos*, Vol. 51, pp. 99–116.

———. 2017. *Ofensiva Megaminería China en los Andes. Acumulación por Desposesión en el Ecuador de la Revolución Ciudadana*. Quito: Abya-Yala.

Sacher, William, and Cooney, Paul. 2019. "Transnational Mining and Accumulation by Dispossession." In: Paul Cooney and William Sacher (eds.), *Environmental Impacts of Transnational Corporations in the Global South. Research in Political Economy*, Vol. 33 (Chapter 1). Bingley, UK: Emerald Publishing.

Santarcangelo, Juan E. (ed.). 2019. *The Manufacturing Sector in Argentina, Brazil, and Mexico: Transformations and Challenges in the Industrial Core of Latin America*. London: Palgrave.

Schorr, Martín, and Ortiz, Ricardo. 2020. "Argentina: factores de impulse al proceso de reprimarización reciente." En: *Territorios primarizados en Argentina. Viejas y nuevas fragilidades socioeconómicas* (pp. 73–91). Buenos Aires: UNS.

Slipak, Ariel M. 2014. "Un análisis del ascenso de China y sus vínculos con América Latina a la luz de la Teoría de la Dependencia." *Realidad Económica*, No. 282.

Smith, W.C. 1989. *Authoritarianism and the Crisis of the Argentine Political Economy*. Stanford: Stanford University Press.

S&P Global. 2018. "World Exploration Trends." *A Special Report from S&P Global Market Intelligence for the PDAC International Convention*, March 2018.

Svampa, Maristella. 2012. "Consenso de los commodities, giro eco-territorial y pensamiento crítico en América Latina." *Osal*, año XIII, 32 (noviembre).

Teubal, M. 2006. "Expansión del modelo sojero en la Argentina. De la producción de alimentos a los commodities." En *Realidad Económica*, No. 220, Buenos Aires, 16.05–30.06.

Treacy, Mariano. 2014. "Transformaciones en el agro argentino y conflictos socio-ambientales en el Siglo XXI." Presentado en COLCA, UNGS.

Trindade, J.R, and Cooney, Paul. 2016. "Reprimarización, Minería Transnacional y el Medio Ambiente en la Amazonia Brasileña" presented at the *IX Jornadas de Economía Crítica*, 25–27, agosto, 2016, Cordoba, Argentina.

Trindade, J.R, and Cooney, Paul. 2017. "Dependency Approach in Latin America: Confronting Challenges of the 21st Century" presented at the *X Jornadas de Economía Crítica*, septiembre, 2017, UNGS, Buenos Aires, Argentina.

Trindade, J.R, Cooney, Paul, and De Oliveira, W. 2016. "Industrial Trajectory and Economic Development: Dilemma of the Reprimarization of the Brazilian Economy." *RRPE*, Vol. 48, No. 2, pp. 269–286.

Wilkinson, John. 2009. "Globalization of Agribusiness and Developing World Food Systems." *Monthly Review*, Vol. 61, No. 4, p. 238.

CHAPTER 8

Social and Environmental Impacts of "New Development Paths"

8.1 Introduction

After two lost decades, Latin America made a clear leftward shift during the first decade of the twenty-first century. For example, several elections were won by the left in a short time span: the election of Hugo Chávez in Venezuela in 1998; Lula Da Silva in Brazil in 2002; Néstor Kirchner in Argentina in 2003; Evo Morales in Bolivia in 2005; Rafael Correa in Ecuador in 2006; Tabaré Vázquez in Uruguay in 2004, and Fernando Lugo in Paraguay in 2008, and some could also argue that the election of Michelle Bachelet in Chile in 2005 should be included. Evidently, there are major differences among these different progressive governments, and the changes of social and economic policies which were implemented, not to mention several successors, such as Dilma Rousseff in Brazil, Cristina Fernandez in Argentina, José Mujica in Uruguay and Nicolás Maduro in Venezuela. In addition, at present many of these presidents are no longer

---

This chapter is partially derived from my chapter titled "Current paths of development in the Southern Cone" in Westra (editor), *The Political Economy of Emerging Markets: Varieties of BRICS in the Age of Global Crises and Austerity* (2017a).

P. Cooney, *Paths of Development in the Southern Cone*, Palgrave Insights into Apocalypse Economics,
https://doi.org/10.1007/978-3-030-67673-5_7

considered progressive, especially given their track record after being in office.

In the cases of Argentina and Brazil in the first years of the twenty-first century the newly elected progressive governments pursued policies distinct from neoliberal orthodoxy, and this was portrayed as a new path of development: neodevelopmentalism.[1] As argued and presented in earlier chapters, as a result of neoliberal globalization and in particular the impact of the rise of China in the global economy and the robust and strong growth associated with the commodities boom, among other factors, both Argentina and Brazil have experienced a notable process of reprimarization. In spite of some advances for manufacturing industry, both Brazil and Argentina have observed or experienced a growing role of agribusiness and the production of raw materials or primary products, during recent decades. This chapter will evaluate both social and environmental impacts for each country in light of the deepening of reprimarization and the shifts associated with neodevelopmentalism.

In previous chapters, we examined the impacts of more orthodox neoliberal policies in Brazil with Color de Mello and Cardoso in Chapter 6, and the case of Menem and the *Plan Cavallo*, in Argentina in the case of the 1990s in Chapter 5. One of the goals of this chapter is to identify the changes in economic policies which were implemented during the period when the PT was in government, 2003–2016: Lula (2003–2010) and Dilma (2011–2016) in the case of Brazil, and from 2003 to 2015, in Argentina with the Kirchners, Nestor Kirchner (2003–2007) and Cristina Fernández Kirchner (2007–2015).

Before examining the shifts in policies by both countries, a brief summary of the principal theoretical positions of the defenders of neodevelopmentalism will be presented to bear in mind when evaluating the nature of the new development paths in Argentina and Brazil. The subsequent section will evaluate the changes in policies and their subsequent social impacts for each country. A number of key socioeconomic indicators or variables, relevant for the general populations, are presented and evaluated: GDP growth, wages, unemployment, the informal economy, poverty, and inequality. In addition, an evaluation of a number of key

[1] As mentioned previously, the term neodevelopmentalism or new developmentalism, which is also used in English, is the translation of the Spanish term *neodesarrollismo* or *novo desenvolvimentismo* in Portuguese.

social programs are presented. The following section then examines the impacts for the environment as a result of reprimarization, which was examined in part in the previous chapter. After considering both the socioeconomic and environmental impacts of these recent tendencies, for both countries, an overall evaluation of neodevelopmentalism in practice is presented.

A key aim is to identify to what degree, neodevelopmentalism is making a break from the past, and to what degree there is a continuity, for example, with respect to the tendency of reprimarization. Finally, an overall assessment is made of the shifts by the PT in Brazil and by the Kirchners in Argentina, thus assessing the new model of development, debating its validity and efficacy with respect to advancing upon a new development trajectory, and to what extent it was or could be beneficial for the majority of each respective country.

8.2 Neodevelopmentalism—A New Development Trajectory

Several Keynesian authors argue that neodevelopmentalism is a new economic path, distinct from neoliberalism.[2] For example, Bresser-Pereira (2011) argues that this perspective defends the need for a strong state and also a strong market and the importance of sustainable growth based on improved social equality and a more competitive exchange rate, which is necessary to compete in global markets. Many aspects are very similar to the previous defense of the Import Substitution Industrialization (ISI) model of development, rooted or based upon Keynesian policies and arguing for industrial policy to maintain the growth of wages equal to productivity and to achieve the expansion of sectors with high value added.

Bresser-Pereira argues that the contrast between the old and new developmentalism is that the new developmentalism does not pursue protection to the same extent and aims to keep an economy more open. Therefore, this is a position oriented more toward free trade, or at the

[2] In 2010, there was a meeting of heterodox economists to discuss neodevelopmentalism, organized by the Ford Foundation and among those that participated included the following economists: Robert Boyer, Osvaldo Sunkel, Paul Davidson, James Galbraith, Jan Kregel, Gabriel Palma, José Antonio Ocampo, Ha-Joon Chang, Roberto Frenkel, Thomas Palley, Fred Block, Luciano Coutinho, Aldo Ferrer, and Marcó del Pont (Azcurra 2011).

very least, more open markets without tariff protection and other policy tools, such as subsidies, associated with industrial policy during ISI. Some advocates of neodevelopmentalism place more emphasis on the importance in supporting and defending industry compared to the position of Bresser-Pereira, especially with the concern of the risk that the Brazilian economy is more and more oriented to the production of primary goods and less toward manufacturing industry.[3] Bresser-Pereira and others argue that they are less concerned with the current account and more interested in the capital account. However, given the reality of the division of labor between the producers of primary goods vs. those that produce manufactured goods, this strikes one as rather naïve and seems to be forgetting the lessons of Prebisch and other developmentalists of another generation.[4]

They refer to the need to aim for a maximum rate of the accumulation of capital which is environmentally sustainable, based upon the incorporation of technical change and yet maintaining the primary objective of the pursuit of full employment of all labor recourses available. It is also argued that the demand side must be considered and that there is a need to ensure high levels of wages and remuneration, and at the same time argue for the need to be competitive at an international level. There is a declared aim to return the growth of wages to coincide with the growth of productivity, which had been the dominant case in the decades after World War II, but not in the case of recent decades. In terms of being competitive internationally, there is a reference to the risk of the Dutch disease and argue for the need to achieve and maintain a competitive rate of exchange.

Overall, there is a very strong degree of naivete, in thinking it is possible to achieve full employment, while being competitive at the global level and achieving maximum accumulation and being sustainable, given the domination of foreign transnational corporations. There is a need to make some choices, a healthier and clean environment will not come with higher levels of growth, no matter how much one may wish to believe

[3] In contrast is the author, Han Joon Chang, who is quite critical of neoliberal policies and "free trade" discourse by first world politicians and advocates of neoliberal views and he is probably the most realistic of all the authors associated with the debates around neodevelopmentalism.

[4] One author (Jepson 2020) that carries out an examination of the relation between the commodity boom and developmental strategies, presents an analysis of neodevelopmentalism in Argentina and Brazil, though also fails to recognize the importance, if not necessity, of ISI style protectionism and industrial development.

in the new Green Capitalism. There is also a more profound naivete, perhaps wishing to appear as solid Keynesians, defending workers' rights but ignoring the recent patterns of transnational capital accumulation with a downward spiral of wages and worsening conditions across the globe. There is a serious contradiction between maintaining higher wages, defending workers' rights and also ensuring environmental sustainability, and yet somehow also, being more competitive in the global economy, all at the same time.

Another key point, which produces the contrast with the earlier period of ISI thinking, is the change in terms of class alliances. During the period from the 1930s through the 1970s, for countries, such as Argentina and Brazil, industrialization took place with an alliance between the rising industrial bourgeoisie and the urban and industrial working classes. At the present point in time, the industrial bourgeoisie is minimally existent at best, and instead the elites are seeking alliances with other parts of the transnational capitalist class. The world has changed since the 1970s, currently with TNC-dominated neoliberal globalization, one must recognize that the role of the nation-state is not the same as before; it has not been eliminated, but it is no longer a defender of national industrial policy, at least not in the periphery. In order to promote a new development project, such changes must be clearly incorporated into new strategies for an alternative approach to development, which is not neoliberal, but which can be industrial without substituting classes that no longer exist or have become mere specters from a foregone time.

In spite of the rather critical view presented of the theoretical advocates of neodevelopmentalism, it is still incumbent upon us to make an evaluation of what took place in terms of the efforts of change by the Kirchner governments of Argentina and the PT governments in Brazil. Thus, we now consider each country and their recent experiences with respect to economic and social policies.

8.3 Socioeconomic Assessment of Neodevelopmentalism

As described above, the new progressive governments of Lula da Silva and Nestor Kirchner arrived in power in 2003, needing to confront a number of structural problems, especially in Argentina, coming out of a depression. In the case of the latter, there were also political mandates to break from the neoliberal orthodoxy of the recent past in order to accommodate the demands of the working classes and more vulnerable and poorer sectors of society. In any case there was clearly a challenge to try and achieve higher growth, which was substantially accomplished through a competitive exchange rate and very low wages, leading to a surge in investment and very robust growth. In terms of Brazil, strong growth was elusive although there was growth in the banking and financial sectors, and of course those sectors tied to reprimarization, especially in the Amazon. However, there were still a number of serious structural problems related to unemployment, the large informal economy and poverty that continued to be a challenge for both economies. Nevertheless, seeking a balance of an acceptable economic performance while also accommodating the demands for greater social inclusion seemed to be a working policy, especially given the commodities boom.

In terms of breaking from neoliberal policies, Argentina, made more of a break, especially as the country needed to not only recover from the nadir of a depression and obtain serious growth of GDP, but also increase wages and accommodate the more vulnerable sectors of a society coming out of their worst economic crisis ever. Such formulas often collide with neoliberal orthodoxy. Argentina had entered in default on its foreign debt and was in a process of hard negotiations with those unwilling to accept a major, though necessary, reduction in the debt owed them and they also placed more controls on finance and foreign exchange.

This was the opposite case in Brazil, where there was a strong accommodation of international finance,[5] seeking to attract capital flows, both for direct investment and also of the portfolio or speculative variety. The strategy, begun under Cardoso, was to maintain the highest rates of interest on the globe, thereby encouraging arbitrage and the financial speculative flow of money into Brazil, especially with the commodities boom. As a result, their currency was strengthened and thus hurt industry from being more competitive, both in terms of the exchange rate but also in terms of higher interest payments. Of course, the largest Brazilian transnationals, had their breaks and did not suffer, as many small and medium manufacturing firms did.

[5] In fact, prior to taking office, Lula had made a commitment to the financial sector, namely that his government would maintain the support for the interests of the financial sector in Brazil (see Marquetti, Hoff and Miebach 2016).

In any case, neither country could break from a neoliberal trade policy, as they were by necessity, members of the WTO. For any individual country to attempt to break from the WTO would be economic suicide[6]; only a block of countries could achieve a successful break, but this will be discussed in the next chapters.

For the time being, neither government was seeking to privatize national firms and in fact, Argentina ended up re-nationalizing two key state enterprises, namely the state oil company, YPF (Yacimientos Petroleras Fiscales) and the state airline, Aerolíneas Argentinas. In terms of monetary policy, unfortunately both Lula and Nestor accommodated the IMF in maintaining, and in the case of Brazil, increasing their primary surpluses. In the case of Argentina this made no sense, since they were coming out of a depression, not seen as the ideal time to save, just consider someone having been laid off for months and then finally gets a job, not the time to start making loans.

In the evaluation below, the issue of GDP growth is considered first, and then a range of key variables are analyzed, namely those which are arguably most relevant for the majority of the population, not necessarily for the countries' elites. Thus, the labor market is examined, considering wages, unemployment, underemployment, the informal economy, poverty, inequality and finally social programs. The social programs were basically a set of welfare programs, and can be seen as a safety net for the poorest and most vulnerable or precarious in society. Such programs, once again, did not fit with neoliberal orthodoxy, which tends to push countries to eliminate or reduce such programs. First, a summary of the performance of the Argentine economy for the period of the Kirchners is presented. After considering Argentina, the same evaluation will be carried out for the case of Brazil and the PT governments.

8.3.1 Argentina

8.3.1.1 Growth

Argentina was able to obtain a significant GDP growth after the difficult experience of hyperinflation during the end of the 1980s and the beginning of the 1990s. This had to do with the intensification of neoliberal

[6] See the discussion of the role of the WTO in Chapter 2.

policies associated with the *Plan Cavallo*, including financial deregulation, trade liberalization, and privatizations, as discussed in Chapter 5. Although there was a decline in growth caused by the "Tequila" effect in the middle of the 1990s, the recessionary tendency began in 1997, culminating in the worst economic crisis in Argentina's history from 2001 to 2003, where GDP dropped by more than 10% in 2002 (see below).

After abandoning the regime of convertibility and then the devaluation of the peso in 2002, the local economy began a process of gradual recovery.[7] As a result of a higher rate of exchange, there was an increase in the level of effective protection for local production. This combined with a strong contraction of wages, as a result of the significant devaluation (approximately 75%), brought about a strong recovery of profitability, especially for manufacturing industry. As a result of these factors, the economy registered an annual growth of approximately 8% during 2003–2008, seen as a sign of economic success for the years that Nestor Kirchner was President and for the beginning of the first period of Cristina Fernandez.

As can be observed in Fig. 8.1, after these auspicious beginnings, came the global financial crisis of 2008–2010, and entering into a recession, with a major drop in GNP growth from 9% in 2007 down to almost a negative 6% in 2009 and then shooting up to over 10% in 2010; a classic V-shaped curve. Argentina achieved a quick and strong recovery, significantly due to the increased role of China as a trading partner. Nevertheless, in spite of achieving a growth rate of over 10% in 2010 and then 6% in 2011, there was another serious decline with GDP growth dropping down to −1% in 2012. After that, growth began to oscillate between plus and −2.5%, reflecting a lack of steady growth, and also the increasing problem of inflation. The latter was around 10% from 2005 through 2013 but then it took off and became out of control, with inflation reaching its highest level in 2019 of over 53% during Macri's last year as President.

It is necessary to mention that the data for Argentina presented in other chapters or in other publications present notable discrepancies for

[7] See Grigera and Eskenazi (2013) for an important contribution analyzing the period of pos-convertibility, in identifying an initial period of recovery in 2002, dominated by reutilizing installed capacity, followed by a proper growth period with investment in industry from 2003–2008.

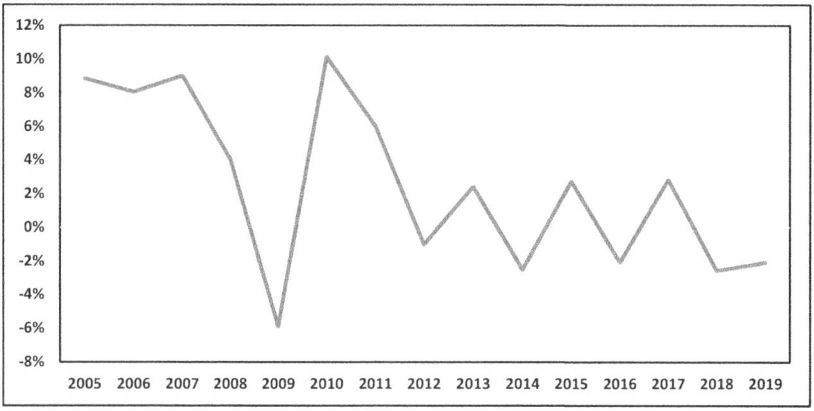

Fig. 8.1 Growth Rates of GDP for Argentina- 2005–2019[9] (*Source* Data from INDEC [2016, 2020] and elaborated by author)

certain years, compared with the data above.[8] For example, during the worst year of the crisis or depression in 2002, previous official data showed a drop of over 11%, in contrast to 10%; and in the case of the crisis of 2008–2009 the low point was just above zero, a significant drop, but not close to −5.92%. The analysis summarizing the economic performance of the Macri government will be addressed in the next chapter. Nevertheless, a major concern is that after 2017, Argentina has been experiencing a recessionary trend with growing inflation—the infamous stagflation.

Returning to the period 2003–2008, the Argentine economy bounced back from the nadir of 2002 fairly strongly, producing a recovery which

[8] It is fairly common knowledge that there have been significant changes in the methodology for data series at INDEC in recent years, often where the changes or manipulations reflect political interests. There are claims that this has taken place by both Cristina Fernandez's government as well as by the Macri government. Although this may not be so novel for Argentina, the changes appear to be rather more drastic than other instances over recent decades. In fact, the reality is that all countries' governments attempt to influence the data of their statistical institutions, in spite of attempts to ensure institutional autonomy, Brazil included.

[9] The data points for 2000–2004 are from the same source as the rest of the data, nevertheless 2016, and the last two points 2018–2019 are provisional.

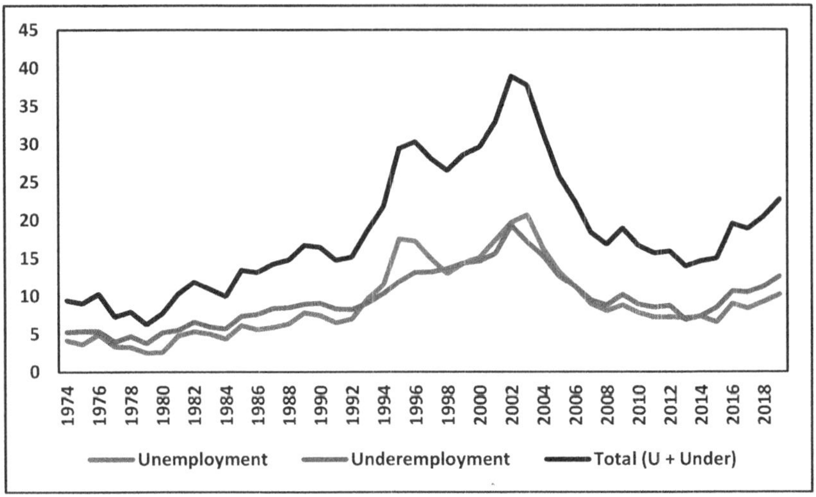

Fig. 8.2 Unemployment and Underemployment in Argentina, 1974–2019 (*Source* INDEC/EPH (2007–2020) and calculations by Iñigo Carrera)

had a significant impact on employment. In fact, the total number of new jobs generated between 2003 through 2010 was approximately 4 million, and the industrial sector was leading the way with the recovery during the first years of the expansion. Moreover, there was a recovery of wages, but eventually the increase in the growth of GDP began to decrease after 2007. In Fig. 8.2, the tendency of unemployment, underemployment, and the sum of the two series, total unemployment[10] can be observed from 1974 through to 2019.

The government of Néstor Kirchner made an effort to reactivate manufacturing industry, implementing changes which favored manufacturing over finance and agribusiness. This push was an attempt by the Kirchner government to reverse the trend of deindustrialization. In fact, Argentine manufacturing industry grew more rapidly between 2003 and 2007 than any other five-year period with the exception of the first period of Perón. The high rate of exchange functioned as protection for local industry and combined with the strong contraction of wages, as a result of the strong

[10] From here on, the term total unemployment refers to the sum of unemployment and underemployment.

devaluation, produced a recovery of manufacturing profitability and these changes helped facilitate the growth of GDP, reaching 8% for several years. However, one has to bear in mind that any economy coming out of a depression after hitting the lowest point or nadir, the rates of growth after the rebound will tend to be particularly high.

8.3.1.2 Labor Market

Although a given country's labor market can be weak and not in labor's favor, this can be a clear advantage for greater growth of capital, as was the case during the economic recoveries experienced in Germany and Japan after WWII. This pattern is similar to the case of Argentina, where the substantial growth coming out of the depression of 2001 was partially due to very low wages. Moreover, the sum of unemployment and under-employment: total unemployment, reached the level of 40% in 2002, but fortunately this changed as employment increased from a low of 34% in 2002. The downward tendency of total unemployment went from 40% down to approximately 14% in 2013. However, since then the total unemployment increased and was approaching 23% in 2019. Unfortunately, the predictions for 2020, as are the majority of economic statistics for most countries, are only going to get worse, and thus this series will certainly increase in 2020 and quite probably in the coming years as well.

During the 1990s, the principal problems that led to the crisis of 2001, were the overvalued peso (connected to convertibility), the overdependency of agribusiness, speculative capital, capital flight, and the problems of the debt, all intertwined with the issues of finance, as well as the trade deficit (see Chapter 5). For example, the percentage of GDP represented by manufacturing had fallen from being 27% in the early 1970s down to only 15% in 2002. Therefore, it is evident that the Kirchner government discontinued many of the neoliberal policies dominant in the 1990s and as a result achieved strong growth in terms of GDP, but also in terms of employment. Let us now consider perhaps the most important variable for the majority of populations across the globe, namely that of real wages.

8.3.1.3 Real Wages

Although one would prefer to examine real wages overall, the best option available is for industrial workers in Argentina, which is quite important,

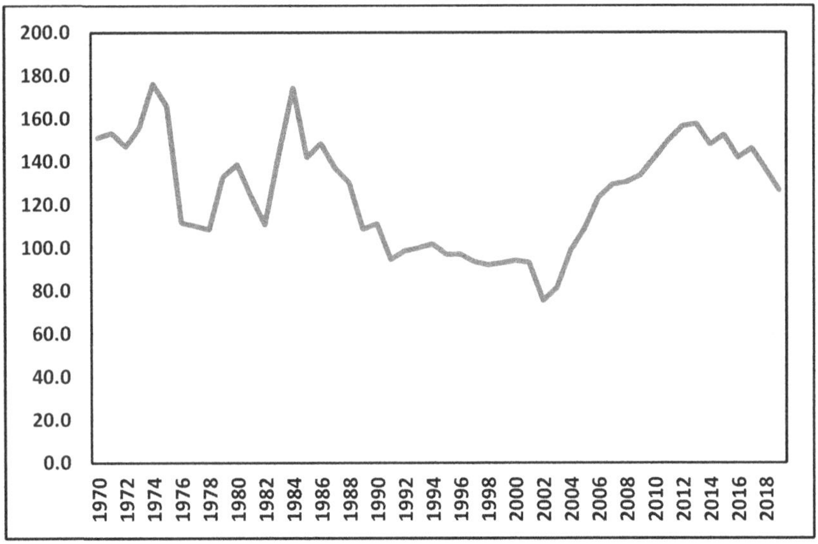

Fig. 8.3 Real Wages for Industrial Workers, Argentina 1970–2018 (1993 = 100) (*Source* Elaboration by Iñigo Carrera using data from INDEC [2020])

though not comprehensive. Once again, as is the case for data series on wages from many countries, there have also been inconsistencies in these data series. After the devaluation in 2002, the index for wages had dropped to 75.3 (1993 = 100) but given the rebound of industry, the wage index grew steadily until 2013, reaching 157.7, evidence of a clear gain for industrial wages. Nevertheless, there is a concern of how the wages of informal workers and those in agriculture and in rural areas fared for this period, especially given the tendency for them to be significantly lower than industry. After 2013, the decline of industrial wages down to 126.7 in 2019 can be observed in Fig. 8.3 reflecting a stagnating labor market or minimal increases in employment and the flip side being an increase of total unemployment reaching roughly 23% in 2019.

8.3.1.4 *Informal Employment*

A major growing problem associated with neoliberal globalization is the increase in the informal economy worldwide. Clearly derived from the

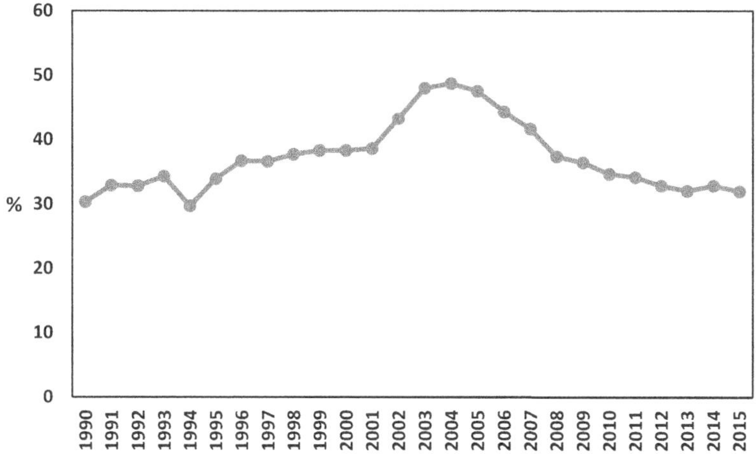

Fig. 8.4 Rate of Informal Employment: Argentina (1990–2015) (*Source* Elaboration by author, using data from INDEC [2020] and INDEC/EPH [2020])

drive for flexibilization of labor or breaking from the euphemistic terminology, the elimination of worker's rights globally to accommodate the transnational corporations desire for flexibility.[11] In the case of Argentina, worker's rights had been a force for many decades, at times requiring military dictatorships to be suppressed, although Menem's neoliberalism also achieved this. The erosion of workers' rights became evident through the 1990s and the increase of the informal economy was a clear example of this. Taking roughly 30% as the previous base of informal labor in 1990, there is a clear increase in the percentage of non-registered or informal workers throughout the 1990s, and reaching a maximum of almost 50% in 2004, right after the low point of the depression. This is evident in Fig. 8.4, as well as the steady decline of informal labor after 2004 down to roughly 32% between 2013 and 2015. Unfortunately, this is the last year that official data is available.

[11] Evidently, the interest in lowering wages is not limited to only transnational capital, however, they have had the greatest success, through their influence in achieving this change.

8.3.1.5 Poverty

A major barometer of how well government policies are working out is the level of poverty for society. When there are serious problems of growth, this implies problems for employment and therefore also for wages. However, when there are both problems of low wages and limited employment, including the growth of the informal economy, there tends to be an increase in poverty. Unfortunately for many Argentines, the crisis of 2001 was the worst level of poverty experienced by the country on record and the official statistic at the time of the crisis in 2003 was roughly 63%. The official numbers today have reduced this maximum to approximately 59%. In any case, so, so many people were suffering in Argentina, searching for food in garbage cans, all over the capital city, including outside the Congress and in many middle-class neighborhoods, which had never observed such phenomena. Prostitution reached shocking levels, garbage collecting turning into a new vocation as scavengers came to be advocates of recycling and were forced to make a living out of it. The villas or poorest neighborhoods are always going to have serious problems of both poverty and indigence, but at the height of the crisis, they reached levels that were unheard of and into neighborhoods that had not witnessed such poverty.

As can be seen above in Fig. 8.5, after 2003, poverty declines from almost 60% to under 30% by 2011. As a result of growing problems in the economy, it grew again and moved back above 30% in 2014, before declining again and dropping to 25% in 2017. The last upturn of poverty in Fig. 8.5, shows it reaching 35.5% in 2019; and it will surely increase through the COVID-19 crisis. In the case of indigence, as can be seen above it reached 21% at the height of the crisis in 2003 and moved downward and declined from roughly 6 to 5% between 2011 and 2017 but has increased again reaching 8% in 2019.

8.3.1.6 Inequality and the Gini Coefficient

The most commonly used measure of inequality is the Gini coefficient for income and therefore we examine it here. There are clearly other measures, from deciles of income to other ratios and measures. Ideally, we should also include the Gini coefficient for wealth inequality, generally a much more severe and telling measure, but for lack of availability and time and space limitations, it is not included. It does not seem necessary to explain the way in which the coefficient is generated with the Lorenz

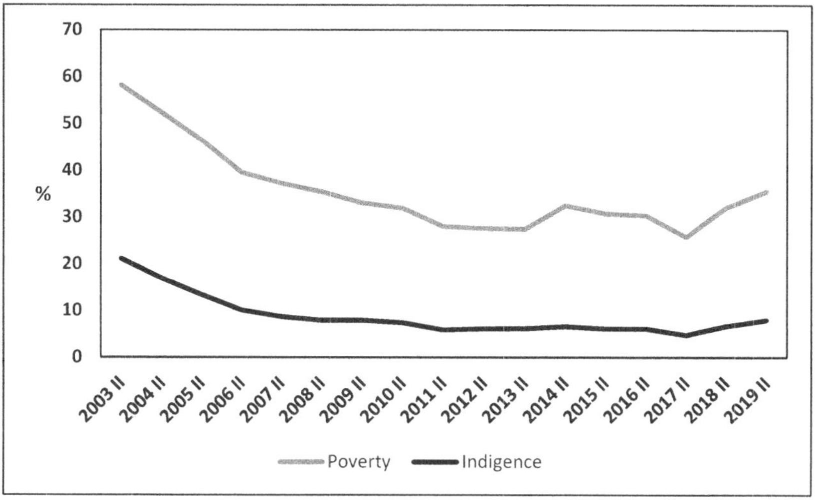

Fig. 8.5 Poverty and Indigence in Argentina (%): 2003–2019 (*Source* World Bank [2021])

curve, but just as a friendly reminder, the maximum value of 1 is the most unequal a society can be, while a value of 0 would be the exact opposite.

As evident from the graph of the Gini coefficient in Fig. 8.6, in the case of Argentina there was a maximum reached (0.48) at the time of hyperinflation in 1989 under Alfonsín and then a new maximum (almost 0.54) was attained in 2002 during the depression of 2001–2003 with Duhalde as President. Since that point, the Gini declined to roughly 0.41 in 2014 with a slight increase to 0.42 in 2016 and it stayed near that value through 2018. Across the globe, the values of Gini coefficients are expected to increase in this particularly strange and difficult crisis, and already evident with the outrageous increases in wealth of the most affluent billionaires on the planet, such as Bezos, Buffet, Zuckerberg, upward of over US$600 billion between just March and July 2020. The reason being is that it is usual in times of crisis that the wealthiest are able to shift much of the burden to the poorest or most vulnerable. It will be a concern to see how inequality worsens in the current and post-COVID-19 period, both in terms of the contrast of income between the wealthy and the poor, but also the contrast of the number of deaths.

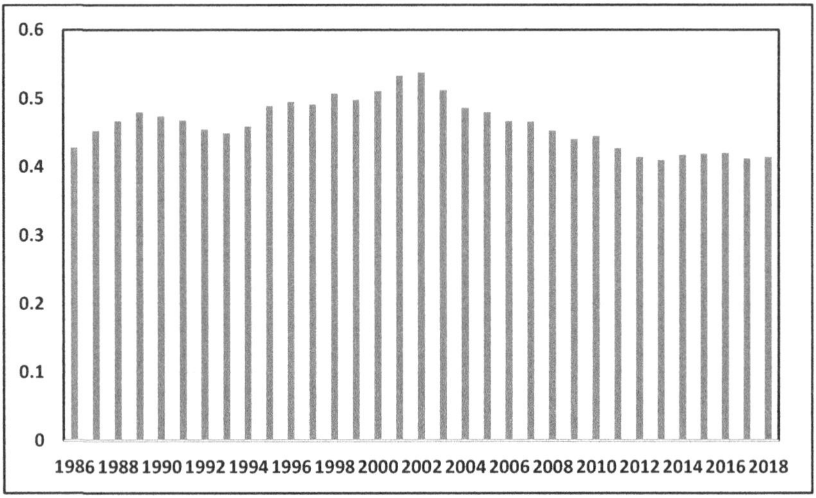

Fig. 8.6 Gini Coefficient in Argentina: 1986–2018 (*Source* World Bank [2018])

8.3.1.7 *Social Programs*

The first social program implemented during the crisis of 2001–2003 was the Unemployed Heads of Households Program (*Programa Jefes y Jefas de Hogar Desocupados*), created in 2002, when Duhalde was the President. The program consists of a direct transfer of 150 pesos given to the unemployed heads of households, with children up to 18 years old, though with the exception of older children that have disabilities. The maximum number of beneficiaries was during the first year of the program in 2002, reaching 1,990,735, while the number of beneficiaries was 77,041 in February 2010, where 65.6% were women and 34.4% were men. Between 2003 and 2010, of all beneficiaries only 643,411 were incorporated into the labor market, and of them, 53.7% were women and 43.3% were men.

There were four other social programs aimed to assist the most vulnerable populations. The program Universal Child Assistance (*Asignación Universal por Hijo*) began in 2009 and consisted of a subsidy per child, designed to assist poor families, whose children lacked health coverage or Social Security. In December 2015 there were 3,684,138 beneficiaries and in June 2019 there was a total of 3,923,040 beneficiaries. Another program: Youth Program for More and Better Employment (*Programa Jóvenes con Más y Mejor Trabajo*), began in 2008, for youth between 18 and 24 years old. It was designed for assisting, in part, through a subsidy for economic assistance, but also training and assistance for obtaining a job. More than half of the beneficiaries were women, and were linked to care or commercial activities, and domestic services, such as cleaning or cooking. In the case of men, it was for those working in construction, industrial, and commercial activities. According to the ILO (International Labor Organization), between June 2008 and December 2011 there were 438,460 beneficiaries.

Additionally, during the government of Cristina Fernández de Kirchner, in 2009, a program referred to as a Plan for Social Inclusion with Work (*Plan Ingreso Social con Trabajo*) was created, also known as Argentina Works (*Argentina Trabaja*), and through December 2015 there were 126,450 cooperative members that had benefitted from this plan. Another similar program established in 2013 is referred to as Women Do It Program (*Ellas Hacen*) and through 2015, it had benefitted 92,420 women. Both of these new plans provided incentives to earn income by working with cooperatives, though in some way, this was an institutionalization of informal employment.

This has been a brief summary of the socioeconomic performance during the years of the Kirchners, and including the social programs aimed at reducing social exclusion. Overall, it provides a sense to what extent these governments broke with neoliberal orthodoxy in pursuing neodevelopmentalism. The next section presents an analysis of socioeconomic policies implemented under the PT governments of Lula and Dilma, and also including social programs aimed to reduce social exclusion.

8.3.2 Brazil

Above we examined the degree to which Brazil continued neoliberal policies and how this was more evident than in Argentina, mainly considering the issues of finance, interest rates, and the exchange rate of the *Real*. These policies, as well as the lack of an industrial policy, contributed toward the continued deindustrialization and the deepening of the tendency of reprimarization, as seen in Chapter 7. In order to evaluate these policies, in socioeconomic terms, the tendency of GDP growth is considered first.

8.3.2.1 Growth

As can be observed in Fig. 8.7, in contrast to Argentina, the highs and lows in Brazil are less marked for this period. This is understandable, given the fact that Argentina experienced a depression between 2001 and 2003 and then had an accelerated recovery with rates of growth of 8–9 percent for several years. In the case of Brazil, the rates of growth were clearly less for the period 1989–1999, with the exception of the period 1993–1995, evidence of the initial positive effect of the *Plano Real*. Yet by the end of the 1990s the negative effects of the *Plano Real* had become evident and afterward the currency crisis of 1999 arrived.

The Brazilian economy according to official statistics grew rather slowly during Lula's first years and was described as comparable to the low growth associated with Cardoso's term, but updated statistics by the IBGE results in a better start for Lula. Nevertheless, there is still an improvement for the second term, achieving a rate of growth of 6% in 2007. However, as a result of the global economic crisis from 2008–2010, the rate of growth of GDP went negative, though barely for 2009. The most significative growth achieved in Brazil in recent years

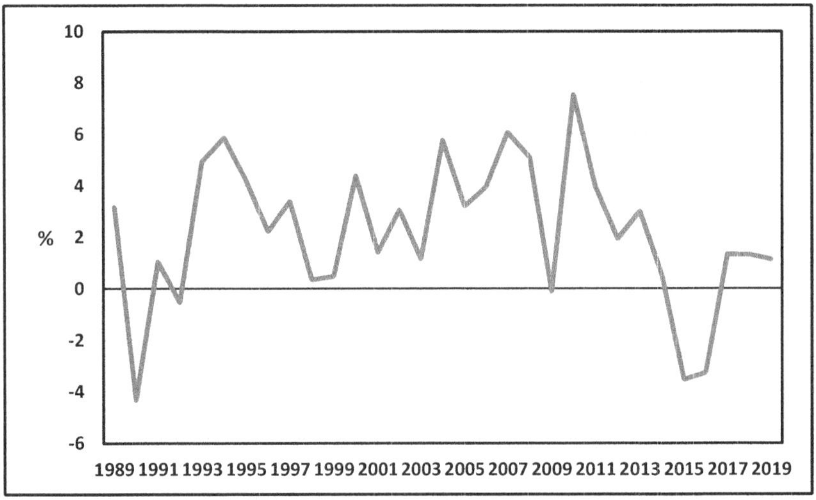

Fig. 8.7 Growth Rates of GDP for Brazil, 1989–2019 (*Source* IBGE [2020])

was the recovery of 2010, reaching an annual rate of 7.5%. However, since 2011 the economic performance of Brazil appeared rather weak, only 1.9% in 2012, though bouncing back to 3% in 2013, but rather anemic after that with only 0.5% in 2014, and then -3.55% in 2015, -3.2% in 2016 and finally returning to positive growth in 2017 with a rate of 1.32% and then dropping slightly to 1.14% in 2019. As expected, 2020 brought a recession, with a decline of –4.1%; a combination of the global trend combined with the horrendous manner in which the Bolsonaro government is dealing with the pandemic and the economy.

In spite of some quarters or years of reasonable growth, the average annual rate of only 3% for the period 1992–2010, remains very far from the average annual rate of 7.3% registered for the period 1960–1980. This is a clear demonstration that the Brazilian economy had a much better performance during the ISI period compared to the neoliberal one in terms of the growth of GDP, even when strict neoliberal orthodoxy was not dominant as in the case of the governments of Lula and Dilma. There is still a need to recognize to what extent there was and was not a break from neoliberal policies; in part this becomes evident in examining a range of variables associated with the labor market, poverty and inequality. An overall evaluation will be discussed further in Sect. 8.5, after considering a number of social variables as well as environmental impacts in recent years.

Having considered the key mainstream statistic for evaluating the overall performance of the Brazilian economy, namely examining GDP growth rates, we now shift to examining the range of variables relevant for the majority of the population. Thus, wages, unemployment, and under-employment, and the informal economy, are considered, followed by how this connects and relates to poverty and the concern over inequality, and therefore examining the Gini coefficient. Lastly, we will examine the efforts to push for more social inclusion as promoted by the PT government and in particular the renowned social welfare program, namely the *Bolsa Família*.

8.3.2.2 Real Wages

One of the policy shifts that has been cited as a key gain for the working classes of Brazil by the PT, was the increase in the real wage in Brazil. As can be seen in Fig. 8.8, there was a continual increase in real wages, for Major Metropolitan Areas in Brazil, between 2003 and 2014, and in fact this was an increase of 4.77% annually. This is not the overall

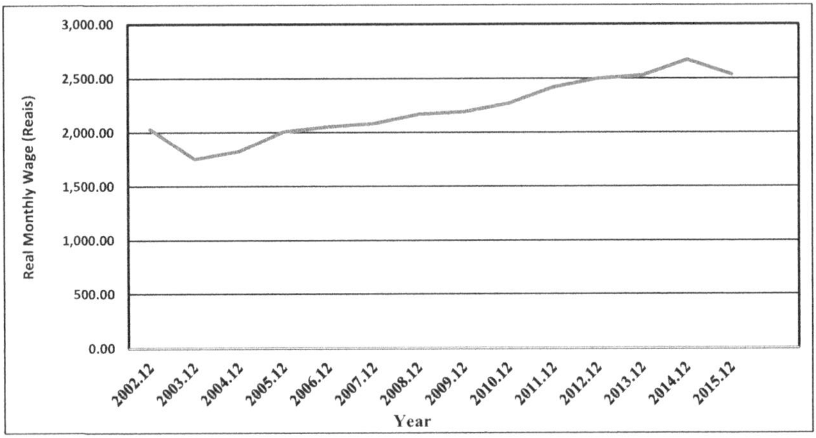

Fig. 8.8 Average Real Income in Major Metropolitan Areas in Brazil (2002–2016) (*Source* IBGE [2020])

real wages for all of Brazil, but rather the average real income in major metropolitan areas in Brazil, namely in large urban cities, and thus, it is excluding the lowest wage levels which occur in the more rural parts of the country. Nevertheless, this improvement is in line with what was hoped and expected by many workers and poor in Brazil. However, since 2014 there has been a worrisome decline, in part, the result of austerity measures implemented by Joaquim Levy, the former Economics Minister under Dilma and then further exacerbated with the interim conservative government of Temer, but this period and that of Bolsonaro will be further discussed in the next chapter.

In contrast to average urban wages shown in Fig. 8.8, there has been a concern for the gap between the minimum wage and the needs of which correspond to a basic basket of consumption goods. In spite of a steady increase from the time of the Plan Real even till Bolsonaro, given the cost of living and inflation (averaging around 3–4% in recent years) the gap between the official minimum wage and the minimum income necessary to avoid poverty continues to grow.

As can be seen in Fig. 8.9, this gap grew from R$635 in 1995 to over R$4000 in 2019, perhaps an improved percentage but a clearly worsening situation. The data for the minimum income necessary is from DIEESE (*Departamento Intersindical de Estatística e Estudos Socioeconômicos*), a

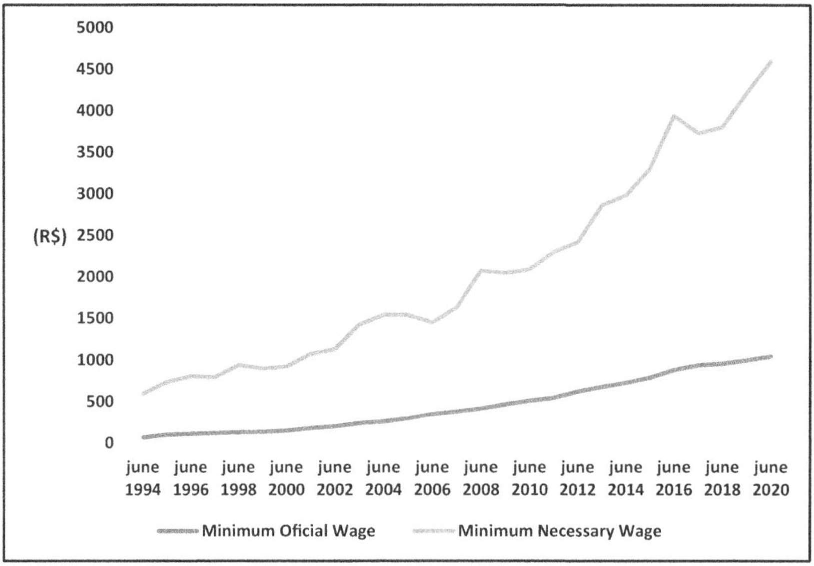

Fig. 8.9 Official Minimum Wage vs. Necessary Minimum Wage Brazil (1994–2020) (current R$) (*Source* DIEESE [2020])

well-recognized progressive Union-Based Research Institute. This is a serious concern when addressing the basic needs of all workers and calls into question a least one aspect of social policy that differs from what the position a Worker's Party should be, in terms of wages, especially minimum wages, which affects so many of the more vulnerable in Brazilian society. Of course, such a criticism needs to bear in mind the Brazilian reality, where the policies implemented previously by Cardozo or those in recent years by Temer and now Bolsonaro continue to be much worse than what was achieved by the PT. In fact, this reality is consistent with the norm of Brazil, where very low wages are maintained in general, even during the 'Miracle' period of accelerated industrialization.[12] Nevertheless, this should not preclude progressives from a critical

[12] In part, the extremely low wages during the dictatorship were key for capital and therefore for Brazil to achieve such amazing rates of growth, over 11% between 1968 and 1973, calling it a Miracle (see Fig. 4.2).

assessment of PT policies when many were far from ideal, even during the best years.

8.3.2.3 *Unemployment*

Although the key aim for governments is to generate new jobs, it is most common to examine unemployment when assessing whether a given government was successful or not, especially since new jobs alone do not tell the full story, and they must be compared with the total population and the economically active population. Unfortunately, most statistics of unemployment have changed the methodology they use to define PEA (Economically Active Population), eliminating those that have been searching and searching and finally give up; not to be translated as being employed, they are still unemployed. They are still a part of a social problem, especially unemployment under capitalism, but so that this blemish of twenty-first-century capitalism does not appear, they are removed from the statistics. It is worth noting that Lula's government first pursued a Program of Zero Unemployment (*Desemprego Cero*) but after several months they realized this is much more easily said than done and changed their emphasis to a program of Zero Hunger (*Fome Cero*), a much more reasonable goal to pursue.

In Fig. 8.10, it is observed that when Lula began, the level of unemployment was roughly 10.5% and it fell through most of his tenure, though jumping up in 2009 to 9%, given the world financial crisis, but continuing downward afterward and reaching a low of 6.73% in 2012 during Dilma's first term. After that point, it grew under Dilma, and was near 10% when she was impeached and Temer took over. After that point it kept growing and reached 13.2% in 2017 until finally dropping to 12.60% in 2018. Since that time, it has grown again and continues increasing with Bolsonaro, especially with the current COVID-19 crisis with a provisional estimate of around 14.3% for 2020 and growing.

8.3.2.4 *Informal Employment*

As discussed above for Argentina, in recent times, the informal economy has grown in general across the globe. In the case of Brazil, the informal economy has been particularly higher than the world average and especially in rural areas and the states of the North and Northeast. As can be seen in Fig. 8.11, there has been a fairly steady decline of the percentage of workers that are part of the informal economy, declining from a level of almost 61% in 1999, which is outrageous, and achieving a significant reduction declining down to below 50% to 45.5% in 2013, during Dilma's

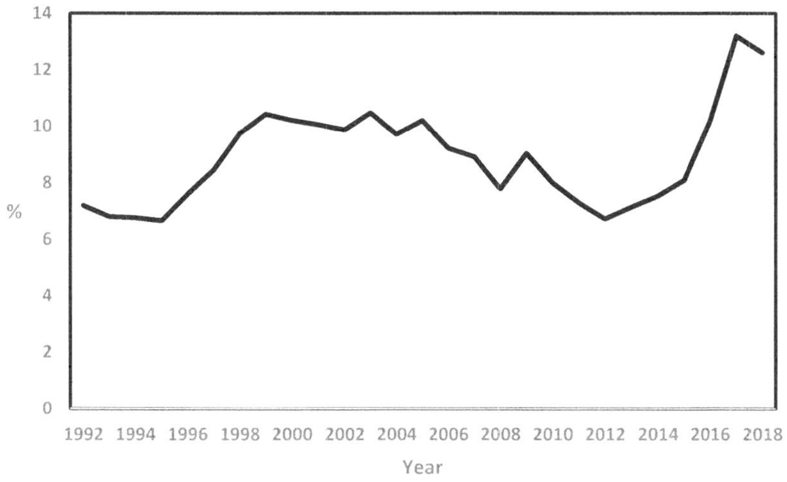

Fig. 8.10 Unemployment Rate in Brazil, 1992–2018 (*Source* IBGE [2020] and PNAD [2020])

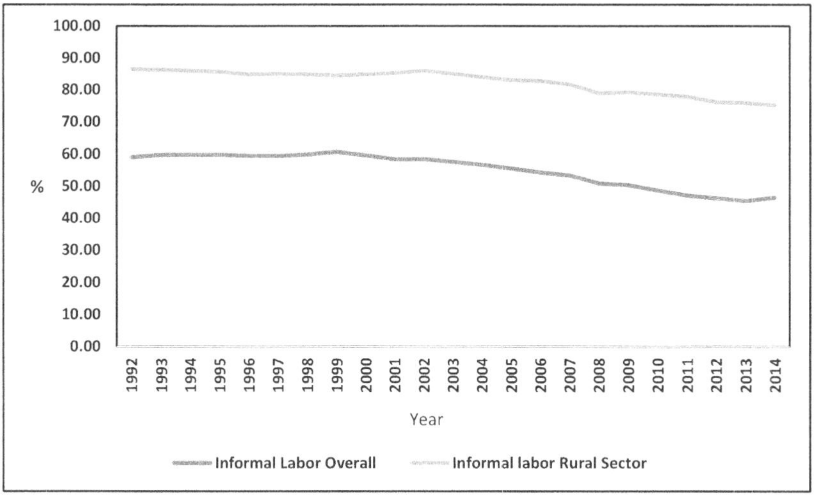

Fig. 8.11 Rate of Informal Employment in Brazil, 1992–2014 (*Source* Elaboration by author using IPEA [2020])

first term. It then began increasing again reaching 46.5% in 2014. Unfortunately, the IBGE has not made the last 5 years available on their website, which is an issue that began with the PT. In any case, to the extent that the variables of unemployment, wages, and poverty worsened during this period, it is most likely that the informal economy has grown again since 2014.

In spite of the socially unacceptable levels of the informal economy in Brazil, the situation in rural areas is even more shocking, reaching levels of 86.5% back in 1992 and declining down to 75% in 2014, which is clearly a disgrace for the twenty-first century. Therefore, it can be argued that in spite of a decline of 10% for the period just mentioned, this is far from a sufficient decline for a country pursuing a new path of development and an area that any government should be giving much greater priority. Unfortunately, the votes from these poorer and rural sectors, often peasants of indigenous or minority populations, are seen as expendable or not relevant. The situation has clearly worsened in recent years, especially with Bolsonaro's government.

There continue to be serious problems in rural areas in terms of worker's rights or lack thereof, causing high unemployment, low wages, extreme levels of informality, and high levels of poverty and inequality. These problems all tie together as an outcome related to the problems of reprimarization as Brazil shifted away from manufacturing, and prioritizing the primary sector, though not achieving improvements for rural workers in general. The worsening conditions in the countryside also have a downward pressure on wages in urban areas as well, and this clearly does not bode well for Brazilian workers in general for the near future.

8.3.2.5 Poverty

Figure 8.12 shows an impressive decline in poverty in Brazil.[13] This improvement is clearly due to a number of key policies and programs on the part of the PT governments, especially the *Bolsa Familia*, which

[13] For most data, but especially that of poverty, it is very important to pay attention to methodological changes, so as to distinguish between real change and a change of methodology. Due to the lack of consistent data for the period being analyzed, the data from the World Bank was used in this instance. However, one must always be careful with their data, given some questionable methods (See Pogge and Reddy 2003). Unfortunately, more and more countries are adopting their methodology, which has a strong ideological bias of aiming to show that especially poverty and unemployment have been reduced with the domination of neoliberalism when in fact it is usually the exact opposite.

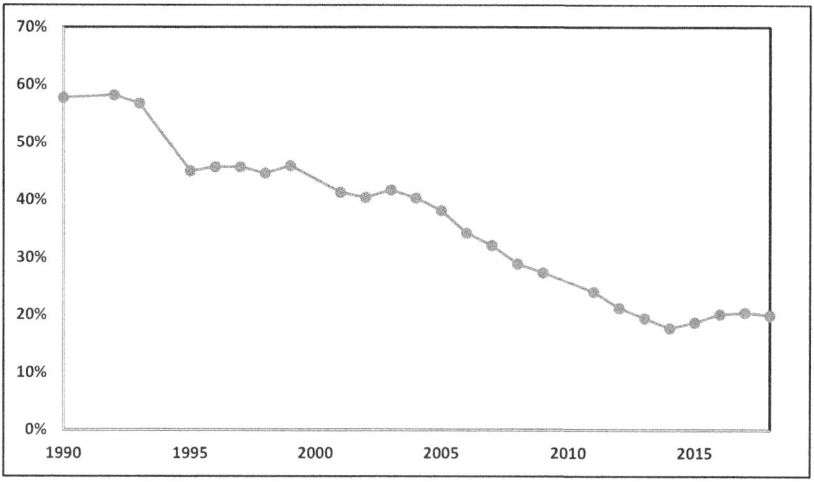

Fig. 8.12 Poverty in Brazil (%): 1990–2019 (*Source* World Bank [2021])

will be discussed in more detail shortly. The Figure below shows the level of poverty declining from 57.8% in 1990 down to 17.7% in 2014, an amazing reduction of 40%, and implying the removal of 75-80 million people out of poverty. This is extremely impressive and to the extent that it was due to social programs, such as *Bolsa Familia*, it is very commendable and something reflecting a change toward a new development path. However, there is still the problem of the need to improve the employment wage situation, which will be revisited shortly.

Most questionable in this data is that in spite of one of the worst crises in recent years, poverty is shown to be 28.9% in 2008, then 27.4% in 2009 (where most countries showed notable increases), no data for 2010 and then a drop to 24%, thus showing a continuous decline of poverty between 2008 and 2010, when anyone who experienced this period in Brazil, including myself, would tell you the opposite took place and most other countries observed an increase in poverty due to the crisis. But such is the nature of what data is available at the present time, including data available from the IBGE, which only gives you a series up until 2014 even though we are already half way through 2020.

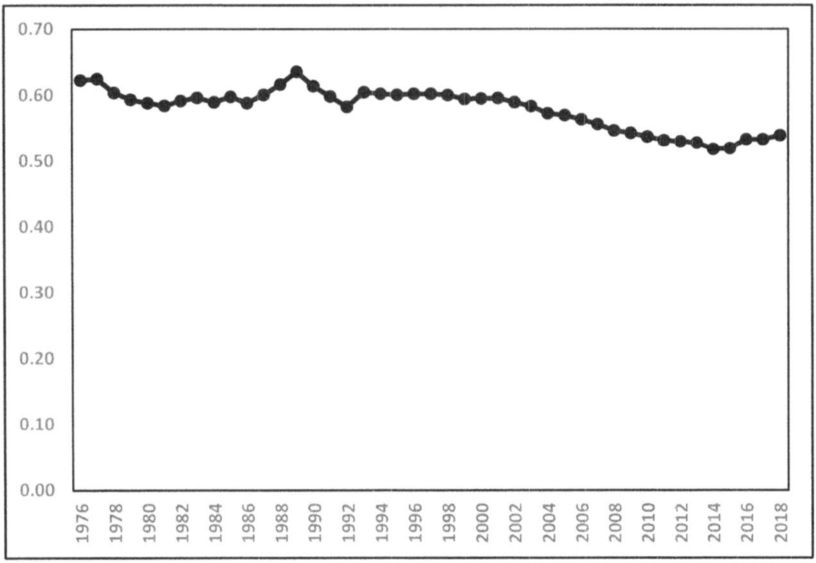

Fig. 8.13 Gini Coefficient in Brazil: 1976–2018 (*Source* Elaboration by the author using data from IPEA [2020] and World Bank [2021])

8.3.2.6 Inequality

In Fig. 8.13 one can clearly see the decline of the Gini coefficient in Brazil from a maximum of 0.63 in 1989 with a steady downward trend toward 0.518 in 2014. In part, this is a reflection of the social programs under Lula and Dilma, and in particular, the program *Bolsa Família*. After 2014, there was a slight increase to .539 in 2018, reflecting the end of Dilma's term, prior to impeachment, and then the government of Temer. It is expected that inequality will continue to increase, especially given the conservative orientation of Bolsonaro, and the conviction on the part of the ruthless elite supporting Bolsonaro that they have had a part of their wealth stolen from them through corruption and accommodation of the "left-wing communists" associated with the PT.

8.3.2.7 Social Programs

From a progressive perspective, one of the most positive initiatives by the administrations of Lula and Dilma was the *Bolsa Familia* program, designed to improve the situation for the Brazilian poor and indigent.

The *Bolsa Familia* program was created in 2003 and converted into Law in 2004, and this program sought to support or help families that were either poor or experiencing extreme poverty, and to improve their access to education and health services. It was basically an income transfer program, providing roughly US$40–80 a month for the poorest of Brazil, totaling some R$27.7 billion, between 2003 and 2007 and reaching over 11 million households. Through 2016, 14 million families had benefitted; 28% of the Brazilian population, with a total investment of 0.5% of GNP. In fact, *Bolsa Familia* is recognized as having been the largest transfer program (welfare program) of its kind in Brazil and in the world for its level of coverage and provision of economic resources. In addition to reducing poverty, it was perhaps even more significant in reducing inequality since it was aimed at the lowest income strata (COPROFAM 2018; Marques et al. 2018; Peixoto 2013).

Several other smaller programs were fused into or extensions of the *Bolsa Família* program, thus combining several other programs designed to provide money for food, gas, and schooling for Brazil's poorest. In addition, there were other programs implemented between 2003 and 2016, the period of Lula and Dilma governments, that focused on reducing poverty, and improving access to health and education. There were a number of social programs aimed at reducing social exclusion: My House, My Life (*Minha Casa Minha Vida*) aimed at obtaining access to housing; one for improving access to the University-PROUNI. In addition to these programs, the PT made major inroads with respect to quota policies for increasing University access for minorities in Brazil, the creation of new universities, and the expansion of public employment in the areas of higher education, health, and Social Security.

Since 2011, the above cases were complemented by other programs with the Brazil Cares Program (*Programa Brasil Carinhoso*) and Brazil without Misery Program (*Plano Brasil sem Miséria*), strengthening the access to education, childcare, free medicine and vitamin supplements, professional training, promotion of solidary economic activities, labor intermediation, and micro-enterprises; in rural zones, technical assistance to agricultural peasant families and construction of cisterns in semi-arid regions.

In spite of all the positives just described regarding the main social program under the PT governments, namely the *Bolsa Família* program, there are some criticism with respect to other priorities. Its budget during 2003–2007 was $27.7 billion, while that paid out to foreign bankers was R$263.3 billion. Thus, service for the foreign debt was almost ten times what was spent to alleviate poverty temporarily. In fact, what Brazil truly needs, is a jobs program to reduce unemployment and improve real wages in order to make a serious dent in addressing its perennial problem of income and wealth inequality and maybe a suspension of interest payments on foreign debt until some basic living conditions are achieved. Such contrasts, provide an unfortunate, though sobering insight with respect to the true priorities of a government allegedly representing the interests of workers. In fact, many have argued that the *Bolsa Família* program was also seen as instrumental in the reelection campaign of Lula in 2006 (also in 2010 and 2014), when the number of families receiving the transfer had almost doubled: increasing from 6.5 million families in March 2005, to 11 million families in March 2007.

In evaluating a progressive vision, of course the support for programs promoting social inclusion, are important, such as the *Bolsa Familia*. However, a welfare program that alleviates poverty in the short run but does not deal with the structural problems that cause poverty, is simply not enough if we are considering alternative development paths. In any case, such programs are not addressing the main problem and more difficult one to resolve, which is the problem of employment and also the high level of informal labor, which continues to be around 50% of workers. Similar to Argentina, Brazil also tried to reduce their dependence on the IMF and thus reduced their debt with the international institution for a number of years, but then the foreign debt has increased significantly, once again.

The next set of issues to examine are the impacts on the environment as a result of the current paths of development, for both Argentina and Brazil, which can arguably be considered more of a continuity of reprimarization and deindustrialization. In the case of Brazil, this also includes a mix of some developmentalist policies and still with certain neoliberal policies in place. In contrast, Argentina made more of a break from neoliberal policies, especially as they were coming out of a depression, and there was not the same commitment or promise to finance, in spite of the influence of the *patria financiera*[14] in Argentina.

[14] The reference to the *patria financiera* in Argentina was described in Chapter 5; most notable has been the degree to which this financial sector is intertwined with transnational agribusiness and finance.

8.4 Neodevelopmentalism, Reprimarization, and the Environment[15]

As seen above, the experiences of the progressive governments of the Kirchners in Argentina and Lula and Dilma in Brazil led to a continuation of the tendency of reprimarization, in spite of the "new development path," namely, neodevelopmentalism. This section examines the consequences for the environment, as a result of the reprimarization tendencies in Argentina and Brazil. There are a range of key impacts on the environment that are connected to this tendency and which deserve examination, the most notable being: (1) deforestation of the Amazon Rain Forest linked to the expansion of lumber, minerals, petroleum, cattle, and soy; (2) air, water, and soil pollution as a result of mining and petroleum; and the use of chemicals in agriculture, where numerous agrochemicals are employed, especially for soy; (3) soil erosion as a result of mining and soy and the eventual risk of desertification; and (4) major socioenvironmental issues associated with the construction and operations of hydroelectric power plants or dams, often strongly tied to mining, as will be seen in the case of Brazil. Before discussing deforestation of the Amazon, the discussion of the environmental problems associated with soy and pesticides will be considered first.

8.4.1 Environmental Problems with Soy, Pesticides, and GMOs

In Chapter 7 the expansion of soy in both Argentina and Brazil and the particular connection to the growth of China and its increasing role with both countries was examined. The main environmental issues associated with soy are the health impacts of agrochemicals, such as fertilizers, pesticides, and herbicides, especially glyphosate. As described in the previous chapter, the genetically modified seed "Roundup Ready" is a variant of a soybean seed particularity resistant to glyphosate. As a result, the intensive use of RR "*zero tillage*" seeds increased productivity and reduced the level of erosion initially. However, after some time, the opposite occurs, the use of the toxic cocktail ends up depleting the soil of nutrients, particularly impacting the microbial mechanisms, necessary for a healthy subsoil. The

[15] Parts of the text in this section are derived from an RRPE article (Cooney 2016) and also Sacher and Cooney (2019).

reality is that pesticides do not just kill the particular pest that is hurting one's productivity; in the right doses, they can kill many other forms of life, be it other insects, worms, or subsoil microbes key for maintaining fertility. The soil eventually suffers an erosion worse than the initial one which was avoided, and destroys key aspects of the biosphere.

In fact, according to Pengue (2005) the intensive use of fertilizers, associated with soybean production, "increased from 300,000 metric tons in 1990 to 2,500,000 tons in 1999." Some have argued, that as a result, the Argentine pampas have actually experienced a decline in soil fertility and also an increase in soil erosion (Prego et al. 1997), Moreover, given the design of Roundup Ready, which involves intensive use of the pesticide glyphosate, over time this results in also causing weeds or *malezas* to become glyphosate-tolerant and therefore requiring much more glyphosate. Farmers argue that they need to use three times or more glyphosate now compared to when they started growing soy in the 1990s. Evidence of this trend is confirmed in Fig. 8.14, showing the major increase of pesticide imports into Argentina, many of which are imported from China. In 1990, the total is almost 13 million tons, but by the year 2017, this has increased to a total of more than 97 million tons.

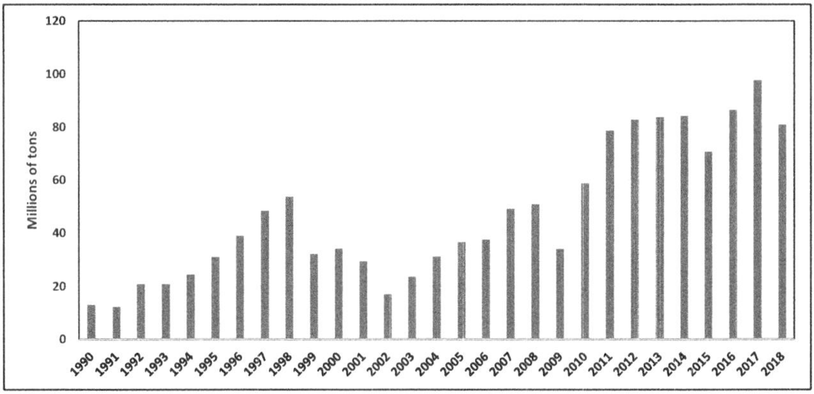

Fig. 8.14 Pesticides Imported by Argentina: 1990–2018 (millions of tons) (*Source* FAO [2020])

There is also the issue of the costs of inputs required for this new technological package of genetically modified zero-tillage seeds (GMOs), be it for soy, maize, or cotton. This is a key economic issue, especially in the context of the discussion on ground rent, as discussed in Chapter 7. Nevertheless, environmental and health issues may constitute an even greater concern. The use of pesticides also affects the agricultural workers applying the pesticide or working the fields, and moreover, pesticides are transported through the air, impacting adjacent communities, and causing general health problems, as well as more serious illnesses, such as cancer or anencephaly (Pengue 2005). A major concern is the exposure to pesticides which have been an increasing problem for air and water pollution in Argentina (as well as Brazil), and is the basis for a health crisis in the province of Entre Rios due to glyphosate getting into the water table. In addition, there is the concern for products which have the residues of glyphosate, be it oatmeal sold by Quaker or the glyphosate appearing in cotton products, whether cotton for health and medical uses, or for children, as well as cotton used for tampons among other health products.

These are issues which many a politician attempts to ignore, given the economic importance of soy, but these are problems that are not going to go away, in fact they are often worsening, and should force society to take a close look at what risks "modern technology" are creating for our lives. There is a need for a very serious evaluation of the implications of transgenic soy, including the agrotoxics, for all of society, for both Argentina and Brazil. Besides the consequences just considered, the combination of the expansion of soy, cattle, lumber, and mining in the north of Brazil, are risking the destruction of the lungs of the planet, namely the Amazon Rain Forest.[16]

[16] The Amazon is the longest and largest river in the world, and the Amazon Rain Forest is the largest rainforest on the planet with an area of almost 8 million hectares, extending over nine different countries. The Amazon Rain Forest is shared between Brazil, Peru, Ecuador, Colombia, Bolivia, Venezuela, Guyana, Suriname and the French Guyana, and the Brazilian Amazon constitutes 64.4% of the total.

8.4.2 *Deforestation of the Amazon Rain Forest*[17]

The Amazon currently constitutes a frontier for capital accumulation, with a strong presence of TNCs. In recent decades, the economic expansion in the Amazon has been increasingly integrated with world markets, primarily for soy, cattle, lumber, and minerals.[18] A common trajectory is the removal of trees for the lumber industry, in order to establish cattle ranching. This is often followed by the planting of an intermediate crop prior to the planting of soy, given the need for reestablishing the nutrients in the soil lost during livestock production. Although soy is heralded as a green and environmentally friendly alternative to cattle ranching, it is often the motor, combined with cattle, behind the process of deforestation in the Amazon, especially given its higher profitability.

As new spaces for capital accumulation become available in the Amazon rainforest through the occupation of new lands (or reoccupation of land used for extensive cattle production), the clearly undesirable "collateral damage" is the clearing of major swathes of the Amazon. Such environmentally irresponsible behavior may only be curbed through increased pressure by social movements, serious enforcement by the Brazilian government, or, perhaps more importantly as global public awareness spreads, the threat of not being able to sell their products on the global marketplace. Free market forces are proving wholly inadequate to achieve a solid and lasting reduction in deforestation in this ecologically crucial region.

The annual deforestation rates in the Brazilian Amazon averaged a disturbing 22,091 square kilometers per year from 2000 to 2004, although this rate was reduced to an average value of 12,692 square kilometers for the period from 2005 to 2009. Though deforestation rates may have slowed for a number of years, significant deforestation is recently increasing again, as the circumstances that brought it about have by no means disappeared from the region. The cause of deforestation cannot be merely reduced to the greed of ranchers or soy farmers; rather it is a consequence of the social nature of capitalist accumulation combined with new global competitive conditions driving it forward—a force that

[17] Parts of the discussion in this section have been derived from an article which examines reprimarization in the Amazon and deforestation (Rivero and Cooney 2010).

[18] The discussion of the expansion of soy, cattle and mining in the Amazon was discussed in Chapter 7.

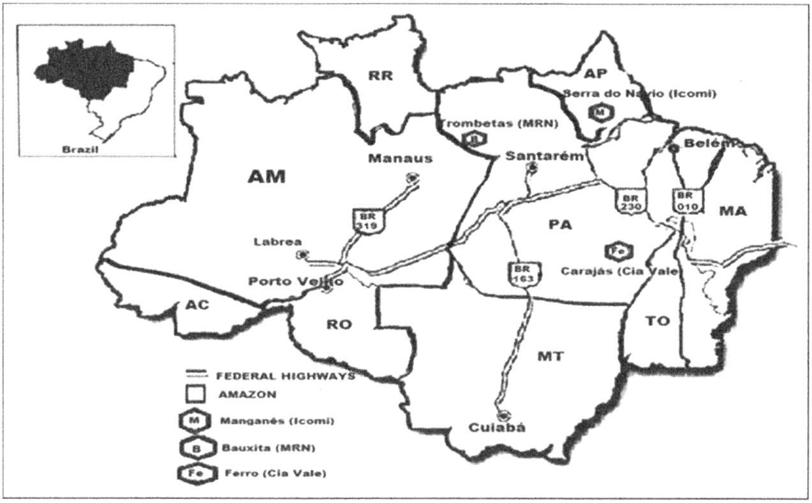

Fig. 8.15 Map of the Brazilian Amazon. *Legend*: AC—Acre; AM—Amazonas; AP—Amapá; MA—Maranhão; MT—Mato Grosso; PA—Pará; RO—Rondônia; RR—Roraima; TO—Tocantins; [these are the states that constitute the legal category of the Amazon in Brazil- (Amazônia Legal)] (*Source* IBGE [2015] modified by my colleague José Raimundo Trindade)

has thus far overcome efforts to control deforestation either by NGOs or the Brazilian government[19].

As described in Chapter 7, the three states in the Amazon where deforestation has been greatest are Mato Grosso, Rondônia and Pará, which can be identified in Fig. 8.15, using the legend. These states are also where the growth of cattle and or soy has been the strongest in recent decades. Moreover, it is also worth noting that the greatest level of deforestation in 2019 was in the state of Roraima in the north, and this is exactly where they are currently experiencing a mining boom. On the map above (Fig. 8.15), Roraima is identified as RR.

[19] Although there were forces promoted by the PT government leading to increased deforestation, there were also forces and ministries making efforts to reduce deforestation. At present, it has clearly become dominated by the first set of forces and Bolsonaro even attempted to shut down the Environmental Ministry, and upon failing to do so, placed a Minister there, Ricardo Salles, that is more committed to deforest than to the contrary (Marques de Souza 2019a).

At present, the Bolsonaro government is doing its best to ignore international pressure and as reflected by his own self-given nickname, Captain Chainsaw, is committed to the "development" of the Amazon, as in huge profits, but at the expense of the populations that live there, the flora, the fauna, and the Amazon rainforest overall. Not surprisingly, the rate of deforestation has jumped up in recent years, and according to INPE (*Instituto Nacional de Pesquisas Espaciais*) exceeded 10,000 square kilometers this year, the first time since 2008 (Butler 2020). In fact, between 2018 and 2019 deforestation increased by 34.4%. A number of the problems that started with the Temer government, have clearly worsened with Bolsonaro. Converting many protected lands into ones available for cattle ranchers or other sectors has been one major problem. A second problem is scaling back personnel available for the enforcement of illegal logging activity, and reducing penalties for those found guilty. In Fig. 8.16 below, shifts in deforestation can be observed, including the increase in deforestation in the last couple of years, since Temer and Bolsonaro have been in government.

The issue of deforestation is not just a Brazilian issue, but is especially relevant due to concerns of climate change for the planet as a whole. In addition, there has been significant deforestation taking place in Argentina; for example, in the Gran Chaco of Argentina, there was a total of 5 million hectares razed in the last 25 years. The Gran Chaco region

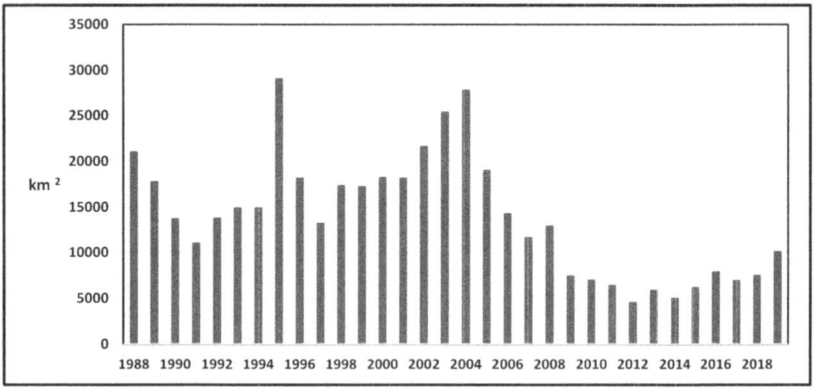

Fig. 8.16 Deforestation in the Brazilian Amazon: 1988–2019 (km^2) (*Source* PRODES/INPE [2020])

in Argentina includes the Chaco province, and parts of the provinces of Santiago del Estero and Salta. First, there were droughts in the Chaco during several years, including 2019, and most recently in 2020 it has suffered major floods. These are results linked to the problems of soil erosion and loss of nutrients described earlier in the context of heavy pesticide use necessary for the production of soy. In fact, the expansion of soy in this region actually began in 1996 with transgenic soy and other crops.

In Chapter 7, the amazing levels of expansion of cattle and soy were examined. This is clearly connected to the problem of deforestation and as can be observed in Fig. 8.16, the level of deforestation was almost 22,000 then more than 25,000 and almost 28,000 km^2 in 2004, and thus the pressure on Brazil and within Brazil to implement better control for illegal logging and other activities linked to soy. This was key in pushing for the moratorium on Soy (SoyM) declared in 2006. Basically, it was a voluntary agreement for major soybean traders to sign the SoyM, and agreeing not to purchase soy grown on lands deforested after July 2006. Evidently, the great majority of soy was produced on lands deforested but this was an effort to reduce new deforestation. As can be expected, as it was a voluntary agreement, it had some impact but other pressure by environmental groups inside and outside Brazil was more significant and from 2004 to 2012 there was a significant drop of new deforestation. However, after 2012 there has been an increasing tendency and as mentioned breaking the 10,000 km^2 mark in 2019 once again. In spite of the Moratorium, the area planted for soy has quadrupled since 2006 (Rodrigues 2018).

Evidently, there are numerous activities that contribute to the problems of deforestation and not just cattle and soy, though they are the primary drivers. Evidently, there is an interest in logging but other key sectors are mining, petroleum and gas exploration and the hydroelectric power plant projects which require major deforestation and expropriations.

In addition to the expropriation of communities, be it peasants or indigenous people, there is also the environmental destruction, effecting both the human populations and issues such as hunting or fishing, but also the impact on the flora and fauna. A significant impact of these activities tied to deforestation implies a major reduction in biodiversity and this becomes even worse as the dominant monoculture such as soy and other transgenic crops continue to expand.[20]

8.4.3 *Climate Change*

The issue of climate change has many dimensions and debates but it is a known fact that the Amazon rain forest constitutes the largest carbon sink on the planet and so the process of deforestation clearly implies a worsening situation of carbon dioxide, given the reduction of a carbon sink, not to mention the effect of the generation of methane gases through livestock farming. In addition, in the instances of petroleum extraction, such as what is planned for with the Solimões oil and gas project, in the Amazonas state (see Fearnside 2020), will also extract more petroleum and natural gas, eventually contributing to additionally global warming through the burning of these fossil fuels.

The fact that many of the pessimistic predictions in terms of the increase of the ppm (parts per million) of carbon dioxide in the atmosphere and the increase in the oceans' temperature and the melting ice and glaciers especially in the Arctic and also Antarctica are already occurring, it appears that the worst-case scenarios are increasing their probabilities (NYT, July 2020). In any case, whether human activity is the main driver or even if it is exacerbated by sunspot activity, the right course is employing the precautionary principle and this means not to worsen what can be avoided. This implies that continued deforestation is not the best option, especially as there are alternatives to such expansion in the Amazon and secondly, we (humans) will be better off reducing or ending our dependence on fossil fuels sooner as opposed to later. The concerns for climate change and consequences, which could threaten our species very existence, not the planet, are all valid arguments to advocate reducing deforestation and preventing an expansion thereof, as is currently taking place with Bolsonaro.

Prior to examining mega-mining and the environment it is appropriate to return to a theoretical discussion from Chapter 2, namely the 2nd contradiction of capitalism as developed by O'Connor. Due to space and time limitations this will not be as extensive a discussion as it deserves. Previously, it was argued that the basis of the 2nd contradiction in a

[20] This has been exacerbated as a result of the increase of forest fires in the Amazon, with Bolsonaro in power and especially since August of 2019 (see Chapter 9).

nutshell is that the problems of reproduction, translated as the broad sense of the environment, human and natural, if you will, comes into contradiction with the drive for accumulation with the profit motive. The worsening conditions of the environment end up leading to increases in costs to the point that they actually can jeopardize, or at the very least, worsen profitability. This is a similar, yet distinct, version of the falling rate of profit argument in Marx. The criticism made previously was that it is not clear to what extent environmental impacts will necessarily lead to a decline in profitability for capitalist firms. It was argued that it is more likely that the global TNCs, given their economic and political power, at present, will be able to shift or defer the burden or problem or paying for the cleanup to local communities, workers, or countries. The upshot tends to mean that capitalist firms experience minimal negative impact in terms of their bottom line; recent history seems to be more supportive of this latter view.

Nevertheless, at some point, the current domination of neoliberalism can come to an end, just as major social movements changed the balance of power between capital and labor for a number of decades in the twentieth century, a global environmental movement could achieve similar success. The one area where O'Connor's argument may have the greatest validity is in the context of global climate change, given the fact that the environmental damage is potentially so great that production conditions could radically change and capitalist firms and even TNCs could end up experiencing a profitability crisis. As previously alluded to, if there were a new rejuvenated global environmental movement, shifting the balance of forces toward human rights and away from corporate rights, then scenarios vindicating O'Connor's thesis could take place. This would probably require advances at the level of laws and restrictions on the part of TNCs, so that many of the damages and ecological devastation that has been caused by TNCs, would have to be paid for by them. At present, and considering the processes of reprimarization in Brazil and Argentina, the environmental damages and problems do not tend to be paid for by the TNCs, although there are instances, such as the cases of a couple of recent landslides associated with Vale in Brazil, where they have been held financially responsible. In any case, the importance of understanding the environmental implications of economic processes, is arguably fundamental, especially in struggling toward a red-green front to promote the transition away from capitalism and eventually toward a post-capitalist world.

8.4.4 Environmental Impacts and Resistance in Mining[21]

In Latin America, at least 14 countries made changes to accommodate TNC investment in mining in recent decades. Between 1991 and 1999, Latin America went from being the fourth to the first most common destination for investment in mineral exploration, as a result of a 500% increase in investment. The amazing growth of China then led to the surge in the prices of metals at the world level, quadrupling between 2002 and 2007. As a result, many Latin American countries, experienced an increased role of the State in mining and associated infrastructure projects, be it for highways, waterways, or hydroelectric dams. The importance of the latter is clearly related to the intensive need for electricity for the processing of minerals. This has brought about a number of serious social and environmental conflicts during recent years, as discussed below. Another environmental problem with mining involves the generation of toxic waste, the processing and chemical treatment of thousands of tons of rock, which lead to substantial quantities of both solid and liquid waste. There are diverse forms of chronic contamination and accidents which impact the air, soil and water, deforestation, and irreversible changes to the water table, etc. These are all issues generating negative effects for public health.

According to the Observatory of Mining Conflicts in Latin America (OCMAL),[22] in 2020, there were 294 social conflicts cited around the mining areas in Latin America, reflecting the negative impacts on peasant and indigenous communities. In the case of Brazil there are 26 cases listed, with half of them being in the Amazon. In the case of Argentina, OCMAL documented 28 social conflicts linked to large-scale mining projects over the period of the last 2 decades, from the provinces in the north, such as Jujuy through Patagonia, such as Santa Cruz. There are numerous examples of communities becoming organized around environmental issues related to mining and soy among other issues, many involved with the Union of Citizen Assemblies (Unión de Asambleas Ciudadanas-UAC), composed of concerned communities all

[21] For more on reprimarization in Latin America, especially for mining, see Cooney and Sacher (2015).

[22] See OCMAL (2020). https://mapa.conflictosmineros.net/ocmal_db-v2/, accessed on July 28th, 2020.

over Argentina.[23] There are many other relevant cases of serious conflicts and resistance in Argentina and Brazil, but due to space limitations, they cannot be elaborated upon here.

Numerous articles, books, and other academic studies around the world provided evidence of the broad variety and scope of the impacts produced by mega-mining at a political, economic, environmental, social, cultural and psychosocial, and public health level. This documentation demonstrates how the massive removal of rocks (typically various tens of thousands of metric tons a day, and up to hundreds of thousands in the case of the biggest mines) as well as the use of toxic reagents release large quantities of pollutants and acidifies the environment with the phenomenon of acid rock drainage. These contaminations usually have irreversible consequences for water (in qualitative as well as quantitative terms), air, soil, and the ecosystems and biodiversity in general. The pollutions come from chronic release of pollutants in the environment as well as accidents, typically with the breakdown of tailings dams[24] containing the toxic wastes as a consequence of earthquakes, flooding, and human negligence. This documentation also shows how the pollution generated by mega-mining can affect areas located at tens or even hundreds of kilometers away from the extraction sites, as toxins can be transported through the air or water. The industrial activities also contribute to sound pollution and are a source of intensive deforestation and biodiversity loss.

With these various forms of toxic pollution, mega-mining generates disastrous impacts on public health, such as cancer, skin and respiratory diseases, nervous and reproductive disorders; serious pathologies at the level of psychological health and including the spread of sexually transmitted diseases. Specific sectors of the population may be more exposed to these impacts. Recent research around large-scale copper mining projects in Ecuador show that the impacts affect women and children in a differentiated and more serious manner (Sacher 2017). Mega-mining presence and activities tend to go hand in hand with militarization and the presence

[23] See Página 12, 18 December 2015. "Por el crecimiento, pero verde."

[24] A tailings dam is typically an earth-fill embankment dam used to store by-products of mining operations after separating the ore from the gangue. Tailings can be liquid, solid, or a slurry of fine particles, and are usually highly toxic and potentially radioactive.

of a large population of young male workers. This leads to the intensification of pre-existing patriarchal dynamics, with degraded living conditions for women.

The large-scale pollution associated with mining, particularly the pollution of water, often only deepens and intensifies the negative impacts of these dispossession and migration processes. In a study by Sacher in 2015, it was shown how the dispossession processes implied by mega-mining activities are not only associated with the massive land grabbing, but also with the destruction of the environment and the hoarding or contamination of vital resources, water being the most illustrative case. From this perspective, it is appropriate to consider the destruction of the environment in general as accompanying the processes of dispossession in the context of mining operations, affecting more directly and dramatically the peasant and indigenous communities, which are particularly vulnerable to the destruction of ecosystems and the depletion of aquifers. Moreover, there are the indirect impacts for urban populations that depend on remote areas for their drinking water supply (Sacher 2015; Galafassi 2010; Machado Aráoz 2010; Garibay Orozco 2010; Perreault 2013; Gordon and Webber 2008).

8.4.5 Hydroelectric Power Plants

With respect to environmental problems associated with the tendency of reprimarization, just as relevant has been the installation of hydroelectric power plants. The latter lead to major displacements and problems of loss of biodiversity, environmental problems due to shifting the natural flows of rivers and the subsequent impacts for farming, hunting, and other activities of peasant and indigenous communities in the vicinity of the land or territory which has been destroyed or transformed in order to construct or operationalize the dams. There have been numerous conflicts related to several hydroelectric dams, where the demand for electricity was more closely linked to mining activity, especially as mining is electricity intensive and thus often the driver behind the arrival of a new hydroelectric dam project.

There have been major conflicts, such as Rio São Francisco in the northeast of Brazil and Belo Monte, in the State of Pará. In the case of Belo Monte, it is the third largest hydroelectric dam in the world, based on electricity potential (4571 MW/h) and costing over US$11 billion. In spite of what seems like a great advance, this project and its functioning have been embroiled in conflict for many years even before construction began in 2011. Even though Lula was in opposition to the construction of the Itaipu hydroelectric plant back in the day, he recently was the main cheerleader for the Belo Monte dam in spite of large social opposition. As a result of this construction there was a displacement of 24,000 people, many of which were from peasant and indigenous communities.

Given the negative outcomes, from the flooding of 500 square kilometers and the expropriation of a significant population, this clearly fits the concept of accumulation by dispossession, as described in the previous chapter. There was also a huge increase in prostitution, drug use, poverty and violence, which came along with this engineering feat. In addition, there was an increase of femicides, increasing from 6.1 to 9.6% between 2008 and 2015. Other concerns include loss of biodiversity, lower quality of life in the surroundings of the dam, between noise and a change of habitat, impacting hunting and agricultural activities. And lastly, is the concern of the impact of reservoirs and increases in the generation of methane gas. When the principal drive for such a hydroelectric power plant is the generation of electricity for the benefit of mining operations in the region and when the local populations are clearly in opposition, one needs call into question whether such developmentalism is for the benefit of the people, or more for the lining of the pockets of the big contractors and transnational corporations.

The other infamous case in recent years in Brazil was that of Rio São Francisco where there have been social protests over a number of years, critical of agribusiness's disproportional access to water but also the problem of pesticides which contaminates all the plants and animals in the region, not to mention humans. Thus, local populations that live near the river, not only have reduced access to water, but their livelihood and surroundings are negatively impacted. Thus, hydroelectric power plants do not only cause the problem of reduced water supply, but combined with accommodating the accumulation needs of mining or agrobusiness companies are also responsible for a number of other social and environmental problems. Another major issue, for large projects like hydroelectric dams, as well as for major infrastructural projects or for petroleum exploration as in the offshore Pre-Sal discovery between Rio and Santa Catarina, is the many opportunities for serious corruption with international financial institutions, be it the World Bank or BID (Banco

Interamericano de Desarrollo), among other financial entities, such as Banco Santander or HSBC.[25]

8.4.6 *Petroleum and Gas*

Petroleum and gas exploration are other sectors associated with the tendencies of reprimarization in Argentina and Brazil and there have been a number of new discoveries. In Brazil, the state oil company, Petrobras recently discovered Pre-Sal oil deposits in the Rio de Janeiro area while in Argentina, YPF expects major expansions with the Vaca Muerta oilfields in Neuquén. In addition to the problems associated with displacement of populations, often peasant and indigenous communities, many of the same environmental problems mentioned in the case of mining projects are the same: loss of biodiversity, use of toxic chemicals, jeopardizing health and safety of workers and surrounding communities, in addition to the problem of deforestation required first to obtain access to an oilfield. Another major problem is that of oil spills, and Brazil has had a number of recent disasters, not to mention landslides in the context of mining operations, in particular Vale. In the case of oil spills, the worst ever in Brazil took place in August 2019, impacting 4334 km of coastline in 11 states between the Northeast and Southeast and destroying the livelihood of fishing communities, not to mention tourism and the health of people living in and around these seaside communities.

As TNCs, such as Vale, or state companies, such as Petrobras or YPF, in seeking to cut costs, and improve profits, make poor decisions, involving high risks. Such poor planning and greed lead to results, that can end up being major environmental and human disasters. The example above of the worst oil spill ever for Brazil, which has yet to have a clear resolution of who is responsible for cleaning it up, or in the case of Vale and the landslide caused by the breaking of a dam; a water reservoir for Vale's mining operations in Minas Gerais, leading to the destruction of whole communities and many deaths, not to mention environmental impacts, are problematic and not uncommon. In this latter case, the warnings about this risk had been communicated several times, but nothing was done. Although Vale is having to pay in this instance, way too often these companies get away with impunity and the poor communities pay the price. There are numerous problems associated with petroleum and gas

[25] See Gudynas (2019), for a discussion on the issue of corruption and large projects, be it mining hydroelectric dams or the drilling for oil.

extraction, independently of specific disasters, just the interruption and displacement of pipelines and problems of pollution, but there are the range of problems associated with climate change and the concerns of our overdependence on fossil fuels.

Due to time limitations an analysis of biomass or biofuels was not examined and yet it is another activity which has expanded significantly, especially in Brazil, including the Amazon in recent years. At times, it can appear, and is, a useful alternative to fossil fuels, substituting ethanol for gasoline or as in the case of many hybrid cars, being able to use both types of fuel. However, there is also the false biomass examples of green energy, as presented in the film by Michael Moore's protégé, Jeff Gibbs, exposing a number of "pro-environment" green capitalists. Each case needs to be examined carefully to determine its direct and indirect contributions to environmental problems or to environmental solutions. For further discussion, see Fearnside (2020) and NRDC (2020).

As this chapter began, an examination of neodevelopmentalism was made, first from a theoretical angle and then followed by a socioeconomic assessment. Having just presented the environmental impacts of recent years in both Argentina and Brazil, the majority of the problems are strongly linked to reprimarization. Therefore, there seems to be a contradiction between a development approach, referred to as neodevelopmentalism, associated with sustainable development and a better environment, and the real-world tendency of reprimarization, which was promoted by these neodevelopmentalist governments. In the next section an attempt will be made to provide a summary of this debate in evaluating the nature of the recent period in Brazil with the PT and in Argentina with the Kirchners.

8.5 Summary of Social and Environmental Impacts of Neodevelopmentalism

Above we evaluated the socioeconomic impacts of the governments of Lula and Dilma with the PT in Brazil and that of the Kirchners in Argentina, and thereby making an assessment of neodevelopmentalism. On the one hand it was evident that both countries made a break from neoliberal orthodoxy, though with varying degrees, but at the same time there was a continuation, if not deepening, of the processes of deindustrialization and reprimarización. In the case of deindustrialization, during Nestor Kirchner's first term, manufacturing as a percentage of GDP increased by 2% to roughly 17% but during the following five years it declined by one percent (see Fig. 7.1). In the case of Brazil, there was an increase of manufacturing as a percentage of GDP by roughly one percent between 2003 and 2004 just shy of 18% but it then decreased down to 12% in the year 2015 (see Fig. 7.2).

Several orthodox neoliberal policies were continued for a longer time in Brazil than in Argentina, for example, during Lula's government, the rates of interest continued being the highest in the world and also a clearly overvalued currency was maintained. It was only with the government of Dilma when the rate of interest was seriously reduced, and strongly linked to this, was the increase in the rate of exchange of the *real*. Moreover, during Lula's first term there was more of a continuity of neoliberalism, and this is reflected in both the Economics Minister, Antonio Palocci (*Ministro de Fazenda*) and the head of the Central Bank, Henrique Meirelles, but over time, and more so with Dilma, changes took place which reflected less neoliberal orthodoxy and a government oriented toward a greater role of the State in the economy in terms of investment, production, and especially infrastructure.

As discussed above in Sect. 8.2, the defenders of neodevelopmentalism argue that it is necessary to have a strong state and a strong market in order to promote solid growth and social inclusion and many have argued that the industrial protection associated with ISI of the twentieth century is unnecessary today as one needs to have a more neoliberal economy. This perspective seems to have resonated with a number of the economists of both countries, though more so in Brazil, in spite of the problems elaborated earlier. Nevertheless, such a view can be rather consistent with both a path of reprimarization, and greater coherence and integration with the interests of transnational capital. The point is not to present just how neoliberal these governments were, though this is relevant, given many claims, which suggest that neoliberalism came to an end, but rather, what were their main priorities, as evident in reality, not just from speeches.

In terms of breaking from neoliberal policies, it cannot be argued that either country broke from a neoliberal trade policy, given the fact that being members of the WTO, a country is locked into a neoliberal approach. In accordance with the WTO, tariff protection and subsidies geared to favorably assist national firms and industries differentially from TNCs or firms from other countries, are subject to sanctions by those countries (see Rodrik [2018], Khor [2006], Edelman [2020]). In other words, the WTO will not sanction a country, but provides a legal framework, based on their rules, that a country, such as Japan, who took Canada to court to eliminate a program in Ontario giving incentives and subsidies to firms for the production of solar panels (see Klein 2014).

The role of transnational corporations at times was questioned or criticized by Lula, Nestor, and Cristina, but it was clear that these governments were disposed to accommodate the majority of the TNC's demands, and in many ways this is necessary if one does not wish to be excluded and are only one country battling against an oligopoly block of TNCs. In terms of finance and monetary issues, evidently Argentina was more willing to or needed to break from being a good pupil, given their debt situation and coming out of a depression. For example, Argentina did not follow neoliberal rules with respect to controls over foreign exchange or the battle with the Vulture-Funds[26] in terms of the renegotiation of Argentine debt. However, they did follow the IMF's demands in 2003, when Nestor Kirchner established a 3–4% primary surplus, in spite of coming out of a depression.

In contrast, Brazil played a significant role in facilitating the major flows of finance, into and out of Brazil, with an arbitrage scheme, and therefore keeping the highest rate of interest in the world for numerous years. With respect to their primary surplus, the Lula government was committed to increase it and kept it in the range of 4–5%, clearly a rather neoliberal stance, as it was even higher than what the IMF was demanding. Moreover, concerns with capital flight were notable for both countries and it is difficult to identify for which country it was a greater concern. Let us now turn to the economic results presented above.

In terms of growth, Argentina had a significant recovery after the depression of 2001–2003 and observed major growth of industry through at least 2008. After that, there was the global crisis of 2008–2010 with a notable drop, though followed by a major leap to 10% GDP growth, seemingly an outlier. The period after 2008 as a whole was clearly distinct from that between 2003 and 2008, as growth oscillated between plus and minus two to three percent. For Brazil, growth was less than auspicious, though stronger than the Cardozo period preceding it. Nevertheless, Brazil also suffered during the global crisis and similarly

[26] Vulture funds (or fondos Buitres in Spansih) refers to the high-risk speculative capital which purchases debt of countries with serious economic problems and which try and squeeze countries of the periphery to pay up in spite of economic crisis or even depression, as was the case of Argentina. After 14 years of holding out, an agreement was made between Argentina and the Vulture Funds, and associated with the most recognized vulture: Thomas Griesa from New York.

experienced a leap in 2010 to 7.5%, but after that, there were a couple years of acceptable growth, followed by a recessionary trend, if not anemic growth, especially after 2014.

At the beginning of Nestor Kirchner's term, emerging out of crisis, it is understandable that the labor market was rather difficult, although there is the link between his election victory, promising a swing to the left and an improvement for the situation of the working classes and poor. So, in spite of starting out with very low wages in 2003, which were 80% of the value of real wages in 1993, they grew steadily till 2013, as can be observed in Fig. 8.2, and this corresponded to 160% of real wages in 1993. However, after that they began to decline as economic growth had become less solid and stable, and after 2015 it was even worse, as the Macri government definitely did not have working-class real wages as a priority. With respect to unemployment and underemployment these declined from 2003 through 2013 as well, reflecting growth rates, connected to the commodities boom beginning in 2002, though evidently fading by 2013.

In the case of real wages in Brazil, unemployment was quite high when the PT came to power but declined significantly from roughly 10% down to 6.5% in 2012, at which point it began to grow as economic problems grew as well as political instability. In terms of the informal economy, this declined in general from roughly 60% down to below 50%, but unfortunately the informal economy in rural areas remained obstinately high, having been close to 90% in the early 1990s but only dropping to roughly 75% in 2014. This remains a serious concern for Brazilian society, reflecting the problems of the labor market, especially in the poorer states and rural areas.

In the case of real wages, in Brazil, the official statistics show a notable increase for metropolitan areas, roughly a 4.77% annual increase from 2003 through 2014, before declining. Nevertheless, this series does not reflect the whole country. In comparing this data with that of Fig. 6.6, in rough terms the level of real wages reached in 2014 reflects an increase of approximately 20% compared to 2003 and therefore is still less than 80% of the level of real wages in 1985. Though not shown, the level of wages in rural areas is much lower than the series presented and remains a critical area that needs to improve, in addition to wages in general. Another concern, from the perspective of workers and the poor, is the gap between the Official Minimum Wage and the Necessary Minimum Wage in Brazil, as calculated by DIEESE and as shown in Fig. 8.9, implying a significantly worsening gap, even through the years of the PT.

Nevertheless, if there were limits to how much labor could gain under PT governments, things clearly worsened under Temer[27] and one should expect far less, in spite of the needs of the population, to have improvements transpire under Bolsonaro or other conservative governments in the short term. In fact, the view by many of the elite, is that the share going to labor increased by too much and thus led to the revolt on the part of the Brazilian Congress against Dilma, contributing to her downfall (see Marquetti et al. 2016).

Lastly, consider poverty and inequality in the two countries: poverty declined significantly, as expected, after such a devastating depression in Argentina, dropping from close to 60% to less than 30% by 2011. Poverty was a growing concern during the last years of Cristina Fernandez but a greater increase, reaching 35%, has taken place under Macri. As mentioned above, in the case of Brazil, the decline in poverty was very significant declining from around 40% to below 20% in 2014, even in spite of some doubts with respect to shifts in the methodology. As far as the Gini coefficient and inequality in Brazil, the worst point was in 2003 (.53) but since then a decline down to .41 in 2014 was achieved with some minor increases since.

Most notable for Argentina was the increase of wealth for the top decile from 1980 to 2002, growing from 30 to 40% of all income in Argentina (ECLAC 2004). At present in 2019, the wealthiest decile earns roughly 33% of all income and that corresponds to 21 times what the poorest decile earns. As far as inequality, Brazil was able to achieve a major decline especially with the social program aimed to reduce poverty for the most vulnerable, namely the *Bolsa Família*, and this is in spite of the fact that the wealthiest decile or 5% were actually improving their percentage, especially reflected by record profits in the banking and finance sector for numerous years during Lula's tenure.

It is quite common today, in many countries of the periphery, to argue that accommodating the transnationals or the elite is a necessary evil in order to achieve growth and foreign exchange required for social programs. However, when the budget for the Bolsa *Familia* program was a mere tenth of what is paid for foreign debt, it is legitimate to call into question just how progressive the PT governments were and who benefitted the most from their economic policies.

[27] The discussion of the Brazilian economy under Temer and Bolsonaro is presented in Chapter 9.

The implications of reprimarization for the environment were examined above for Argentina and Brazil. In the case of the Brazilian Amazon, it was shown that the problems of deforestation, pollution, and social disruption were clearly linked to the expansion of lumber, cattle, soy, petroleum, and mining. Moreover, the expansion of soy and the use of pesticides, were seen as causing a number of public health issues. In addition, there are concerns of soil erosion and pollution, given the intensive use of toxic chemicals in agriculture, not to mention concerns for food production for local populations, not just exports. Lastly, the range of socioenvironmental problems associated with mining and petroleum, in particular, environmental accidents, were briefly discussed.

In contrast to the Cardoso government, the role played by the Brazilian State for infrastructure projects increased significantly, and is associated with the Program for the Acceleration of Growth (PAC) begun in 2007 under Lula.[28] Nevertheless, the majority of these infrastructural projects were associated with projects linked to reprimarization, such as hydroelectric dams, transport systems, and energy. In the case of Argentina, a recent agreement with China reflects the latter's increased role supporting infrastructure in Latin America, where it facilitates the production and transport of principally primary goods. The major concerns are with respect to air, water and soil pollution, in addition to the socioenvironmental impacts of hydroelectric dams, promoted primarily for mining, and often leading to major displacement of local and indigenous populations, as evidenced by social conflicts described above.

8.6 Conclusions

Around the turn of the century, Latin America experienced a shift toward the left, sometimes referred to as a Pink Tide, and several Latin American countries broke from orthodox neoliberal policies. In the case of the two largest economies of South America, namely Argentina and Brazil, several authors describe the changes there, as constitutive of a new model of economic development, namely, neodevelopmentalism.[29] In Sect. 8.2

[28] The PAC stands for *Programa de Aceleração do Crescimento* which began in 2007 under Lula (PAC1), with a budget of R$504 billion, and PAC2 began in 2010 under Dilma, with a budget of R$ 1.6 trillion.

[29] Authors associated with new developmentalism include Bresser-Pereira, Aldo Ferrer, Davidson, Palley, Chang, among others (Sicsú et al. 2005).

a number of the key theoretical elements associated with this new development path were considered. This was followed by an empirical analysis of the recent periods of the specific cases of the Kirchners and the Justicialista Party in Argentina and then the PT in Brazil, evaluating a range of key socioeconomic variables. Lastly, an evaluation was made regarding environmental impacts that have resulted from the continuation or deepening of the tendency toward reprimarization in both countries. The latter appears to be a more adequate description of the development path which both countries are currently pursuing, in spite of the break from orthodox neoliberal policies in both countries.

In order to evaluate the changes that have taken place in Argentina and Brazil, several key socioeconomic variables were considered, beginning with growth rates, and including real wages, unemployment, informal employment, poverty, and inequality, as well as social programs. The growth rates were arguably reasonable for the neoliberal period but by no means was there a solid period of growth that would be striking, nor were there major crises such as that of 2001 in Argentina or like 1999 in Brazil. The levels of unemployment, wages, and the informal economy remain an area of seriously needed long-term improvement in spite of some gains for a number of years in both countries.

With respect to redistribution and social programs, the most notable by the PT government was the *Bolsa Familia*, a welfare program by the State to the poorest and most vulnerable families. More than 13 million families benefitted from this program and there was a significant reduction in poverty as a result. Similar to Brazil and the *Bolsa Familia* program, Argentina under the Kirchners implemented several welfare programs,[30] in order to assist the poor and most vulnerable families. Both sets of programs in Brazil and Argentina were significant in reducing inequality and providing a safety net for the most vulnerable. Nevertheless, these policy changes did not address in a lasting way, the structural problems of unemployment, low wages, and the informal economy, associated with peripheral capitalist economies.

It is necessary to recognize the accomplishments of the new tendencies in Argentina and Brazil but also their serious limitations. Although

[30] Two major programs are *Asignación Universal por Hijo*, support for low income or poor parents and *Jefes y Jefas de Hogares Desocupados*, a program of support for unemployed heads of households.

the PT and Kirchner governments are clearly preferred to their predecessors or conservative replacements, there is an important need to have a serious critical discussion and not one that is simply drawn along party lines. This is argued, not as one in clear opposition to the PT in Brazil or the Justicialistas in Argentina, but considering the quality of life of the majority of their populations and their needs as a priority from a progressive perspective. Secondly, and more importantly, is the continuation of a development path associated with, first, deindustrialization and now reprimarization, accommodating the needs of the circuits of transnational capital accumulation. This discussion will be continued and developed in the last two chapters.

If "neodevelopmentalism" has been pursued and the dominant result is reprimarization, with its negative consequences for the environment and limited social gains, one must ask the question what is meant by developmentalism, and what are the goals that progressive governments are seeking to achieve. A shift in strategy toward primary exports, because it is a period of high commodity prices, is by no means a serious strategy to achieve long-term development, just consider Prebisch and Singer's arguments back in the 1950s.

The tendency of deindustrialization followed by reprimarization is not suggestive of a favorable development path for the majority of the populations of either country. Let us recall that every first world country went through a process of serious industrialization in order to become part of the "developed" world; with the last new members being South Korea and Taiwan. If there were at least a tradeoff, in terms of greater employment, perhaps it could be encouraging, but the activities such as soy, mining, and petroleum are capital intensive and not major generators of employment. Instead, it is more consistent with a strategy to maximize the gains for the TNCs and elites of a given country. The strategies pursued suggest that the plan was to accommodate the working class and poor, through social inclusion programs like Bolsa Familia, and improvement in labor markets, so as to strengthen a social base to insure reelection. Evidently the commodity boom has not continued, and thus the capacity economically and politically to continue pursuing this model of "neodevelopmentalism" seems to have reached a limit.

In summary, the results of the recent development paths pursued in Argentina and Brazil showed that there was a clear shift away from the orthodox neoliberal model, however, the push by both the government and the elites for a "neo-extractivist" model, emphasizing primary goods production, implied the continuity of the tendency of reprimarization. The pursuit of a strategy of reprimarization can be criticized but it is necessary to seriously evaluate, what options, politically and economically, are currently available for a country of the periphery in the present world, given the domination of TNCs, and the necessity to adhere to WTO rules. The reality is that any country that is a member of the WTO has by necessity a neoliberal trade policy, and this reduces, if not eliminates, the possibility of independent industrial policies. This has resulted in the loss of autonomy for countries to pursue policies aimed at fomenting national development as had existed through the 1950s, 1960s and 1970s.

In the next chapter we seek to provide an assessment of the present situation in both countries, having experienced swings to the right and in the case of Brazil, a move toward fascism. Even where the Kirchneristas have returned to power, it is far from an ideal moment, especially as the world is confronted with the worst pandemic since the time of World War I, and the economic crisis brought about by the pandemic was feared to rival the Great Depression of the 1930s. In any case, it is assumed that within several years the world will get beyond this crisis, though scarred and with significant loss of human life. In Chapter 9, an evaluation of the present but also future paths of development will be presented, seeking to discern a silver lining in the dark clouds on the horizon.

References

Azcurra, Fernando Hugo. 2011. "Las diez tesis sobre el Nuevo Desarrollismo elaboradas por economistas heterodoxos en un encuentro financiado por la Fundación Ford en el 2010."

Bresser-Pereira, Luís Carlos. 2011. "An Account of New Developmentalism and Its Structuralist Macroeconomics." *Brazilian Journal of Political Economy*, Vol. 31, No. 3 (123) (July–September/2011), pp. 493–502.

Butler, Rhett A. 2020. "Brazil Revises Deforestation Data: Amazon Rainforest Loss Topped 10,000 sq. km in 2019." *Mongabay Series: Amazon Conservation, Global Forests*.

Cooney, Paul. 2016. "Reprimarization: Implications for the Environment and Development in Latin America: The Cases of Argentina and Brazil." *RRPE*, Vol. 48, No. 4.

———. 2017a. "Current Paths of Development in the Southern Cone: Deindustrialization and a Return to the Agro-export Model." In: Richard Westra (ed.), *The Political Economy of Emerging Markets Varieties of BRICS in the Age of Global Crises and Austerity*. New York: Routledge.

COPROFAM. 2018. *Políticas Públicas para la Agricultura Familiar de Brasil.*

DIEESE (Departamento Inter Sindicato da Estadística e Estudos Socioeconômicos). 2020. www.dieese.org.br.

ECLAC. 2004. *Statistical Yearbook for Latin America and the Caribbean.* http://www.eclac.cl.

Edelman, Marc. 2020. "Bringing the Moral Economy Back into the Study of 21st Century Transnational Peasant Movements." *American Anthropologist* Vol. 107, No. 3 (2005).

FAO. 2020. https://www.fao.org/data/en/.

Fearnside, Philip. 2020. "Oil and Gas Project Threatens Brazil's Last Great Block of Amazon Forest." Mongabay Series: Amazon Conservation.

Galafassi, Guido. 2010. "Megaminería en Patagonia, Argentina, saqueo y nuevos cercamientos en un renovado proceso de acumulación por desposesión." In: G.C. Delgado (ed.), *Ecología política de la minería en América Latina.* México: UNAM-CEEICH.

Garibay Orozco, C. 2010. "Paisajes de acumulación minera por desposesión campesina en el México actual". In: En Delgado Gian Carlo (ed.), *Ecología Política de la minería en América Latina.* México: UNAM-CEEICH.

Gordon, Tedd, and Webber, Jeffery. 2008. "Imperialism and Resistance: Canadian Mining Companies in Latin America." *Third World Quarterly*, Vol. 29, No. 1, pp. 63–87.

Grigera, Juan and Matías Eskenazi. 2013. "Capítulo 7: Apuntes sobre la acumulación de capital durante la Posconvertibilidad". En Grigera, Juan (ed.), *Argentina después de la convertibilidad (2002–2011).* Buenos Aires: Imago Mundi.

Gudynas, Eduardo. 2019. *Extractivismos y Corrupción: Anatomía de una íntima relación.* Quito: Abya Yala.

IBGE. 2016–2020. www.sidra.ibge.gov.br/. Accessed July 2020.

INDEC. 2003–2020. www.indec.gov.ar/. Accessed July 2020.

INDEC/EPH. 2007–2021. www.indec.gov.ar/eph. Accessed July, 2021.

IPEA. 2010–2021. www.ipeadata.gov.br/. Accessed July 2021.

Jepson, Nicholas. 2020. "Neodevelopmentalist Type: Argentina and Brazil." In: N. Jepson, *In China's Wake: How the Commodity Boom Transformed Development Strategies in the Global South.* New York: Columbia University Press.

Klein, Naomi, 2014. *This Changes Everything: Capitalism vs. the Climate.* New York: Simon and Schuster.

Khor, Martin. 2006. "The WTO's Doha Negotiations and Impasse: A Development Perspective". *Third World Network* (November): 16.

Machado Aráoz, H. 2010. "El Agua Vale Más que el Oro. Grito de resistencia descolonial contra los nuevos dispositivos expropiatorios." In: Delgado Gian

Carlo (ed.), *Ecología política de la minería en América Latina*. México: UNAM-CEEICH.

Marques, Rosa María, Salomão Barres Ximenes and Camila Kimie Ugino. 2018. "Governos Lula e Dilma em matéria de seguridade social e acesso à educação superior". *Brazilian Journal of Political Economy*, Vol. 38, No. 3.

Marques de Souza, Gilberto. 2019a. *Amazônia- Riqueza, Degradação e Saque*. São Paulo: Expressão Popular.

Marquetti, Adalmir, Hoff, Cecilia, and Miebach, Alessandro. 2016. "Lucratividade e Distribuição: A Origem Econômica da Crise Política Brasileira."

NRDC. 2020. "Our Forests aren't Fuel" FROM Natural Resources Defense Council. https://www.nrdc.org/resources/our-forests-arent-fuel. Accessed May 8th, 2020.

OCMAL. 2020. https://mapa.conflictosmineros.net/ocmal_db-v2/. Accessed July 28, 2020.

Peixoto Ávila, Milene. 2013. "El Programa Bolsa Familia y la pobreza en Brasil: mucho más que números a considerar." *Revista Sociedad & Equidad*, No. 5, enero de 2013.

Pengue, Walter. 2005. "Environmental and Socio Economic Impacts of Transgenic Crops Releasing in Argentina and South America: An Ecological Economics Approach." *Bulletin of Science, Technology & Society*, Vol. 25, No. 4 (August 2005), pp. 1–9.

Perreault, T. 2013. "Dispossession by accumulation? Mining, Water and the Nature of Enclosure on the Bolivian Altiplano." *Antipode*, Vol. 45, No. 5, pp. 1050–1069.

PNAD (Pesquisa Nacional por Amostra de Domicílios). 2020. www.ibge.br.

Pogge, Thomas and Reddy, Sanjay, 2003. "Unknown: The Extent, Distribution, and Trend of Global Income Poverty." http://www.socialanalysis.org/.

Prego, J., Ruggiero, R.A., Conti, H.A., Panigatti, J.L., Chebez, J., and Hoffmann, J.A. 1997. *El deterioro del ambiente en la Argentina (suelo-agua-vegetación-fauna)* [Environment Deterioration in Argentina (Land, Water, Vegetation and Fauna)] (3rd ed.). Buenos Aires, Argentina: Fundación para la Educación, la Ciencia y la Cultura.

PRODES/INPE. 2020. http://www.obt.inpe.br/OBT/assuntos/programas/amazonia/prodes.

Rivero, S., and Paul Cooney. 2010. "The Amazon as a Frontier of Capital Accumulation: Looking Beyond the Trees." *Capitalism, Nature, Socialism*, Vol. 21, No. 4.

Rodrigues, Sabrina. 2018. "Área de cultivo de soja na Amazônia quadruplicou desde 2006." *O Eco*. https://www.oeco.org.br/noticias/area-de-cultivo-de-soja-na-amazonia-quadruplicou-desde-2006/. Accessed August 16, 2020.

Rodrik, Dani. 2018. "The WTO Has Become Dysfunctional." *Financial Times*, August 5, 2018.

Sacher, William. 2015. "Megaminería y Desposesión en el Sur: un análisis comparativo." *Íconos*, Vol. 51, pp. 99–116.

———. 2017. *Ofensiva Megaminería China en los Andes. Acumulación por Desposesión en el Ecuador de la Revolución Ciudadana*. Quito: Abya-Yala.

Sacher, William, and Cooney, Paul. 2019. "Transnational Mining and Accumulation by Dispossession." In: Paul Cooney and William Sacher (eds.), *Environmental Impacts of Transnational Corporations in the Global South. Research in Political Economy*, Vol. 33 (Chapter 1). Bingley, UK: Emerald Publishing.

Sicsú, J., De Paula, L.F. and Renaut, M. (eds.), 2005. *Novo-Desenvolvimentismo: Um Projeto Nacional de Crescimento com Equidade Social*. Barueri, SP: Editora Manole and Konrad Adenauer Stiftung.

World Bank. 2018–2021. https://data.worldbank.org/.

CHAPTER 9

Present and Future Paths, Development and Dependency

9.1 Introduction

This chapter begins with an assessment of the recent swings to the right in both countries. Although the *Kirchneristas* or perhaps the Peronists[1] have returned to power in Argentina, it is far from an ideal moment, between the state of the economy after Macri, and especially as the world is confronted with the worst pandemic since the time of World War I, and the economic crisis brought about by this COVID-19 pandemic threatens to rival the Great Depression of the 1930s. In any case, it is assumed that within several years, the world will get beyond this crisis, though scarred and impacted in many ways, and with significant loss of human life.[2] In this chapter, an evaluation of the present paths of development is presented, and the final chapter analyzes potential future paths

[1] The *Kirchneristas* is a more left leaning grouping within Peronism, however, the current government with Alberto Fernandez as President and with the support of more centrist Peronists, such as Masa, its base is arguably more Peronist, not merely *Kirchnerista*, as it was with Nestor Kirchner and then Cristina Fernandez previously.

[2] This chapter will not enter into an extensive analysis of the pandemic COVID-19 crisis nor the related economic crisis (writing as of August 2020) but given its relevance for future developments in both Argentina and Brazil, a post-script to the final chapter will present a brief discussion of these issues.

P. Cooney, *Paths of Development in the Southern Cone*, Palgrave Insights into Apocalypse Economics, https://doi.org/10.1007/978-3-030-67673-5_8

of development, seeking to discern a silver lining in the dark clouds on the horizon.

Therefore, a brief summary of (1) the economic problems at the end of Cristina Fernández's second period leading to the election of Macri, will be presented, followed by (2) a summary of policy shifts with Macri and the state of the economy at the end of 2019. This will be followed by a brief summary of the end of Dilma's second term, followed by the arrival of Temer and a brief summary of the beginning of the presidency of Bolsonaro. After the discussion of the present period, the chapter will present a discussion of what future paths, are possible, probable, or feasible, and the relationship between dependency, in its current form, and the possibility of serious and real development, in the medium term for the populations of Argentina and Brazil.

A range of analysis for both countries was presented, arguing that it is clear that the tendencies of deindustrialization and reprimarization are here to stay, not only in the short run, but most likely in the medium run, for both Argentina and Brazil and this has significant implications. An evaluation was made of the strategies of neodevelopmentalism associated with both countries, seen as representing a new development trajectory seeking improved growth, higher wages, and sustainable development, but upon closer examination the end result was more of a type of reformism, that did not produce a truly new development path. Clearly there were positive results for both Argentina and Brazil, especially in reducing social exclusion, particularly for the working classes, the poor and most vulnerable in society. Most notable were reduction in poverty and inequality for both countries. However, there were serious limitations in terms of shifting to a new development path, though before entering this discussion, an evaluation of the events and changes with respect to the economy in the last few years is presented.

9.2 The Macri Government

As observed in the last chapter, a number of economic problems continued to undermine the continuity of *Kirchnerismo* in power after the end of the second term for Cristina Fernandez. The main economic problems had been a negative rate of growth of –2.5% in 2014, a year before the election, growing inflation, reaching over 25% in 2015, and linked to this, was the ever-increasing dollar exchange rate. Moreover, the growth of poverty and unemployment and the concerns over exchange controls, all contributed to an undermining of the support for *Kirchnerismo*. A number of problems derived from the end of the commodities boom, about which Cristina had no control over, but the range of economic problems, and biased media coverage, especially with regard to several scandals related to corruption,[3] among other issues discussed in previous chapters, contributed to a victory by Macri.

After winning the presidential elections in 2015 by a narrow margin, and leading a conservative political coalition referred to as Alliance of Change (*Cambiemos Alliance*), Mauricio Macri ended twelve years of Kirchner governments. His government pushed through more neoliberal policies, and more orthodox neoliberal policies. Some *Kirchneristas* will try to argue that Macri brought back neoliberalism, but they are in denial of the fact that some of the policies with the Kirchners, had a neoliberal slant, though not orthodox, as discussed earlier. Independently, the orientation of Macri was to accommodate his base, which was much more the upper class and higher income middle class, not the working classes and poor. Nevertheless, a significant portion of this latter social strata came to support Macri in this election.

The shifts were achieved through a range of policies, from (1) reducing taxes for the wealthy, (2) increasing prices for public services, though often embattled with Congress, so not so clearly or easily achieved; (3) a reduction of exchange controls, and (4) a shift away or reduction in the social programs associated with the Kirchners.

After GDP[4] growth of 2.73% in 2015, which was the last year of Cristina's government, the first full year of Macri had negative 2% growth. Fortunately for Macri there was then a rebound to 2.82% in 2017, though followed by a negative 2.57% in 2018 and though slightly improving in 2019, it was still a negative 2.09%. These oscillations going from positive to negative growth after 2012, are in part explained by the end of the commodities boom, and thus cannot be simply attributed to the policies of one government or the other.

[3] The main corruption scandals associated with Cristina Fernandez were related to Nisman, the Economics Minister Moreno, and the Vice President Amado Boudou, in addition to her own trials. For a Peronist defense of Cristina, see *Página* 12 (2015) and for a take from the Macri or conservative perspective, see the newspaper Clarín.

[4] The graph of GDP for this period can be observed in Fig. 8.1, and that of unemployment is presented in Fig. 8.2

There were some ups and downs but more negative growth than positive; similarly, unemployment increased through the Macri years, roughly 7.6% in 2016 which grew to 10.7% in 2019, and if taking into account underemployment, the total unemployment[5] was almost 23%. In terms of poverty, this also grew from roughly 30% up to 40% in 2019. The promised foreign investment that Macri was so confident about, never really arrived, thus contributing to a lackluster economy and combined with unfulfilled campaign promises.

Another major critique of the economic policy of Macri was creating an artificial need to go to the IMF for a loan, and after the loan, resulting in an increase of debt from US$240 billion, 52.6% of GDP, in December 2015 to US$324 billion and 88.5% of GDP, in early 2019. This increase is clearly linked to the largest loan emitted by the IMF, namely US$ 57 billion, negotiated by Macri in 2018. Such a huge increase in debt has now become an inherited problem for the Fernandez government, leading to the default in 2020. Although Macri could not achieve a return of the commodities boom, the combination of neoliberal policies clearly led to a worsening of distribution or to one favoring the rich, which was expected, given his neoliberal orientation and social background. As a result, it isn't a surprise that the Peronists, namely Alberto Fernandez and Cristina Fernández were able to win the election in 2019. Having presented a brief summary of the shift to the right in Argentina, the next section turns to look at the situation in Brazil and the subsequent shifts that have taken place since 2015.

9.3 Brazil: From Dilma to Temer to Bolsonaro[6]

Economic problems began to surface soon after Dilma began her Presidency in 2011, and GDP growth dropped down to 1.9% in 2012. A critical move by Dilma's government back in 2011, was the reduction of the rate of interest for public debt bonds, namely, the SELIC. This drop began in August 2011 and by October 2012 had fallen from 12.5% down to 7.25%. This was the lowest value since the series was tracked as of

[5] As mentioned earlier, the term total unemployment refers to the combination of unemployment and underemployment.

[6] This section has benefitted from two articles with quality analysis on both economic and political issues: Marquetti et. al. (2016) and Anderson (2019).

1986; though new records would be reached in 2018–2019. The counterpart to this was the increase in private investments in infrastructure (PAC), as mentioned in the last chapter.

A key event, which would have negative implications and beyond Dilma's control, was that in 2013, the U.S. Federal Reserve announced it would stop buying bonds. The upshot was that the arbitrage scheme, where investors borrowed cheaply from the US and invested in Brazil, which had worked for many years, was no longer feasible, especially given the decline in the SELIC, described above. Starting with the *Plano Real* under Cardoso and then continued with Lula, maintaining the SELIC (Brazilian Federal Funds rate), for many years as the highest rate of interest globally (between roughly 25–13%), facilitated a huge influx of financial flows into Brazil (see Fig. 9.1). As a result, beginning in 2013, much of foreign finance left Brazil, and thereby increasing the problem of capital flight. Subsequent problems were a weakening of balance of payments and an increasing rate of inflation, not to mention the end of the commodities boom. In a nutshell, the best economic years of the PT were over (Marquetti et al. 2016).

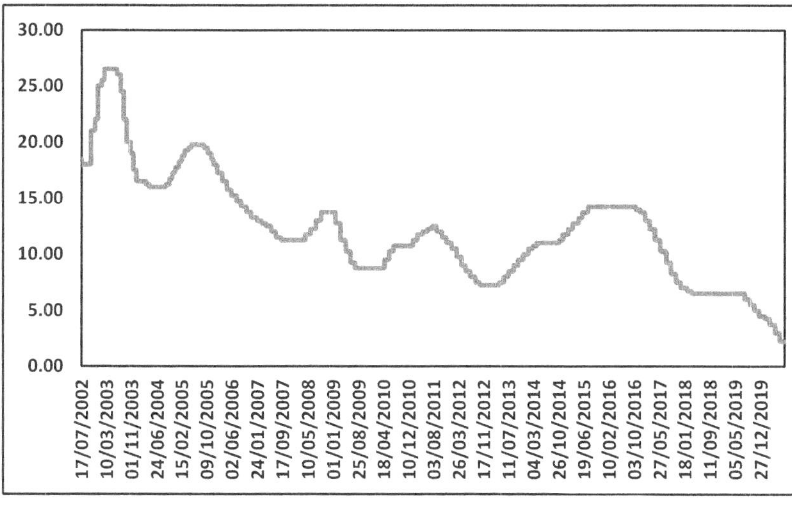

Fig. 9.1 SELIC- (Brazilian Federal Funds Rate): 2002–2020 (%) (*Source* Banco Central do Brazil 2020)

Back in 2013, there was increasing discontent by the middle classes and rising prices were causing popular tension in the big cities. In fact, in 2013, initially protests were connected to the cost of public transportation, but rapidly expanded to other issues, such as the improvement of public services and Dilma was then being attacked from both the right and the left. There came to be an increasing presence of the right wing in these demonstrations. In a rather short period, Dilma's approval ratings had dropped from 57 down to 30 percent. Given what took place in 2013 when Dilma ran for reelection in 2014, she faced a far more dangerous and aggressive opposition than in 2010.

Dilma Rousseff was reelected in 2014, with the support of diverse sectors of the left, especially in the second round. During the campaign the PT argued that a victory by the opposition PSDB would represent a return to neoliberal economic policy with negative effects regarding employment, wages, and spending on social programs. A major contrast was fundamental for the Dilma victory and such a contrast combined with her carrying out what she swore she would not, and this was crucial in leading to the massive protests against the PT, the ex-President Lula, and Dilma herself in 2015.

Dilma also indicated that she would be making a change of her economic team in the case of reelection. Therefore, it was a shock when she brought in Joaquim Levy as economics minister, and she was subject to many criticisms, especially by the left, and rightfully so. Besides bringing in someone from the University of Chicago, who had worked for the IMF, Levy had been working in finance prior to his nominations, and he ended up pushing through neoliberal economic policies.

Opposite to what she promised in the elections, Dilma opted for a strategy of neoliberal inspiration. Apparently, the idea was to repeat the success of the measures implemented in 2003. However, contrary to that period, there was not the same scenario with favorable external conditions, such as a commodities boom, which would allow for growth of exports, resulting in the appreciation of the *Real* and control of inflation. The political situation, after the close election and the denouncing of the corruption involved in the *Lava Jato* case[7], kept things far from

[7] There had been Federal police wire-taps regarding the money-laundering operations in a Brasília "Car Wash" (*Lava Jato*), with widespread corruption involving Petrobras, the state-owned petroleum enterprise, referred to in Chapter 8. This major inquiry carried out by the Supreme Court judge Sergio Mora, resulted in a major corruption scandal,

under control. Dilma made an attempt to appease the Brazilian elite, and the neoliberals, and thus she sought to make concessions that she hoped would convince them, but this strategy completely backfired.

Unfortunately for Dilma, the conservative forcers operated to undermine her and the best track was pursuing impeachment, which they achieved through a technicality. The issue was that Dilma deferred payments on public accounts to improve them anticipating the election. Although this had been the norm for many previous Brazilian governments, did not matter. Therefore, in spite of being one of the least corrupt politicians in the PT, Dilma was removed from office by the Summer of 2015 and replaced by her Vice President Michel Temer from the PMDB.

An excellent summary of this lightning attack of neoliberal orthodoxy achieved an immediate rollback on workers gains by implementing orthodox neoliberal policies to last for decades. As Anderson argues:

> the new regime passed three classical pieces of neoliberal statecraft in short order, altering the economic constitution of the country at a stroke. Within a month, legislation freezing social expenditures for twenty years.... No sooner was it passed with a two-thirds majority than the labor code was comprehensively scrapped: the legal limit of a working day was extended from eight to 12 h; permissible lunch breaks cut from an hour to thirty minutes; protection of employees, full or part-time, reduced; the check-off of union dues abolished; plus sundry other deregulations of the labour market. A third law gave a generalized green light to the outsourcing of employment and zero-hour contracts. Next up was radical pension reform, increasing contributions and raising retirement ages, to bring down the costs of constitutionally mandated social security in the name of reducing the national debt. (Anderson 2019)

The stabilization plan accompanying Temer's initial neoliberal measures had ended the Dilma recession, but it produced a weak recovery, with problems of unemployment and poverty, thus worsening Temer's low credibility. As a result, the PMDB chose to go with the finance minister, who had presided over the recovery, Henrique Meirelles,[8] for

involving kickbacks and bribes, in which, many PT politicians were implicated, including Lula (Milenio Digital y Agencias 2020).

[8] One should recall that Meirelles was the first President of the Central Bank under Lula; apparently greedy neoliberals are not too picky about what party they belong to.

president in 2018. He received a mere 1 percent of the vote. Nevertheless, Temer was quite skilled at bringing about major neoliberal shifts in the short period of time that he was president and had helped set the stage for an even more rightward shift for the coming period.

Although it is clear that Bolsonaro has a neoliberal orientation in general, it is not absolute, as he was once in opposition to privatizations. One also must observe to what extent he is able to push through legislation and what type of support he can expect in Congress. Much of this scenario has been shifted due to the COVID-19 crisis, which will be addressed in the final chapter. Of relevance in terms of neoliberal policies, Bolsonaro's choice for the minister of economics was Paulo Guedes, a well-trained neoliberal from the University of Chicago, who taught in Chile under Pinochet. His primary solution to economic problems at present is to privatize all state enterprises and assets in order to pay down the national debt, and also push for major deregulation reform.

Bolsonaro's new economic plans include reforming the pension system, and keeping with the neoliberal unofficial mantra, redistribution from the poor and working classes to the wealthiest and capitalist classes. Besides these neoliberal schemes, with a clear class dimension, additional cuts in public spending are also anticipated. A major part of the plan will be privatizations advertised as the way to pay off the debt. As Anderson has claimed: "A hundred state holdings of one kind or another – the plums are in infrastructure: motorways, ports, airfields – are scheduled for disposal or closure, naturally also in the name of efficiency and better service." It is expected that this next wave of privatizations, will also see a number of sweet deals for TNCs or international banks, similar to what took place under FHC (Cardoso), e.g., such as the case of *Vale do Rio Doce*. Fortunately, Bolsonaro has come to alienate a number of his allies in Congress and elsewhere, thus reducing the chance that he will be able to push through all of his plans for new legislation, but the legacy of the Bolsonaro presidency is still very much to be determined.

An important development in Bolsonaro's first year of office reached international dimensions in August of 2019, and it continues to generate major concern in the field of human and environmental rights. Bolsonaro called for a "Day of Fire" which was a call to arson or forest fires, prompting major concerns, both for the impact on the rain forest, deforestation, and major loss of biodiversity, especially animals being burned alive, but more sinister, regarding the call to burn down indigenous villages. There was a disproportionate increase in forest fires or fires of peasant and indigenous lands in the Amazon during August of 2019. There was a total of 26,795 fires for the month of August through August 25, 2019. Ancestral practices often involve the burning of land to recover the fertility of the land but this is on average much less, averaging 22 thousand for this same period. Loggers are considered to be the primary source of those responsible, given their interests and the pattern of cutting down trees in these areas, which are deemed off-limits and therefore illegal[9] (see Marques de Souza 2019b).[10]

After these incidents, involving the burning of serious swathes of land, and also the real threat of genocide for certain indigenous groups, Bolsonaro was brash in defending his actions calling for a "Day of Fire," and was very defensive regarding the criticism of deforestation by mainly Europe and other countries, declaring "the Amazon is ours." His posture has changed somewhat, as there has been increased pressure by certain countries not to buy products from Brazil, such as soy, oil, or cattle, if associated with deforestation and illegal logging (Londoño and Casado 2020).

The development path or perhaps more adequately termed Bolsonaro´s "path of destruction" is not only sinister, sadistic, and fitting for apocalyptic scenarios, but clearly and deserves further attention for several reasons. However, the aim of this book was regarding the processes of reprimarization and its impacts such as deforestation associated with the development paths pursued by progressive governments in Brazil and Argentina. Although there are a number of continuities in Brazil after the PT governments, with respect to the tendencies of deindustrialization and reprimarization, this would deserve a separate analysis, beyond the original plan of this book. It clearly requires close vigilance, especially given the proto-fascist tendencies of Bolsonaro and the real risk of a military coup not just the technical coup that brought Temer to power.

[9] The term illegal wood (*madeira ilegal*), implies cutting down trees in these areas, be it ecological reserves, indigenous reserves, or simply environmental restrictions where it is considered illegal to carry out logging.

[10] An important piece of analysis of the fires and deforestation in the Amazon associated with Bolsonaro's call for a "Day of Fire," on the 10th of August 2019, is an extreme example of the social problems related to reprimarization and the sectors most associated with deforestation (Marques de Souza 2019b).

9.4 Problems of the Current Paths

The first part of this chapter has presented a summary, however brief, of several of the main policy changes related to the political economy of Argentina and Brazil since the PT and Kirchners left government. Now, the overall discussion of problems with the current path of development will be considered, identifying its major limitations and moving toward proposing alternatives, rooted in the reality of both countries at present in 2020. In evaluating the new development paths of both governments, whether one refers to them as neodevelopmentalism or not, the main point is that this development project or approach constituted the continuation, if not deepening, of the tendencies of reprimarization and deindustrialization. Therefore, given the discussion in the last chapter, there is a need to revisit the principal limitations and problems associated with these tendencies and the underlying dependence on transnational corporations and the WTO, limiting, if not controlling, national policies with regard to industry, social priorities, and public policies.

The scope of the relevance of such policies includes a range of major issues: distribution in terms of income and wealth; sustainable growth, including GDP; real wages, employment, and poverty; sustainability for the environment; and the identification of priorities, including choices of allies and alliances. It seems imperative to confirm that one´s population, including the working classes and poor, should have priority over TNCs, not vice versa. Evaluating this range of issues, enables one to move toward seeking viable alternatives in the short to medium run, not discussing what the Southern Cone may look like in 2200, but rather within 20–30 years from the present year, 2021.

As seen previously, the results of the recent development paths pursued in Argentina and Brazil was a clear shift away from the orthodox neoliberal model, however, there was a continuity by both the government and the elites for a "neo-extractivist" model (Gudynas 2015), emphasizing primary goods production, and the tendency of reprimarization. It is evident that the current trajectory of reprimarization reflects an economy dominated by the interests of increasingly transnationally oriented elites, including the TNCs themselves. Therefore, the idea that an industrial bourgeoisie can either be reconstituted (as in Argentina) or re-empowered (as in Brazil) and convinced to establish an alliance with the working classes, as many a *kirchnerista* or *petista* has suggested, namely a return to a class alliance associated with industrialization and ISI, is more and more an illusion, and does not reflect the current reality. In spite of a number of progressive changes in Argentina and Brazil, partially breaking from neoliberalism, and thus achieving improvements regarding social inclusion, they did not make structural changes necessary for pursuing a new model of development, capable of sustained improvements, in employment and wages and in the standard of living for the majority, and not for just a few years.

It is a structural problem to pursue a strategy dominated by the accumulation needs of the TNCs, in spite of discourse to the contrary, and this is the primary cause of the economic limitations of the current model. It is the dominant form of dependency on TNCs and their global model in the countries of the periphery across the globe. Even economies, such as Argentina and Brazil, that had achieved significant levels of industrialization, end up being forced to find niches within transnational global value chains, and often with minimal levels of value added.[11]

A key concern is the problem of compromises with these TNCs, argued to be for the benefit of all, but which have not resulted in viable tradeoffs, and thus too many of these compromises are simply not acceptable. Examples abound, especially in the cases of mining, such as the Glacier Law (*Ley de Glaciares*) with Cristina Fernandez in Argentina, giving mining TNCs the right to extract minerals from under existing glaciers. Moreover, in the discussions in Chapter 7 about the expropriation of populations from their territory, including to the point of genocide in the Amazon, and this has become a major human rights issue again with Bolsonaro in the Amazon, especially in this period of the pandemic. Another major compromise was with respect to genetically modified organisms (GMOs) or crops, as took place in Brazil under Lula. Soybean production in Brazil had been dominated by non-GMOs for many years and the European market meant that this was still viable economically. Succumbing to the pressure by both Monsanto and China to make the transition, which is now close to 100% of soy production in Brazil, was a grave error, and not only for Brazil. Accommodating

[11] See discussion of low levels of value added and reprimarization in Bolinaga and Slipak 2015, and the discussion of the conflict over exporting soy products with greater value added with China in Chapter 7.

a TNC such as Monsanto,[12] now Bayer, is the opposite of looking for an alternative development path. Instead we should be putting our resources and scientists into projects expanding the capacity of growing food with existing agricultural producers, farmers, family farms (which currently provide approximately 70% of food worldwide) and pursuing or expanding agroecology, with much greater potential for achieving sustainable development. Such projects are ones in which Bayer will never be in agreement with, as their primary aim, besides profits, is to control the world food supply, while selling as many agrotoxics as possible.

Another set of problems are related to the issue of social conflict, and the tendency for many countries, be it in the first world or the periphery, to criminalizing resistance. Attempts to set up a mining operation or expand on expropriated land or install an unwanted hydroelectric power plant, often occurs without consultation with the local populations and in numerous cases, involves serious social conflicts. The posture of many governments, such as Canada and the US, but also including Argentina and Brazil, has been the criminalizing of resistance movements.

This is extremely problematic for progressive governments, who have often criticized their predecessors, for the same strategy, where the violence of the State (be it federal, provincial, or municipal) is employed against legitimate protest and resistance of operations by transnationals, that are not taking into account the rights of communities in a given region. In other words, having to accommodate these interests, be it Barrick Gold or JBS or Vale, in order to have the mega projects with a major source of foreign exchange, needs to be seriously questioned as constitutive of a progressive development path. It is therefore also imperative to recognize that a progressive alternative development approach needs to prioritize human and social rights above the demands of TNCs. Given the track record of so many TNCs, where they have violated human rights, with impunity, time and time again, be it Shell in Nigeria, Texaco in Ecuador, Coca-Cola in Colombia, Monsanto (Bayer) in India, Mexico, etc. (Robin 2008a), Vale in Brazil, or Barrick Gold in Argentina.

A fundamental issue is recognizing the problems with respect to social conflict and democratic and human rights in the context of a development path wedded to TNCs. Whether it be expropriations necessary for

[12] An excellent critical and very well-documented book about Monsanto (Bayer) and the threat to our food supply, see Robin (2008b), in addition to her documentary by the same name (2008a).

mega-mining, lumber, cattle ranching, soybeans, petroleum, etc., these have tended to involve violations of human rights and in many cases, such as in the Brazilian Amazon, the State apparatus has been used against the public. Evidently, this was worse with the military government and at present with Bolsonaro, but there have also been cases when the PT was in government. As discussed in Chapter 7, this fit with Harvey's concept of "accumulation by dispossession." Harvey, refers to the violence associated with accumulation of capital through dispossession, and how this often leads to social protest and struggle. The social demands are not limited to expropriations, they also involve issues of health, the need to reduce, clean up, or eliminate the contamination associated with activities such as mining, which often uses cyanide, mercury, lead, etc., without sufficient safety and health precautions. In addition, the activities associated with agribusiness involving extensive use of agrochemicals, which are dangerous, both for workers and communities' health.

Again, the concern or conflict between human rights and transnational rights, where the priority should clearly be human rights first, but given the treaties that dominate in the present period of neoliberal globalization it is usually the reverse. National governments must call this into question, be it in terms of new treaties or previously existing ones, such as NAFTA. Strong examples of the problems of human rights taking a back seat to the priority of TNC profits. Consider the example when the Ethyl corporation took Canada to court for its lost profits because of a health law banning the use of carcinogens, and therefore their gasoline additive MMT, a known carcinogen. Not only did they win their case in the courts of NAFTA, forcing Canada to reimburse them for lost profits, Canada was forced to change their law protecting the health and safety of the citizens to permit this carcinogen to be used in gasoline sold in Canada. (Weissman 1996). It really does not get much more perverse than this and yet we are continuing down this road where transnational rights are given priority over human rights.[13]

[13] Another shocking example of where the right to profits is clearly seen as a greater priority than the pursuit of sustainable development on the planet is when the WTO ruling in favor of Japan and the EU, forced Ontario to suspend the successful program of subsidizing the development of solar panels to reduce our fossil fuel dependency. This is another example of the rule of transnationals overriding human interests through the framework of the WTO (see Chapter 2 and the reference to Klein (2014).

9.5 Mercosur—Problems of the Past; Potential for the Future

As seen throughout the book, in spite of the advances in terms of industrialization for both Brazil and Argentina, the shifts that have taken place during the period of neoliberal globalization, reversed these advances. This reflects in part the overdependence on foreign transnationals, but also the priority of accommodating both local elites as well. It is the TNCs operating in Argentina and Brazil which dictate the nature of both industrial and trade policies, in spite of the fact that they are the two principal members of Mercosur. Just consider the cases of the automobile industry, and also the soy and mining sectors. Lastly, in spite of many solid efforts and discussion for advancing Mercosur, the problem of the agenda and strength of TNCs, clearly limits what a genuine progressive government or group of governments can seek to accomplish. This condition clearly undermines the possibility of the development of a serious regional industrial policy.

In spite of advances made by recent progressive governments to strengthen Mercosur and develop progressive autonomous institutions such as the *Banco del Sur* or *Unasur*,[14] first during the heyday of Lula, Nestor, and Chavez and then also with Dilma and Cristina, but since roughly 2015 things have changed significantly. The Macri government, Temer, and now Bolsonaro, have no interest in a progressive block as envisioned by the progressive governments several years back. They even made efforts in seeking to dismantle what little advances had been achieved, and this became worse with the arrival of Moreno in Ecuador in 2017, the recent coup in Bolivia in 2019, as well as the sad state of affairs in Venezuela.

The scenario of greater regional integration of Mercosur, in spite of many problems, seemed to provide a more optimistic possibility for strengthening industrialization and redistribution in South America, and thus achieving greater results in terms of development. Unfortunately, the current economic and political conjuncture suggests that this is impossible

[14] *Banco del Sur*, translated as the Bank of the South, was a monetary fund and lending organization established on September 26, 2009 by Argentina, Brazil, Paraguay, Uruguay, Ecuador, Bolivia, and Venezuela with promises of initial capital of US$20 billion. Unasur or Union of South American Nations is an intergovernmental regional organization that once comprised twelve South American countries; but as of 2019, most countries have withdrawn, given the splits between right and left Latin American governments.

at present and may not be feasible for quite some time to come. Nevertheless, this may the basis for a future regional project advocating a truly alternative development path, not one so dependent on TNCs and accumulation needs, but rather based on a mixed economy, not just capitalist relations of production.

Currently, in the case of Argentina, with the return of Peronism with Alberto Fernandez, winning the Presidency and Cristina Fernandez his vice president, it is assumed that they will attempt to continue policies similar to what was pursued prior to the four years of Macri. Given the COVID-19 pandemic and associated crisis, the short term is rather difficult to predict. It is even less clear what the near-term conjuncture will be for Brazil, given the current crisis and the unpredictable government of Bolsonaro. It will clearly be more conservative, if not reactionary and seek to implement orthodox neoliberal policies to the extent that they can be passed by the legislature. In spite of the many uncertainties, this topic will be addressed in the concluding chapter.

In any case, for both Argentina and Brazil, continuing with reprimarization is a certainty, with attempts of advancing manufacturing industry, at a minimum. Although such a strategy has had success with the recent commodities boom, a new one is rather unlikely, given the continuing economic crisis due to the COVID-19 pandemic, in the short run. In line with Prebisch's predictions, which as a long-term tendency continue to be valid, historically, the prices of primary goods tend to be more volatile and with declining terms of trade, in relation to the first world or when exchanged with manufactured goods. Therefore, improvements in economic performance and the quality of life for the working classes and poor of Argentina and Brazil, unfortunately appear unlikely in the short run.

9.6 Future Development Paths

There is a need to recognize that the development paths pursued by the progressive governments in Argentina and Brazil were overly accommodating the TNCs, and that this is NO longer viable, if serious development is the goal. There is a need to put human rights and needs as the principal priority for any progressive government. The improvements achieved by the PT and the Kirchners are now seen as short-lived; the improvements and gains for the poor and working classes were for some 10 years only. Moreover, the governments that followed, have tended to undermine many of these gains, given the orthodox neoliberal orientations (or worse) of Temer, Macri, and Bolsonaro.

At one level, the problems of neodevelopmentalism, reprimarization, and deindustrialization are rooted in the problems of capitalism and the inherent conflict over distributing wealth between capital and labor, in addition to the structural problem of imperialism and dependency. Evidently, a single country cannot try to fight against the world, as in David and Goliath, but rather a coalition of countries demanding change could bring about serious transformation, but not overnight. No struggle is simple or straightforward, whether one is seeking to abolish slavery, or obtaining the right to vote for women, or countries seeking to break from colonialization. Such movements all require commitment, mobilization, patience, and political education, not to mention general education as well as resources.

Besides the specific discussion about the economic trajectories of Brazil and Argentine, and in particular the problems of the tendencies of deindustrialization and reprimarization, there is a broader issue at stake, namely the need for countries of the periphery to break from the dependency model in order to pursue viable development paths in the future. Many will argue that this requires overthrowing capitalism, and that may be the case. However, at present the populations of Argentina and Brazil are currently not demanding such a change, nor is a political transformation, given the limitations of the left parties in these countries, about to take place in the short run. Instead, a shift away from the TNC-dominated model is a necessary and more realistic step needed to prevent these populations from suffering even more over the next fifty or more years. The final chapter presents a discussion of potential paths of development looking toward the future.

References

Anderson, Perry. 2019. "Bolsonaro's Brazil." *London's Review of Books*, Vol. 41, No. 3 (February 7, 2019).

Banco Central do Brasil. 2004–2021. https://www.bcb.gov.br/.

Bolinaga, L., and Slipak, A. 2015. "El consenso de Beijing y la reprimarización productiva de américa latina: El caso argentino." *Revista Problemas Del Desarrollo*, Vol. 46, No. 183, pp. 33–58.

Gudynas, Eduardo. 2015. *Extractivismos. Ecología economía y política de un modo de entender el desarrollo y la Naturaleza*, 1ª ed. Lima: Cedib y ClAES.

Klein, Naomi. 2014. *This Changes Everything: Capitalism vs. the Climate*. New York: Simon and Schuster.

Londoño, Ernesto, and Casado, Letícia. 2020. "As Bolsonaro Keeps Amazon Vows, Brazil's Indigenous Fear 'Ethnocide'." *New York Times*, April 19, 2020.

Marques de Souza, Gilberto. 2019b. "Derrotar Bolsonaro para Defender a Amazônia: Presidente estimula queimadas e desmatamento na região".

Marquetti, Adalmir, Cecilia Hoff and Alessandro Miebach. 2016. "Lucratividade e Distribuição: A Origem Econômica da Crise Política Brasileira."

Milenio Digital y Agencias. 2020. ¿Qué es el 'Lava Jato' la trama de corrupción por la que Lula da Silva estuvo preso? November 8, 2019.

Robin, Marie-Monique. 2008a. (Director) *The World According to Monsanto*. A documentary Film.

Robin, Marie-Monique. 2008b. *The World According to Monsanto: Pollution, Corruption, and the Control of the World's Food Supply*. New York: The New Press.

CHAPTER 10

Conclusions

10.1 Summary of the Book

Starting from the agro-export period for both Argentina and Brazil, this book traversed over one hundred years of the histories of two of the countries of the region that achieved industrialization and major advances economically, then followed by deindustrialization and reprimarization, and analyzed how these transformations took place. Through these transformations, reference to the different phases of dependency was alluded to, reflecting the condition of dependency for countries of the periphery, resulting in transfers of wealth to the center but also limits on their autonomy, economically and politically.

During the first phase their main insertion in the world economy was exporting primary products, be it coffee, sugar, and rubber from Brazil or beef, wool, and wheat from Argentina. Based upon the famous analysis of Prebisch, this was the classic case of unequal exchange of exporting primary goods in exchange for manufactured goods from the center, and given the deterioration of terms of exchange over time, countries of the periphery produce and export more in exchange for less. In this first phase of dependency, both economies were oriented toward exporting primary goods, primarily to Great Britain and the US, where the role of rent was key, as the higher fertility lands for producing beef, wheat, or coffee facilitated their capacity to earn foreign exchange, so as to import manufactured goods.

P. Cooney, *Paths of Development in the Southern Cone*, Palgrave Insights into Apocalypse Economics, https://doi.org/10.1007/978-3-030-67673-5_9

Then the period of transition to ISI, implied the slow but sure development of light industry, first connected to the food and beverage sectors and then extending further. It was evident that Brazil and Argentina developed at different paces and with varied emphasis, regarding the role of the State. Brazil made major advances in its first phase of industrialization with the governments of Vargas, while in the case of Argentina it was under the guidance of Perón, and the union and worker movements, he was able to influence and control, that the first phase of ISI took place for Argentina.

The second phases of ISI were also examined as in the case of Kubitschek and his Plan de Goals and eventually the military government of Geisel leading Brazil to the third phase of industrialization and even the production of industrial capital goods. In the case of Argentina, the governments of Frondizi and others pushed forward the second phase of industrialization, reaching a point where two thirds of their exports were manufactured goods. This period of ISI corresponded to the second stage of dependency. On the one hand, both countries were first able to produce light consumer goods, though still requiring the importation of consumer durables and capital goods.

Over time, heavy industry developed, producing consumer durables, though often with or through the presence of MNCs. This was a step forward, insofar as reducing their dependence on manufactured consumer goods, albeit with a greater dependence on capital goods imports, in particular, machinery. Therefore, there was clearly an advance and a change in terms of dependency, although, this still involved a net outflow of surplus value, given the differences in value added between the imports and exports, especially as much of the latter were still primary goods. Although these transfers of value, as reflected in the theoretical category of unequal exchange, constitute transfers of wealth, by the 1970s, there was now a new and rapidly growing additional source of transfers, namely the growth of foreign debt. Evidently, as is the case for most investments, initially, the net flow is positive, but the long term plan is for the net flow to be negative for the receiving country, such as Argentina, and the net flow positive to the lending country, as in the US.

However, this is where a major historical shift took place, namely the rise of neoliberal ideology and doctrine and eventually the implementation of neoliberal economic policies. Argentina was one of the three first infamous cases of neoliberal experiments, combined with military governments in the 1970s, along with Chile and Uruguay. This period for Argentina actually began a process of deindustrialization and a move toward the return of the primary sector, though not simply a return to the previous agro-export economy, strictly dominated by the Pampean oligarchy and the British; agribusiness was distinct in terms of character and international links. The world economy was changing, and this was the beginning of a new phase of capitalist globalization, with a new global actor—the transnational corporations with their global commodity chains.[1]

The examination of neoliberal policies and their impacts in Latin America starting with the debt crisis was evaluated. Moreover, eventually Brazil began its own process of deindustrialization and it was in the 1990s when neoliberal polices and the domination by transnationals led to transformations under the general category of globalization. Major shifts in terms of trade liberalization, deregulation of finance, privatizations, and last, but not least, the flexibilization of labor, took hold in country after country across the entire planet.

As in all the phases of dependency, there is always the internal and external dimension; it is not sufficient to simply claim that a given foreign government, such as the US, is simply imposing its will,[2] at least not in this current period of imperialism. In the cases of Argentina and Brazil, the shift of their insertion within the global economy in recent decades implied the tendencies of deindustrialization and reprimarization. On the one hand, as has been argued and presented (see Chapters 2 and 7) joining the WTO meant adhering to rules which severely limited the continued pursuit of industrialization. Evidently, the governments of Collor de Melo and Cardoso were clearly committed to facilitate the shifts of their local economies for the advantages that would come with a strengthening of links with transnational capital. Again, the return to the dependency on primary exports is a return to the same problems outlined by Prebisch. The difference from the agro-export period is that it is no longer just simply local agro-exports, but rather local agribusinesses, that

[1] Although the grand majority of TNCs were originally MNCs, their nature and way of operating in terms of production, investment and exchange had been transformed, and thus the new term, transnational corporations (Robinson 2004).

[2] Of course, there are instances of U.S. invasions, be it in Puerto Rico, Nicaragua, Cuba and the list goes on. Though, even in these instances, there are local elites that are willing to make alliances with the foreign occupiers, that accept the military invasion of their countries.

are inserted into more complex transnational chains, involving high-tech inputs, such as transgenic seeds, fertilizers, pesticides and technologies for extracting minerals, oil, etc.

Once again, the perennial problem of external vulnerability, exporting in order to earn foreign exchange, required for imports, and also paying interest payments, more than anything, for an ever-increasing foreign debt. This stage is more complex, and one could argue, more dependent, especially as the agrarian rent or mining rent which was controlled by local elites, now has to be shared substantially with the TNCs operating in the country, be it for RR seeds or new technologies, such as fracking or new mineral extraction techniques. Therefore, the problems of transfers of wealth continue and thus the control of the surplus is less available for the local population, and the elites are more wedded to transnational capital than ever before. In part, because they identify themselves as part of the transnational capitalist class, even if they are the junior partners. Moreover, given the continuation of the problem of foreign debt, serious problems can also result in increasing internal debt, as seen in Chapter 6 for the case of Brazil.

In most discussions of development problems and macroeconomic issues, it is rare to address the question of why does a country need so much foreign exchange, what is it used for, imports yes, but which imports and for what and for whom? How many luxury items, airline travel (mostly by the upper classes, the wealthy and political elite) is necessary NATIONALLY? In other words, for what and for whom is there such a need for foreign exchange and this combines with the problem of trade deficits and the growth of debt, not to mention debt crises, that continue, decade after decade, if not century after century. Evidently, there is a need to demand a more detailed analysis and society-wide debate.

This is not to argue for autarky and consider becoming like Albania in the 1970s, disconnecting from the world economy, but it is necessary to address and examine a perennial problem for the grand majority of countries on the globe. There is also a need to recognize, as had been the case 60 years ago, that there are structural problems, even Prebisch, a neoclassical economist and former Central Banker, clearly recognized this. Today any Central Banker in Latin America tends to be a hard-core neoliberal, just consider Meirelles with Lula; times have undoubtedly changed, but many of the problems of underdevelopment have not gone away.

In Chapter 7, the two major tendencies of deindustrialization and reprimarization were examined in detail for both countries. In addition, an evaluation of the process of reprimarization historically was carried out and the concept of accumulation by dispossession was considered, as one examined the main sectors associated with this tendency: cattle and livestock farming, soy and other transgenic crops, mega-mining, etc.

Subsequently, in Chapter 8, an attempt to produce on overall assessment of the neodevelopmentalism associated with the progressive governments of the Kirchners in Argentina (Nestor and Cristina) and the PT (Lula and Dilma) in Brazil was carried out. The aim was to evaluate the extent to which these progressive governments were actually achieving a new path of development. The limitations of neodevelopmentalism were presented in Chapter 8, and the problems of the current path considered in Chapter 9. It was concluded that there were major shortcomings of these projects, in terms of both social issues, and with regard to the environment. In order to elaborate on elements necessary for future alternatives, a summary of these issues is now presented.

The first set of issues are general macroeconomic problems, related to GDP growth, and problems of the labor market, whether it was high unemployment, high underemployment or the growth of the informal economy, not to mention the problem of low wages. This group of problems, when combined, as they often are, consistently lead to increases in poverty and indigence. The neoliberal model, when functioning well, for the economic elites, clearly leads to increases in inequality and this is one of the problems inherent to capitalism, although it is much more acute when the laissez-faire mentality dominates, as has been the case with neoliberalism for some 40 years. The other concern is to what extent the growth of GDP and employment are stable or not. As mentioned in Chapter 9, the upshot is that there were some 10 years of reasonable improvement for the working classes, and the poor and vulnerable, in Brazil and Argentina. Evidently, this is arguably positive, but this has been undermined since roughly 2013, and how long will it be, or how much worse do things have to become, before another push for ending social inclusion is possible. In both countries the real wages of decades past are much higher than today; this translates into a failure in terms of the basics of development, though not in terms of the goals of neoliberalism.

In terms of sectoral issues, one often thinks of manufacturing industry as capital intensive and that the primary sector is more labor intensive and therefore involves more employment, however, several key sectors linked to the tendency toward reprimarization are in fact rather capital intensive.

Soy is very capital intensive, as presented in Chapter 9 with the contrast, which deserves to be repeated: "For each 1000 Ha, the soybean crop employs 15 workers... the sugar cane 350 workers and ...the citric crop employs 1,300 workers" (Haro Sly 2017, p. 5). This contrast is amazing and issues of employment must always be considered when discussing the pros and cons of a given sector. Although soy production generates substantial foreign exchange, it is less in percentage terms than many other agricultural crops, given the costs of imported inputs and secondly, maybe more importantly, it involves proportionally much lower levels of employment.

Mining is also very capital intensive, and so is the petroleum sector. Therefore, several of the main activities associated with the reprimarization in Argentina and Brazil do not translate into more employment, but rather come to exacerbate the employment situation, causing increases in unemployment and therefore downward pressure on wages. A trade-off away from manufacturing could be more acceptable, if at the very least, there were an increase in jobs. Such a possibility would be the case for certain agricultural sectors, as considered below.

Continuing with the concerns with respect to the main sectors of soy, mining, petroleum and cattle, there have been solid evidence of the problems of displacing populations from their lands, through the process of accumulation of dispossession, as discussed in Chapter 7, and this has sadly involved the use of violence even in the twenty-first century. In the case of indigenous populations, there were cases of genocide pursued by the military government of Brazil back in the 1980s and shockingly enough this is a problem once again with the proto-fascist Bolsonaro in power, especially in the context of promoting the burning of parts of the Amazon, causing forest fires, and threatening the very existence of certain communities, as seen in Chapter 9.

Clearly related to this are the range of environmental issues in both Argentina and Brazil. In terms of the Amazon rain forest, the growth of primary sectors, have led to incredible levels of deforestation during the first decade of the century. Fortunately, this was followed by an improvement after major pressure internally and externally, however, since Temer and now Bolsonaro in power, there has been a major increase in deforestation once again. In addition, the problems have grown due to the sectors just mentioned, but also due to the establishment of hydroelectric plants, which also involves major displacement of populations.[3]

Other major environmental problems are the contamination or pollution caused by mining and the incredible levels of waste as described in Chapter 8, not to mention the toxic chemicals and mineral waste which contaminate the rivers, lakes, and other sources of water; necessary for communities to drink, and also used for agriculture, among other activities. Moreover, in the case of soy, there has been a social disaster in the province of Entre Rios of Argentina, due to the levels of pesticides in the water, not to mention problems with flooding (La Biodiversidad 2019). The other problem is that pesticides, such as glyphosate, end up leaving residues in the final products, be it oats, cotton, among other fruits and vegetables. Another problem with the excessive use of pesticides, with which the dependence has only grown, is the issue of glyphosate-resistant weeds or *malezas*, as pointed out by Pengue (2005), an Argentine agronomist. Another issue is that it is not clear what effects genetically modified organisms will have on biosystems over time, and in terms of other eco-balances.

Therefore, the set of environmental problems associated with these primary sectors and their level of seriousness alone calls into question the validity of this development path and should force us to truly consider a path based on sustainable development. But truly sustainable development is not one that jeopardizes the health of so many communities, increases the risks of fires as in August of 2020 in Argentina (Página 12 2020) or in Brazil in the inferno of August 2019, not to mention deforestation, causing loss of biodiversity and which is linked to the major problem of climate change for the planet. Since the Amazon Rain Forest is the largest natural sink for carbon dioxide, it plays an extremely important role in reducing the accelerated pace of climate change.

There are a range of additional health problems associated with the toxins in our air, rivers, and soil, ranging from cancer, skin problems,

[3] Consider the role of China in the case of the hydroelectric plant of Santa Cruz, Argentina-China (Gandini 2019).

and a range of diseases, including anencephaly. Moreover, science still has not established all the links between pollution and health problems.[4] Another environmental problem which derives from major displacements of natural habitats, and in part linked to the use of excessive agrotoxics is the problem of erosion, sometimes leading to major landslides, and this has been the case for several locations in Brazil, associated with the mining TNC Vale. In addition, there are the problems of a lack of safety controls, such as the oil spill in 2019 along the coast of Brazil from the Northeast all the way down to the Southeast and as of August 2020 there is not an identifiable culprit (Brazilian Report 2019). If a situation such as this continues unabated and without proper treatment and political resolve, this can come to impact economic activities quite negatively, along the lines of O'Connor's 2nd contradiction at a small scale, though not impacting TNCs.

10.2 Future or Alternative Paths of Development

There are many legitimate arguments to envision a future beyond capitalism and it should be apparent that we humans can do a much better job than the current state of affairs with capitalism in the twenty-first century, between the problems of poverty, inequality, disease, even pandemics, environmental disasters, and unprecedented climate migration beginning to transpire. A major part of the problem is evident given the major contradictions between human priorities and corporate (TNCs) priorities. What is being proposed here is first off, a transition beyond capitalism, as this will not take place overnight, just consider the fact that the transition between feudalism and capitalism took centuries. Of course, the discussion below will promote many skeptics from the left and right as to its viability. In any case, it is a proposal, though arguably a necessary proposal. The reason being is that what has been the *modus operandi* is not functioning, namely the attempts by "progressive" governments to pursue an alternative development path. Such attempts should not be considered as a viable alternative for either the short or medium term. Moreover, it is also absolutely necessary to ensure a new path corresponds to the will of the majority, respecting democratic process.

[4] In addition, the corporate interests that dominate the EPA and FDA inhibits the proper functioning of these public institutions, allegedly to protect the well-being of the U.S. population (see Robin 2008a, 2008b).

10.2.1 Transition Away from TNC-Dominated Capitalism

In Chapter 9 the problems of the current paths that had been pursued with the *Kirchneristas* and the PT and their limitations, especially given the overdependency on TNCs were summarized. In a recent article discussing the progressive governments of the Pink Tide, Robinson (2017) pointed out, that in spite of the advances of a greater role of the State, seeking to reduce social inclusion and achieve some level of redistribution of income, there was arguably more critical rhetoric. In fact, the "Pink Tide states were able to push forward a new wave of capitalist globalization with greater credibility than their orthodox and politically bankrupt neoliberal predecessors" (Robinson 2020).

Evidently, as observed in earlier chapters, thanks to the commodities boom, various governments were able to finance and implement social programs, in particular raising the standard of living of the working class and poor. As a result, poverty and indigence were reduced and some improvements in wages took place, yet the problems of unemployment and the informal economy remained resilient. This is consistent with the early change by the Lula administration from the symbolic program of "Zero Unemployment" (*Desemprego Cero*) to a much more attainable "Zero Hunger" (*Fome Cero*). The problem of unemployment is structural and is very much linked to the functioning of labor markets under capitalism; reality over many decades provide solid evidence that the concept of Full Employment is merely a myth.

The world financial crisis between 2007 and 2010, combined with the end of the commodity boom, clearly showed the limits of these progressive attempts to achieve some distribution of income in workers' favor. Subsequently, there were increasing economic problems, be it low growth, unemployment, and inflation, which led to increasing political problems, if not protests, as in Brazil, and thus opening up space for a resurgent right-wing to take power. Robinson presents a lucid analysis of what took place in Brazil:

> Brazil was most indicative of the mild reformist thrust of many Pink Tide governments, and the most tragic for the popular classes. President Luiz Inácio Lula da Silva won the 2002 election only after his wing of the Workers' Party moved sharply toward the political center and promised not to default on the country's foreign debt. In Brazil, as elsewhere, the Pink Tide state remained a part of the larger institutional networks of the global financial system and beholden to transnational finance capital. The

> Workers' Party government demobilized the mass social movements that brought it to power and then imposed austerity after the collapse. Only in this light can we understand the brazen return of the far right (Robinson 2017).

This concise assessment makes it even more clear that, at this point in time, an alternative, distinct from the recent attempts in Argentina and Brazil must be considered, and discussed by society. There is a clear need for change, but it is necessary that the basis for this change be rooted in progressive social movements and popular forces. The movements must include unions and worker movements, feminist movements, indigenous movements, anti-racist movements, such as Black Lives Matter,[5] and environmental and ecological movements.

As emphasized numerous times, problems with the current development paths are rooted in the dependency on TNCs in the context of neoliberal globalization and the necessity to adhere to the international rules of the WTO. As described earlier, a single country, or a few countries, could choose to exit the WTO at a given moment, yet this would constitute economic suicide. However, there is a strong probability that a block of countries, say twenty or thirty countries could push to exit *en masse* and have political success, in either exiting or forcing a full-scale reworking of the WTO. Given the lack of possibility of viable development, a fundamental human right, such as improvement of real wages, should not be seen as extreme, but necessary to avoid social chaos or worse in many countries, especially if the worst-case scenarios of climate change with concomitant environmental refugees start to manifest themselves. It will become more and more evident that continuing to work with the current framework of the WTO is extremist and absurd.

As discussed, and evaluated previously, the condition of economic dependency, in the current TNC-dominated global economy, brings a range of problems and limitations, and not long-term solutions for serious development. Therefore, there is a need to identify what elements are necessary for a viable alternative. When using the term viable, it is not

[5] Although Black Lives Matter is a movement rooted in the US, in recent months, after the brutal murder by the police of George Floyd in Minneapolis in May 2020, significant solidarity was expressed in many countries across the world. Evidently there is a range of similar anti-racist movements globally, including in Latin America. Consider the example of the Mapuche people, in the south of Argentina and Chile, or indigenous movements in Brazil, such as the Aliança dos Povos Indígenas do Brasil (APIB).

only from the feasibility in political economic terms, such as whether cooperatives in peasant and family agriculture can be productive and effective, beyond subsistence, but feasible in terms of *Realpolitik*. This latter point means being able to achieve changes at the national level, but also at the international level. In terms of the national level, the majority of populations in Latin America came to recognize the failure of neoliberal policies to achieve development and the false promises of the neoliberal politicians, whether it was Cardozo, Salinas de Gortari, or Menem, and were willing to push for a change. In the same vein, the populations of Argentina and Brazil, and other countries of the region or periphery, must recognize the limits of the previous attempts of pursuing new development paths, so-called neodevelopmentalism, by progressive governments, and insist on alternative proposals, which break from the WTO, and seek to go beyond the dependency on TNCs in the not so distant future.

Evidently, Argentina and Brazil are not at the point of revolutionary insurrection at this point in time, nevertheless, the absolute dependency on having to accommodate transnational corporations and their local allies must be broken. It is fundamental to recognize that the elite base of economic power, increasingly transnational, has been the same for progressive governments. Therefore, any government accommodating increasingly transnationalized elites, which have placed their bets on the processes of reprimarization and global financial markets, has basically abandoned national manufacturing industry.[6] Neither in Brazil nor in Argentina, is there a popular push to break from capitalism, in spite of some sectors, parties, or social movements that advocate for it, and thus, in the medium term at least, these peripheral countries will continue to maintain a dependent capitalist economy. In addition, the PT and Kirchners, never advocated a break from capitalism, and in fact, maintained the strategy whereby the interest of transnational capital continued to have precedence, in spite of much progressive rhetoric. It can be argued that without insisting on a clean break from capitalism, there is still serious space for improvement by not being as dependent on transnational capital, but having a goal of expanding the non-capitalist sectors of

[6] A solid example of the difficulties of progressive governments to challenge TNCs or national groups and coalitions linked to agribusiness TNCs was when Cristina Fernández Kirchner unsuccessfully sought a legitimate increase in their tax contributions for bonanza years. However, although the policy change was reasonable, these forces were able to achieve victory (Sartelli 2008).

the economy. Such a proposal is a long-term strategy, requiring mobilization and strategic alliances with other progressive allies, internally, within the region, and in other continents, in particular, the Global South, demanding a break from the WTO, in order to return development, but real development, to the table of negotiation. Fundamental in this discussion and demands is the necessity to put human rights and needs as the principal priority for any progressive government, not transnational corporate rights.

Of course, one cannot purport to prescribe an exact set of plans for a major structural shift, even though it is not about a revolutionary transformation, it is more a revolutionary reform, if you will. An attempt to finally break from neoliberal capitalism, but not capitalism itself, will tend to be pursuing an alternative socially oriented capitalism, which involves a much greater role for the State. The latter includes much greater planning and social inclusion, but the idea is very distinct from the perspective of neodevelopmentalism. One must recognize that the idea of attempting to be competitive in the global economy and working hand in hand with TNCs is NOT viable for development in the medium term. As far as a greater role of the state it is crucial to identify a means of industrial restructuring, so as to reduce foreign dependence, not autarky, and preferably, through a bloc of countries from the periphery seeking to pursue a new development path, seen as necessary as a transition beyond capitalism. One aspect is the importance of reindustrializing, though selectively and strategically, especially Brazil, but also Argentina, and preferably as part of a framework of a revamped Mercosur, ensuring a democratically constituted regional bloc.

Another major issue is the need to emphasize family and peasant agriculture but with serious efforts at improvements and pursuing agroecology and breaking from a monoculture approach in order to achieve a sustainable agriculture, even if for many years it will be less efficient compared to the maximum productivities of Monsanto agrotoxic agriculture. In contrast, more people will have jobs and better wages and environmental issues will be much improved, avoiding environmental disasters, not to mention a much healthier approach with respect to nature and human health. Evidently, a major effort of research and development must be pursued with significant resources, such as what Monsanto invested, in research over many decades so as to arrive at their wonderful form of Frankenfoods. In addition, agriculture for a given country, but even more advantageously, for a given region, should be oriented toward what is being consumed locally, along the lines of food sovereignty (Bello 2009; Shiva 2015; Flores Chamba 2020) not just food security. In such an approach, the surplus beyond social consumption can then be exported, instead of orienting agricultural production around exports, which cannot be consumed locally. If the export market does not stay strong, such as at the end of the 1990s and at the end of the recent commodities boom, then one has a serious problem of overproduction, limited accumulation and most likely trade deficit problems, if not worse.

In the instance of trade deficit problems, immediately at issue is the concern of foreign exchange. Of course, it is critical to discuss the source of foreign exchange, which will be necessary, for a range of inputs, at the very least, be it capital goods, or certain consumer goods. However, much of the use of foreign exchange has been required for paying off debt, often accumulated by military and previous anti-democratic governments, which probably cannot be paid, and in fact should be questioned, as many a negotiation took place between the IMF and a military dictatorship.[7] Moreover, there is the previously referred to issue of the use of foreign exchange, much of which has not been for the needs of the majority, but for much of the elite's luxury consumption habits. This must be carefully analyzed since the burden of the crisis is always on the poor and working-class families and the wealthy tend to not pay their share or what they could afford to pay. This reality is ever so evident here during the COVID-19 crisis and the wealthiest simply get absurdly wealthier[8] while major portions of populations in the periphery are choosing between going hungry or the risk of contagion and death.

Finding real solutions to the current set of environmental problems that confront Argentina and Brazil in the present day is a major challenge. Nevertheless, they could begin with a serious break from the dependence on foreign TNCs, but also local TNCs, such as Vale, JBS, Techint, and Maggio, and this means elevating human rights above corporate rights. Just what is meant by corporate rights—the corporation's rights to higher levels of profitability, not to avoid being hungry, but just the right to earn more and more billions. When such arguments are made one tends to

[7] It is also critical to note, as campaigns against foreign debt in the periphery, there are precedents, such as for Germany after WWII.

[8] Consider the shameful irony of how the CEO of Amazon, Bezos, has become the first person to own over US$ 200 billion, during the COVID-19 crisis, while his company is permanently laying off thousands of workers.

be given the response of how pushing for redistribution, such as taxing billionaires, will mean they will not invest.

The point is a society should not need to push in the opposite direction of human rights to make the conditions propitious for the TNCs. In fact, the goal should be a more just and equitable society, where such ridiculous concentration of wealth does not require governments, public agencies and institutions, and the grand majority of the population to accommodate their greed, by offering ever worsening wages. This flows in with the reality of accommodating TNCs often means relaxing environmental regulations or at the very least making them less stringent, more attractive than in the first world. In other words, the TNC formula forces the periphery to prostitute itself or offer conditions against the interest of populations or societies and the shared environment, just so they will invest and then rob the lion's share of wealth at the end of the day. This is the exact opposite of sustainable development.

Along the lines of the argument of Robinson (2004), during recent decades there has been the emergence of a transnational capitalist class, which is an effective coalition of the elites of the periphery and the elites of the first world[9]; and they seem to have things quite clear. Especially given the fact that during the neoliberal period, there has never been such an unprecedented transfer of wealth from the poor and middle classes to the wealthy, more than at any time in human history (Dumeníl and Lévy 2004; Harvey 2005). On the one hand, it can be argued that this appears to be a very serious indictment of capitalism, and that cannot be denied. Many would argue that the next step is the overthrow of the capitalist system, however, this is premature at the present time, primarily because this not what the majority of the populations of the periphery are currently demanding. And although it is this population which is suffering the most from this extremely unequal and anti-democratic system, they are not as a whole pushing for a systemic change at present. In part, because they had given their efforts and faith for progressive governments, which in several ways, let them down, and some are wary of new promises by "progressive" politicians.

A fundamental point, in proposing an alternative to TNC-dominated neoliberal capitalism is the promotion of a transition beyond capitalism,

[9] There is not a particular institution which one could argue represents the transnational capitalist class, but an organization such as the World Economic Forum, which meets each year in Davos, does come rather close.

and therefore the need for an alternative to promote a non-capitalist sector. Secondly, there is a need to have a solid commitment, not simply a minor percentage of some 2 or 3% of a government budget, dedicated to non-capitalist production, be it cooperatives, in manufacturing, or agriculture, especially for family and peasant agriculture, and not of the Soviet style collectivizations, but rather encouraging a solidarity or community-based economy,[10] and from the bottom up, with significant autonomous planning, research, and development. The idea that progressive solutions can come from the top down has reached its limit of being a credible option. A more serious effort has to be made to democratize the discussion of economic options, including paths of development, but actually carried out and done in a serious fashion. There should be democratic processes in place for truly evaluating different projects, be it mining, petroleum, soy, etc., but considering all angles of a project, not just the version according to Monsanto or a Chinese development corporation or Vale or the Ministry of Mining. The experiences of neighborhood assemblies or committees, discussing a range of issues at the local, provincial, and national level in Argentina, at the turn of the century, had a significant amount of success, and in spite of certain problems, these could be pursued once again. The experiences of democratic participatory budgets, with the PT, as in Porto Alegre, Brazil, are examples which can be built upon.

As described above, the role of human rights is crucial and should be placed front center when considering the different development paths. The sad reality that many human rights are being violated at present and often because of the need to push forward the mega-projects of the TNCs, whether foreign or local, such as Vale in Carajás, soy farmers in Acre or the mining projects expropriating the Mapuches in Neuquén. This not only involved forcibly pushing people off their land, namely, expropriations, which involved violence, and even murder, and in extreme cases, it has led to genocide of indigenous tribes and even now in the twenty-first century, the leader of Brazil is threatening to commit genocide again.[11] This should not really be surprising, as this is a leader that

[10] There has been extensive research and projects around a solidarity economy (*Economía Solidaria*), and so on, authors such as Coraggio (2011b), Razeto (1999), and Gaiger (2007).

[11] Besides the issue of forest fires and the burning down of communities (see Chapter 9), and the promotion thereof by Bolsonaro, in addition, in April 2020, there

praises the former military government of Brazil and considers Pinochet to be a hero. The scarier thing is so many people in Brazil voted for him and even in the middle of 2020, with the national disaster taking place with regard to the pandemic and economic crisis, he is the only leader that was worse than Trump and that is not easy.

The issues of human rights and the right to protest have grown globally and are part of the root problem associated with the turmoil and protest over police brutality in the US in 2020, as well as across the globe, including Latin America.[12] Democracy has regressed significantly, across the globe, and even progressive governments, end up accepting this, and not opposing the criminalization of resistance, and the militarization of many police forces. As seen previously, this problem has also been present in Argentina, against mining companies, for example, and in the protests in Brazil, over environmental problems and illegal logging or the rights of indigenous people to their land or protecting their sacred lands from destruction. How would the Irish or Italian Catholics of NYC react, if suddenly a major development project meant they were going to tear up cemeteries in Queens or Brooklyn? Yet, in the US, you have had the very same thing taking place with the Dakota Access pipeline protests, where Obama and Trump have both accepted sending in federal troops, maybe with the former President playing dumb, and the other actively being a cheerleader in suppressing the human rights of these indigenous people.

Criminalization of resistance movements or the right to free speech is by no means a minor issue, especially given the increase of the treaties for trade (and investment) which strongly defend the rights of profits of transnationals, and often foreign firms, over the human rights of the citizens of a given country. Consider the case mentioned above, of the Ethyl Corporation and the carcinogen MMT in Canada and many other cases, where the WTO becomes the supreme court that always defends the rights of TNCs over human rights. If serious changes are not made

was serious violence with firearms against locals on land taken from them by Vale and a security agency, accused of major violations of human rights (Prosegur), in the Amazon (see Angelo 2020).

[12] Recent examples in Latin America include the cases of Chile, Ecuador, and Bolivia in 2019 and the Chocobar Doctrine (*Doctrina Chocobar*) in Argentina in 2018, not to mention the current atmosphere in Brazil with police, the military and militias having free reign in many instances.

soon, these precedents get more difficult to be reversed and if leaders like Bolsonaro and Trump continue to not just appear on the scene, with their armed reactionaries, but actually win elections, the future looks very dark and bleak.

Therefore, be it the issue of human rights or in pursuit of a new development path, there is an urgent need to seek alliances with a range of social movements, rooted in crucial issues and defending the right to a more tolerant society, and in opposition to those that are white supremacist, xenophobic, misogynist, or homophobic. An alternative is urgently needed with a more inclusive social contract instead of just the apathetic response of "that's capitalism" or "that's neoliberalism" as Margaret Thatcher advocated in her infamous "There is NO Alternative." Although many say that you cannot fight city hall, the reality is that it is NEVER easy, but yes you can fight City Hall. The struggles continue!

10.3 Post-script on COVID-19

Evidently, as the research and theoretical development pursued in the writing of this book advanced, such a crisis like that of COVID-19, could not have been anticipated. Nevertheless, given the importance of the health and economic situation in both Brazil and Argentina, with the COVID-19 crisis, and the potential impact for development, in the near and medium terms, a brief discussion was deemed appropriate and thus I chose to add this post-script.

First off, this is the worse pandemic since the Spanish flu over 100 years ago, and the economic crisis that is accompanying it, due to the need for social isolation, etc. and was threatening to be as bad as the 1930s, and worldwide still has the potential to be one of the worst capitalist crisis in the history of the system. A clear distinction is that the root cause is not capitalist contradictions, although the hangover from the crisis of 2007–2010, is still playing a role in the evolution of the current COVID-19 economic crisis.

There is a range of analyses, including the rosiest versions that a V-shaped recovery is expected by the end of 2020, to the opposite side of the spectrum arguing that we may be headed to a decade of depression.[13]

[13] Relevant articles discussing the economic crisis related to COVID-19 are: Roubini (2020), Rodrik and Stantcheva (2020), Stiglitz (2020), and Ocampo and Faccio (2020).

With regard to the former view, there are many from the Wall Street world, arguing that the worst took place between March and June of 2020, that the markets took their hits and now we are on course for the V-shaped recovery. Famous for predicting the mortgage crisis very early on, Nouriel Roubini, has been nicknamed Dr. Doom, given his pessimistic, or perhaps more realistic view of the world economy. He has argued that this crisis could not only be as bad as the 1930s but it could also last 10 years. He has also argued that a recovery could take place followed by a second wave, in other words, after a minor recovery, a more serious collapse. The latter would not even be a slow recovery as in a U-shaped curve, but rather an L-shaped curve, going down and staying stagnant (Roubini 2020).

Back in April 2020, Roubini laid out a set of 10 potential phenomena that could occur. For many, this would be a set of worst-case scenarios and for most, preferably distinct crises, but Roubini argues that some combination of the 10, if not all 10, have the possibility of occurring. His analysis ranged from standard economic issues, such as interest rates, inflation, deflation, but also considered the geopolitical constellation, which includes the US-China tensions, not to mention a range of other problems, including climate change. For many this can seem to be the set of plagues associated with Armageddon itself and that along those lines some could also argue that Trump is the Antichrist.

Avoiding such truly Apocalyptic visions and evangelical approaches to economic analysis, let us consider some of the facts so far and some reasonable predictions of what scenarios should be expected. Subsequently, we shall attempt to discern to what extent these scenarios, mostly depressing and negative economic news, could mean for the potential of alternative or future paths of development for the Southern Cone of South America, but more specifically for the two countries that have been the subject of this book, namely Argentina and Brazil.

For the year 2020, the world experienced a negative 3.27% growth rate, even given the exception of China. Though even with China for 2021 and beyond, it is not clear, since they do depend significantly on exports and the worse the economy becomes for other countries, the weaker is their capacity to pay for foreign goods or buy Chinese goods. Although China has spoken about and has begun to make policy shifts to increase the demand from its internal economy, this still takes time and will mean increasing real wages in China with its associated negative effects for profits. Moreover, the time frame for developing an internal market could still mean China experiences setbacks, including a recession. But even if they stay in the black, the majority of the world will be experiencing a recession, given the fact that many countries are still having lockdowns, even in Europe, as of June 2021. The problems of COVID-19, including a lack of vaccines, for so many countries, continues to generate major political and health crises, such as in Brazil and India.

In spite of many countries beginning vaccine programs by the middle of 2021, the majority of the world will not be completely vaccinated till some point in 2022, if not 2023. A major economic problem, is still the need for social distancing and controls, if not tests, so as to avoid the high-level contagions. In many parts of the periphery, the system of public health has been gutted, and subject to austerity programs and its functioning is often at maximum capacity with much greater risks of deaths. In countries such as Brazil, India and Ecuador, it is imperative to not risk getting infected because the hospitals are hopelessly unprepared, understaffed, undersupplied and the risk of dying is much higher especially for the more vulnerable populations, primarily the poor and elderly. The reality is that many countries are making the push to open up controls so as to have the economy moving toward normal but this has produced some horrendous results, such as in numerous states in the US, not to mention in Latin America and elsewhere. A number of countries should have made a push together to demand cheaper loans from the IMF for this period or forced the billionaires to pay their share for once, especially given that we are enduring the worst planetary and humanitarian crisis since WWI.

Until the pandemic is under control, meaning that the vaccine becomes generally available only then can a real world economic recovery begin. At present, for the periphery, it is anticipated that economic problems will continue to worsen for some time, especially as there has not been a sufficient push for a global solution, including the wealthier countries, banks, etc. assisting the poorer parts of the globe, in spite of some advances or the proclamations of the G-7 in Cornwall in June 2021. As Naomi Klein has said in the context of the climate crisis, this is once again Bad Timing; neoliberal capitalism is not known for promoting compassion and care for fellow human beings as one of their priorities. It is rather sad that instead it seems that survival of the fittest still reigns and if this is the best that we can do here in the twenty-first century, it is a sad legacy for humanity.

With regard to the future development paths for Argentina and Brazil, overcoming the pandemic is the first priority and at a very minimum that the governments, even Bolsonaro, guarantee that the populations are able to access basic necessities. Secondly, depending on what has taken place for the global economy, both countries will evidently need a significant period to come out of a recession and seek some return to normalcy, including struggling to ensure that human rights are guaranteed, given the fact that many human rights have been violated during this crisis so far.

In order for serious efforts in pursuing discussion over alternative development trajectories as discussed above, several conditions would preferably be met. The first is that both countries overcome the pandemic and also have positive growth rates and some level of economic stability. Secondly, that they have progressive parties in power, thus requiring that Bolsonaro is not reelected, nor a right-wing conservative, and that Argentina continues to have a Peronist/Kirchnerista in the government. In spite of the limitations of the PT and the Kirchneristas, the potential to moving toward a more serious development alternative has much greater feasibility with progressive parties in power compared to the right-wing or proto-fascists.

References

Angelo, Maurício. 2020. "Novo ataque de seguranças da Vale a agricultores acirra conflito pela terra no Pará." *Reporter Brasil* (June 27, 2020).

Bello, Walden. 2009. *The Food Wars*. London: Verso.

Biodiversidad, La. 2019. "Inundaciones y modelo productivo". February 4, 2019.

Brazilian Report. 2019. "Brazil's Mistakes in Containing Massive Oil Spill." October 30, 2019.

Coraggio, José Luis. 2011b. *Economía social y solidaria. El trabajo entes que el capital*. Quito: Ediciones Abya-Yala.

Dumeníl, G., and Lévy, D. 2004. *Capital Resurgent. Roots of the Neoliberal Revolution*. Cambridge, MA: Harvard University Press.

Flores Chamba, Enith. 2020. "El Modelo Extractivista y los Peligros para la Soberanía Alimentaria en el Caso Ecuatoriano." *SaberEs*., Vol. 12, No. 1, pp. 1–19.

Gaiger, Luis Ignacio. 2007. "La economía solidaria y el capitalismo en la perspectiva de las transiciones históricas". En *La economía social desde la periferia. Contribuciones Latinoamericanas*, organizado por José Luis Coraggio, 79–109. Buenos Aires: Universidad nacional General Sarmiento/Altamira.

Gandini, Nicolad. 2019. "Represas de Santa Cruz, la avanzada china en infraestructura energética." *Econo Journal* (June 6, 2019).

Haro Sly, Maria José. 2017. "The Argentine Portion of the Soybean Commodity Chain." *Palgrave Communications*.

Harvey, David. 2005. *A Brief History of Neoliberalism*. Oxford: Oxford University Press.

Ocampo, José Antonio, and Tommaso Faccio. 2020. "Making Multinationals and the Wealthy Pay." *Project Syndicate*, June 30th, 2020.

Página 12. 2020. "Incendios en el Delta: todos los caminos conducen a los productores agropecuarios." 6 August. www.pagina12.com.ar/283103-incendios-en-el-delta-todos-los-caminos-conducen-a-losprodu?utm_source=gravitec&utm_medium=push&utm_campaign=rss.

Pengue, Walter. 2005. "Environmental and Socio Economic Impacts of Transgenic Crops Releasing in Argentina and South America: An Ecological Economics Approach." *Bulletin of Science, Technology & Society*, Vol. 25, No. 4 (August 2005), pp. 1–9.

Razeto, Migliaro Luis. 1999. "La economía solidaria: concepto, realidad y proyecto." http://www.luisrazeto.net/.

Robin, Marie-Monique. 2008a. (Director) *The World According to Monsanto*. A documentary Film.

Robin, Marie-Monique. 2008b. *The World According to Monsanto: Pollution, Corruption, and the Control of the World's Food Supply*. New York: The New Press.

Robinson, William I. 2004. *A Theory of Global Capitalism—Production, Class and State in a Transnational World*. Baltimore: The John Hopkins University Press.

Robinson, William I. 2017. "Passive Revolution: The Transnational Capitalist Class Unravels Latin America's Pink Tide." In *Truthout*, June 6, 2017.

Robinson, William I. 2020. "Global capitalism post-pandemic." *Race and Class*, Vol. 62, No. 2 (2020).

Rodrik, Dani, and Stefanie Stantcheva. 2020. "The Post-Pandemic Social Contract." *Proyect Syndicate*, June 11, 2020.

Roubini, Nouriel. 2020. "The Coming Greater Depression of the 2020s." *Project Syndicate*, April 28, 2020.

Sartelli, Eduardo (dir.). 2008. *Patrones en la Ruta: El conflicto agrario y los enfrentamientos en el seno de la burguesía, marzo-julio de 2008*. Buenos Aires: Ediciones Razón y Revolución.

Shiva, Vandana (ed). 2015. *Seed Sovereignty, Food Security: Women in the Vanguard of the Fight against GMOS and Corporate Agriculture*. Berkeley, CA: North Atlantic Books.

Stiglitz, Joseph E. 2020. "Priorities for the COVID-19 Economy." *Project Syndicate*, July 1st, 2020.

References

AAPRESID (Asociación Argentina de Productores en Siembra Directa). 2012. Evolución de la superficie en Siembra Directa en Argentina. www.aapresid.org.ar/.

Alvarez, Juan. 1929. *Temas de la Historia Económica Argentina*. Buenos Aires: Ateneo.

Anderson, Perry. 2019. "Bolsonaro's Brazil." *London's Review of Books*, Vol. 41, No. 3 (February 7, 2019).

———. 2011. "Lula's Brazil." *London's Review of Books*, Vol. 33, No. 7 (March 31, 2011).

Angelo, Maurício. 2020. "Novo ataque de seguranças da Vale a agricultores acirra conflito pela terra no Pará." *Reporter Brasil* (June 27, 2020).

Antunes, Ricardo. 1992. *A rebeldia do trabalho: o confronto operário no ABC paulista: as greves de 1978/80* (2° ed.). Campina (SP): Editora da UNICAMP.

Aranda, Darío. 2015. "Por el crecimiento, pero verde." *Página 12*, December 18, 2015.

Arceo, Enrique. 2003. *Argentina en la Periferia Próspera. Renta Internacional, dominación oligárquica y modo de acumulación*. Buenos Aires: Universidad Nacional de Quilmes Ediciones.

Ashman, S., and Callinicos, A. 2006. "Capital Accumulation and the State System: Assessing David Harvey's, The New Imperialism." *Historical Materialism*, Vol. 14, No. 4.

Aureliano, L.M. 1981. *No limiar da industrialização*. São Paulo: Editora Braziliense.

P. Cooney, *Paths of Development in the Southern Cone*, Palgrave Insights into Apocalypse Economics, https://doi.org/10.1007/978-3-030-67673-5

Azcurra, Fernando Hugo. 2011. "Las diez tesis sobre el Nuevo Desarrollismo elaboradas por economistas heterodoxos en un encuentro financiado por la Fundación Ford en el 2010."

Azpiazu, D., and Schorr, M. 2004. "Los impactos regresivos de las privatizaciones en la Argentina: ¿"errores de diseño" o funcionalidad frente a los intereses del poder económico?". In: R. Boyer and J. C. Neffa (eds.), *La economía argentina y su crisis (1976–2001): visiones institucionalistas y regulacionistas*. Buenos Aires: Miño y Dávila.

Baker, Dean, and Weisbrot, M. 2002. "The Role of Social Security Privatization in Argentina's Economic Crisis." *Center for Economic and Policy Research*, April 16, 2002, Washington, DC.

Bambirra, Vania 1978. *Teoría de la dependencia: una anticrítica*. Mexico City: Ediciones Era.

Banco Central do Brasil. 2004–2021. https://www.bcb.gov.br/.

Bastos, P.P. 2006. "Controle de capitais: uma comparação internacional." Presented at the *3rd Latin American Political Science Congress*, Unicamp, Campinas, Brazil, September 2006.

Basualdo, Eduardo M. 2001. *Sistema político y modelo de Acumulación en la Argentina*. Buenos Aires: Universidad Nacional de Quilmes.

———. 2003. "Historia económica: Las reformas estructurales y el plan de convertibilidad durante la década de los noventa, El auge y la crisis de la valorización financiera." *Revista Realidad Económica*, Número 200, 16 de noviembre–31 de diciembre 2003, Buenos Aires.

Bello, Walden. 2009. *The Food Wars*. London: Verso.

Bensaïd, Daniel. 2008. *Les dépossédés- Karl Marx, les voleurs de bois et le droit des pauvres*. Québec: Lux Éditeur.

Bielschowsky, Ricardo. 2004. *Pensamento econômico brasileiro: o ciclo ideológico do desenvolvimentismo* (5ª ed.). Rio de Janeiro: Contraponto.

Biodiversidad, La. 2019. "Inundaciones y modelo productivo". February 4, 2019.

Biondi, Aloysio. 1999. *O Brasil privatizado: Um balanço do desmonte do Estado*. São Paulo: Editora Fundação Perseu Abramo.

———. 2000. *O Brasil privatizado II: O assalto das privatizações continua*. São Paulo: Editora Fundação Perseu Abramo.

Bolinaga, L., and Slipak, A. 2015. "El consenso de Beijing y la reprimarización productiva de américa latina: El caso argentino." *Revista Problemas Del Desarrollo*, Vol. 46, No. 183, pp. 33–58.

Bond, Patrick. 2006. *Looting Africa: The Economics of Exploitation*. New York: Zed Books.

Brazilian Report. 2019. "Brazil's Mistakes in Containing Massive Oil Spill." October 30, 2019.

Brenner, Robert. 1998. "The Economics of Global Turbulence." *New Left Review*, Special Issue 229, May/June 1998.

———. 2006. *What Is, and What Is Not, Imperialism? Historical Materialism*, Vol. 14, No. 4, pp. 79–105.

Bresser-Pereira, Luís Carlos. 2011. "An Account of New Developmentalism and Its Structuralist Macroeconomics." *Brazilian Journal of Political Economy*, Vol. 31, No. 3 (123) (July–September/2011), pp. 493–502.

Brondizio, E.S. 2004. "Agricultural Intensification, Economic Identity and Shared Invisibility in Amazonian Peasantry: Caboclos and Colonists in Comparative Perspective." *Culture & Agriculture*, Vol. 26, pp. 1–24.

Buck, Daniel. 2009. "On Primitive Accumulation and Its Shadowy Twin, Subsumption." *Human Geography*, Vol. 2, No. 3.

Buenos Aires Times. 2020. "China Overtook Brazil as Argentina's Largest Trading Partner in April." 6 April. Accessed at https://www.batimes.com.ar/news/economy/china-overtook-brazil-as-argentinas-largest-trading-partner-in-april.phtml.

Bunker, Stephen G. 1985. *Underdeveloping the Amazon*. Chicago: University of Chicago Press.

Bunker, Stephen, and Paul Ciccantell. 2005. *Globalization and the Race for Resources*. Baltimore: Johns Hopkins University Press.

Butler, Rhett A. 2020. "Brazil Revises Deforestation Data: Amazon Rainforest Loss Topped 10,000 sq. km in 2019." *Mongabay Series: Amazon Conservation, Global Forests*.

Canitrot, Adolfo. 1981. "Teoría y práctica del liberalismo. Política antiinflacionaria y apertura económica en la Argentina, 1976–1981." *Desarrollo Económico*, No. 82, pp. 131–189.

Cano, Wilson. 1977. *Raízes da concentração industrial em São Paulo*. São Paulo: Difel.

———. 1999. *Soberania e Política Econômica na América Latina*. São Paulo: UNESP.

Carcanholo, Marcelo Dias. 2017. *Dependencia, super-explotación del Trabajo y Crisis: una interpretación desde Marx*. Madrid: Ediciones Maia.

Carcanholo, R. 2007. "La Experiencia Brasileña: Deuda Externa, FMI y Política Económica." *Revista de SEPLA*, No. 1, set. 2007.

Cardoso, Fernando H. 1972. "Dependency and Development in Latin America." *New Left Review*, No. 74 (June–August 1972), pp. 83–95.

Cardoso, Fernando H., and Faletto, Enzo. 1979. *Dependency and Development in Latin America*. Berkeley: University of California Press.

———. 2011. *Dependência e Desenvolvimento na América Latina*. Rio de Janeiro: Civilização Brasileira.

Carneiro, Ricardo. 2002. *Desenvolvimento em crise: a economia brasileira no último quartel do século XX*. São Paulo: Editora UNESP, IE – Unicamp.

———. 2008. *Impasses do desenvolvimento Brasileiro: a questão produtiva. Campinas*. SP: Unicamp. IE. 56 p. (*Texto para Discussão*, n. 153).

Carvalho, Carlos Eduardo. 2004. "Dívida pública: um debate necessário." In: João Sicsú, L.F.R. Paula, R. Michel (orgs.), *Novo-Desenvolvimentismo: Um projeto nacional de crescimento com equidade social*. Rio de Janeiro: Fundação Konrad Adenauer.

———. 2007. "A Dívida Interna: Custos, Restrições ao Crescimento, Alternativas." IEEI versão revista, April 24, 2007.

Castro, Antonio Barros De, and Francisco Eduardo Pires De Souza. 1987. *Economia Brasileira em Marcha Forçada*. Rio de Janeiro: Paz e Terra.

Chang, Han-Joon. 2002a. *Kicking Away the Ladder—Development Strategy in Historical Perspective*. London: Anthem Press.

——— (ed.). 2002b. *Rethinking Development Economics*. London: Anthem Press.

———. 2007. "Kicking Away the Ladder: The Real History of Free Trade." In: Anwar Shaikh (ed.), *Globalization and the Myths of Free Trade: History, Theory and Empirical Evidence*. New York: Routledge.

Chilcote, Ronald. 1981. "Issues of Theory in Dependency and Marxism." *Latin American Perspectives, Dependency and Marxism*, Issues 30 and 31, Summer and Fall, 1981, Vol. VIII, Nos. 3 and 4, pp. 3–16.

Cibils, A., Weisbrot, M., and Kar, D. 2002. "Argentina Since Default. The IMF and the Depression." *Center for Economic and Policy Research*. Briefing paper, September 3, 2002. Washington, DC.

CIFRA. 2011. "Rentabilidad, empleo y condiciones de trabajo en el sector agropecuario." *Documento de Trabajo*, N. 8, febrero.

The Commoner. 2001. *Enclosures, the Mirror Image of Alternatives*, No. 2 (September).

Cooney, Paul. 2001. "The Mexican Crisis and the Maquiladora Boom—A Paradox of Development or the Logic of Neoliberalism." *Latin American Perspectives*, Vol. 28, pp. 55–83.

———. 2007a. "Argentina's Quarter Century Experiment with Neoliberalism: From Dictatorship to Depression." *Revista de Economia Contemporânea*. Rio de Janeiro, Vol. 11, No. 1 (January/April).

———. 2007b. "Evaluando el Neoliberalismo en América Latina: Los casos de Argentina, Brasil y México." Presented at the *XII Encontro da SEP*, June 2007.

———. 2008a. "Uma Avaliação Empírica da Lei Geral da Acumulação Capitalista no Período Atual de Globalização Neoliberal." *Revista de Economia UFPR (Curitiba)*, Vol. 35, pp. 51–76.

———. 2008b. "Dos décadas de Neoliberalismo en México: resultados y retos." *Novos Cadernos NAEA*, No. 11, pp. 15–42.

———. 2010. "Late Neoliberalism." In: Richard Westra (ed.), *Brazil: Social and Economic Impacts of Trade and Financial Liberalization in Confronting Global*

Neoliberalism—Third World Resistance and Development Strategies. Atlanta: Clarity Press.

———. 2013. "El Estado del Mercado de Trabajo Informal en el Cono Sur: los casos de Argentina y Brasil." Presented at the *VI Jornadas de Economía Crítica*, Mendoza, Argentina, 2013.

———. 2014. "Desindustrialización y Reprimarización en el Cono Sur: una comparación de Argentina y Brasil en décadas recientes." Ponencia en las *Jornadas de Economía Crítica*, La Plata, Argentina, 16 a 18 de octubre de 2014.

———. 2015. "Evaluación de la validez de la caracterización de la economía Argentina como neodesarrollista para el período de pos-convertibilidad." Presented at *Jornadas de Enseñanza en Economía*, UNGS, Buenos Aires, Argentina.

———. 2016. "Reprimarization: Implications for the Environment and Development in Latin America: The Cases of Argentina and Brazil." *RRPE*, Vol. 48, No. 4.

———. 2017. "Current Paths of Development in the Southern Cone: Deindustrialization and a Return to the Agro-export Model." In: Richard Westra (ed.), *The Political Economy of Emerging Markets Varieties of BRICS in the Age of Global Crises and Austerity*. New York: Routledge.

———. 2020. "Argentina y Brasil: tendencias de desindustrialización y reprimarización." PICTO in Sergio Emiliozzi and Karina Forcinito (compiladorxs), *Políticas de ciencia, tecnología e innovación: La emergencia de los instrumentos sectoriales en Argentina y Brasil*. Prov. de Buenos Aires: Ediciones UNGS.

———. 2021 (forthcoming). "Transnationals, Dependent Development and the Environment in Latin America in the 21st Century." In: *Handbook of Latin America and the Environment*. London: Routledge.

Cooney, Paul, and Sacher, W. 2015. "Reprimarización en Argentina y Brasil y la relevancia del concepto de 'acumulación por desposesión'." Presented at the VIII JEC, Rio Cuarto, Argentina.

Cooney, Paul, and Santarcángelo, Juan E. 2011. "La industria en Argentina y Brasil a comienzos del siglo XXI: Avances y desafíos." Trabajo presentado en las *Jornadas de Economía Crítica*, agosto 2011, Cordoba, Argentina.

Cooney, Paul, and Trindade, José R. 2016. "Reprimarización, Minería Transnacional y el Medio Ambiente en la Amazonia Brasileña." Presented at the *IX Jornadas de Economía Crítica*, agosto 25–27, 2016, Cordoba, Argentina.

Cooney, Paul and Trindade, José R. 2017. "Dependency Approach in Latin America: Confronting Challenges of the 21st Century." Presented at the *X Jornadas de Economía Crítica*, September 2017, UNGS, Buenos Aires, Argentina.

COPROFAM. 2018. *Políticas Públicas para la Agricultura Familiar de Brasil*.

Coraggio, José Luis. 2011a. "Alcances y desafíos de las prácticas de Economía Social y Solidaria." Presented in the panel "Interrogantes y desafíos" del *Foro 2000–2010: Diez años de Economía Social Otro Siglo—Otra Economía*, abril 30, 2011.

———. 2011b. *Economía social y solidaria. El trabajo entes que el capital.* Quito: Ediciones Abya-Yala.

Coriat, B., and Sabóia, J. 1988. "Regime de acumulação e relação salarial no Brasil: um processo de fordização forçada e contrariada." *Ensaios FEE*, Vol. 9, No. 2, pp. 3–45.

Costa de Assis, Francisco. 2000. *Formação Agropecuária da Amazônia: os desafios do desenvolvimento sustentável.* Belém: NAEA.

Damill, M., Frenkel, R., and Juvenal, L. 2004. "Las cuentas públicas y la crisis de la convertibilidad en la Argentina." In: R. Boyer and J.C. Neffa (eds.), *La economía argentina y su crisis (1976–2001): visiones institucionalistas y regulacionistas*. Buenos Aires: Miño y Dávila.

Davis, Mike. 2017. *Late Victorian Holocausts: El Niño, Famines and the Making of the Third World.* New York: Verso.

Dean, W. 1976. *A industrialização de São Paulo* (2^a ed.). São Paulo: Difel.

De Oliveira, F.A., and Nakatani, P. 2007. "The Brazilian Economy Under Lula: A Balance of Contradictions." *Monthly Review*, Vol. 58, No. 8 (February).

Díaz Alejandro, C.F. 1975. *Ensayos sobre la historia económica argentina* (2^a ed.). Buenos Aires: Amorrortu.

DIEESE (Departamento Inter Sindicato da Estadística e Estudos Socioeconômicos). 2020. www.dieese.org.br.

Dinerstein, A. 2003a. "The Battle of Buenos Aires. Crisis, Insurrection and the Reinvention of Politics in Argentina." *Historical Materialism*, Vol. 10, No. 4, London.

———. 2003b. "Power or Counter Power? The Dilemma of the *Piquetero* Movement in Argentina Post Crisis." *Capital & Class*, Vol. 81, London.

Di Tella, Guido, and Zymelman, Manuel. 1967. *Las Etapas del Desarrollo Económico Argentino.* Buenos Aires: Editorial Universitaria de Buenos Aires.

Dorfman, A. 1983. *Cincuenta Años de Industrialización en la argentina 1930–1980.* Buenos Aires: Ediciones Solar.

Dos Santos, Theotônio. 1970. "The Structure of Dependence." *American Economic Review*, Vol. LX (May), pp. 231–236.

Duarte, M. 2002. "Los impactos de las privatizaciones sobre el mercado de trabajo: desocupación y creciente precarización laboral." In: D. Azpiazu (ed.), *Privatizaciones y Poder Económico.* Buenos Aires: Universidad Nacional de Quilmes.

Dumenil, G., and Lévy, D. 2004. *Capital Resurgent: Roots of the Neoliberal Revolution.* Cambridge, MA: Harvard University Press.

———. 2011. *The Crisis of Neoliberalism*. Cambridge, MA: Harvard University Press.

Dunn, B. 2007. "Accumulation by Dispossession or Accumulation of Capital? The Case of China." *Journal of Australian Political Economy*, Vol. 60.

Dussel, E. 1997. *La Economía de la Polarización—Teoría y Evolución del Cambio Estructural de las Manufacturas Mexicanas (1988–1996)*. México, D.F.: Editorial Jus.

ECLA. 1958, 2008. http://www.eclac.cl.

ECLAC. 2004. *Statistical Yearbook for Latin America and the Caribbean*. http://www.eclac.cl.

Edelman, Marc. 2020. "Bringing the Moral Economy Back into the Study of 21st Century Transnational Peasant Movements." *American Anthropologist* Vol. 107, No. 3 (2005).

EJOLT. 2020. *Environmental Justice Organisations, Liabilities and Trade*. www.ejolt.org. Last visited July 12, 2020.

FAO. 2020. https://www.fao.org/data/en/.

Fearnside, Philip. 2020. "Oil and Gas Project Threatens Brazil's Last Great Block of Amazon Forest." *Mongabay Series: Amazon Conservation*.

Fearnside et al. 2019. "Deforestation Control in the Brazilian Amazon: A Conservation Struggle Being Lost as Agreements and Regulations Are Subverted and Bypassed." *Perspectives in Ecology and Conservation*, No. 17.

Féliz, Mariano. 2019. "Neodevelopmentalism and Dependency in Twenty-first Century Argentina: Insights from the Work of Ruy Mauro Marini." *Latin American Perspectives*, Vol. 46, No. 1 (224), pp. 105–221, January 2019.

Feliz, Mariano, and Lopez, Emiliano. 2010. "¿Por qué neodesarrollismo? Hacia una caracterización de la nueva modalidad de desarrollo capitalista en la Argentina reciente" *VI Jornadas de Sociología de la UNLP*, La Plata, Argentina.

Filgueiras, L. 2000. *História do Plano Real*. São Paulo: Editorial Boitempo.

Fine, Ben. 2006. "Debating the 'New' Imperialism." *Historical Materialism*, Vol. 14, No. 4, pp. 133–156.

Flores Chamba, Enith. 2020. "El Modelo Extractivista y los Peligros para la Soberanía Alimentaria en el Caso Ecuatoriano." *SaberEs.*, Vol. 12, No. 1, pp. 1–19.

Ford, A.G. 2009. "Las inversiones británicas y el desarrollo de la economía argentina, 1880–1914." In: David Rock (ed.), *Argentina en el siglo veinte: economía y desarrollo político desde la élite conservadora a Perón-Perón* (pp. 33–64). San Isidro: Lenguaje Claro Editora.

Foster, J.B., and Holleman, H. 2010. "Financial Power Elite." *Monthly Review*, Vol. 62, No. 1 (May 2010), pp. 1–19.

Frank, André G. 1967. *Capitalism and Underdevelopment in Latin America: Historical Studies of Chile and Brazil*. New York, Monthly Review Press.

———. 1969. *Latin America: Underdevelopment or Revolution*. New York: Monthly Review Press.
Furtado, Celso. 2006. *Formação Econômica do Brasil*. São Paulo: Companhia Editora Nacional.
Gaiger, Luis Ignacio. 2007. "La economía solidaria y el capitalismo en la perspectiva de las transiciones históricas". En *La economía social desde la periferia. Contribuciones Latinoamericanas*, organizado por José Luis Coraggio, 79–109. Buenos Aires: Universidad nacional General Sarmiento/Altamira.
Gala, Paulo. 2006. "Dois padrões de política cambial: américa latina e sudeste asiático." Presented at the *3rd Latin American Political Science Congress*, Unicamp, Campinas, Brazil, September 2006.
Galafassi, Guido. 2010. "Megaminería en Patagonia, Argentina, saqueo y nuevos cercamientos en un renovado proceso de acumulación por desposesión." In: G.C. Delgado (ed.), *Ecología política de la minería en América Latina*. México: UNAM-CEEICH.
Gandini, Nicolad. 2019. "Represas de Santa Cruz, la avanzada china en infraestructura energética." *Econo Journal* (June 6, 2019).
Garibay Orozco, C. 2010. "Paisajes de acumulación minera por desposesión campesina en el México actual". In: En Delgado Gian Carlo (ed.), *Ecología Política de la minería en América Latina*. México: UNAM-CEEICH.
Goldenstein, L. 1994. *Repensando a dependência*. Rio de Janeiro: Paz e Terra.
Gonçalves, R. 1999. *Globalização e Desnacionalização*. São Paulo: Paz e Terra.
Gordon, Tedd, and Webber, Jeffery. 2008. "Imperialism and Resistance: Canadian Mining Companies in Latin America." *Third World Quarterly*, Vol. 29, No. 1, pp. 63–87.
Grigera, Juan and Matías Eskenazi. 2013. "Capítulo 7: Apuntes sobre la acumulación de capital durante la Posconvertibilidad". In: En Grigera, Juan (ed.), *Argentina después de la convertibilidad (2002–2011)*. Buenos Aires: Imago Mundi.
Gudynas, Eduardo. 2010. "La ecología política del progresismo sudamericano: los límites del progreso y la renovación verde de la izquierda." *Sin Permiso*, No. 8 (diciembre 2010), pp. 147–167, Barcelona (España).
———. 2015. *Extractivismos. Ecología economía y política de un modo de entender el desarrollo y la Naturaleza*, 1ª ed. Lima: Cedib y ClAES.
———. 2019. *Extractivismos y Corrupción: Anatomía de una íntima relación*. Quito: Abya Yala.
Guillén Romo, Héctor. 2002. "México: del desarrollo 'hacia adentro' al desarrollo 'hacia afuera'." *Realidad Económica*, Vol. 191 (octubre/noviembre 2002), pp. 56–77.
Hardt, M., and Negri, A. 2000. *Empire*. Cambridge, MA: Harvard University Press.

Haro Sly, Maria José. 2017. "The Argentine Portion of the Soybean Commodity Chain." *Palgrave Communications*.
Harvey, David. 1982. *Limits to Capital*. London: Penguin Books.
———. 2003. *The New Imperialism*. Oxford and London.
———. 2005. *A Brief History of Neoliberalism*. Oxford: Oxford University Press.
Hayek, F. 1944. *The Road to Serfdom*. London: Routledge Press.
Hecht, Susan. B. 1985. "Environment, Development and Politics: Capital Accumulation and the Livestock Sector in Eastern Amazonia." *World Development*, Vol. 13, No. 6, pp. 663–684.
———. 1993. "The Logic of Livestock and Deforestation in Amazonia." *BioScience*, Vol. 43, No. 10, pp. 687–695.
Henwood, D. 1995. "The Contract with México." *Left Business Observer*, No. 68, pp. 1–7.
Historical Materialism Symposium. 2006. Vol. 14, No. 4.
Hora, R. 2000. "Terratenientes, empresarios industriales y crecimiento industrial en la Argentina: los estancieros y el debate sobre el proteccionismo (1890–1914)." *Desarrollo Económico*, Vol. 40, No. 159, pp. 465–492.
Ianni, O. 1986. *Estado e Planejamento Econômico no Brasil*. Rio de Janeiro: Editora Civilização Brasileira.
IBGE/SIDRA. 2010–2020. www.sidra.ibge.gov.br/. Accessed July 2020.
IBGE (Instituto Brasileiro de Geografia e Estadística). 2010–2021. www.ibge.gov.br/. Accessed July, 2021.
IEDI (Instituto de Estudos para o Desenvolvimento Industrial). 2018. "A Produtividade Industrial no Período Recente." Julho 2018.
INDEC. 2003–2021. www.indec.gov.ar/. Accessed July 2021.
INDEC/EPH. 2007–2021. www.indec.gov.ar/eph. Accessed July, 2021.
INEGI (Instituto Nacional de Estadística, Geografía e Informática). 1999–2021. www.inegi.gob.mx.
Iñigo Carrera, Juan. 2002. "Estancamiento, crisis y deuda externa: evidencias de la especificidad de la acumulación de capital en la Argentina." *Ciclos en la historia, la economía y la sociedad*, No. 23, Buenos Aires.
———. 2004. "La crisis de la representación política como forma concreta de reproducirse la base específica de la acumulación de capital en Argentina." *Revista da Sociedade Brasileira de Economia Política*, No. 27, Rio de Janeiro.
———. 2007. *La formación económica de la sociedad argentina. Volumen I. Renta agraria, ganancia industrial y deuda externa 1882–2004*. Buenos Aires: Imago Mundi.
International Monetary Fund. 1998. "Argentina: Recent Economic Developments." IMF Staff Country Report No. 98/38, Washington, DC.
IPEA. 2010–2021. www.ipeadata.gov.br/. Accessed July 2021.
Jepson, Nicholas. 2020. "Neodevelopmentalist Type: Argentina and Brazil." In: N. Jepson, *In China's Wake: How the Commodity Boom Transformed*

Development Strategies in the Global South. New York: Columbia University Press.

Katz, Claudio. 2018. *La Teoría de la Dependencia, cincuenta años después*. Buenos Aires: Batalla de Ideas.

Katz, Jorge, and Kosacoff, B. 1989. *El proceso de industrialización en la Argentina: evolución, retroceso y prospectiva*. Buenos Aires: Centro Editor de América Latina.

Kejsefman, I. 2014. "El 'nuevo' agro argentino: Transformaciones productivas en el sector y la inserción de la Argentina en el actual capitalismo mundial (1990–2012)." *mimeo*.

Khor, Martin. 2006. "The WTO's Doha Negotiations and Impasse: A Development Perspective." *Third World Network* (November): 16.

Kicillof, Axel. 2011. "Serie canal encuentro: La etapa agro-exportadora." Texto no publicado.

Klein, Naomi. 2014. *This Changes Everything: Capitalism vs. the Climate*. New York: Simon and Schuster.

Kosacoff, B., and Azpiazu, D. 1989. *La industria argentina: desarrollo y cambios estructurales*. Buenos Aires: Centro Editor de América Latina.

Lazzari, Ricardo. 2011. "Estrategias de acumulación de las clases dominantes de Argentina y Brasil bajo la dinámica cíclica de los modelos primario exportadores (1870–1914)." Trabajo presentado en las *Jornadas de Economía Crítica*, agosto 2011.

Lenin, Vladimir I. 1974. *Imperialism: The Highest Stage of Capitalism*. New York: International Publishers.

Lipietz, Alain. 1988. *Miragens e Milagres: problemas da industrialização no terceiro mundo*. São Paulo: Nobel.

Londoño, Ernesto, and Casado, Letícia. 2020. "As Bolsonaro Keeps Amazon Vows, Brazil's Indigenous Fear 'Ethnocide'." *New York Times*, April 19, 2020.

Machado Aráoz, H. 2010. "El Agua Vale Más que el Oro. Grito de resistencia descolonial contra los nuevos dispositivos expropiatorios." In: Delgado Gian Carlo (ed.), *Ecología política de la minería en América Latina*. México: UNAM-CEEICH.

Malheiro, B.C., Michelotti, C., and Guedes Sabino, T.A. 2020. *Aqui o capitalismo não! espoliação e brutalidade em tempos de pandemia, o que a Amazônia tem a dizer?* In Geographia Vol. 22, No. 48. Niterói, Universidade Federal Fluminense. Brasil.

Mandel, E. 1975. *Late Capitalism*. London: Verso.

Mantega, Guido. 1984. *A economia política brasileira*. Petrópolis: Editora Vozes.

Marcelino, Maria Fernanda, and Fernandes Maso, Tchenna. 2020. "La hidroeléctrica de Belo Monte: problemas sociales, fracasos del Estado y la lucha de las mujeres por modelos energéticos alternativos." Heinrich Boll

Stifting, Bogota. https://co.boell.org/es/2020/04/20/la-hidroelectrica-de-belo-monte-problemas-sociales-fracasos-del-estado-y-la-lucha-de-las.
Marini, Ruy Mauro. 1973. *Dialética da dependência*. México: Era.
Marques, Rosa María, Salomão Barres Ximenes and Camila Kimie Ugino. 2018. "Governos Lula e Dilma em matéria de seguridade social e acesso à educação superior." *Brazilian Journal of Political Economy*, Vol. 38, No. 3.
Marques de Souza, Gilberto. 2019a. *Amazônia- Riqueza, Degradação e Saque*. São Paulo: Expressão Popular.
———. 2019b. "Derrotar Bolsonaro para Defender a Amazônia: Presidente estimula queimadas e desmatamento na região."
Marquetti, Adalmir. 2004. "A Economia Brasileira no Capitalismo Neoliberal: Progresso Técnico, Distribuição, Crescimento e Mudança Institucional." *Seminário USP/IPE*.
Marquetti, Adalmir, Hoff, Cecilia, and Miebach, Alessandro. 2016. "Lucratividade e Distribuição: A Origem Econômica da Crise Política Brasileira."
Martins, Carlos E. 2011. *Globalização, Dependência e Neoliberalismo na América Latina*. São Paulo: Boitempo.
Marx, Karl. 1977 *Capital: Critique of Political Economy, Vol. I*. New York: Vintage Books.
———. 1981 *Capital: Critique of Political Economy, Vol. III*. New York: Penguin Books.
Mattoso, J. 1995. *A Desordem do Trabalho*. São Paulo: Scritta.
McMichael, Phillip. 2013. "Land Grabbing as Security Mercantilism in International Relations." *Globalizations*, Vol. 10, No. 1, pp. 47–64.
MDIC. 2012–2020. http://www.mdic.gov.br/sitio/. Accessed December 2020.
Meiksens Wood, Ellen. 2005. *Empire of Capital*. New York: Verso.
Mello, J.M. Cardoso de. 1982. *O Capitalismo Tardio*. São Paulo: Brasiliense.
Milenio Digital y Agencias. 2020. ¿Qué es el 'Lava Jato' la trama de corrupción por la que Lula da Silva estuvo preso? November 8, 2019.
Ministerio de Economía, Argentina. 2005. https://www.argentina.gob.ar/economia.
Minsburg, N. 2001. *La economía pos-menemista- ¿atrapada sin salida?* Buenos Aires: EUDEBA.
Monbiot, George. 2016. *How Did We Get into This Mess?: Politics, Equality, Nature*. London: Verso.
Neffa, Julio C. (coord.) 2008. "La informalidad, la precariedad laboral y el empleo no registrado en la provincia de Buenos Aires." CEIL-PIETTE, Ministerio de Trabajo.
———. 2010a. "Naturaleza y significación del trabajo/empleo precario." En: Mariana Busso y Pablo Pérez (coords), *La corrosión del trabajo. Estudios sobre informalidad y precariedad laboral*. Buenos Aires: Miño y Dávila/CEIL-PIETTE/Trabajo y Sociedad.

———. 2010b. "El trabajo no registrado como modalidad límite de precariedad." En: Mariana Busso y Pablo Pérez (coords), *La corrosión del trabajo. Estudios sobre informalidad y precariedad laboral*. Buenos Aires: Miño y Dávila/CEIL-PIETTE/Trabajo y Sociedad.

NRDC. 2020. "Our Forests aren't Fuel" FROM Natural Resources Defense Council. https://www.nrdc.org/resources/our-forests-arent-fuel. Accessed May 8th, 2020.

Ocampo, José Antonio, and Tommaso Faccio. 2020. "Making Multinationals and the Wealthy Pay." *Project Syndicate*, June 30th, 2020.

OCMAL. 2020a. https://mapa.conflictosmineros.net/ocmal_db-v2/. Accessed July 28, 2020.

———. 2020b. *Observatorio de Conflictos Mineros de América Latina*. www.ocmal.org. Last visited July 12, 2020.

O'Connor, James. 1988, "Capitalism, Nature, Socialism: A Theoretical Introduction." *Capitalism, Nature, Socialism*, Vol. 1, No. 1.

———. 1998. *Natural Causes: Essays in Ecological Marxism*. New York: Guilford Press.

Oliveira, A.U. de. 2005. "BR-163 Cuiabá-Santarém: Geopolítica, grilagem, violência e mundialização." In: *Amazônia Revelada: Os descaminhos ao longo da BR-163*. Brasilia: CNPq.

Oliveira, F. de. 1988. "A formação do anti-valor." In: *Novos Estudos CEBRAP*, No. 22. São Paulo: CEBRAP.

Oreiro, José, and Feijó, Carmem. 2010. "Desindustrialização: conceituação, causas, efeitos e o caso brasileiro." *Revista de Economia Política*, Vol. 30, No. 2 (118) (abril–junho/2010), pp. 219–232.

Ortega, Max. 2002. *Política Laboral y Movimiento Sindical. El Primer Año del Gobierno Foxista*. México: Editorial Itaca.

Osorio, J. 2012. "América Latina: o novo padrão exportador de especialização produtiva – estudo de cinco economias da região". In: Carla Ferreira, Jaime Osorio e Mathias Luce (orgs.). *Padrão de reprodução do capital: contribuições da teoria marxista da dependência*. São Paulo: Boitempo.

Oviedo, Eduardo Daniel. 2015. "Actors in the Argentina-China Soybean Trade and in Chinese Immigration to Argentina." In: E. Dussel Peters and Ariel C. Armony (coord.), *Beyond Raw Materials-Who Are the Actors in the Latin America and Caribbean-China Relationship?*

Página 12. 2020. "Incendios en el Delta: todos los caminos conducen a los productores agropecuarios." 6 August. www.pagina12.com.ar/283103-incendios-en-el-delta-todos-los-caminos-conducen-a-losprodu?utm_source=gravitec&utm_medium=push&utm_campaign=rss.

Peixoto Ávila, Milene. 2013. "El Programa Bolsa Familia y la pobreza en Brasil: mucho más que números a considerar." *Revista Sociedad & Equidad*, No. 5, enero de 2013.

Pengue, Walter. 2005. "Environmental and Socio Economic Impacts of Transgenic Crops Releasing in Argentina and South America: An Ecological Economics Approach." *Bulletin of Science, Technology & Society*, Vol. 25, No. 4 (August 2005), pp. 1–9.

———. 2015. *Dinámicas y Perspectivas de la Agricultura actual en Latinoamérica: Bolivia, Argentina, Paraguay y Uruguay*. Santiago: Fundación Heinrich Böll Cono Sur.

Perreault, T. 2013. "Dispossession by accumulation? Mining, Water and the Nature of Enclosure on the Bolivian Altiplano." *Antipode*, Vol. 45, No. 5, pp. 1050–1069.

PNAD (Pesquisa Nacional por Amostra de Domicílios). 2020. www.ibge.br.

Pochmann, Mario. 1996. "Efeitos da internacionalização do capital no mundo do trabalho no Brasil." In: Enrique de La Garza Toledo y Carlos Salas (eds.), *NAFTA y MERCOSUR: Procesos de Apertura Económica y Trabajo*. Ciudad de México: CLACSO.

———. 1999. *O Trabalho sob Fogo Cruzado*. São Paulo: Editora Contexto.

Pogge, Thomas, and Reddy, Sanjay. 2003. "Unknown: The Extent, Distribution, and Trend of Global Income Poverty." http://www.socialanalysis.org/.

Prego, J., Ruggiero, R.A., Conti, H.A., Panigatti, J.L., Chebez, J., and Hoffmann, J.A. 1997. *El deterioro del ambiente en la Argentina (suelo-agua-vegetación-fauna)* [Environment Deterioration in Argentina (Land, Water, Vegetation and Fauna)] (3rd ed.). Buenos Aires, Argentina: Fundación para la Educación, la Ciencia y la Cultura.

PRODES/INPE. 2020. http://www.obt.inpe.br/OBT/assuntos/programas/amazonia/prodes.

Rapoport, M., et al. 2000. *Historia económica, política y social de la Argentina (1880–2000)*. Buenos Aires: Ediciones Macchi.

Razeto, Migliaro Luis. 1999. "La economía solidaria: concepto, realidad y proyecto." http://www.luisrazeto.net/.

Reddy, Sanjay G., and Minoiu, Camelia. 2007. HAS WORLD POVERTY REALLY FALLEN?. *Review of Income and Wealth*, Vol. 53, No. 3, pp. 484–502.

Rego, J.M., and Marques, R.M. (org.). 2006. *Economia Brasileira*. São Paulo: Editora Saraiva.

Rivero, S., and Cooney, Paul. 2010. "The Amazon as a Frontier of Capital Accumulation: Looking Beyond the Trees." *Capitalism, Nature, Socialism*, Vol. 21, No. 4.

Robin, Marie-Monique. 2008a. (Director) *The World According to Monsanto*. A documentary Film.

———. 2008b. *The World According to Monsanto: Pollution, Corruption, and the Control of the World's Food Supply*. New York: The New Press.

Robinson, William I. 2004. *A Theory of Global Capitalism—Production, Class and State in a Transnational World*. Baltimore: The John Hopkins University Press.

———. 2008. *Latin America and Global Capitalism—A Critical Globalization Perspective*. Baltimore: The John Hopkins University Press.

———. 2017. "Passive Revolution: The Transnational Capitalist Class Unravels Latin America's Pink Tide." In *Truthout*, June 6, 2017.

———. 2020. "Global capitalism post-pandemic." *Race and Class*, Vol. 62, No. 2.

Rocha, Geisa M. 2002. "Neo-Dependency in Brazil." *New Left Review*, No. 16, pp. 55–86.

Rock, D. 1987. *Argentina 1516–1987—From Spanish Colonization to Alfonsín*. Berkeley: University of California Press.

———. 2002. "Racking Argentina." *New Left Review*, No. 17 (September/October 2002), London.

Rodrigues, Sabrina. 2018. "Área de cultivo de soja na Amazônia quadruplicou desde 2006." *O Eco*. https://www.oeco.org.br/noticias/area-de-cultivo-de-soja-na-amazonia-quadruplicou-desde-2006/. Accessed August 16, 2020.

Rodrik, Dani. 2018. "The WTO Has Become Dysfunctional." *Financial Times*, August 5, 2018.

Rodrik, Dani, and Stefanie Stantcheva. 2020. "The Post-Pandemic Social Contract". *Proyect Syndicate*, June 11, 2020.

Roubini, Nouriel. 2020. "The Coming Greater Depression of the 2020s." *Project Syndicate*, April 28, 2020.

Saad-Filho, A., and Morais, L. 2002. "Neo-Monetarismo Tropical: A Experiência Brasileira nos Anos Noventa." *Revista de Economia Política*, Vol. 22, No. 1 (85).

Saboia, J. 1985. *A questão salarial*. São Paulo: Brasiliense.

Sacher, William. 2015. "Megaminería y Desposesión en el Sur: un análisis comparativo." *Íconos*, Vol. 51, pp. 99–116.

———. 2017. *Ofensiva Megaminería China en los Andes. Acumulación por Desposesión en el Ecuador de la Revolución Ciudadana*. Quito: Abya-Yala.

Sacher, William, and Cooney, Paul. 2019. "Transnational Mining and Accumulation by Dispossession." In: Paul Cooney and William Sacher (eds.), *Environmental Impacts of Transnational Corporations in the Global South. Research in Political Economy*, Vol. 33 (Chapter 1). Bingley, UK: Emerald Publishing.

Santarcángelo, Juan E. (ed.). 2019. *The Manufacturing Sector in Argentina, Brazil, and Mexico: Transformations and Challenges in the Industrial Core of Latin America*. London: Palgrave.

Sartelli, Eduardo (dir.). 2008. *Patrones en la Ruta: El conflicto agrario y los enfrentamientos en el seno de la burguesía, marzo-julio de 2008*. Buenos Aires: Ediciones Razón y Revolución.

Schorr, Martín, and Ortiz, Ricardo. 2020. "Argentina: factores de impulse al proceso de reprimarización reciente." En: *Territorios primarizados en Argentina. Viejas y nuevas fragilidades socioeconómicas* (pp. 73–91). Buenos Aires: UNS.

Schvarzer, Jorge. 1986. *La política económica de Martínez de Hoz*. Buenos Aires: Hyspamerica Ediciones.

———. 1998. "Nuevas perspectivas sobre el origen del desarrollo industrial argentino (1880–1930)." *Anuario IEHS*, 13. Tandil: UNC.

———. 2001. "Terratenientes, industriales y clase dominante en el ya antiguo debate sobre el desarrollo argentino." *Desarrollo Económico*, Vol. 41 (1961), pp. 121–126.

SEADE. 2007–2008. *Fundação Sistema Estadual de Análise de Dados*. https://www.seade.gov.br/.

Sevares, J. 2002. *Por qué cayó la Argentina-Imposición, crisis y reciclaje del orden neoliberal*. Buenos Aires: Grupo Editorial Norma.

Shaikh, Anwar. 1978. "An Introduction to the History of Crisis Theories." In: *U.S. Capitalism in Crisis*. New York: Union for Radical Political Economy.

———. 1983. Mimeo from Advanced Political Economy 204–205 New School.

———. 1987. "The Falling Rate of Profit and the Economic Crisis in the U.S." In: Robert Cherry et al. (eds.), *The Imperiled Economy, Book I*. New York: Union for Radical Political Economy.

Shiva, Vandana (ed). 2015. *Seed Sovereignty, Food Security: Women in the Vanguard of the Fight against GMOS and Corporate Agriculture*. Berkeley, CA: North Atlantic Books.

Sicsú, J., De Paula, L.F., and Renaut, M. (eds.). 2005. *Novo-Desenvolvimentismo: Um Projeto Nacional de Crescimento com Equidade Social*. Barueri, SP: Editora Manole and Konrad Adenauer Stiftung.

Silva, Sérgio S. 1976. *Expansão cafeeira e origem da indústria no Brasil*. São Paulo: Alfa Omega.

Sims, Jocelyn and Jessie Romero. 2013. "Latin American Debt Crisis of the 1980s: 1982–1989." *Federal Reserve History*. https://www.federalreservehistory.org/essays/latin-american-debt-crisis.

Singer, Paul. 1989. *A Crise do Milagre*. Rio de Janeiro: Paz e Terra.

Sklair, Leslie. 2001. *The Transnational Capitalist Class*. Oxford: Blackwell.

Slipak, Ariel M. 2014. "Un análisis del ascenso de China y sus vínculos con América Latina a la luz de la Teoría de la Dependencia." *Realidad Económica*, No. 282.

Smith, W.C. 1989. *Authoritarianism and the Crisis of the Argentine Political Economy*. Stanford: Stanford University Press.

Solberg, C.E. 1981. "Argentina y Canadá: Una Perspectiva Comparada sobre su Desarrollo Económico, 1919–1939." *Desarrollo Económico*, Vol. 21, No. 82 (julio–setiembre 1981).

S&P Global. 2018. "World Exploration Trends." *A Special Report from S&P Global Market Intelligence for the PDAC International Convention*, March 2018.

Stedman Jones, Daniel. 2012. *Masters of the Universe: Hayek, Friedman, and the Birth of Neoliberal Politics*. Princeton: Princeton University Press.

Stein, S.J. 1979. *Origens e evolução da Indústria têxtil no Brasil—1850/1950*. Rio de Janeiro: Campus.

Stiglitz, Joseph E. 2020. "Priorities for the COVID-19 Economy." *Project Syndicate*, July 1st, 2020.

Suzigan, Wilson. 2000. *Indústria Brasileira: Origem e Desenvolvimento*. São Paulo: Editora Hucitec, Editora da Unicamp.

Svampa, Maristella. 2012. "Consenso de los commodities, giro eco-territorial y pensamiento crítico en América Latina." *Osal*, año XIII, 32 (noviembre).

Svampa, Maristella, and Pereyra, S. 2004. "La experiencia piquetera: Dimensiones y desafíos de las organizaciones de desocupados en Argentina." *Revista da Sociedade Brasileira de Economia Política*, No. 27, Rio de Janeiro.

Tavares, Maria dá C. 1972. *Da Substituição de Importação ao Capitalismo Financeiro*. Rio de Janeiro: Zahar.

———. 1974. *Acumulação e industrialização no Brasil*. Tese de livre-docência. Rio de Janeiro. Faculdade de Economia e Administração da Universidade Federal do Rio de Janeiro.

———. 2010. "O processo de substituição de importações como modelo de desenvolvimento na América Latina." In: J. Sicsú e P. Douglas (eds.), *Desenvolvimento e Igualdade: homenagem aos 80 anos de Maria da Conceição Tavares* (pp. 39–66). Rio de Janeiro: IPEA.

Teubal, M. 2006. "Expansión del modelo sojero en la Argentina. De la producción de alimentos a los commodities." En *Realidad Económica*, No. 220, Buenos Aires, 16.05–30.06.

Treacy, Mariano. 2014. "Transformaciones en el agro argentino y conflictos socio-ambientales en el Siglo XXI." Presentado en COLCA, UNGS.

Trindade, J.R., and Cooney, Paul. 2019. "Empresas Transnacionais, Territorialidade e Impactos Ambientais na Região Amazônica Oriental Brasileira." Presented at *ENEP XXIV*, Victoria, Brazil.

Trindade, J.R, Cooney, Paul, and De Oliveira, W. 2016. "Industrial Trajectory and Economic Development: Dilemma of the Reprimarization of the Brazilian Economy." *RRPE*, Vol. 48, No. 2, pp. 269–286.

Vasconcellos, M.A.S., et al. 1996. *Economia Brasileira Contemporânea: para cursos de economia e administração*. São Paulo: Atlas.

Versiani, F.R., and Versiani, M.T. 1977. "A industrialização Brasileira antes de 1930: uma contribuição." In: F.R. Verisani and J.R.M. Barros (org.), *Formação Econômica do Brasil: a experiência da industrialização*. São Paulo: Saraiva.

Villanueva, J. 1972. "El Origen de la Industrialización Argentina." *Desarrollo Económico*, Vol. XII, No. 47.

Villela, A., and Suzigan, W. 1973. *Política do Governo e Crescimento da Economia Brasileira, 1889–1945*. Série Monográfica, 10. Rio de Janeiro: IPEA/INPES.

Weisbrot, M., and Baker, D. 2002. "What Happened to Argentina?" *Center for Economic and Policy Research*, January 31, 2002, Washington, DC.

Weissman, Robert. 1996. "Another NAFTA Nightmare." *Multinational Monitor*, Vol. 17, No. 10, p. 7.

Wilkinson, John. 2009. "Globalization of Agribusiness and Developing World Food Systems." *Monthly Review*, Vol. 61, No. 4, p. 238.

World Bank. 2018–2021. https://data.worldbank.org/.

Wrenn, Mary V. 2016. "Immanent Critique, Enabling Myths, and the Neoliberal Narrative." *Review of Radical Political Economics*, Vol. 48, No. 3, pp. 452–466.

Index

P. Cooney, *Paths of Development in the Southern Cone*, Palgrave Insights into Apocalypse Economics, https://doi.org/10.1007/978-3-030-67673-5

J

K

N

O

P

The manufacturer's authorised representative in the EU is Springer Nature Customer Service Centre GmbH, Europaplatz 3, 69115 Heidelberg, Germany. If you have any concerns regarding our products, please contact ProductSafety@springernature.com

Printed and bound by CPI Group (UK) Ltd, Croydon, CR0 4YY
30/09/2026
02225455-0014